P9-DOG-844

501 GMAT® QUESTIONS

501 GMAT® QUESTIONS

LEARNINGEXPRESS®

NEW YORK

Copyright © 2013 LearningExpress, LLC.

All rights reserved under International and Pan American Copyright Conventions.
Published in the United States by LearningExpress, LLC, New York.

Library of Congress Cataloging-in-Publication Data

501 GMAT questions.—First edition.
     pages   cm
   ISBN 978-1-57685-920-9
   1. Graduate Management Admission Test—Study guides.   2. Management—
Examinations, questions, etc.   3. Business—Examinations, questions, etc.   4. Verbal
ability—Examinations, questions, etc.   5. Mathematics—Examinations, questions, etc.
6. Universities and colleges—United States—Graduate work—Examinations—Study
guides.   I. LearningExpress (Organization)   II. Title: Five hundred one GMAT
questions.   III. Title: Five hundred one GMAT questions.
   HF1118.A14 2013
   650.076—dc23

                                                                  2013001029

Printed in the United States of America

9 8 7 6 5 4 3 2 1

First Edition

ISBN 978-1-57685-920-9

For more information or to place an order, contact LearningExpress at:
   80 Broad Street
   Suite 400
   New York, NY 10004

Or visit us at:
   www.learningexpressllc.com

*GMAT is a registered trademark of the Graduate Management Admission Council® (GMAT®),
which was not involved in the production of, and does not endorse, this product.

Contents

Introduction

Congratulations! By purchasing this book, you're investing in your future by taking a step toward obtaining an MBA degree, which in turn will sharpen your business and analytical skills. *501 GMAT® Questions* will familiarize you with the Graduate Management Admission Test (GMAT®) and its format.

When you take the test, remember that the GMAT is a computer adaptive test (CAT), which means that as you answer each question, a harder question or an easier question will appear. Therefore, you will not be able to skip a question and come back to it later, or change your answer to any previous questions. If you find that you are having trouble with a particular question, try to eliminate some of the wrong answer choices, reread the passage one more time, and then make your best guess. Do not leave any questions unanswered.

How to Use this Book

This book is divided into four distinct sections, each representing a section on the official GMAT: Writing, Verbal, Integrated Reasoning, and Quantitative.

Review the instructional sections in each chapter before answering the questions in that chapter. The answers to all questions are at the end of each corresponding chapter. Each answer is fully explained, so if you have trouble with a particular question, you will be able to figure out how to arrive at the correct answer. Take your time; refer to the instructions as frequently as you need to, and be sure you understand the answer explanations at the end of each chapter. This book provides the practice; you provide the initiative and perseverance. Good luck!

SECTION 1

GMAT
Writing Section

Strong writing skills are a prized asset in the business world. The ability to make a cohesive argument and communicate it clearly is something that you can use in any facet of the business world. The GMAT Analytical Writing Assessment aims to test these skills.

Analytical Writing Assessment

The Analytical Writing Assessment (AWA) is designed to measure your ability to think critically and to cohesively express your ideas. The AWA consists of one 30-minute essay: Analysis of an Argument.

The test will use topics of general interest connected to business or a variety of other subjects to generate your prompts. No specific knowledge of the essay topic is necessary to write a high-scoring essay—only your capacity to write analytically will be measured.

You will be asked to analyze the reasoning behind an argument that is provided and then write a critique of that argument. You will not be asked to present your own views on the subject.

All AWA prompts share a similar format that includes a backdrop for the prompt, the prompt statement, and instructions. It looks like this:

> The following appeared in the editorial section of a corporate newsletter:
>
> *The common notion that workers are generally apathetic about management issues is false, or at least outdated: a recently published survey indicates that 79 percent of the nearly 1,200 workers who responded to survey questionnaires expressed a high level of interest in the topics of corporate restructuring and redesign of benefits programs.*
>
> Discuss how well reasoned you find this argument. In your discussion be sure to analyze the line of reasoning and the use of evidence in the argument. For example, you may need to consider what questionable assumptions underlie the thinking and what alternative explanations or counterexamples might weaken the conclusion. You can also discuss what sort of evidence would strengthen or refute the argument, what changes in the argument would make it more logically sound, and what, if anything, would help you better evaluate its conclusion.

Developing Your Essay

When developing your essay, consider the following:

- What questionable assumptions underlie the thinking behind the argument?
- What alternative explanations or counterexamples might weaken the conclusion?
- What sort of evidence could help strengthen or refute the argument?

The AWA tests your ability to construct a thoughtful and unified critique of a specific statement based on a specific line of reasoning. An effective way to approach your argument is to create a brief, organized outline. Within this outline, create:

- an introduction that states a clear position in response to the prompt with some brief support
- a body that elaborates on each supportive idea with relevant details and examples or experiences that define each supportive idea
- a conclusion that ties together all the parts of your argument

Improving Your Score

In order to improve your score, be aware of proper grammar, spelling, and vocabulary. Using varied vocabulary and sentence structure (as long as both are used effectively) will have a positive impact on your score.

Another way to boost your score is to employ some tactics that will separate your essay from the masses. Some ways to do this:

- Correctly use relevant facts, statistics, and historical examples. *(Almost one-third of freshmen entering high school will graduate.)*
- Make well-known literary references. *(To quote Dickens, "It was the best of times, it was the worst of times," for everyone who remained employed at the peak of the recession.)*
- Craft relevant and intelligent metaphors. *("All the world's a stage, and upon it our elected officials are merely players.")*

A smart way to make your position stronger is to offer thoughts on the other side of the argument. Briefly addressing these counterpoints and exposing their weaknesses can only strengthen your argument. It is easier to make your position appear *right* after you have dispelled assumptions from opposing perspectives.

Timing

It is important to keep track of time while developing your argument for the AWA and to pace yourself accordingly. An incomplete essay will have a negative impact on the overall scoring of the AWA section of your exam.

Here is a good guideline to keep in mind for the usage of your allotted time:

- consider your issue or argument (1 minute)
- choose your position, develop an outline (4–6 minutes)
- create the body of your essay (22–24 minutes)
- proofread (1–2 minutes)

Understanding Your Score

Each essay in the AWA section will be given two independent ratings, one of which may be performed by an *automated essay-scoring engine*. The automated essay-scoring engine is an electronic system that evaluates over 50 structural and linguistic features, which include the organization of ideas, syntactic variety, and topical analysis.

If the two ratings differ by more than one point, a separate and third evaluation by an expert reader is required to resolve the discrepancy and determine the final score.

The two scores are then used to create an average score. Scores range from 0 to 6, including half-point intervals. These scores are computed separately from the multiple-choice sections of the GMAT and will not affect your Verbal, Quantitative, or Total scores.

College and university faculty members trained as readers for the AWA will consider the following:

- the overall quality of your ideas about the argument presented
- your overall ability to organize, develop, and express those ideas
- the relevant supporting reasons and examples you used
- your ability to control the elements of standard written English

Business schools that receive your GMAT score will also receive your AWA score. While most business schools will not place a great deal of importance on a mediocre score, a good score can help boost your application.

Examinees whose first language is not English will have their essays considered with some sensitivity to the elements of standard written English.

Set 1

Create a response to the following sample prompts.

1. The following appeared in the opinion column of a financial magazine:

   A powerful business tycoon is in a better position to influence the legislation, and ultimately the destiny, of a society or nation than any political leader or government official can in their position.

   Discuss how well reasoned you find this argument. In your discussion be sure to analyze the line of reasoning and the use of evidence in the argument. For example, you may need to consider what questionable assumptions underlie the thinking and what alternative explanations or counterexamples might weaken the conclusion. You can also discuss what sort of evidence would strengthen or refute the argument, what changes in the argument would make it more logically sound, and what, if anything, would help you better evaluate its conclusion.

2. The following appeared as part of a newspaper editorial:

   Throughout our society's history there have been people who dedicate themselves to changing the norms and set the bar anew for generations to come. To leave such a mark on society takes immense ambition, and we remember best the people who broke the rules to achieve success.

   Discuss how well reasoned you find this argument. In your discussion be sure to analyze the line of reasoning and the use of evidence in the argument. For example, you may need to consider what questionable assumptions underlie the thinking and what alternative explanations or counterexamples might weaken the conclusion. You can also discuss what sort of evidence would strengthen or refute the argument, what changes in the argument would make it more logically sound, and what, if anything, would help you better evaluate its conclusion.

3. The following is an excerpt from a memo written by the head of a governmental department:

> *Organizations should attempt to remove the large number of positions and salary levels that categorize employees by skill and experience, because a flat structure is more likely to foster a congenial working environment within the company.*

Discuss how well reasoned you find this argument. In your discussion be sure to analyze the line of reasoning and the use of evidence in the argument. For example, you may need to consider what questionable assumptions underlie the thinking and what alternative explanations or counterexamples might weaken the conclusion. You can also discuss what sort of evidence would strengthen or refute the argument, what changes in the argument would make it more logically sound, and what, if anything, would help you better evaluate its conclusion.

4. The following appeared in the editorial section of a college newspaper:

> *In a world of ever-changing economic climates, it seems clear the global impact of a nation should be weighed by its artistic and scientific accomplishments rather than its accomplishments in business and economic progress.*

Discuss how well reasoned you find this argument. In your discussion be sure to analyze the line of reasoning and the use of evidence in the argument. For example, you may need to consider what questionable assumptions underlie the thinking and what alternative explanations or counterexamples might weaken the conclusion. You can also discuss what sort of evidence would strengthen or refute the argument, what changes in the argument would make it more logically sound, and what, if anything, would help you better evaluate its conclusion.

5. The following appeared in a blog about education:

> *In order to maximize students' potential, educators should create an atmosphere of freedom and spontaneity in a learning environment, rather than maintain a highly structured environment that emphasizes discipline, punctuality, and routine.*

Discuss how well reasoned you find this argument. In your discussion be sure to analyze the line of reasoning and the use of evidence in the argument. For example, you may need to consider what questionable assumptions underlie the thinking and what alternative explanations or counterexamples might weaken the conclusion. You can also discuss what sort of evidence would strengthen or refute the argument, what changes in the argument would make it more logically sound, and what, if anything, would help you better evaluate its conclusion.

6. The following appeared as part of an article in a trade magazine:

> *Because there are already so many personal distractions to be had at work, such as Facebook and texting, employees should keep their private lives and personal activities as separate as possible from the workplace. In this way, an employee can focus on work and little else.*

Discuss how well reasoned you find this argument. In your discussion be sure to analyze the line of reasoning and the use of evidence in the argument. For example, you may need to consider what questionable assumptions underlie the thinking and what alternative explanations or counterexamples might weaken the conclusion. You can also discuss what sort of evidence would strengthen or refute the argument, what changes in the argument would make it more logically sound, and what, if anything, would help you better evaluate its conclusion.

7. The following appeared in a research paper written for an introductory economics course:

> *Competition in the marketplace is beneficial to businesses because it inspires changes and improvements to the status quo. Businesses that are ill-equipped to compete in a bustling market will not likely last very long. The true mettle of a company and its product and services is tested within the open market.*

Discuss how well reasoned you find this argument. In your discussion be sure to analyze the line of reasoning and the use of evidence in the argument. For example, you may need to consider what questionable assumptions underlie the thinking and what alternative explanations or counterexamples might weaken the conclusion. You can also discuss what sort of evidence would strengthen or refute the argument, what changes in the argument would make it more logically sound, and what, if anything, would help you better evaluate its conclusion.

8. The following appeared in the opinion column of a financial magazine:

> *These are times in which people find themselves strapped for cash while working multiple jobs or unemployed with little notice. The average job listed online or in local classifieds can sometimes have up to seventy applicants, if not more. With this in mind, the upcoming crop of soon-to-be college graduates should consider financial compensation as the main factor in deciding on a career path.*

Discuss how well reasoned you find this argument. In your discussion be sure to analyze the line of reasoning and the use of evidence in the argument. For example, you may need to consider what questionable assumptions underlie the thinking and what alternative explanations or counterexamples might weaken the conclusion. You can also discuss what sort of evidence would strengthen or refute the argument, what changes in the argument would make it more logically sound, and what, if anything, would help you better evaluate its conclusion.

9. The following appeared in the media section of a magazine on trends and lifestyles:

> *Because there is such a range of diverse cultures that make up the world, the degree of censorship for improper content and language in arts and entertainment media varies in different countries.*

Discuss how well reasoned you find this argument. In your discussion be sure to analyze the line of reasoning and the use of evidence in the argument. For example, you may need to consider what questionable assumptions underlie the thinking and what alternative explanations or counterexamples might weaken the conclusion. You can also discuss what sort of evidence would strengthen or refute the argument, what changes in the argument would make it more logically sound, and what, if anything, would help you better evaluate its conclusion.

10. The following appeared in an article in a consumer products magazine:

> *When considering an array of advertising from a smattering of different cultures from around the globe, one thing appears true: the ideas of a nation become clear when observing its advertisements. All aspects of a nation's advertisements draw together to paint a cultural story that moves with the population.*

Explain what you think this quotation means and discuss how true or false it may be. Develop your argument with reasons and/or specific examples drawn from history, current events, or your own experience, observation, or reading.

Answers—Set 1

Each sample essay below represents a score-6 response.

1. This statement, *a powerful business tycoon is in a better position to influence the destiny of a society or nation than any political leader or government official*, has a good deal of truth to it, but it should be noted that a powerful business tycoon can easily influence politicians to do what is in their interests as well. It is well-known that lobbyists, who work in the interests of powerful businesses, have a major influence on policy in Washington. Business tycoons, and corporations, also have the power to greatly influence elections with their money by funding campaigns, buying airtime, and producing ads to achieve their personal ends. Furthermore, tycoons and corporations can influence the destiny of a nation by developing media and products that change the way people do things.

   Lobbyists are influential people who work for powerful companies, or groups of companies, to secure their interests in Washington. Lobbyists will often spend millions to influence politicians regarding legislation and the positions they take on certain issues. While the actual tycoons are not out there meeting directly with politicians, their lobbyists are doing this work for them. Lobbyists' influence on legislation is far more profound than most citizens realize.

   Another way that tycoons and corporations with large amounts of money can influence the destiny of a nation is through campaign contributions. Perhaps one of the most effective ways to influence the people's vote is to control the message sent to the voting public. Buying airtime and creating campaign press that will influence the way people perceive a candidate can change the outcome of an election, particularly if the tycoon happens to be a media magnate.

   On another level, a tycoon or successful corporation can influence the destiny of a nation on a basic level—creating something that is integral to the cultural fabric of the nation. This can be anything from pharmaceuticals to media. Two examples of this are Dow Chemical and Rupert Murdoch. Dow is an umbrella company for most of the creators, researchers, and providers of chemical content in everything from cosmetics to pesticides; therefore, its presence in our daily lives is highly pervasive. Rupert Murdoch, who owns and operates NewsCorp, is behind Fox News Channel, which is available to upward of 102 million homes in the United States. It is easy to influence a nation when you are a daily part of its life.

While it is not necessarily a healthy truth, it is a truth nonetheless that tycoons (or otherwise powerful entities) are in a better position to influence the destiny of a country than any politician. They are, in fact, in positions to influence the politicians themselves to a great extent, consequently influencing legislation and eventually our everyday lives.

2. There are several ways to understand the statement, and not every angle is favorable or even true. It is not definitive to say that the people we remember best are remembered because they broke the rules. A great many people in history who are remembered for their contributions to society are memorable because their accomplishments benefited the masses, regardless of how they achieved the ends. Also, to remember someone for breaking the rules may not be a positive memory, as is the case with infamous criminals. It might be more honest to say that the people who we remember for changing the game did so by breaking the rules.

It is not entirely true that we remember people because they broke the rules. Many people, like Mother Teresa and Gandhi, built a lifetime of accomplishments by sticking very closely to the rules in everything they did. Of course we can think of many, like Steve Jobs and Rupert Murdoch, who certainly have achieved monumental success for having done things their way, against the grain, but it would be incorrect to use them as definitive examples.

Additionally, rule breakers whose accomplishments are remembered are not necessarily positive forces in our society. Bernard Madoff would be considered a breaker of rules. He did everything he wasn't supposed to do and benefited greatly financially, yet he destroyed the lives of many people and families who trusted him. While we may remember him, it isn't because he did anything good.

Perhaps a more refined way to state the sentiments would be to say that "the people we remember best are the ones who played the game by their own rules." Intrinsic in this statement is that the person in question had an independent mind-set and did not give up on his or her dreams when things seemed difficult. By bringing to light a person's individuality rather than insubordination, this statement can remain a positive inspiration to others.

In sum, it is not a reliable statement to say we remember those who broke the rules. To put it this way lends this statement to much interpretation that isn't necessarily positive or useful. To say that we remember those who did things their own way would be more appropriate.

3. While the fundamental premise of the argument, that a *flat structure* is likely to foster a more congenial work atmosphere, may be true, it could prove disastrous for the organization. Not every position at every organization requires the same amount of daily hours or the same skill set from the individual occupying said position. Some positions may require extensive and specific education, while other positions at the same organization may not require any secondary education or training at all. While it might be fair to imply that the disparity between some people at the very top of the organizational structure and the rest of the organization's employees is unjust, imposing a flat salary structure would be too drastic. Furthermore, to initiate such a drastic policy could end in a mass exodus of higher-level employees and spell the end for an organization.

To say to an employee with an applicable secondary degree that he or she will now be compensated on the same level as another employee who may lack the same credentials can easily be taken as an insult. Engineers and technicians who work at the same automobile factory will have different tasks in their positions. They may all be equally important in the grand scope of fabricating a car, but it would be unfair to say that every job at that automobile plant requires the same skill set and experience level. While the people who design the cars, the people who test the cars, and the people who build the cars are all working toward the same end, they have committed to their craft on different levels. Also, different employees in the same position may have varying degrees of experience as well as education.

Another reason why it would be a bad business plan to change an existing salary structure to a flat rate is that the change would have far too drastic an impact on some employees' finances. Once a person has become accustomed to living with certain means, or salary, it is very difficult to change that salary without causing the employee great stress. Imagine living on a salary that gets reduced by a third or even a quarter: Some sacrifices must be grudgingly made to adapt. A disgruntled employee is rarely a productive employee.

Lastly, when you have a business full of top employees who are undervalued, you risk a mass exodus of prime employees. Of course, there will be a great many employees on the lower scale who will be happy, but one must consider whether these employees are more vital than the ones whose pay will be reduced. Once all the people who design or create your automobiles have left the organization, you would have to start from the bottom to rebuild. This could quickly end up costing the company far more than it ever hoped to save from changing its salary structure.

To be fair, all employees at any organization should be paid with considerable generosity to maintain a healthy work environment. People do not generally work hard when they feel undervalued, and the same goes for the employees who work at the very top of the salary, and position, pyramid.

4. It is impossible to judge the value of a nation solely on its contributions to the arts and sciences. Historically, it is the impact of various factors within a society that shape the standard of living of a nation. Business and economic progress set the stage for success in arts and sciences research and accomplishments. A healthy economy and global business engagement can only increase the internal wealth and infrastructure of a country, which can advance a nation in its cultural accomplishments.

To assert that only artistic and scientific accomplishments can define a nation's worth is heavily one-sided. While the massive totem heads found on Easter Island are largely considered a magnificent accomplishment in art and sculpture, is it fair to say that this Pacific island nation should be valued as a most accomplished nation? A tribal nation that lacked the infrastructure to prosper as a first world country should hardly be in the same category as, say, Italy for its respective achievements in art. It is an incongruous comparison at best.

In most countries where the economy is growing, people tend to have more formal education. This is in large part because a growing economy requires all sorts of people in varying professions to be successful in their pursuits. These pursuits can be exporting and importing goods, creating software, or telecommunications. Businesses that engage with the economies of other nations also open the door to other cultures, and therefore increase a nation's understanding of the world and humanity.

Furthermore, a robust economy creates a heartier cash flow for a nation's citizens. When food and shelter are stable, it enables a society to pursue more intellectual fields and consequently develop ideas and research in the arts and sciences. Countries that have a high or competitive GDP also tend to be countries with highly educated citizens and a high percentage of people with secondary degrees. This type of intellectual slant on society creates the right environment for success and accomplishment in the arts and sciences.

So, you see it would be folly to sum up a nation's value relying only on a tally of accomplishments in the arts and sciences. While achievements in the arts and sciences are a good indicator of a nation's cultural progress, they are by no means an overall illustration of standards. A better method of calculating a nation's value would be to consider all accomplishments in the arts and sciences as well as its economic progress and business achievements.

5. People learn in many different ways and find inspiration in a variety of environments. Some students require the structure and discipline of a routine-heavy system of learning, while others may shut down in this environment. Conversely, a learning environment with little restrictions and an inclination toward creativity and spontaneity may be very inspiring to some, but others may need help focusing on tasks and topics. The latter is a method that can surely inspire advanced thinking, but either method could easily alienate either type of learner.

While a free-learning environment would be the most inspiring, for some students it is a challenge to remain focused on a task for an extended period of time. A significant portion of students in today's classrooms could potentially be classified within a wide range of learning disabilities. These disabilities could be easily treated with medication, or by creating the boundaries of an effective routine. For students like these, a free-learning environment may pose a challenge or even a threat. While some students will thrive in a free-learning environment, others will unfortunately become alienated by this method.

Other students, who perhaps are more creatively inclined or experimental-minded, will thrive in an open, spontaneous learning environment. In preschool this is referred to as "free-play," where students can decide what games they play and what they will learn. In this scenario, the teacher allows the student to lead the way and supports the student's exploration. Some students respond to this freedom with an enhanced desire to learn and a drive to explore tasks and topics with even greater depth. For students who can handle this type of setting, it can be a mind-opening experience that stokes the flames of curiosity. Furthermore, it impresses in the young student's mind that learning can be a thrilling experience and he or she can feel great inspiration by controlling the process. Particularly advanced students may become bored with tasks and topics within a routine-heavy and structured environment.

The most successful classrooms and learning environments will incorporate both styles of education effectively. It falls upon the educators, as well as the families of the students, to work to better understand the minds of each and every student in a classroom, so that an environment that strives not to alienate anyone is born. This is a task that may seem impossible for a lone teacher with a classroom full of students, but there can be ways around this conundrum. For example, a teacher might assign students to groups that tackle the same exact tasks and topics in different ways.

In sum, it is not effective to rely on one method of teaching to maximize all students' potential. Even though an open learning environment may prove to be more inspiring and motivational, it can potentially alienate students who are not prepared for these scenarios. Also, students who require more responsibility so that they remain interested in tasks and topics may lose interest in lessons. The ideal learning environment is one that is sensitive to students' individual needs and responds to those needs accordingly.

6. This statement is essentially great advice, but in reality it may be difficult to follow. In cases where an individual works in a profession that requires her or him to be social, it may prove to be almost impossible to draw such a hard line between professional and personal aspects of life. Some professions will require so much of one's time that it would require one to basically live behind a *facade*. Still, in most settings it is the safest approach toward one's job whenever possible.

Some professions require people to be socially, and even emotionally, available to others. One such profession is sales. Whether a person is selling insurance, cars, or ideas, he or she will be expected to spend a great deal of time interacting with clients. In this situation it might prove disastrous to keep your clients at a distance. Most people who do this type of work walk a fine line between being genuine and being disconnected. Additionally, it behooves a good salesperson to know his or her market/clientele in order to keep providing them with the goods and services that are most relevant to them. In order to do this, salespeople must be ready to *give* of themselves so that they may *get* some of the others.

Professionals like lawyers, doctors, and journalists may spend unusual amounts of time at work with others. In these situations a person may become depressed or unmotivated after long stretches of time without connecting to anyone. Perhaps getting a drink with some coworkers at the end of the day and chatting about each other's lives and interests may bond them so that they can work together more effectively. While engaging in this behavior is always a risk, and could end up in social divisions or rifts, it might be unavoidable.

Despite the human need to make connections with each other, there are still some professions in which fraternizing may become detrimental to one's position. While teachers may enjoy creating personal connections with each other, it would be inappropriate for a teacher to engage in similar relationships with his or her students. Similarly, while social workers explore their clients' personal lives and activities, they should largely remain an anonymous presence in their clients' lives to maintain professionalism.

Employees certainly should strive to maintain their personal lives and activities as separate from work as possible, but in some cases this is not likely or emotionally healthy. This philosophy is certainly the easiest and most effective way to reduce potential for things like prejudice and emotional confusion between coworkers, but, unfortunately, it is not always the most realistic approach.

7. Competitive businesses tend to grow and adapt at a fast and flexible rate. In the struggle to remain on top of a particular market, a business must understand the needs and expectations of its client base. One method of collecting this data is to assess and analyze the models of competitive businesses. In doing so a business learns more about itself in relation to the marketplace, and also readies itself to compete with rival businesses. Sometimes this leads businesses to adopt methods and models "outside the box" in order to stay one step ahead of their rivals. Adapting and changing the perspectives and expectations of how a business should be run increases the business's ability to survive and rise to the top.

   The lifeline of a business is its connection to its clientele. Success in business is a codependent relationship with its clients. When several businesses are in competition to serve the same demographic, it makes perfect sense to monitor the methods of rival businesses. For example, when Apple develops a new phone, it is imperative for Samsung and other competitors to find out as much as possible about this new product before it even hits the market. The more data these rival companies can collect, the more likely they can come up with a competitive phone before they lose a portion of their business to this new product. The only way to stay new and popular is to constantly try to outperform other businesses in your marketplace.

   In some cases a competitive marketplace will lead a business to change its internal model on a regular basis. This is good because change in the marketplace is less likely to happen when the internal workings of a business remain stagnant. This also helps reduce bloating of staff and unnecessary protocol. A regular restructuring and purge of unnecessary positions is vital to maintaining a healthy business model. Much like the rivalry between Microsoft and Apple, it makes sense to emulate the model of a more successful business in a shared marketplace. By creating competitive products and functioning with a competitive business model, a business continues to increase its chances of remaining relevant to its client base.

More importantly than emulating its rivals, a company must always be able to conceive of ways to stay one step ahead of them. Necessity is often an impetus to radical invention, and while no business wishes to find itself in a desperate situation, it certainly increases the likelihood of risk-taking. In situations where a business must struggle against a very competitive market, it pays to think of unconventional ways of reaching and satisfying the clientele.

In summation, competition in the marketplace is vital for the growth and survival of any company. Without competition, a business risks becoming irrelevant, antiquated, and out of touch.

8. It is an age-old struggle for young people: deciding on a path for the future. When carving out a career path, what factors should be most important? Some may say it is a better life decision to do what makes you happy. Others believe the most important thing in a career is stability and financial security. Some people are lucky to find themselves inclined to pursue a career that is lucrative and also makes them very happy. Still others may dedicate themselves to the struggle of doing what they love without the promise of steady pay. I feel that if you do not enjoy your profession, there is no amount of money that can make you happy.

Many people choose fields of study in college that will guide them toward a reliable career with opportunities for growth and exponential financial compensation. Some such fields may include medicine or law. In either of these fields of study, the possible careers one may forge are complicated and deeply engrossing. Most lawyers and doctors are prone to work long, intense hours under massive amounts of pressure, but the compensation for their invested time is substantial. Furthermore, doctors and lawyers will always have a professional place in society. This may all be true, but one can hardly imagine dedicating one's life to such professions without receiving some sort of personal satisfaction.

Others decide to pursue livelihoods doing what they love most, even if it may not be financially secure. For example, take the notion of the "starving artist" as an illustration of someone who pursues a career in a financially unstable field. Actors, writers, and musicians can easily fit this description, although many artists do get to enjoy a great deal of professional and financial success. Being able to spend most of one's time doing what one loves most may prove to be highly fulfilling, but it often does not guarantee any sort of financial security for the future. While this professional fulfillment may be profound, as time passes it is overshadowed by a lack of stability.

The luckiest people are those who take great joy in the professions they have chosen in financially viable fields. Doctors who love to study medicine and lawyers who get a thrill from practicing law have the best of both worlds. To do what one loves best and be amply compensated from this work is truly to have it all.

In the end, a person may pursue a lifetime of work that he or she is not passionate about, but the financial compensation may never be enough for this sacrifice. Conversely, even though it may be thrilling to dedicate your life to pursuing your passion, it may get old when there is never any stability. The best confluence of factors would be to find a lucrative way to do something that makes you happy.

9. Censorship in arts and entertainment varies from country to country, as cultures and media will vary. In most cases the result is a confluence of two factors: a country's media infrastructure (access to the Internet, cable/satellite, etc.) and that country's cultural inclinations (religion, type of government, etc.). A third factor when considering a government's control over media content is relevant demographics. A country's power of censorship should be primarily driven by these three factors to provide a fair and relevant cultural experience for its people.

Available access to media is something that varies greatly across the globe. While many nations, like the United States, can easily connect to the Internet from the home, there are many nations that still largely rely on public access to the Internet, such as cafes. In cases of countries that lack a pervasive electrical grid that extends power to the individual homes of its inhabitants (e.g., tribal areas of Africa), access to the Internet or TV may be a greater problem than regulation, thereby limiting the government's ability to control what type of content the people can access. Countries that engage in open flow of content exchange, such as purchasing international media to run on national TV and radio, will have greater opportunities to shape that nation's programming and to fine-tune the message of that content.

Perhaps the greatest regulator of a culture's media is its government type and religious inclinations. China's firewall and close surveillance of Internet content is a perfect illustration of that country's powerful communist administration. To deregulate the flow of media in China would greatly undermine the staunch values and focused message of Chinese-generated media. By contrast, countries like the United States that are founded on principles like freedom of speech would greatly undermine their fundamental values by allowing the government too much control of their media. Religious affiliations and inclinations may have even more specific regulatory effects in places like Afghanistan and Saudi Arabia, where it is a violation of the Koran to depict Allah, and the role of women in society requires them to wear traditional garb at all times.

A country's access to media and its cultural orientation are expressly guided by its internal demographic. While a government has the ability to restrict or release media, it makes no difference when no one is watching. There is a basic aspect of supply and demand, or viewership, with regard to programming. For example, the most expensive commercial airtime on American TV every year is during the Super Bowl. Drawing an average of 111 million viewers in recent years, it is one of the most watched sporting events in the world.

In conclusion, the extent to which a governing body should be allowed to regulate public media varies from country to country. Power over the media should be relevant to the founding principles of a nation and should not undermine certain funda-mental tenets of a society. The power a governing body has over a nation's media is relative to the peoples' access to programming and content. Viewership and demographics play a substantial role in shaping that media, perhaps more powerfully than the govern-ing body itself.

10. This statement can be interpreted in various ways. The *ideas* of a nation can be a broad array of topics, particularly in a country like the United States, where people feel nationalistic pride to express their minds. Beyond seeing the desires and needs of a country based on the supply and demand of its product and service consumption, advertising also tells us a lot about demographics. To define the limits and motives of a nation's advertising is to recognize its demographics and thereby somehow define the *ideas* and preferences of the people within those demographics.

First, we should define exactly what we mean by the *ideas* of a nation and how they relate to advertising. If by *ideas* we mean to say ideologies, then I do agree that we can ascertain this from a sampling of advertising. Clearly, if a nation is primarily religious it isn't likely that we will see advertising containing overt sexual innuendo, nudity, or other images that challenge those religious views.

If we define the *ideas* of a nation to refer specifically to widely accepted notions, I believe advertising is not a reliable source of data. Things like trends, styles, and much-observed topics are the fabric of pop culture. This cultural fabric is an eclectic quilt of varying demographics, and the audience will vary from product to product and media format to media format. Therefore the *ideas*, in this sense, would be too broad to define so simply.

Demographic information is a revealing tale of who makes up the most influential groups of a nation. For example, we can assume that a country in which a majority of the women in each household with children leave the home to go to work must have a reliable infrastructure of childcare. Because of this large demographic, the consumption of products and services in the field of childcare will likely be greater than the demand for these products and services in countries where women of the household traditionally stay at home to raise their families. If there is a negligible market for this area, it will be reflected as a lack of a country's advertising in that field.

Somehow, by factoring together these aspects of a nation's advertising, we can grasp a broad notion of its ideas as they relate to the established demographics present in that nation, but the previous statement remains far too broad in its verbiage. Perhaps it would make more sense to say that we can tell the demographics of a nation by its advertising.

SECTION 2

GMAT
Verbal Section

To be successful in the business world, you'll need to recognize how sentences work, how arguments are constructed, and how written English is used and understood. These skills will be tested in the GMAT Verbal section with three types of multiple-choice questions—Reading Comprehension, Critical Reasoning, and Sentence Correction.

Critical Reasoning

When you take the GMAT, critical reasoning sections will be interspersed throughout the Verbal section. Critical reasoning questions use passages that are shorter than those in the reading comprehension section, and passages will have one or two questions. The passage will remain visible on the screen for each question.

Critical reasoning questions test the reasoning skills involved in constructing an argument, evaluating an argument, and formulating or evaluating a plan. You do not need to have any familiarity with the subject matter of the questions in order to answer them. Furthermore, you will want to be wary of any prior knowledge that you have about any field written about in a critical reasoning question because outside knowledge may cause you to make assumptions about the correct answer.

Following are the directions for the critical reasoning questions. Read them carefully and understand them clearly so that you will not need to spend time reviewing them when you sit for the test: *Each of the critical reasoning questions is based on a short argument, a set of statements, or a plan of action. For each question, select the best answer of the choices given.*

Argument Construction

Examples of argument construction question types are: identify the basic structure of the argument, draw the argument's conclusion, identify the assumption, draw an inference, explain the hypothesis, and identify parallels between arguments with similar structures.

Identify the Basic Structure of the Argument

These questions test you on your ability to recognize components of an argument and how the argument is put together. This question may actually quote a speaker and ask you to identify what that speaker is doing. These questions may also quote a speaker and then list the response of a different speaker. Examples:

- X responds to Y by
- The phrase in bold plays which of the following roles in the argument above?
- A supports his conclusion by

Draw the Conclusion

These questions ask you to identify the conclusion that most logically follows from the passage.

- Which of the following most logically completes the argument given below?
- The statements above, if true, best support which of the following as a conclusion?
- Which of the following conclusions CANNOT be drawn from the statements above?

Identify the Assumption

Look for an unstated premise that must be true in order for the argument to be valid.

- The conclusion above is properly drawn if which of the following is assumed?
- The conclusion drawn above is based on the assumption that
- Which of the following assumptions would make the conclusion above properly drawn?

- The argument above relies on which of the following assumptions?

Draw an Inference
Look to see what inferences you can draw from the information in the passage.

- Which of the following can be inferred from the argument above?
- If all of the statements above are true, then which of the following must also be true?
- Which of the following is best supported by the passage?

Explain the Hypothesis
These questions ask you to resolve an apparent contradiction in the passage or to pick the answer choice that would be most helpful to assess the argument.

- Which of the following, if true, helps to explain the discrepancy described above?
- All of the following statements help to explain . . . EXCEPT

Identify Parallels Between Arguments with Similar Structures
These questions ask you to find the answer choice that imitates the argument in the passage.

- Which of the following uses the same method as the author in the above statements?
- Which of the following has the same structure as the above passage?

Argument Construction Test-Taking Strategies

1. Identify the premises of the argument.
Premises could consist of an actual fact ("larger cars usually burn more fuel"), a report or study ("the city's survey shows that the majority of people want the X subway line expanded"), or a reason ("most people eat broc-

coli instead of French fries because they want to lose weight"). Be aware that critical reasoning questions will often clog the statements with extraneous information that is not part of the argument. Mentally set that information aside and focus on the premises. Jot them down on scratch paper if necessary.

2. Identify the conclusion.

The conclusion of the argument is the reason that the argument exists in the first place. Conclusions exist in various forms, such as a recommendation for a future course of action ("In order to increase revenue, Company X should offer a sale during the upcoming holiday"), an opinion ("Farmers believe that this new irrigation technique will result in greater crop yields"), or an interpretation ("Polling companies concluded from the survey that most citizens of Nation Z will vote for Candidate Y"). If the passage does not have a conclusion and the question asks you to identify the answer choice that has the correct conclusion, try to paraphrase a conclusion in your own words and look for the answer choice that best matches the conclusion you already formed.

3. Identify the assumption.

An assumption is the gap in the reasoning of the argument. Not all arguments in life have assumptions. For example:

All people are warm-blooded. Laura is a person. Therefore, Laura is warm-blooded. There is no gap in the reasoning here. However, GMAT® critical reasoning questions use arguments with a gap in the reasoning. This kind of gap, an assumption, would make the above argument look like this:

All people are warm-blooded. Laura is warm-blooded. Therefore, Laura is a person. The link between the conclusion and the supporting facts is flawed because there is an assumption here, which is that all warm-blooded beings are people. This is obviously not true, but the conclusion assumes that it is. If you reject the assumption, then you must reject the conclusion.

To identify the assumption, you will want to be familiar with the most common forms of assumptions on the GMAT®. One kind of assumption is a **causal connection**, in which the argument assumes that one causal connection in the supporting facts also proves an additional causal connection. Example: *People who enroll in MBA programs are more likely to earn a high salary in their career. Therefore, enrolling in an MBA program causes a person to find a better job.* The argument assumes that because enrollment in an MBA program causes higher salaries, then enrollment also causes people to find better jobs.

Another kind of assumption is a **similarity** between terms in the supporting facts and those in the conclusion. Example: *Sixty percent of people with MBA degrees in New York City indicate that they earn over $100,000 a year. Therefore, 60% of people with MBA degrees earn over $100,000 per year.* The argument assumes a similarity between people in New York City with MBA degrees and people overall with MBA degrees.

A third kind of assumption is a **shift** in the terms in the supporting facts and the conclusion. Example: *People with MBA degrees tend to have more knowledge about computer information systems. Therefore, people with MBA degrees know more about conducting business at the corporate level.* The argument shifts from knowledge about computer information systems to knowledge about conducting business at the corporate level.

The most straightforward way to attack an assumption question is to test each answer choice against the conclusion. Could the conclusion still be valid if the assumption were negated? If so, then that answer choice is not the assumption of the argument.

4. Identify the inferences that go too far.

Inference questions ask you to identify the answer choice with the inference that *must* be true, not the choices that *might* be true. Therefore, be wary of answer choices that state facts that the passage itself does not actually state. For example, suppose an answer choice says: *Defense attorneys have abused their positions.* If the passage does not say anything about defense attorneys abusing their position, then this answer choice probably goes too far. You want to pick the answer that says something that you can definitely conclude from the passage and that is within the scope of the passage.

5. In resolve the discrepancy questions, identify other possible causes for the end result.

Resolve the discrepancy questions tend to be about a plan or a study that set out to achieve or prove one thing, and the end result was not what was expected. Think of other reasons that could be the cause for the end result and then look at the answer choices. Is that answer choice a plausible explanation for the result? Second, does that answer choice thoroughly explain the end result? Be wary of answer choices that would partially explain the result, but fail to address the entire issue.

Set 2

Now it is time to answer GMAT Critical Reasoning practice questions that have been designed to test your argument construction skills. Good luck!

11. Louis: The financial industry will suffer greatly from the new government regulations over derivatives. Compliance with these regulations will cost the industry $5.5 million annually because companies in the industry will have to double the size of their proxy statements in order to disclose all the required information. Companies in the industry will then lose profits and have to lay off other employees. Therefore, these regulations will have an adverse effect on the nation's economy.

Peter: The $5.5 million that companies in the finance industry will have to spend will be profits for other types of companies in the private sector. Profits and jobs may be lost in the finance industry, but they will be gained by other companies.

Peter responds to Louis by

   a. agreeing with Louis's conclusion by offering additional information to support it.
   b. offering information that suggests that Louis has overlooked a mitigating consequence.
   c. agreeing with Louis's conclusion but suggesting that the outcome is positive rather than negative.
   d. challenging the tenability of the facts that serve as the basis of Louis's argument.
   e. demonstrating that Louis's conclusion is not based on relevant facts.

12. A cellular phone company spent tens of thousands of dollars in the past year fixing cell towers damaged by extreme weather conditions. In order to reduce the company's overall budget this year, the company plans to cover the base of its towers with a better type of steel and to move certain towers to different locations so that fewer overall are needed.

    Which of the following would NOT be required for the cellular phone company to achieve its aim?
    a. The cost of the steel would have to be lower than the cost of the repairs to the cell towers during the previous year.
    b. The cost of evaluating the most efficient placing of cell towers would have to be lower than the cost of the repairs to the cell towers during the previous year.
    c. The cost of covering the towers with the better type of steel would have to be lower than the cost of the repairs to the cell towers during the previous year.
    d. The cost of the repairs to the cell towers during the previous year would have to be lower than the price of the steel construction crews' wages to cover the cell tower bases.
    e. The cost of shipping the steel would have to be lower than the cost of the repairs to the cell towers during the previous year.

13. Kathryn has a higher GPA than Pamela. Madelyn has a higher GPA than Adrienne. Shane has a higher GPA than Madelyn. Thus, it follows that Kathryn has a higher GPA than Adrienne.

    Which of the following, if introduced into the argument as an additional premise, makes the argument above logically incorrect?
    a. Madelyn has a higher GPA than Katherine.
    b. Katherine has a higher GPA than Madelyn.
    c. Adrienne has a higher GPA than Pamela.
    d. Pamela has a higher GPA than Madelyn.
    e. Adrienne has a higher GPA than Shane.

14. The Braman Rule states that someone who leaves property to another in a will cannot leave property that the deceased did not own at the time of death. Humphrey Monroe left Claire McGinnis a cottage in his will. Claire McGinnis stated in her will that all her property would be left to her niece, Sharon. Claire McGinnis died before Humphrey Monroe. Therefore, the cottage was not inherited by the person whom Claire McGinnis wanted to inherit it.

Which of the following assumptions would make the conclusion above properly drawn?

a. Claire McGinnis wanted Sharon to inherit the cottage.
b. Humphrey Monroe wanted Sharon to inherit the cottage.
c. Sharon wanted to inherit the cottage.
d. Claire McGinnis did not want Sharon to inherit the cottage.
e. Humphrey Monroe did not want Sharon to inherit the cottage.

15. A franchise restaurant pays its employees in State A $2.00 per hour above the minimum wage, and pays its employees in State B $1.00 per hour above the minimum wage. The franchise has three times as many employees in State A as in State B. The franchise's total expenditures on hourly wages for its employees must therefore be higher in State A than in State B.

The argument above relies on which of the following assumptions?

a. The franchise employees in State A do not each work significantly less hours than the franchise employees in State B.
b. The franchise has a greater number of restaurants in State A than in State B.
c. The franchise employees in State B each work significantly more hours than the franchise employees in State A.
d. The law in State A requires the franchise to pay its employees a higher wage than the law in State B.
e. The franchise is planning to decrease the wages paid to employees in State A to $1.00 per hour above the minimum wage.

16. The cost of buying diamonds in the country of Luvania is 40% more than the cost of buying diamonds in the country of Oretania. When one adds the expenses of travel and the tax on purchases by foreigners in Oretania, buying diamonds in Oretania is still less expensive for a citizen of Luvania than buying diamonds in Luvania.

The statements above, if true, best support which of the following as a conclusion?

a. The ground in Oretania breaks more easily under the force of a pickaxe than it does in Luvania.

b. The tax on purchases by foreigners in Oretania is less than 40% of the cost of buying diamonds in Luvania.

c. The cost of traveling to Oretania from Luvania is more than the 40% of the cost of buying diamonds in Luvania.

d. Diamond mining costs are higher in Luvania than in Oretania.

e. Buying diamonds in Luvania will eliminate some retail jobs in jewelry stores in Oretania.

17. After reports from three schools of too much chlorine in their drinking water, the city hired a plumbing company to revamp its running water system. The plumbing company replaced the filtration system after the point in which groundwater is collected. We can conclude that the three schools will no longer have a problem with too much chlorine in their drinking water.

Which of the following does the argument depend on as an assumption?

a. Not all faulty water filtration systems will allow too much chlorine into the drinking water.

b. Water filtration systems are not the only source of too much chlorine in the drinking water.

c. The city has been able to successfully filter water at its water filtration plant.

d. The excess chlorine was not introduced into the schools' water supply at some point later than groundwater collection.

e. Not all faulty water filtration systems are likely to produce excess chlorine in a drinking water supply.

18. The number of people who quit smoking every year is on the rise. The most common reasons that people cited in a survey for quitting smoking are wanting to improve their health, wanting to save money, and wanting to appear physically appealing. Out of the people who quit smoking that cited health reasons, 85% of them also cited wanting to appear physically appealing. The last question in the survey asked whether physical appearance was important to the respondents. 100% of survey respondents answered affirmatively.

Which of the following, if true, does NOT explain the discrepancy described above?

a. Some respondents felt that although their physical appearance was important to them, it was not important enough to quit smoking.

b. Some respondents believed that holding a cigarette enhanced their physical appearance.

c. Some respondents believed that cigarette smoking would not have an adverse effect on their physical appearance.

d. Some respondents felt superficial in admitting that their physical appearance was important to them.

e. Some respondents believed that cigarette smoking had little to no connection to their physical appearance.

19. Rental prices are usually lower on the basement and ground floors of an apartment building, and highest at the top of the building. Rental prices are also usually higher for buildings that receive more sunlight. In addition, rental prices are determined by the number of bedrooms in an apartment. There are six floors in building #153. Cathy lives on the sixth floor, David lives on the fourth floor, Krystal lives on the ground floor, and Oscar lives in the basement. Out of the four tenants, Krystal pays the highest rent and Oscar pays the lowest rent.

Which of the following conclusions CANNOT be drawn from the statements above?

a. Oscar lives in a 1-bedroom, David's apartment receives the most sunlight, and Krystal lives in a 3-bedroom.

b. Cathy lives in a 3-bedroom, Oscar lives in a 3-bedroom, and Krystal lives in a 1-bedroom.

c. Krystal lives in a 1-bedroom, David's apartment receives the most sunlight, and Cathy lives in a 3-bedroom.

d. David lives in a 2-bedroom, Cathy's apartment receives the most sunlight, and Oscar lives in a 1-bedroom.

e. Cathy lives in a 3-bedroom, Cathy's apartment gets the most sunlight, and Krystal lives in a 5-bedroom.

20. A university study showed that women who spent more money on their exercise clothes went to the gym more often. However, the women who spent more money on their exercise clothes did not lose more weight than the women who spent less money on their exercise clothes.

　　Which of the following statements does NOT help to explain the results of the study?

a. The women who spent more money on their exercise clothes did not exercise as hard as those who spent less money because they were too concerned about looking good at the gym.

b. The women who spent less money on their exercise clothes worked out more frequently than those who spent more; they just did not work out as frequently at the gym.

c. The women who spent more money on their exercise clothes focused their workouts more on strength training and less on fat and/or calorie burning exercise.

d. The women who spent more money on their exercise clothes were, on average, already at their ideal weight.

e. The women who spent more money on their exercise clothes had higher memberships in weight loss programs.

21. In the past, doctors would often prescribe antibiotics to patients with viruses purely for purposes of patient satisfaction. Antibiotics only successfully treat bacterial infections and do not actually treat viruses, which must merely run their course. Doctors have since decreased the percentage of patients for whom they prescribe antibiotics.

　　All the following statements help to explain the decrease in the percentage of patients prescribed antibiotics EXCEPT:

a. Doctors are less concerned with patient satisfaction.

b. Doctors are more concerned about patients developing an immunity to antibiotics.

c. A larger percentage of patients today are diagnosed with viruses.

d. A smaller percentage of patients today are diagnosed with ailments that require antibiotics.

e. A larger percentage of patients today are diagnosed with bacterial infections.

22. A publishing company derives revenue from three main areas. Digital products constitute 30% of sales and earn 40% of the profits. Books constitute 60% of sales and earn 50% of the profits. Audiobooks and other mediums constitute 10% of sales and earn 10% of the profits.

    Which of the following can be inferred from the statements above?
    a. Digital products earn higher profits per sale than books or other mediums.
    b. Digital products earn more profit than books or other mediums.
    c. The area of digital products is growing more rapidly than books.
    d. Each digital product is more profitable than each book product.
    e. Books earn less profit than digital products and products in other mediums combined.

23. Major businesses have begun near-shoring, which is a practice that involves moving jobs from cities with a higher cost of living to lower cost of living locales. The rationale behind near-shoring is that employees with a lower cost of living will not demand as high salaries. High-level positions that involve a lot of face time with clients will remain in the higher-cost-of-living cities. High-level employees will travel to the lower-cost-of-living locales when they need to meet with staff.

    Which of the following conclusions, if true, provides the strongest support for the practice of near-shoring?
    a. Employees will be willing to relocate in order to keep their jobs.
    b. The cost of travel for high-level employees will not negate the savings in moving jobs to locations with a lower cost of living.
    c. Clients will not need to travel to the lower-cost-of-living locales.
    d. Cities with a higher cost of living will not offer financial incentives to businesses to stay.
    e. Clients will not move out of the cities with a higher cost of living.

24. In order for humanitarian effort to relieve starving that results from a drought to succeed, there must be an efficient transportation system for water and support from several relief organizations. At least a dozen trucks that hold liquid are required for an efficient transportation for water. Each relief organization involved has pledged to supply trucks. Thus, relief will be brought to drought victims in the country of Y.

    Which of the following is the most important item be ascertained in order to evaluate the argument presented above?
    a. the number of relief organizations involved
    b. the availability of gasoline for the trucks
    c. the availability of water for transportation
    d. the amount of time it would take for the trucks to transport the water to drought victims
    e. the amount of time it would take to begin transporting the water to drought victims

25. Alexandra has more money than Courtney. Marnie has more money than Courtney. Alexandra has less money than Danielle. We can conclude that Courtney has less money than Josie.

    Which of the following, if true, would make the argument above logically incorrect?
    a. Danielle has more money than Marnie.
    b. Danielle has less money than Courtney.
    c. Alexandra has more money than Josie.
    d. Josie has more money than Danielle.
    e. Josie has less money than Marnie.

26. Taylor: The requirement that financial institutions register with the Securities and Exchange Commission all securities offered for sale to the public is pointless because people never read through all those piles of paper before they buy securities.

    Sophia: I disagree. The registration provides a paper trail that people can use to hold financial investors responsible in the event that securities were not accurately represented.

    Sophia responds to Taylor's argument by

    a. providing evidence that people who buy securities actually read the paperwork about them beforehand.
    b. shifting the discussion away from the paper that registration generates and toward the illegal activity that often occurs in securities sales.
    c. pointing out a benefit of registration, which Taylor's argument failed to consider.
    d. objecting to Taylor's dismissal of securities purchasers' financial literacy.
    e. rejecting Taylor's argument while suggesting that registration with the Securities and Exchange Commission be required of all securities.

27. The two methods available to ABC Car Company to increase fuel efficiency in its vehicles are installing a new type of engine in its cars and using a lighter metal for the car frames. The use of a lighter metal in the car frames will increase efficiency more than installation of a new type of engine. Therefore, by using a lighter metal in the car frames, ABC Car Company will be doing the most it can to increase fuel efficiency in its cars.

   If the statements above are true, which of the following must be true?

   a. ABC Car Company has several options for a lighter metal to use for the car frames.

   b. Fuel efficiency cannot be increased more by using both methods together than by only using a lighter metal in the car frames.

   c. The cars that ABC Car Company manufactures are already quite fuel efficient.

   d. ABC Car Company is unsure whether it should bother with increasing fuel efficiency.

   e. Installing a new type of engine will be more expensive than using a lighter metal in the car frames.

28. Demand for olive oil has remained constant during the past few years. Production and prices have also remained the same during the past few years, yet Crunchy Organics has seen an increase in its profits from olive oil by more than 20% over last year's profits.

   The conclusion above would be more reasonably drawn if any of the following were inserted into the argument as an additional premise EXCEPT:

   a. An economic recession has enabled Crunchy Organics to find workers who will work for lower wages.

   b. Crunchy Organics installed insulation and other energy-saving measures in its facilities, which resulted in significant decreases in utility bills and a hefty tax refund.

   c. Increased rainfall resulted in a more plentiful olive crop.

   d. Crunchy Organics was featured in a nationwide news segment about ethical small businesses, which was viewed by over 10 million people.

   e. The demand for olive oil has decreased, and most companies that produce olive oil have increased their distribution.

29. Which of the answer choices best completes the argument below?

More cosmetic companies should follow the marketing plan of Company G. Women want to see how products look on women who look like themselves because they can get a better idea of how the makeup will actually look on them. Women are also tired of being confronted with images _____.

a. of women who can clearly afford more expensive cosmetics than the average woman.

b. of supermodels who wear evening makeup when most women shop for a daytime look.

c. of supermodels who perpetuate the stereotype of unrealistic beauty.

d. of models who fail to make cosmetics look glamorous.

e. of models wearing makeup that is not of a good quality.

30. Township P conducted a survey in which over half of its residents admitted that they do not recycle, and the township's recycling plant has threatened to lay off employees due to a lack of work. In order to increase recycling, Township P should install recycling machines in the town center, in which residents can turn in their bottles, cans, and other recyclables in exchange for five cents apiece. This plan would dramatically increase the number of residents that recycle and save the jobs of many residents.

Which of the following are assumptions made in drawing the conclusion above?

a. Saving the jobs at the township's recycling plant would not result in corresponding layoffs at the township's trash plant, and the 5-cent refund would pay for the cost of recycling the additional materials.

b. The township's recycling plant can handle the increased quantity of materials to recycle, and an increase in recycling would save the jobs that the recycling plant has threatened to eliminate.

c. The recycling machines would induce residents to recycle more, and the 5-cent refund would pay for the recycling machines over time.

d. The 5-cent refund per item would eventually pay for the cost of the recycling machines, and the township could afford to pay the workers that the recycling plant has threatened to lay off.

e. The recycling machines and the 5-cent refund per item would induce residents to recycle more, and an increase in recycling would save the jobs that the recycling plant has threatened to eliminate.

31. Reporter: The Q Virus is a serious disease that can make people deathly ill. Starting in 1990 and continuing in every subsequent year, approximately 10,000 people became infected. Before 1990, there were only about 3,000 cases per year. We can conclude that the Q Virus has become a dire public health threat.

Public Health Expert: But before 1990, the population was only one quarter the size that it is now.

The public health expert challenges the reporter's argument by doing which of the following?

a. pointing out that the argument makes a conclusion based on a small sample of the population

b. pointing out that the argument treats facts about some people in a group as if they were true about all people in that group

c. presenting information that refutes the argument's assumption of an incremental increase

d. introducing information that casts doubt on an assumption of the reporter's argument

e. questioning the argument's information about the people in a particular group

32. Computer programming classes are offered in the College of Math and Science. A middle range percentage of students is enrolled in courses of the College of Math and Science. Economics classes are offered in the College of Business. The largest percentage of students is enrolled in courses in the College of Business. Business writing courses are offered in the College of Humanities. The lowest percentage of students is enrolled in courses in the College of Humanities. Therefore, computer information system classes should be offered in the College of Business.

     The conclusion above would be more reasonably drawn if which of the following were inserted into the argument as an additional premise?

   a. Courses should be offered in the college in which a greater percentage of students is enrolled.
   b. Computer information systems courses are more like business than they are like computer science.
   c. More majors in the College of Business require courses in computer information systems than majors in the College of Math and Science.
   d. Computer information systems courses have no relevance to the humanities.
   e. More students major in business because business majors have the greatest chance of finding a job.

33. The press reports sensationalist stories in order to get people to pay attention to the news. In order to generate high ratings, reporters must only report on topics with great scandal that will compel people to pay attention. The general public is, therefore, uninformed about basic current events.

     The conclusion drawn above is based on the assumption that

   a. the press only cares about high ratings.
   b. only scandalous topics will generate high ratings.
   c. the general public obtains all its news information from news outlets that generate high ratings.
   d. the press should be rewarded for high quality journalism.
   e. the press has tried to generate high ratings with quality news, and has failed.

34. This year, the police department of City X reported a relatively substantial increase in petty crime. The voters of City X congregated at a city council meeting to express their concern about this problem. A leader of a community action group stood up and urged the city council to rehire the 300 police officers it laid off due to budget cuts in the previous year. The city council president responded that the increase was in the actual number of victims who bothered to report petty crime to the police.

The city council's statements, if true, best support which of the following as a conclusion?

a. The previous presence of an extra 300 police officers deterred criminals from committing petty crime.

b. The laid-off police officers committed petty crime because they were no longer earning a salary.

c. The budget cuts were a symptom of an economic downturn, which is usually a cause behind a rise in petty crime.

d. It is possible to determine how many people were victims of petty crime in a year.

e. The percentage of victims of petty crime in the past year is no larger than the percentage of victims of petty crime this year.

35. Which of the answer choices most logically completes the argument given below?

Retail Expert: Companies that manufacture and sell name brand products often operate under the common misconception that manufacturing generic products would not be as profitable because they sell for a lower price. Even though name brand products sell for a higher price, the cost of production for generic products does not include any marketing expenses. Thus, the profits generated from the manufacture and sale of name brand products and generic products are usually comparable because ____.

a. the market for generic products is large enough and the cost of production is sufficiently low enough to offset the lower prices charged to customers

b. the market for name brand products is large enough and the cost of production is sufficiently low enough to offset the higher prices charged to customers

c. the respective markets for name brand products and generic products are about the same size

d. consumer demand will always exist for name brand products despite their higher prices

e. most companies are savvy enough to manufacture and sell both name brand and generic products, and they can purposely balance out those markets

36. Many people complain that standardized tests do not actually measure knowledge because people simply direct their studies toward the actual test and not the subject. However, standardized tests do measure knowledge because test takers have no way of anticipating the questions on the test and therefore have to study the entire subject.

The conclusion above is properly drawn if which of the following is assumed?

a. Standardized tests merely ask particular types of questions on which certain test takers excel.

b. Test takers must be able to anticipate test questions on any standardized test in order to direct their studies toward the actual test and not the subject.

c. If a standardized test has questions that cover the entire breadth of a subject, then the test actually measures knowledge.

d. People who direct their studies toward an actual test do not study an entire subject for the test.

e. Non-standardized tests actually measure knowledge.

37. Many companies offer their employees the option of flex time. Flex time is the practice of allowing employees to work their allotted number of hours on whatever schedule that they choose. Flex time permits employees to work during the most convenient hours for them, and results in increased productivity because employees are no longer as distracted by convenience issues.

Any of the following, if true, is a valid reason for a company to offer flex time to its employees EXCEPT:

a. The majority of workers in any industry report that they often conduct e-mail correspondence outside of traditional work hours.

b. Reports show that employees who work from home are often less productive, and employees who often utilize work from home options usually opt for flex time instead when their employers offer it.

c. Employees who work traditional hours often miss time at work because of health care appointments.

d. The majority of clients report that they prefer to conduct business over the telephone rather than via e-mail.

e. Employees often exceed their lunch hours because they are running personal errands that are more convenient to do midday.

Argument Evaluation

Examples of argument evaluation questions are: analyze the argument, strengthen the argument, weaken the argument, identify reasoning errors in the argument, or recognize aspects of the argument's development.

Flaw Questions
These questions ask you to identify the answer choice that makes the argument incorrect.

- Which of the following is a flaw in the above argument?
- The flaw in the argument is that it fails to consider. . . .
- Which of the following, if true, identifies a flaw in the argument above?

Strengthen Questions
This type of question requires that you identify the assumption and pick the answer choice that would strengthen the assumption.

- Which of the following, if true, would most strengthen the conclusion drawn above?
- Which of the following, if true, would lend the most support to the view . . . ?

Weaken Questions
This type of question requires that you identify the assumption and pick the answer choice that would weaken the assumption.

- Which of the following, if true, would most weaken the conclusion drawn above?
- Which of the following, if true, would most undermine the argument?
- Which of the following, if true, casts the most doubt on the conclusion above?

Evaluate the Argument
These questions ask you to identify what would be the most useful to assess the argument in the passage.

- Which of the following would be most helpful in evaluating the argument above?
- Which of the following would be most useful to know in assessing the conclusion above?

Argument Evaluation Test-Taking Strategies

1. Identify the assumption.

Identify whether the assumption is a causal connection, a similarity, or a shift. Strengthen and weaken questions require that you identify the assumption and pick the choice that would either strengthen or weaken it. Ask yourself whether the passage creates a causal connection, similarity, or a shift between two things that does not actually exist. These two items may be quite similar, designed to trip you up by assuming that they are in fact related.

2. Identify the relationships between the numbers.

Many GMAT questions use a lot of quantitative information designed to cause you to assume relationships between sets of numbers when in fact there is not one. Critical reasoning questions will often use dollar amounts, quantitative amounts, percentages, interest rates, and inflation. Do not assume that dollar or quantitative amounts necessarily correlate with percentages. Furthermore, ask yourself whether interest rates or inflation, if mentioned in the prompt, will actually have a particular effect on the numbers in the passage. After you read the question and reread the prompt, discard any extraneous numbers clogging the passage that you do not need to consider.

3. Remember "except," "not," and other opposites.

GMAT questions will occasionally flip the standard format and list a series of answer choices that strengthen, weaken, or explain the argument. These questions will ask you to identify the answer choice that does NOT strengthen, weaken, or explain. Test takers often get tripped up when working on these questions and start looking for the opposite of what the question is asking for. For questions such as these, jot down what the question is asking for on your scratch paper. For example:

Which of the following, if true, does NOT strengthen the argument above

Remember, that "not strengthen" does not necessarily mean "weaken." The correct answer choice may not do either. Note that you should cross off all answer choices that strengthen the argument and pick the remaining one.

4. Note which argument the question addresses.

Some GMAT questions will include the arguments of multiple parties instead of just one. Many test takers have a tendency to skim the question and assume that it is asking you to strengthen, weaken, or point out the flaw in the last argument in the passage. However, the question may want you to work with a different party's argument. For example:

A asserts that the budget is not accurate because it failed to take into account tax credits.

B concludes that there were no tax credits because of an accounting error.

Which of the following, if true, would strengthen A's argument?

Make sure that you are addressing the argument that the question directs you to because one of the answer choices will likely strengthen B's argument and trick you.

5. Right result, wrong reason.

Beware of answer choices that list subject matter that could plausibly strengthen or weaken an argument, be a flaw in the argument, or point out something useful to evaluate an argument, but that employ incorrect reasoning. If multiple answer choices seem plausible to you at first glance, take a closer look at the reasoning in them. For example:

> A dog food company was concerned about failing to adhere to its budget in the current calendar year. In order to solve this problem, the company decided to move its headquarters to a different office building with a lower rent. Upper management concluded that moving the company's headquarters in the next year would result in sufficient savings to meet its budgetary requirements.
>
> Which of the following, if true, would weaken the argument?
>
> **a.** After the company paid for moving costs, it would not earn back the rental savings from the new location for an additional two years—**correct answer**
>
> **b.** The company failed to consider that the new building has higher utility bills—**incorrect answer**

Do you see why? Both answers provide reasons that the new building will not provide the savings that the company believes it will. However, choice **a** specifically negates savings that the company's plan to move will allegedly generate. Choice **b** provides another reason that could plausibly negate the savings, but it is not conclusive because the answer does not specifically say that the higher utility bills would cancel out the savings generated by the lower rent. The reasoning here is not sufficiently thorough to be the best answer to weaken the argument.

Set 3

Now it is time to answer GMAT Critical Reasoning practice questions that have been designed to test your argument evaluation skills. Good luck!

38. Vegetarians tend to live longer than people who eat meat. This does not show that vegetarianism causes people to live longer because vegetarians as a group tend to exercise more regularly than meat eaters.

    Which of the following, if true, most strengthens the argument above?

    a. A vegetarian who does not exercise regularly is more likely to start exercising than a person who eats meat.
    b. Among vegetarians, most of those who start to exercise regularly early in life tend to maintain the practice later in life.
    c. Among people who exercise regularly, those who do not eat meat tend to live as long as those who eat meat.
    d. Vegetarianism tends to cause people to engage in other healthy habits besides regular exercise.
    e. A person who eats meat and gives up regular exercise is much more likely than a vegetarian to never resume regular exercise.

39. The city of Springfield has received a proposal to upgrade its metro system. An environmental group has argued that increasing the number of trains and the metro's area of coverage within the city will result in a 20% increase in rider capacity, reducing the need for people to drive cars. The city of Springfield should grant the proposal to solve the problem of traffic congestion on the city roads.

    Which of the following, if true, most seriously weakens the argument?

    a. Most people in Springfield are unwilling to switch from driving to public transit.
    b. Increasing the metro's passenger capacity will require the trains to travel at a slower speed.
    c. Most people who drive in Springfield commute to places in the city that the metro does not currently reach.
    d. The proposed upgrade to the metro system will increase air pollution.
    e. The metro system is currently not filled to capacity during the rush hour commute.

40. President of Fundraising: Donations to our organization have decreased steadily over the past five years. Many individuals at this meeting have suggested that the poor economy is the reason. I disagree. My research has indicated that donors to this cause tend to donate the same amounts and in the same frequency regardless of their income. I believe that we need to reexamine our mailings so that we can find a better way to remind our donors about the important work that our organization does.

Which of the following, if true, most strongly supports the fundraising president's theory?

a. The majority of the donors to this organization have not suffered financially in the downturned economy.

b. The organization's mailings used to contain prepaid postage on the return envelopes for donations, but have not for the past five years.

c. The organization has decreased its charitable work over the past five years in order to increase its fundraising effort.

d. The organization has not updated its mailing list for the last seven years.

e. The majority of the donors are above age 75 and have difficulty reading smaller print.

41. Dr. Roberts, a dentist, gave a speech to a dental convention in which she argued that the recent rise in tooth enamel decay in the population came from a new brand of toothbrush. This brand used a new type of plastic for the bristles, which Dr. Roberts claimed wears down the enamel of the teeth over time. Dr. Roberts concluded her remarks by stating that the consistent high rate of soft drink consumption was not a significant contributing factor to the recent rise in tooth enamel decay.

Which of the following, if true, most strongly supports the view that the new brand of toothbrush was responsible for the rise in tooth enamel decay mentioned above?

a. The brand Dr. Roberts mentioned is the only brand to use the new type of plastic for the bristles.

b. Consistent heavy consumption of soft drinks does not increase tooth enamel decay over time provided that patients brush twice a day.

c. This brand of toothbrush has a 70% market share.

d. The majority of Dr. Roberts's patients used this brand of toothbrush for a significant period of time.

e. The company that sold this brand of toothbrush sent hundreds of thousands of samples to dentists for free giveaways to dental patients.

42. People between the ages of 40 and 50 purchase more vacations to Mexico than any other age group. Therefore, the Mexico Tourist Board should convince hotels and resorts in Mexico to offer more family friendly packages and services.

Which of the following indicates a flaw in the reasoning above?

a. The author assumes that the majority of people between the ages of 40 and 50 have children.

b. The author assumes that the majority of people between the ages of 40 and 50 want family friendly vacations.

c. The author assumes that the majority of people between the ages of 40 and 50 are married.

d. The author does not supply information about people in other age groups.

e. The author assumes that the majority of people between the ages of 40 and 50 can afford a vacation in Mexico.

43. Last year, approximately 1 million smokers quit smoking. This year, the number of smokers who quit is approximately 3 million. Thus, we can conclude that the number of smokers who will quit is increasing and that the number of smokers who will quit next year will be even higher.

Which of the following statements best supports the conclusion above?

   a. The 1 million smokers who quit last year represented the lowest number in six years.
   b. An increase in government regulation regarding health care usually results in an increase in health care coverage of smoking cessation programs.
   c. This year, a government grant to a program called Light Up No More brought the number of smokers who quit temporarily up from the average number of 1 million per year.
   d. This year, health insurance companies raised premiums 20% for customers who smoke, and they plan to institute a 5% increase for next year.
   e. The estimated number of smokers who quit annually is actually based on a representative sample of the population rather than the entire population.

44. Production of paper has always been costly, but the tariffs on a box of paper currently make domestic paper production less expensive. Therefore, if we want to obtain paper in the cheapest way possible, we should produce all our paper in our own country.

Which of the following, if true, most seriously weakens the argument above?

   a. Producing paper domestically will create more jobs.
   b. Tariffs on boxes of paper are the same flat cost on every box no matter the size.
   c. Companies that produce a product have a high incentive to control the cost of production.
   d. The final price of a product after adding in the tariff is higher than the impact that production start-up costs have on the final price of a product.
   e. Foreign paper producers can produce more paper overall than a domestic producer.

45. The retail industry suffers from the problem of high employee turnover. Since wages remain stagnant for employees who work in stores, employees have no incentive to remain with the same company over time. The Namaste Clothing Co. has a much higher retail employee retention rate than other retail companies. The human resources department published a report that stated that the company's success is due to qualitative factors that the company offers, such as a pension plan, comp time for salaried employees, casual Fridays, water coolers, and high-end computers with great tech support.

Which of the following, if true, identifies a flaw in the argument above?

a. The human resources report assumes that employees care about the qualitative factors listed.

b. The human resources report erroneously lists pension and comp time for salaried employees as qualitative factors, when they are actually related to employee compensation.

c. The human resources report lists qualitative factors that would apply only to company employees who do not work in stores.

d. The human resources report assumes that employees have remained with the company because of something the company has offered them.

e. The human resources report did not list all the qualitative advantages that the company offers its employees.

46. In 2000, women's clothing retailers reported that 20% of their sales were for sizes 0–4, 35% of their sales were for sizes 6–12, and 45% of their sales were for sizes 14–16. In 2010, women's clothing retailers reported that those percentages were 25%, 45%, and 30%, respectively. We can conclude that the average adult woman was the same size in 2010 that she was 10 years ago.

Which of the following, if true, best explains the conclusion above?

a. The amount of clothing purchased in 2010 was greater than the amount of clothing purchased in 2000.

b. Vanity sizing was much more prevalent in 2000 than in 2010.

c. A greater percentage of slimmer woman bought clothing in 2010 than in 2000.

d. The number of women who purchased clothing in 2000 was greater than the number of women who purchased clothing in 2010.

e. Most of the designers who designed clothes in 2010 had not yet earned their degrees in fashion design in 2000.

47. The average law firm pays entry-level attorneys an annual salary of $70,000. Ninety-five percent of law school students have jobs upon graduation. Therefore, of that 95%, the average law student will earn an annual salary of $70,000.

Which of the following, if true, most seriously undermines the argument above?

a. Most law students who have jobs upon graduation were hired by small law firms.

b. The average salary offered by law firms varies by geographical region.

c. Fewer students enroll in law school today than 10 years ago.

d. The law students who do not have jobs upon graduation did not pass the bar exam.

e. Over half of law students who have jobs upon graduation were not hired by law firms.

48. Company XYZ manufactures and sells products that help people quit smoking. This year, Company XYZ reported an increase in sales overall and in each individual smoking cessation product. The entire market for products that help people quit smoking also reported an increase in sales overall. The product with the highest increase was the patch. The product with the lowest increase was the gum. We can conclude from this information that the number of people who have quit smoking has increased this year.

Which of the following, if true, most seriously calls into question the explanation above?

a. Most people who quit smoking reported that their greatest success was with the gum.

b. Most people who quit smoking reported that they did not buy smoking cessation products from Company XYZ.

c. Most people who quit smoking reported that they relapsed in approximately 10 months.

d. Most people who quit smoking reported that they bought multiple smoking cessation products at once.

e. Most people who quit smoking reported that they purchased whatever smoking cessation product their doctor recommended.

49. The rise of college tuition was widely expected to result in an overall increase in the total amount that people in this country spent on college tuition. However, the exact opposite occurred. The rise in tuition occurred along with a rise in merit scholarships. The result is that college students in this country actually spend less on college than previously.

Which if the following would NOT be useful in evaluating the reasoning above?

a. the total cost of tuition and the monetary amount of the scholarships

b. the total cost of tuition and the percentage of students who take advantage of scholarships

c. the total cost of tuition considering scholarships and the cost of room and board

d. the total cost of tuition considering scholarships and the breakdown of student attendance at public versus private colleges

e. the total cost of tuition considering scholarships and the number of students who attend college

50. The state legislature has become concerned with the rise in drunk driving accidents on state highways. In an effort to curtail this problem, the legislature raised the driving age from 17 to 18. The governor lauded this effort, declaring to the press that this new law will drastically reduce drunk driving accidents.

All the following statements strengthen the argument above EXCEPT:

a. Seventeen-year-old drivers were involved in over half of the drunk driving accidents on state highways.

b. A famous study reported that the alcoholism rate in minors was exorbitantly high in this state.

c. A survey of teenagers found that the majority of teenagers did not believe that alcohol consumption significantly impaired their driving.

d. A report issued by the department of highway safety asserted that less driving experience made teenagers slower to react to hazards on the highway.

e. The state police's statistics showed that most drunk driving accidents occurred between 10 P.M. and 6 A.M., and the department of motor vehicles issued only limited drivers licenses to teenagers, which permitted driving only during daylight hours.

51. Ten people were hospitalized for severe stomach problems within one day after drinking Zippo's Cola. The Zippo Cola Company fervently argued that its cola drink was not responsible for the stomach problems and that the company was in no way responsible for anyone's illness. Instead, Zippo Cola released a statement to the public that it believed that the company that makes the soda cans, Carrie's Canning Inc., used an ingredient in the metal that made people sick. Margie Smith, one of the patients, told her doctor that she was convinced that she ate bad shellfish. All 10 patients ate lunch at the same restaurant that day. The doctors concluded that both the restaurant and the cola were responsible for the patients' illness.

Which of the following, if true, would cast the most serious doubt on Zippo's argument?

   a. Carrie's Canning, Inc. also supplied cans from the same can supply to the Bubbles Orange Soda Company, and no one who drank that soda became ill.
   b. All 10 patients ate shrimp scampi as an appetizer at the restaurant that day.
   c. All 10 patients ate meals at the restaurant that had no overlapping ingredients with each other's meals.
   d. Seven of the patients drank regular Zippo Cola and three of the patients drank Diet Zippo Cola.
   e. Margie Smith's lunch was a pasta dish with mussels.

52. The Department of Safe Transportation reported that 73% of all accidents involve people who are supposed to wear glasses or contact lenses. We can reduce car accidents if department employees ask drivers whether they wear glasses or contact lenses, and make a notation on the driver's license, every time drivers renew their license.

The argument is flawed because it fails to consider that

a. drivers who are supposed to wear glasses or contact lenses will wear them while driving.

b. driver's license renewals will catch a fair number of drivers who have not notified the Department that they are required to wear glasses or contact lenses while driving.

c. drivers who are supposed to wear glasses or contact lenses are not aware of it.

d. a vision test will let drivers know that they need to see an ophthalmologist.

e. the departments of transportation in other states will not implement the same policy.

53. University Z created eight intramural sports teams in order to combat obesity among the student population. The university estimated that approximately 55% of students were overweight, including 35% who were obese. Seventy-five percent of students signed up and participated regularly in the intramural sports teams for the entire year. At the end of the year, 55% of students remained overweight, and 35% remained obese.

Which of the following, if true, best explains why the university's plan failed?

a. The students who participated in intramural sports continued to have extremely poor eating habits that exercise could not offset.

b. The students who participated in intramural sports were not active previously.

c. The students who participated in intramural sports included those who also participated in official university sports teams.

d. The students who participated in intramural sports possessed various athletic abilities.

e. The students who participated in intramural sports were somewhat active previously.

54. Dr. Roberts, a dentist, gave a speech to a dental convention in which she argued that the recent rise in tooth enamel decay in the population came from a new brand of toothbrush. This brand used a new type of plastic for the bristles, which Dr. Roberts claimed wears down the enamel of the teeth over time. Dr. Roberts added that the consistent soft drink consumption was not a significant contributing factor to the recent rise in tooth enamel decay. She then concluded her remarks by stating that tooth enamel decay in patients will significantly decrease if every dentist convinces her patients not to use this brand of toothbrush.

The argument is flawed primarily because the author

a. assumed that the cause of increased tooth enamel decay in her patients is the same as in every other dentist's patients.

b. assumed that consistent soft drink consumption was not a significant contributing factor to the recent rise in tooth enamel decay.

c. assumed that the new type of plastic used for the bristles was the cause of the rise in tooth enamel decay in the general population.

d. assumed that this brand of toothbrush is the only brand to use the type of plastic for the bristles that Dr. Roberts claims wears down tooth enamel over time.

e. assumed that because consistent soft drink consumption was not a significant contributing factor to tooth enamel decay in her patients, then it was not in any other dentist's patients.

55. Television Executive: The largest demographic in this country is senior citizens. Senior citizens are also more likely to not work than the rest of the population because they have retired, and therefore spend more time at home. The majority of senior citizens dislike reality television. We can therefore conclude that our network should plan fewer reality TV programs in the future.

Which of the following, if true, would most undermine the television executive's argument?

a. Reality television programs cost less to produce than other types of programs.

b. Senior citizens are not the largest demographic that watches television.

c. A smaller percentage of senior citizens are currently retired than in previous generations.

d. The reality TV program called *The Golden Years* is extremely popular among senior citizens.

e. Retired senior citizens generally spend their daytime hours engaged in activities such as gardening, walking, and taking care of grandchildren.

56. A company has decided to implement a new employee evaluation program in which pay raises will be determined by an employee's overall rating given by his or her supervisor. Upper management concluded that this new evaluation program would result in pay raises for the employees with the most meritorious job performance.

Which of the following, if true, does NOT cast doubt on upper management's belief that the new program will result in pay raises based on merit?

a. Supervisors' judgment of what constitutes "exceeds expectations" is subjective.

b. All employees who meet revenue goals cannot receive "does not meet expectations" on their employee evaluations.

c. The three ratings of "does not meet expectations," "meets expectations," and "exceeds expectations" do not provide enough information to differentiate the various levels of employee job performance.

d. Supervisors who like their employees tend to rate them higher than supervisors who dislike their employees.

e. The new employee evaluation program records the information in a database that the human resources department can access when processing pay raises.

57. A recent economic downturn has reminded people of the importance of saving, both for emergencies and for retirement. The average household saved 5% of its income in the past year, and that number is predicted to grow over the next 10 years. The result will be that banks will have more money to lend to customers to start businesses and buy homes. We can conclude that economic activity will grow over the next 10 years as a result of this ethic in saving money.

Which of the following would most weaken the argument?

a. People who place a greater percentage of their income into their savings accounts have been and will be underemployed over the next 10 years.

b. People who place a greater percentage of their income into their savings accounts will take out loans to start businesses.

c. People who place a greater percentage of their income into their savings accounts will also pay down their credit card debt.

d. People who place a greater percentage of their income into their savings accounts will focus their spending on only necessary home improvements.

e. People who place a great percentage of their income into their savings accounts will enable the banks to curtail fee increases.

58. Retail stores that pay their sales associates based on commission pay their employees wages that vary with the sales dollar amount for which each employee is responsible. In the retail business last year, stores that paid their employees on commission showed that worker productivity was 17% higher than that of their competitors that paid their sales associates an hourly wage.

If, on the basis of the evidence above, it is argued that paying sales associates on commission increases worker productivity, which of the following, if true, would most seriously weaken the argument?

a. Retail stores that pay their sales associates on commission have experienced that costs other than wages, such as rent, utilities, and inventory processing, make up an increased proportion of the total cost of operating each store.

b. Retail stores that pay their sales associates on commission have more troubling hiring workers because many applicants are concerned about making little money on days when the stores have few customers.

c. Sales associates who earn money on commission have paychecks that are 22% higher than those of sales associates who are paid an hourly wage.

d. The productivity results cited for sales associates in retail stores are also true for telemarketers.

e. The majority of customers who shop in retail stores report that they purchase items without assistance from sales associates.

59. College President: This state's families actually do not pay less for tuition at public colleges than private colleges. Each family in this state pays taxes, a portion of which go to state colleges. When you add the amount of those taxes with the cost of tuition at a public college, the cost is actually the same as tuition at a private college.

The college president's argument is flawed because it fails to consider that

a. the cost of tuition at a private college is higher than the cost of state taxes paid toward a public college and tuition at a public college.

b. a portion of taxes that each family in the state pays goes to public colleges even if no members of that family attend college.

c. many private colleges offer scholarships to students who demonstrate superior academic achievement.

d. a portion of every family's taxes in the state goes to public colleges even if members of that family attend a private college, so the taxes are not actually part of the cost of tuition.

e. the price of tuition at a public college depends on the state's budget.

60. Economist: Large price club type stores will eventually drive small, independently owned stores out of business. Price clubs can price their goods much lower per item because they sell products in bulk sizes. Small stores simply cannot compete with those prices.

Which of the following, if true, does NOT weaken the argument above?

a. Price club stores may be able to offer lower prices, but they only sell a limited variety of goods, and customers will need to shop elsewhere to find the remainder of the goods that they want.

b. An increasing majority of customers use public transportation instead of cars, and live in small apartments rather than houses, so they cannot transport or store a large number of goods.

c. Many customers desire to support independently owned businesses, and will shop there rather than at price clubs even if it means paying higher prices.

d. Independently owned stores accept coupons, and most customers report that when they factor in coupons, they wind up paying the same price at independently owned stores as they do in price clubs.

e. Price club customers report that they earn back the price of their membership fee within the first two months of purchases.

61. Osteoporosis is a disease that results in a severe weakening of bones. A diet rich in calcium throughout one's lifetime is commonly known to be the best prevention against osteoporosis. Sources of calcium include legumes, leafy green vegetables, and dairy products. A medical group devoted to raising the awareness of osteoporosis recommends that people consume more leafy green vegetables than dairy products in order to raise their calcium intake.

Which of the following, if true, would most strongly support the position above?

a. Dairy products typically contain fat, and leafy green vegetables do not.

b. Leafy green vegetables provide many other health benefits, most notably a higher iron content.

c. Nutritionists recommend five to eight servings of leafy green vegetables per day, and only three servings of dairy per day.

d. The body's absorption rate for calcium in leafy green vegetables is 50%, and for dairy products is 30%.

e. The farming of leafy green vegetables uses fewer environmental resources than the production of dairy products.

62. Each unit in an apartment complex is supplied with a refrigerator, stove, microwave, and dishwasher. In order to keep the appliances functioning, the apartment complex employs a full-time super who is on call Monday through Friday from 9 A.M. to 5 P.M. Without repairs, the appliances would eventually stop working and would be expensive to replace. We can conclude that the apartment complex should continue to employ the super full-time.

Which of the following, if true, would most seriously weaken the argument above?

a. Most tenants discover that their appliances are not working during the evening hours.

b. Apartment complexes that install dishwashers in their units use a much greater amount of water than those without dishwashers in their units.

c. Appliances become obsolete in only a few years, which makes repairing them less practical and more costly then buying new appliances.

d. Employing a super full-time requires benefits, such as medical insurance and paid vacation time, in addition to a salary.

e. This apartment complex uses electric stoves, and gas stoves usually have lower utility bills.

63. The textbook publishing industry reported a consistent annual increase in e-book sales. For two years, publishers of law textbooks offered a special promotion, in which the e-book version was offered free along with the hard copy. Publishers of law textbooks expected this exposure to e-books to ease law students' transition away from hard copies and result in a decline in sales of hard copies in favor of e-books. Surprisingly, this decline did not occur.

Which of the following would be the most useful to determine in order to evaluate why the publishers' promotion did not achieve the expected results?

a. the average age of law students and their respective familiarity with the e-book format before the promotion

b. the weight of the average hard copy law textbook

c. the percentage of courses covered by the textbooks with the promotion

d. the percentage of law students who previously bought e-books compared to the percentage of undergraduate students who bought e-books

e. the majority of law students who had open-book exams and took their exams on their laptop computers, which required an exam software that blocked student access to all their computer files during the exam

64. The press has consistently reported stories about the adverse effects of soy on people with existing thyroid problems, and about the environmental problems that stem from farming soybeans. A national health organization stated that fewer people reported consuming soy products in place of meat and dairy, and an increasing number of people reported concern that they might be allergic to soy. Therefore, we can conclude that soy consumption will decrease over the next few years.

Which of the following, if true, would most undermine the conclusion above?

a. Soy is a common ingredient in processed foods that contain meat.

b. People do not discover a food allergy until after they have had an adverse reaction to food.

c. Many people suspect that they have a thyroid problem even when they do not actually have one.

d. People base many of their food choices on the effect they have on the environment.

e. Meat and dairy products tend to be more expensive than soy products.

Formulating and Evaluating a Plan of Action

Examples of formulating and evaluating a plan of action questions are: identify the effectiveness of a plan, identify whether the plan is appropriate to address the problem at hand, recognize whether another plan would be more efficient, identify factors that would strengthen a plan, and identify factors that would weaken a plan.

Identify the Effectiveness of a Plan/Recognize Whether Another Plan Would Be More Efficient

These questions will ask you to identify whether a proposed plan will address the actual course of a problem effectively. These questions will also ask you to recognize whether another plan would provide a better solution to the problem.

- Which of the following is the LEAST important to know to determine the success of the plan?

- Which of the following is NOT important to know for the plan?
- Which of the following would help to explain why the plan failed?

Strengthen the Plan

These questions will ask you to identify the answer choice that would strengthen the plan in the passage.

- Which of the following, if true, provides the strongest reason to expect the plan to succeed?
- Which of the following, if added to the plan, would be most effective in helping the above plan?

Weaken the Plan

These questions will ask you to identify the answer choice that would weaken the plan in the passage.

- Which of the following, if true, would provide the most serious disadvantage to the plan above?
- Which of the following, if true, would most likely worsen the plan above?

Formulating and Evaluating a Plan of Action Test-Taking Strategies

1. Identify the assumption.

This strategy is in each section of this book for the Critical Reasoning portion of the GMAT®, but it bears repeating. Most of the plans in this type of question are either business related or government related. Do not let your own knowledge of these subject matters cause you to make assumptions about the plan. Instead, find the gap in the reasoning and identify whether it is a causal connection, shift, or similarity.

2. Identify whether the plan could actually address the problem.

If the passage states that the plan failed, evaluate the plan and see whether it actually could have addressed the problem. What was the flaw in the plan? Did the plan fail to consider something? Did it address an effect of the problem rather than the source? If the answer choices list alternative or additional plans designed to rectify the problem that the original plan failed to solve, look for answer choices with plans that have the same flawed reasoning and eliminate them.

3. Watch out for the numbers.

Since many of the plans that you will evaluate on the test will have to do with business or government, they will likely contain numbers. Watch out for assumed relationships between raw numbers and percentages. You should also be aware of any comparisons between combinations of different variables. If the numbers are vague and you cannot figure out how anyone could eliminate answers, remember that the question may ask you for an answer choice that is the only one for which you can draw a conclusion.

4. Identify reasons for the plan's failure or success.

Many formulating and evaluating a plan of action questions will ask you to identify the answer choice that explains the reason for a plan's failure or success. If you see this type of question and then reread the passage, you could benefit from thinking of your own reasons before looking at the answer choices, much like thinking of an argument's conclusion before reading the conclusions that the answer choices offer in argument construction questions.

Set 4

Now it is time to answer GMAT Critical Reasoning practice questions that have been designed to test your formulating and evaluating a plan of action skills. Good luck!

65. Millipoint is a large city that employs many people from the surrounding suburban communities. Suburban Commute Transportation Company must expand its services for the increasing number of people who commute to Millipoint. Suburban Commute could replace its trains with double-decker trains, add 10% more ferries, or add 25% more buses. Trains typically spend the least amount of time in traffic, which is important because they run every 15 minutes. Ferries have a capacity of 75 people apiece. Buses have a capacity of about 50 people apiece and tend to spend time in traffic. After considering all options, Suburban Commute decided to replace its trains with double-decker trains.

    Which of the following, if true, could represent the most serious disadvantage for Suburban Commute's plan?
    a. Two new highways were constructed that lead into Millipoint.
    b. Double-decker trains require twice the amount of boarding time as single-level trains.
    c. A competitor has significantly increased its use of the same train tracks that Suburban Commute uses.
    d. Double-decker trains running against rush hour traffic tend to be nearly empty.
    e. Double-decker ferries are available.

66. The Consumer Watchdog Agency reports that 65% of red snapper sold in grocery stores and restaurants is actually less expensive types of fish fraudulently labeled. In an effort to clamp down on this fraud, the agency has created a new consumer confidence stamp that would mark packages of red snapper as inspected and verified by the Consumer Watchdog Agency.

Which of the following, if true, provides the strongest reason to expect that the Consumer Watchdog Agency will succeed in decreasing the percentage of less expensive types of fish fraudulently sold as red snapper?

a. Grocery store inventory managers are usually the individuals who place other fish in the red snapper section of the fresh fish counter.

b. Restaurant owners have a common practice of passing off other fish as red snapper.

c. Most customers are unable to tell the difference between red snapper and other types of fish.

d. The majority of red snapper sold is sold fresh off the boat without packaging.

e. The fishing industry is interested in curtailing the fraud in red snapper sales.

67. Potter Shipping, Inc. had a relatively high failure rate in delivering packages on time. In order to address this problem, the CEO promised drivers a 10% year-end bonus if they succeeded in delivering 90% of their packages on time.

All the following, if true, would help to explain why the CEO's bonus incentive plan failed to achieve a significantly better on-time delivery rate EXCEPT

a. highway construction projects caused drivers to spend hours of time sitting in traffic.
b. most company trucks had faulty GPS units.
c. drivers were responsible to pay for their own fuel, which was expensive, and faster driving consumed greater quantities of gasoline.
d. other shipping companies paid their drivers a 15% bonus if they delivered 90% of their packages on time, and many Potter drivers wound up leaving their jobs within six months to work for competitors.
e. most drivers believed the 10% bonus to be a great incentive to increase on-time deliveries.

68. A group called People for the Preservation of the Environment has published a damaging report about the pollution caused by Trikas Oil Refineries. Although not accused of any illegal activity, Trikas has decided that it must decrease the air pollution it generates in order to placate public opinion. In order to accomplish this goal, Trikas plans on upgrading its refineries with the Zeebot Purification System.

The adoption of the Zeebot Purification System would most likely worsen Trikas Oil Refineries' problem if

a. the Zeebot Purification System costs a significant amount of money.
b. the Zeebot Purification System malfunctions 10% of the time.
c. the Zeebot Purification System will take six months to implement.
d. the Zeebot Purification System takes a lot of manpower to maintain.
e. the Zeebot Purification System results in a significant increase in water pollution.

69. The government of Woodrock decided five years ago to increase the number of preventative care medical services covered in the government's free health care program for seniors.

Which of the following would be the LEAST important in determining whether the increased number of preventative care medical services would be likely to achieve better health for Woodrock's senior population?

a. the percentage of seniors who seek preventative care medical services

b. the success rate of preventative care medical services

c. the cost of preventative care medical services

d. the senior population's access to facilities that provide preventative care medical services

e. the percentage of seniors who utilize the government's free health care program for seniors

70. In the upcoming elections, the Grow the Economy Now party's candidates have proposed a government tax break to individuals and companies who invest in start-up businesses. The plan would exempt these individuals and companies from paying any taxes on the profits from these investments for five years.

All the following would NOT be important to know in determining whether the tax break would provide an incentive to invest in start-up businesses EXCEPT

a. the amount of capital required to start a business.

b. the tax bracket of the average individual investor.

c. the most common types of start-up businesses created.

d. the number of years a start-up business requires to earn a profit.

e. the number of candidates in the Grow the Economy Now party who have a history in investing in start-up businesses.

71. The Lightening Tread Shoe Company, in an effort to boost revenue, has decided to offer free shipping on its website for all orders over $22.00. The cost of shipping these orders will reduce the profit by $4.00 per shipment. However, management believes that the savings to customers will result in more orders.

   Which of the following would be NOT be important to know in determining whether this plan will result in an increase in revenue?

   a. the current price of packing materials
   b. whether competitors of the Lightening Tread Shoe Company also offer free shipping on orders over $22.00
   c. changes in the average price of an order
   d. changes in postal rates
   e. whether customers purchased the same amount of merchandise spread out in several smaller orders

72. A citywide survey was conducted in the past year, and revealed that 35% of employees do not know where the fire exits are in their places of employment. Previously, a private safety company would conduct annual fire drills in all commercial city buildings that consisted of more than four floors. In order to increase employee knowledge of the location of fire exits, the city has arranged to pay fire department employees a bonus to conduct a second annual fire drill in these buildings.

   Which additional plan, combined with the plan just outlined, will be most effective in helping the city address the high percentage of employees who do not know the location of the fire exits in their workplace?

   a. hiring the private safety company to conduct annual fire drills in city buildings with less than four floors
   b. paying fire department employees a bonus to conduct a second annual fire drill in city buildings with less than four floors
   c. hiring the private safety company to conduct two annual fire drills in all city buildings
   d. finding a new private safety company to conduct the annual fire drills
   e. threaten to fine companies with over 35% of employees unable to identify the location of the fire exits

73. Plan: The government of Tulpso was concerned about the high level of credit card debt that its average citizen carried, and about the high amount of credit card debt the population carried as a nation. The government convinced the banks in the credit card industry to offer a 4% lower APR for existing debt to any customer who paid off more than the monthly interest. The government subsidized the difference in interest rates.

Result: Many Tulpso citizens still carry the same amount of debt as before.

Further Information: The annual rate of inflation since the government-subsidized reduced interest rate on existing credit card debt has been below 3%, and every Tulpso citizen who carried credit card debt paid more than the monthly interest of their credit card bills.

In light of the further information, which of the following, if true, does most to explain the result that followed implementation of the plan?

a. The most recent reduction in APR was only the second of its kind in the last 20 years.

b. The Tulpso credit card repayment system required citizens to pay their bills in person.

c. The majority of citizens in Tulspo needed this program to pay down their credit card debt.

d. The prices of food and other necessities rose to a level that required citizens to charge similar amounts to what they repaid.

e. The government offered the reduced APR at a time when a large number of people were poverty-stricken.

74. The population in the country of Xusa has remained stable for the last 20 years and is expected to remain so. The airline industry has decided to triple the number of flights offered to current destinations in the next year.

Which of the following would be most helpful to justify the airline industry's plan?

a. The largest segment of the population has reached retirement age.

b. Businesses have reported a substantial rise in attendance at trade shows around the nation.

c. The price of airplane fuel has decreased.

d. Companies that produce airplane meals have offered substantially better wholesale prices to airlines.

e. A famous university study has reported that the percentage of the population with a fear of flying has dropped significantly over the last 10 years.

75. The customer service department of the E-Z Movie Rental Co. has reported a 15% increase in customer service complaints regarding damaged or unplayable discs in the past year. The CEO announced that employees responsible for packing the discs into mailer envelopes are required to perform a new 3-step process to check for scratches and other visible defects on the discs. Over the next year, the customer service department reported a 5% increase in customer complaints regarding damaged or unplayable discs.

All the following, if true, would explain why the new 3-step process failed to achieve the company goal EXCEPT

a. the paper that the mailer envelopes were made of was a particularly abrasive type of paper.

b. the warehouse employees did not comply with the new 3-step process when mailing out discs.

c. most of the customers who complained about damaged or unplayable discs had damaged those discs themselves.

d. the majority of the discs' defects were visible defects.

e. damaged or unplayable discs were not taken out of circulation.

76. The Whigham Insurance Company offers All Risk insurance to hotels, resorts, and other large structures. All Risk insurance covers everything that is not listed in the exclusions. There has been a recent increase in earthquakes and Whigham is concerned that earthquake coverage will be too expensive to maintain. However, Whigham would still prefer to avoid listing earthquakes in the list of exclusions for the future if possible.

   Which of the following strategies would be most likely to minimize Company X's losses on the policies?

   a. insuring only those customers whose buildings did not experience earthquake damage in the past 20 years
   b. insuring only those customers who cannot obtain earthquake coverage through another insurance provider
   c. expanding its marketing campaign to attract customers with buildings far away from fault lines
   d. insuring only those customers who can afford to pay for earthquake coverage for their buildings
   e. insuring other disasters such as tornadoes, hurricanes, and monsoons, in the hopes of maintaining customer loyalty

77. A company that manufactures laundry detergent has decided to switch from petroleum-based ingredients to plant-based ingredients. The company believes that the switch will decrease its environmental footprint and address frequent customer complaints that the detergent tends to cause the color in clothes to fade quickly.

   Which of the following, if true, most helps to provide a justification for the company's planned switch?

   a. The cost of petroleum-based ingredients and plant-based ingredients is the same.
   b. The company plans to move its manufacturing overseas.
   c. The annual sales of laundry detergent have decreased over the past two years.
   d. The company will continue to manufacture stain remover pens that have stronger ingredients.
   e. Consumer spending on higher-quality clothing is anticipated to grow over the next 10 years.

78. Currently, the market for ice cream is dominated by dairy-based ice cream. To increase its revenue, the Simply Soy marketing department developed a new campaign for its line of soy-based ice cream flavors. The marketing team convinced the product development team that it should amplify the food coloring used in all the flavors, and the marketing team would release ads with pictures of the ice cream designed by a food stylist.

What condition will make the marketing department's plan more likely to increase revenue?

a. The food coloring used in the Simply Soy flavors consists of all natural ingredients.

b. The number of people who are lactose intolerant has increased.

c. People who buy ice cream are not bothered by food that contains artificial colors.

d. The public in general is gravitating toward more plant-based foods.

e. People tend to base their grocery shopping decisions based on how appealing the products look.

79. Both universities and the government are concerned about the low level of student achievement in math and science. In addition, the government is also concerned about the rising cost of university tuition. A university suggested that private enterprise could locate some of their research in university laboratories, and provide tuition assistance to promising students who aid in the research.

Which of the following, if true, would be most useful to know in evaluating the university's suggested plan?

a. the size of the student applicant pool for the research program

b. the science and math aptitude of the student applicant pool for the research program

c. the value of incentives that universities would offer private enterprise to conduct research in university laboratories

d. the number of students who would major in math and science as a result of the plan

e. the type of research that private enterprise would conduct in university laboratories

80. Construction Company Y always used power drills that plug into an electrical socket. Power-Z has manufactured a new type of battery-powered drill that uses so little energy that it is much cheaper to use. Thrilled that the price of both kinds of drills is the same, Construction Company Y has decided to replace all its drills with the new Power-Z drill, and estimates that the replacement costs will pay off within three years.

Which of the following, if it occurred, would constitute a disadvantage for Construction Company Y of the plan described above?

a. construction Company Y would need to buy 350 new drills
b. an increase in the market demand for construction work
c. other companies that manufacture power tools introduced similar drills at the same price
d. a significant increase in the price of batteries in the next year
e. a shortage of industrial-sized extension cords in hardware stores

81. A national long distance track coach created a new cross-training program for the team, which includes swimming, weight training, sprinting staggered with jogging, and yoga. The coach has stated to the press that the new cross-training program will result in an Olympic podium sweep by the nation's team.

Which of the following, if true, could present the most serious disadvantage for the coach's cross-training program?

a. The yoga exercises would enhance the runners' breathing capabilities under physical stress.
b. None of the national team's competitors have considered this type of cross-training program.
c. The cross-training program would lead to improvement in some of the runners on the team, but runners on other teams would likely have trouble with it.
d. The program requires additional athletic gear, which is very expensive.
e. The weight training would add muscle to the runners, which would result in a slight weight gain that would slow down their times.

82. Winston University had many cases of meningitis the previous year. The Director of Residence Life presented a plan to prevent this from happening again this year. All university students covered by the student health plan would be required to obtain a meningitis vaccine before moving into the dormitories.

    The answer to which of the following questions would be most important in determining whether implementing the proposal would be likely to achieve the desired result?

a. the percentage of Winston University students who are covered by the student health plan

b. the percentage of Winston University students who live in the dormitories and are covered by the student health plan

c. the percentage of Winston University students who live in the dormitories

d. the percentage of Winston University students who live off campus

e. the percentage of Winston University students who did not receive a meningitis vaccine the previous year

83. A non-governmental organization raised money to donate thousands of anti-malarial mosquito nets to a country in which malaria is a serious public health threat. The organization also operated a chain of free clinics in that country. The organization transported the nets in April of that year. Four months later, the president of the organization announced that the severe decline in malaria outbreaks would continue throughout the remainder of the year, and adjusted the clinic budget by slashing its orders for quinine, the treatment for malaria, in half.

    Which of the following, if true, would most undermine the president of the organization's decision to order half as much quinine for the year?

a. Quinine is used to treat a few other uncommon ailments.

b. The chain of clinics treats on average only 40% of the country's population.

c. The wet season, during which malaria is prevalent, begins in October and ends in March.

d. The percentage of the population that received the anti-malarial mosquito nets is unclear.

e. Other clinics operated by different organizations ordered the same amount of quinine.

84. Foreign language skills are vital in today's international economy. Studies have shown that the earlier a student begins to learn a language, the more proficient that student will become with that language. The school district of M wants to increase student foreign language skills. The superintendent of the M school district concluded that requiring all students to begin studies in a foreign language in fourth grade instead of seventh grade will result in a greater number of students who are proficient in a foreign language.

    Which of the following, if true, would cast the most doubt on the success of the superintendent's plan?

    a. The majority of students who study a foreign language in the school district already speak a foreign language at home.
    b. The instruction time for foreign language study will be significantly less for the earlier grades than for grades 7 and above.
    c. Students will still have a choice between only two languages
    d. Foreign language study for fourth graders will take some instruction time away from social studies.
    e. Most elementary school teachers in school district M do not have training in a foreign language.

85. Trial courts in the state's civil division have found that jurors pay less attention in civil trials than they do in criminal trials, which jurors find to be more interesting. In order to maintain the attention of jurors, the county bar association proposed that all civil litigators use color and/or interactive visual aids.

    Which of the following, if true, provides the strongest reason to expect that the bar association's plan will succeed in getting jurors to pay attention during civil trials?

    a. Jurors will find the color and/or interactive visual aids as interesting as criminal trials.
    b. Jurors will find the color and/or interactive visual aids interesting enough to hold their attention.
    c. Judges will allow the civil litigators to use color and/or interactive visual aids.
    d. Civil litigators will actually want to use color and/or interactive visual aids.
    e. Criminal litigators will not start to use color and/or interactive visual aids.

86. The Everglades has an ecological problem because of its population of Burmese pythons, which are not a native species of the area and were likely introduced by people who dumped them when they were no longer desirable as pets. In order to address this problem, a local ecological group created a procedure for safely capturing the pythons.

Which of the following, if true, would provide the most support for the conclusion that the ecological group will capture most or all of the Burmese pythons in the Everglades?

a. The ecological group has a group of dogs trained to sniff out the location of the Burmese pythons.

b. The local government has increased the fines for people caught releasing animals into the Everglades.

c. The Burmese python is one of several snakes in the Everglades that are not native to the area.

d. Burmese pythons are not venomous.

e. Other environmental groups have also created plans to reduce the Burmese python population in the Everglades.

87. A state has used the speed limit of 65 miles per hour on its highways over the last several years. A study has shown that many drivers pulled over for speeding on these highways were not driving at an unsafe speed. In order to lower the number of drivers pulled over for speeding who were not driving at dangerous speeds, the state has decided to increase the speed limit on its highways to 70 miles per hour.

Which of the following would be most useful in evaluating the state's plan to lower the number of drivers pulled over for speeding who were not driving at dangerous speeds?

a. the number of drivers who will continue to drive at speeds greater than 70 miles per hour

b. the percentage of drivers who were pulled over for speeding as opposed to the percentage of drivers who were pulled over for other reasons

c. the number of the state's voters who believe that speeds of 70 miles per hour and under are not unsafe

d. the number of drivers who were pulled over for driving at speeds between 66 miles per hour and 70 miles per hour

e. the number of drivers on the state's highways during rush hour

88. The Bridgeview shopping mall's customer service department has reported many complaints from customers about a shortage of parking in the parking deck. The Bridgeview mall drafted a plan in which it would construct two additional levels to its parking deck, and would charge each retailer in the mall a $4,000 fee to help pay for it, to which the retailers all agreed.

   Which of the following, if true, would be most useful to evaluate the benefit to the retailers for agreeing to pay the fee in order to enable more customers to shop at the mall?

   a. the percentage of mall customers that drive to the mall, as opposed to taking other forms of transportation
   b. whether the additional number of parking spaces will alleviate the parking shortage
   c. the actual number of complaints to customer service about a shortage of parking spaces
   d. the cost of the plan to the Bridgeview mall after the retailers each paid their fee
   e. whether the $4,000 fee that each retailer would pay toward the additional two levels in the parking deck would actually pay off in sales revenue

89. A municipality is concerned about the number of car accidents that occurred during the winter. The mayor suggested that it consider buying and staffing snowplows in order to alleviate the problem. The municipality purchased four snowplows, and offered a $15 per hour wage to applicants to drive the snowplows when needed.

   Which of the following would be most useful in determining whether the municipality's plan to decrease car accidents during the winter season will actually succeed?

   a. whether job applicants will drive the snowplows for $15 per hour
   b. whether most winter car accidents are a result of snow
   c. whether most car accidents in the municipality occur during winter
   d. whether four snowplows will be enough
   e. whether most cars in the municipality have snow tires

90. Kitchen, Kitchens, Kitchens, Inc.! is a kitchen appliance company that is looking to increase sales for stainless steel appliances. The company designed its new line of appliances to be more energy efficient. Advertisements will show the total of the annual savings in energy costs plus the average government tax rebate to homeowners for increasing the energy efficiency of their homes.

Which of the following, if true, raises the most serious doubt regarding the company's expected success from its new advertising campaign?

a. Competitors plan on highlighting the appearance of the appliances in their advertisements.

b. The savings generated by energy savings and the tax rebate are less than the cost of the new appliances.

c. Stainless steel appliances always have a higher price than appliances in basic colors.

d. Most customers want to buy their kitchen appliances in matching sets.

e. The savings generated by energy efficient appliances and the tax rebate are negligible.

91. Many universities have elected to turn their undergraduate programs into 5-year programs, in order to incorporate mandatory internships for credit. Although students will have an additional year of study, they will gain valuable working experience that will look great on their resumes in this recession and this experience will be worth the cost of the additional year's tuition.

Which of the following, if true, provides the most support for the potential success of attracting undergraduate applicants to 5-year undergraduate programs?

a. Most students take out only a small quantity of money in student loans, and find their monthly payments to be affordable.

b. The recession has meant that employers have their pick of students, and prefer those with experience.

c. Students have the opportunity to intern full-time during their summers.

d. Most of the internships are offered in big cities that students regard to be fun and exciting.

e. About half of undergraduate institutions are planning on offering these 5-year programs.

92. The We Care Insurance Company wants to expand by offering new insurance products. One of the members of the product development team proposed that the company offer pet insurance. The team agreed that it was a good idea, until the member who pitched the idea shared an industry study, which stated that pet insurance clients tend to avoid policies that raise the annual premium based on the number of claims submitted. Since pet insurance cannot legally drop a pet's coverage once the pet becomes ill or significantly injured, the product development team is worried that pet insurance will not be profitable after all.

Which of the following strategies would most likely enable the We Care Insurance Company to offer pet insurance?

a. capping the amount of covered services per pet at the cost of an annual checkup and shots

b. require pet owners to bring their pets only to veterinary practices that participate in the We Care Insurance Company's plan

c. insure only those customers who are wealthy enough to afford many veterinary services for their pets

d. raise premiums based on the age of the pets

e. insure only pets with no history of medical problems

Answers

Set 2

11. **b.** Choice **b** identifies the strategy in Peter's counterargument. Peter points out that Louis did not consider that the financial industry's losses in profits and jobs will result in profit and job increases for others. Choice **a** is incorrect because Peter does not offer additional evidence to support Louis's argument. Choice **c** is incorrect because Peter does not argue that the regulations on derivatives will have a negative effect on the national economy. He argues that the increase in profits and jobs in other industries will compensate for the loss in profits and jobs in the finance industry. Choice **d** is incorrect because Peter does not challenge Louis's facts; he supplements them. Choice **e** is incorrect because Peter does not challenge the relevance of Louis's facts.

12. **d.** Choice **d** is correct because the cost of repairing the cell towers does not need to be lower to justify the cost savings of this plan. Those repairs must cost more than the cost of this plan for the cell towers. Choices **a**, **b**, **c**, and **e** are incorrect because they all mention items that should cost less than the repairs to the cell towers during the previous year.

13. **e.** This is a problem that you should attempt to sketch out. Try to connect the names to make a chain. Katherine has a higher GPA than Pamela and Adrienne. Shane has a higher GPA than Madelyn, who has a higher GPA than Adrienne.

$$P \& A < K$$
$$A < M < S$$

Choice **e** is correct because Adrienne cannot have a higher GPA than Shane. Choices **a** and **b** are incorrect because the argument does not tell you whether Katherine or Madelyn has a higher GPA. Choice **c** is incorrect because the argument does not tell you whether Pamela or Adrienne has a higher GPA. Choice **d** is incorrect because Pamela could have a higher GPA than Madelyn.

14. **a.** The argument shows that Sharon did not inherit the cottage because Claire McGinnis did not own the cottage when she died. Choice **a** is correct because we do not know whether Claire would have left the cottage to her niece, even though Claire left Sharon the rest of her property. Choices **b** and **e** are incorrect because whether Humphrey Monroe wanted Sharon to inherit the cottage is irrelevant to the argument's conclusion. Choice **c** is incorrect because whether Sharon wanted to inherit the cottage is irrelevant. Choice **d** is incorrect because the assumption is about who Claire wanted to inherit the cottage, not who Claire did not want to inherit it.

15. **a.** Choice **a** is correct because it is possible that the employees in State A each work such a low number of hours per week and that the employees in State B work such a high number that the total number of hours paid for is actually higher in State B. Choice **b** is incorrect because there is not necessarily a correlation between the number of employees and the number of restaurants since many employees could work very few hours. Choice **c** is incorrect because the statement would actually contradict the argument's conclusion. Choice **d** is incorrect because there is no indication that state law has anything to do with why employees in State A are paid a higher wage. Choice **e** is incorrect because the argument does not say anything about what might happen in the future.

16. **b.** Choice **b** is correct because in order for buying diamonds to cost 40% more in Luvania, the tax on purchases by foreigners in Oretania and the cost of transportation to Oretania must be 40% less than the cost of buying diamonds in Luvania. Choice **a** is incorrect because the ease of the ground breaking under the force of a pickaxe in Oretania is merely a plausible explanation for the cost difference, but there are also other possible reasons. Choice **c** is incorrect because if the transportation cost is more than 40%, buying diamonds in Oretania would be more expensive. Choice **d** is incorrect because the cost of diamond mining is merely a possible explanation for the cost difference. Choice **e** is incorrect because there is no evidence about retail jobs in jewelry stores in the passage, and the passage also indicated that people would actually be less likely to buy diamonds in Luvania.

17. **d.** Choice **d** is correct because fixing the filtration system at the point of groundwater collection will not change the excess chlorine content if the problem starts later in the process. Choice **a** is incorrect because whether all faulty water filtration systems allow excess chlorine into drinking water is irrelevant. Choices **b** and **e** are incorrect because they introduce assumptions that would disprove the argument. Choice **c** is incorrect because it states a fact listed in the argument.

18. **d.** Choice **d** is correct because whether survey respondents felt superficial in admitting that their physical appearance was important to them does not explain why 100% admitted that it was, yet 15% of respondents did not cite concern over their physical appearance as a reason for quitting smoking. Choice **a** is incorrect because it reflects the possible reason that respondents saw a connection between their physical appearance and cigarette smoking, and did not care enough about it to quit smoking. Choice **b** is incorrect because it indicates the possible reason that respondents saw a positive correlation between their physical appearance and cigarette smoking. Choices **c** and **e** are incorrect because they reflect the possible reason that respondents did not see much, if any, connection between their physical appearance and cigarette smoking.

19. **c.** This problem appears tricky, but it is actually pretty simple if you remember not to make any assumptions about the listed apartment traits and their respective values. The prompt tells you that a higher rental price results from a higher floor, more sunlight, and/or a greater number of bedrooms. What we do not know is how various combinations compare to each other, so it is important not to assume anything, such as a greater number of bedrooms having a higher value than greater sunlight. What you want to look for is the one answer choice that clearly violates the following setup:

Cathy—6th floor
David—4th floor
Krystal—1st floor, $$$$ (highest rent)
Oscar—basement floor, $ (lowest rent)

Choice **c** is correct because it violates the setup. If Krystal lives in a 1-bedroom, David's apartment has the most sunlight, and Cathy lives in a 3-bedroom, then how can Krystal pay the highest rent? She cannot because her apartment would not meet any of the conditions that could plausibly price her rent the highest. In choice **a**, Krystal could pay the highest rent because no one is listed as having an apartment with more bedrooms than hers. Choice **b** appears tricky because Krystal has a smaller apartment than Cathy, but Krystal's apartment might receive far more sunlight than the others. Choice **d** is incorrect because the conditions provided support the fact that Oscar pays less rent than the other two tenants listed in the answer choice. Choice **e** is incorrect because even though Cathy's top floor apartment gets the most sunlight, the additional two bedrooms in Krystal's apartment provide a reason that she pays the highest rent.

20. **e.** Choice **e** is correct because a higher membership in weight loss programs fails to explain why women who spent more money on exercise clothes and went to the gym more often did not lose more weight than other women. Choices **a**, **b**, **c**, and **d** are all reasons why the women who spent more money on exercise clothes, and went to the gym more often, did not lose more weight than those who spent less money on their exercise clothes.

21. **e.** Choice **e** is correct because a larger percentage of patients diagnosed with bacterial infections would not justify a decrease in the percentage of patients prescribed antibiotics. Choices **a**, **b**, **c**, and **d** are all reasons that would explain a drop in the percentage of patients prescribed antibiotics.

22. **a.** Choice **a** is correct because digital products earn a higher percentage of profits than the percentage they make up of sales. Choice **b** is incorrect because books earn the greater percentage of profits. Choice **c** is incorrect because the passage says nothing about growth. Choice **d** is incorrect because the passage does not say anything about the number of products in each group. Choice **e** is incorrect because books earn the same percentage of profits as digital products and products in other mediums together.

23. **b.** Choice **b** is correct because the cost of travel for high-level employees would need to be less than the savings generated by near-shoring in order to justify the practice. Choice **a** is incorrect because the prompt does not say anything about businesses wanting to convince current employees in cities with a higher cost of living to relocate. Choice **c** is incorrect because the prompt does not indicate that businesses would have to pay for any cost of client travel. Furthermore, even if the clients traveled out of the cities with a higher cost of living, that would actually further justify moving employees out of those locations, including higher-level employees who deal with clients. Choice **d** is incorrect because although it provides some support for near-shoring, there is not enough information about financial incentives to provide a comparison to the savings generated by near-shoring. Choice **e** is incorrect because the clients staying put does not provide an incentive for near-shoring.

24. **c.** This question is asking for the MOST important item to ascertain, so be careful with answer choices that list items that are relevant but are not the most important. Choice **c** is correct because water has to be available to the drought victims in order to give them relief. Choice **a** is incorrect because the exact number of relief organizations involved is irrelevant. Choices **b**, **d**, and **e** all list items that are important to know but are not the most important, because without water, the rest of these items will have no impact on the drought relief plan.

25. **b.** This is a formal logic argument, so you should try to sketch it out and make connections between the people. Courtney is the most commonly mentioned name, so try to see where everyone falls in relation to her. Courtney has less money than Marnie, Alexandra, and Josie. Alexandra has less money than Danielle. Therefore:

    C . . . M/A/J
    C . . . A . . . D

    Choice **b** is correct because Danielle cannot have less money than Courtney, since Alexandra has more money than Courtney, and Alexandra has less money than Danielle. The other choices are all possible.

26. **c.** Choice **c** is correct because Sophia pointed out that Taylor failed to consider that registration is a benefit after the purchase of securities, not before. Choice **a** is incorrect because Sophia does not provide evidence that people actually read the securities paperwork. Choice **b** is incorrect because Taylor's argument is not about the volume of paper that registration generates, and Sophia's response merely indicates that buyers of securities will have a remedy against the parties who misrepresented them. Choice **d** is incorrect because Taylor's argument is about the volume of information that registration generates, not about the financial literacy of people who buy securities. Choice **e** is incorrect because Sophia does not suggest that all securities be registered; she only states the advantages of registration for those securities that already must be registered.

27. **b.** Look for the choice that is required for the argument to be true. Choice **b** is correct because both options together cannot result in greater fuel efficiency than only the use of a lighter metal in the car frames. Choice **a** is incorrect because ABC's options for a lighter metal would not change the argument that the use of a lighter metal in the frames would be the most that ABC could do to increase fuel efficiency. Choice **c** is incorrect because the cars' fuel efficiency can still be increased even if it already is good. Choice **d** is incorrect because what ABC wants to do and the most that ABC can do are two different things. Choice **e** is incorrect because cost is not relevant to ABC's best effort to increase fuel efficiency.

28. **e.** Choice **e** is correct because a lower market demand and higher distribution in the overall industry would be reasons for Crunchy Organics' profits to decline. Choice **a** is incorrect because decreased wages would enable the company to earn a greater profit. Choice **b** is incorrect because lower utility bills and a tax refund would result in a greater profit. Choice **c** is incorrect because a larger olive crop means a greater supply of olives, and rainfall does not cost the company money. Choice **d** is incorrect because a feature about the company as an ethical business could reasonably result in more consumers buying olive oil specifically from this company.

29. **c.** Choice **c** is correct because women like to see how a product will look on them, which is a realistic image. Choice **a** is incorrect because the affluence of women in cosmetics advertisements is not relevant to the passage. Choice **b** is incorrect because the passage provides no information that most women actually shop for daytime cosmetics rather than makeup more appropriate for evening. Choice **d** is incorrect because glamorous is not the same as realistic. Choice **e** is incorrect because the passage does not indicate that women are dissatisfied with the quality of cosmetics featured in advertisements.

30. **e.** Choice **e** is correct because the passage does not explicitly say that the installation of the machines in town that give a 5-cent refund per item will motivate people to recycle. Furthermore, the passage does not indicate whether any resulting increase in recycling would be enough to save those jobs. Choice **a** is incorrect because the township's trash plant is irrelevant and the 5-cent refund will not pay for any costs because residents will pocket it. Choice **b** is incorrect because the passage does not question the recycling plant's capacity for additional materials. Choices **c** and **d** are incorrect because the 5-cent refund would go to residents, not for the cost of the machines.

31. **d.** Choice **d** is correct because the public health expert provides information about population size that negates the reporter's claim. Choice **a** is incorrect because the issue is the number of cases of the virus in relation to the size of the entire population. Choice **b** is incorrect because the public health expert does not single out particular people who are infected with the Q Virus. Choice **c** is incorrect because the argument never alleges an incremental increase, only an increase. Choice **e** is incorrect because the expert does not question information about the people, only about the group as a whole and its relation to the entire population.

32. **a.** Choice **a** is correct because the argument draws a conclusion based on the percentage of students enrolled in each college. Choices **b** and **d** are incorrect because the argument does not say anything about the qualities of computer information systems courses. Choice **c** is incorrect because the argument does not say anything about course requirements. Choice **e** is incorrect because the job market is not relevant to the argument.

33. **c.** Choice **c** is correct because people obtaining news from sources that do not have high ratings would undermine the argument's conclusion. Choice **a** is incorrect because the conclusion does not rely on what the press cares about. Choice **b** is incorrect because the argument already made this statement. Choice **d** is incorrect because what the press should do has no role in the argument. Choice **e** is incorrect because whether the press has failed to obtain high ratings with quality news is not an assumption necessary for the conclusion that people will not obtain news elsewhere.

34. **e.** Choice **e** is correct because the city council is arguing that crime did not increase. Do not let the answer's use of percentages fool you. The key is that the percentages did not change year to year. Choice **a** is incorrect because this conclusion follows from the argument by the community action group leader. Choice **b** is incorrect because the passage says nothing about the laid-off police officers committing petty crime. Choice **c** is incorrect because the city council president is not stating causes for an increase in petty crime; she is stating that no increase in petty crime has occurred. Choice **d** is incorrect because the city council's claim that only the number of reported petty crimes has increased does not indicate that it is possible to actually find out how many people were actually victims in a year.

35. **a.** Choice **a** is correct because a large market and low production cost are both valid criteria for offsetting a lower price for generic products. Choice **b** is incorrect because a large market and low production cost for name brand products are not needed to offset higher prices. Higher prices would naturally generate higher profits, and therefore do not need to be offset at all. Choice **c** is incorrect because the passage does not provide any information to link similar profits with a similar market size. Choice **d** is incorrect because the passage says nothing about either of the markets in the future. Choice **e** is incorrect because the argument states that companies that manufacture and sell name brand products are often under this misconception about the difference in their profits, which indicates that most companies are not savvy enough to manufacture and sell both brand name and generic products.

36. **b.** Choice **b** is correct because the argument assumes a connection between anticipating test questions and gearing study toward the question types. Choice **a** is incorrect because the argument is about how people study for standardized tests, not about whether certain people excel on those tests due to question types. Choice **c** is incorrect because the argument does not say anything about tests covering the entire breadth of a subject. Choice **d** is incorrect because the argument concludes that people have to study the entire subject for tests. Choice **e** is incorrect because the argument does not mention non-standardized tests.

37. **d.** Choice **d** is correct because telephone correspondence requires that clients are at work at the same time as employees at the companies that serve clients. Although employees could schedule telephone calls during flex time, this answer provides a circumstance in which flex time is not beneficial, even if it is not detrimental here. Choice **a** is incorrect because it shows that e-mail correspondence occurs at all hours, which could actually make flex time beneficial. Choice **b** is incorrect because it shows that flex time can make a particular group of employees more productive. Choices **c** and **e** are incorrect because they show negative results of employees working regular hours, which flex time can fix.

Set 3

38. **c.** The argument establishes a correlation between regular exercise and longevity, and states that vegetarianism is not the cause of greater longevity. Choice **c** is correct because it strengthens the argument that there is no causal connection between vegetarianism and longevity by showing that both meat eaters and vegetarians have the same longevity when they exercise regularly. Choice **a** is incorrect because it states an association between vegetarianism and the likelihood of exercising regularly, which would weaken the argument. Choice **b** is incorrect because it does not negate the causal connection between vegetarianism and longevity. Choice **d** is incorrect because it promotes an association between vegetarianism and other healthy habits that fails to weaken a causal connection between vegetarianism and exercising regularly. Choice **e** is incorrect because it merely states a correlation between meat eating and unhealthy habits.

39. **a.** Choice **a** is correct because if most people in Springfield are unwilling to switch from their cars to public transit, the upgrade will not significantly reduce the number of drivers on the streets. Choice **b** is incorrect because the speed of the metro trains has no impact on the argument. Choice **c** is incorrect because the current limited reach of the metro supports the argument that increasing its area of coverage would entice drivers to use public transit instead. Choice **d** is incorrect because although an increase in air pollution may counteract additional reasons that the environmental group may have to support the proposed upgrade for the metro, air pollution does not have a relationship in this argument with getting drivers to switch to public transit. Choice **e** hints that people do not desire to ride public transit, but does not weaken any argument that people are unwilling to switch.

40. **e.** The question is asking for the choice that bests supports the president of fundraising's theory that donors are giving less because they are less aware of the work that the organization does. Choice **e** is correct because smaller print, if used in the mailings, could cause the donors to be unable to read about the organization's work, and therefore feel less inclined to donate. Choice **a** is incorrect because the fundraising president stated that the economic downturn did not have a relationship to donation activity. Choice **b** is tricky, but it is incorrect because although the prepaid postage on the donation envelopes has to do with the mailings, it does not inform the donors about the organization's work. Choices **c** and **d** are incorrect because they provide different reasons for the decrease in donations.

41. **c.** Choice **c** is correct because it shows that the majority of people who brush their teeth used this brand of toothbrush. Choice **a** is incorrect because it only establishes that no other brands used the same type of plastic for the bristles, not that a significant number of people used this brand of toothbrush, which would be necessary to show the brand's effect on the tooth enamel of the population. Choice **b** is incorrect because it does not address the brand of toothbrush under discussion, and whether people brushed twice a day is outside of the scope of the dentist's theory. Choice **d** is incorrect because the majority of Dr. Roberts' patients do not provide a basis for making a statement about the general population. Choice **e** is incorrect because the toothbrush company's promotional activities did not necessarily result in a significant portion of the population using those toothbrushes.

42. **b.** Choice **b** is correct because the author makes a faulty assumption that people between the ages of 40 and 50 want a particular style of vacation, when the argument does not provide any information to that effect. Choice **a** is a tricky one, but it is incorrect because the author does not assume that people between the ages of 40 and 50 have children, but that they want to travel with their families as opposed to other people. Choice **c** is incorrect because the author does not assume that people between the ages of 40 and 50 have a family that includes a spouse, but that they want to travel with their family. Choice **d** is incorrect because the argument tells us that people between ages 40 and 50 purchase the most vacations to Mexico. We do not need to know information about other age groups. Choice **e** is incorrect because whether the majority of people in a particular age group can afford a vacation in Mexico is outside of the scope of the argument.

43.   **d.** Choice **d** is correct because it provides a reason that more
smokers chose to quit this year. A higher cost for the following
year would support the conclusion that even more smokers will be
motivated to quit the following year. Choice **a** is incorrect because
the previous year having the lowest number does not tell us
whether the following year will have a higher number than the
current year. Choice **b** is incorrect because the answer does not tell
you whether an increase in government regulation has actually
occurred or will occur in the future. Choice **c** is incorrect because
it merely provides a possible reason for the increase in the number
of smokers who quit this year. It does not provide any information
about whether that grant will be available for the following year.
Choice **e** is incorrect because it does not provide any information
about the following year.

44.   **b.** Choice **b** is correct because fewer larger boxes of paper will
generate lower tariffs and might wind up being less expensive than
domestic paper production. Choice **a** is incorrect because job
creation is not relevant to cost reduction here. Choices **c** and **d** are
incorrect because they actually would strengthen the argument.
Choice **e** is incorrect because the amount of paper produced
overall does not necessarily have relevance here as a foreign paper
producer likely produces and sells paper to several countries.

45.   **c.** Choice **c** is correct because the human resources report fails to
recognize that the qualitative benefits it lists generally do not
pertain to store employees. Choice **a** is incorrect because there is
no information in the prompt that indicates that company
employees do not care about the qualitative factors listed. Choice **b**
is incorrect because whether pension and comp time for salaried
employees relates to employee compensation does not matter; the
point is whether these items actually help retain store employees.
Choice **d** is incorrect because the argument states that the
company has done something to retain employees. Choice **e** is
incorrect because additional qualitative factors that may have
retained employees are irrelevant to the flaw in this argument.

46. **c.** Choice **c** is correct because it explains why a greater percentage of clothing in smaller sizes purchased in 2010 does not show that the average size of adult women has changed in 10 years. Choices **a** and **d** are incorrect because variations in the amount of clothing purchased or in the number of adult women who purchased clothing does not explain the discrepancy between percentages of various sizes purchased and a lack of change in the average adult woman's clothing size. Choice **b** is incorrect because it supports the opposite conclusion than the one posited. Vanity sizing would have to be more prevalent in 2010, not 2000, to explain this conclusion. This is the type of answer choice designed to trip you up because you may have assumed that the correct answer would be vanity sizing before you looked at the answer choices. Choice **e** is incorrect because a change in the majority of people who designed clothes merely hints at the vanity sizing issue mentioned in choice **b**, but does not actually indicate any change in the way the designers designed clothes. Remember that you are looking for the best answer.

47. **e.** Choice **e** is correct because if most law students who have jobs upon graduation were not hired by law firms, then the average annual salary of $70,000 provides no information about their salaries. Choice **a** is incorrect because the argument provides no information about salary in relation to the size of the law firm. Choice **b** is incorrect because geographical region is outside of the scope of the argument. Choice **c** is incorrect because the argument makes a statement about the percentage of law students, not the total number. Choice **d** is incorrect because the argument does not draw a conclusion about law students who did not pass the bar exam.

48. **d.** Choice **d** is correct because multiple purchases by each person who attempted to quit smoking would negate the association between the number of the smoking cessation products purchased and the number of people who quit smoking. Choice **a** is incorrect because the fact that people reported that they had more success with the gum may imply that they might have failed with the other products, which would cast some doubt on the argument, but this statement is not as conclusive as choice **d**. Choice **b** is incorrect because Company XYZ may be one of many companies that manufacture and sell smoking cessation products. Choice **c** is a tricky one, but be careful. Someone who quit smoking and then relapsed *still quit smoking*, albeit temporarily, so choice **c** is incorrect. Choice **e** is incorrect because doctor recommendations are irrelevant in this argument.

49. **d.** Choice **d** is correct because the breakdown of student attendance at public versus private colleges is irrelevant; the actual total in overall tuition is what matters. Choice **a** is incorrect because theoretically a majority of students could have scholarships, but they could be for such low amounts that they barely offset the cost of tuition. Choice **b** is incorrect because even if scholarships offer a large discount on college tuition, a low percentage of students who have them could result in scholarships having a minimal effect on the expense of tuition. Choice **c** is incorrect because the conclusion is about *college*, not *college tuition* specifically. Therefore, room and board is a relevant cost of college. Choice **e** is incorrect because the number of students who attend college affects overall college expenditures.

50. **e.** Choice **e** is correct because teenagers could only legally drive during daylight hours and the most drunk driving accidents occurred during late hours. Choices **a** and **d** are statements that would support the state legislature's belief that drivers under age 18 significantly contribute to or are less capable of avoiding drunk driving accidents. Choices **b** and **c** are statements about teenagers and alcohol that would support an inference that teenagers are responsible for a percentage of drunk driving accidents.

51. **a.** Remember to read the question closely, because this one asks you for the answer that would cast the most serious doubt on *Zippo's* argument, NOT the doctors' argument. Choice **a** is correct because it would cast doubt on the argument that an ingredient in the cans caused the illness. Choices **b**, **c**, and **e** are incorrect because they are about what the patients ate, which does not undermine Zippo's argument. Choice **d** is incorrect because whether the patients drank regular or diet Zippo Cola does not matter: they all got sick.

52. **c.** Choice **c** is correct because if most people who need to wear glasses or contact lenses are unaware of that fact, then they obviously will not notify the department of transportation when they renew their driver's licenses, and the plan will not reduce accidents. Choices **a** and **b** are incorrect because they are assumptions of the argument, not factors that the argument failed to consider. Choice **d** is incorrect because the prompt does not mention a vision test. Choice **e** is incorrect the prompt does not mention anything about out-of-state drivers in relation to car accidents.

53. **a.** Choice **a** is correct because it provides a reason why increased athletic activity among students did not result in any weight loss among the student body. Choice **b** is incorrect because it provides a reason why the program should have succeeded. Choice **c** is incorrect because there is no information regarding what percentage of students who participated in the intramural sports were also on official university athletic teams. Choice **d** is incorrect because athletic ability does not reveal anything about student weight before and after participation in the intramural sports. Choice **e** is incorrect because students being somewhat active before participating in intramural sports merely hints that the increased physical activity was insufficient to result in weight loss.

54. **d.** Choice **d** is correct because Dr. Roberts' conclusion is that the rate of tooth enamel decay will drop if patients stop using this brand of toothbrush. However, the problem is actually the type of plastic in the bristle. If other brands used the same plastic in the bristles, patients would still suffer the same rate of tooth enamel decay. Choices **a** and **e** are incorrect because they merely assume a connection between Dr. Roberts' patients and dental patients in general. Choices **b** and **c** are incorrect because these claims by Dr. Roberts do not address the brand of the toothbrush in the conclusion.

55. **b.** Choice **b** is correct because the television executive assumes that since senior citizens are the largest demographic of the population and spend more time at home due to retirement, they watch the most television. If another age group watched the most television, then the executive should gear programming toward that age group. Choice **a** is incorrect because the mention of cost is not directly tied to viewer popularity, which is the subject of the argument. Choice **c** is incorrect because it merely states that fewer senior citizens spend time at home than previously, not that they necessarily watch less television than other groups. Choice **d** is incorrect because it simply mentions one reality TV show popular among seniors; theoretically, that group may not watch any other reality programs. Choice **e** is incorrect because it only provides reasons that hint that senior citizens do not spend that much time watching television, and those reasons only apply to daytime.

56. **e.** Choice **e** is correct because database storage shows a feature of the program that is efficient for human resources to use. Choices **a** and **d** are incorrect because supervisors can allow personal likes or dislikes to color their evaluations of employees. Choice **b** is incorrect because employees who meet revenue goals may be deficient in other job responsibilities. Choice **c** is incorrect because differences in merit may vary more than at three levels.

57. **a.** Choice **a** is correct because if the people who are saving are underemployed, their income is probably lower than it was previously and an increased percentage of income saved could actually result in less money to spend, which will not increase economic activity. Choice **b** is incorrect because loans to start businesses may generate more economic activity. Choice **c** is incorrect because the public paying down its credit card debt would bring more money to the banks, which would facilitate increased economic activity. Choice **d** is incorrect because spending only on necessary home improvements does not indicate how much or little economic activity is generated by that activity. Choice **e** is incorrect because bank fees are not relevant to the conclusion.

58. **e.** Choice **e** is correct because if the majority of customers purchase items without help from sales associates, then the connection between increased worker productivity and sales rates is broken. Choice **a** is incorrect because wages becoming a smaller proportion of total costs does not weaken the argument. The other costs could have grown faster than the cost of wages. Choice **b** is incorrect because hiring is not relevant to the argument. Choice **c** is incorrect because sales associates who work on commission having higher paychecks supports the argument that they are more productive. Choice **d** is incorrect because other industries are not relevant.

59. **d.** Choice **d** is correct because the money that state residents pay in their taxes is not actually a cost of tuition, and families pay tax even if their children attend private colleges. Choice **a** is incorrect because the college president states that the cost of tuition at a private college equals the cost of tuition at a public college plus the cost of taxes paid toward public colleges. Choice **b** is incorrect because it only explains that everyone pays the taxes. Choice **c** is incorrect because scholarships at private colleges could result in private colleges costing less. Choice **e** is incorrect because the state's budget is not relevant in this argument to the cost that state families pay toward tuition at a public college.

60. **e.** Take note that this question asks for which answer does NOT weaken the argument, NOT which answer strengthens the argument. Therefore, cross off each answer that weakens the argument and choose the one that remains. Choice **a** is incorrect because customers will shop at other stores for goods if price clubs do not sell them. Choice **b** is incorrect because customers who cannot transport or store bulk sizes of goods are unlikely to shop at price clubs. Choice **c** is incorrect because it states that some customers will not shop at price clubs despite the low prices. Choice **d** is incorrect because it negates the claim that price club prices, the reason that customers would presumably choose to shop there over other stores, are not actually lower than those in other stores. Choice **e** is correct because it does not address the price comparison between the two stores.

61. **d.** Choice **d** is correct because it provides justification for the medical group's recommendation of one food item that contains calcium over another in order to lower one's chances of osteoporosis. Choice **a** is incorrect because the argument does not say that fat intake has any effect regarding osteoporosis. Choice **b** is incorrect because the argument does not concern itself with other health issues. Choice **c** is incorrect because the medical group's argument is not about the general daily diet, only about calcium intake. Choice **e** is incorrect because the effect on the environment is not relevant to the argument.

62. **c.** Choice **c** is correct because if the installation of new appliances is less expensive than repairing the current ones, the reason for the complex to employ a full-time super is weakened. Choice **a** is incorrect because the time of day that tenants discover problems with the appliances is not important; what is important is the cost for the complex to have the appliances fixed. Choice **b** is incorrect because the amount of water the appliances use tells us nothing about whether the complex should continue to have the appliances fixed. Although you might infer that more water used means a higher cost, the answer does not provide any information to infer that the cost from greater water use would negate the savings from fixing the appliances. Choice **d** is incorrect because the answer does not provide any information indicating that the cost of the super's benefits would negate the savings of having the super fix the appliances. Choice **e** is incorrect because it does not compare the expense of utility bills with the expense of paying the super. In addition, tenants commonly pay utility bills, which would mean that the utility bill savings suggested here are irrelevant to the argument.

63. **e.** Choice **e** is correct because it provides a reason why law students would not buy the e-book. If a large percentage of students had open-book exams and took them on the computer using software that blocked access to computer files during the exam, these students would not have access to the e-book during the exam; they would therefore have a reason to continue purchasing hard copies. Choice **a** is incorrect because the age and familiarity with e-books before the promotion would not explain why the promotion did not succeed in making more students prefer e-books after the promotion. Choice **b** is incorrect because the weight of a hard copy textbook, if heavy, does not explain why the promotion failed. Choice **c** is incorrect because regardless of the percentage of courses covered by the promotion, some decrease in hard copies purchased would be expected. Choice **d** is incorrect because a comparison to undergraduate students is not relevant to why a decline in the purchase of hard copies of law textbooks did not occur as a result of the promotion.

64. **a.** Choice **a** is correct because the argument states reasons why people plan not to consume soy and fewer people plan to consume soy in place of meat and dairy; if soy is abundant in processed foods that contain meat, people may inadvertently consume an increased amount of soy. Choice **b** is incorrect because the increasing number of people concerned that they might be allergic to soy would presumably have already had an adverse reaction to something they ate, believe that soy was the culprit, and plan on avoiding soy in the future. Choice **c** is incorrect because suspicion of a thyroid problem, even if not well founded, is enough to convince people to avoid soy when they believe that soy will exacerbate the problem. Choice **d** is incorrect because it would actually strengthen the argument. The passage states that soybean farming causes environmental problems. Choice **e** is incorrect because although a price difference is a reason that people would consume more soy, price difference fails to negate one of the reasons the passage listed for less future consumption of soy.

Set 4

65. **c.** Choice **c** is correct because the advantage of the trains was that they do not spend much time in traffic. A competitor significantly increasing its use of the same tracks could result in train traffic problems. Choice **a** is incorrect because it merely presents an advantage of the bus option, not a disadvantage of the train option. The answer also does not indicate whether the construction of two new highways will necessarily alleviate traffic on the road. Choice **b** is incorrect because the passage does not say how long trains take to board in the first place, and the amount of boarding time is unlikely to cause a problem with a train system that runs at 15-minute intervals. Choice **d** is incorrect because the low use of the trains for trips in small demand is not a factor in Suburban Commute's capacity needs for peak trips. Choice **e** is incorrect because it merely presents an advantage of the ferry option.

66. **e.** Choice **e** is correct because the fishing industry's desire to decrease fraudulent red snapper sales could help the Consumer Watchdog Agency. Choice **a** is incorrect because if grocery store inventory managers are placing other fish in the red snapper section of the fresh fish counter, the fish is being sold unpackaged and customers will not see the stamp. Choice **b** is incorrect because restaurants serve prepared, and not packaged, food, so customers would not see the stamp. Choice **c** is incorrect because customers failing to discern red snapper from other fish will not help solve the fraud problem. Choice **d** is incorrect because if most red snapper is sold without packaging, the stamp verification would not appear to be helpful.

67. **e.** This is an EXCEPT question, so note that you are looking for the answer choice that does NOT explain why the plan failed. Choice **e** is correct because the drivers finding the 10% bonus to be an incentive would not explain why they failed to deliver 90% of their packages on time. Choice **a** is incorrect because traffic problems are a plausible reason that delays were beyond the drivers' control. Choice **b** is incorrect because faulty GPS units could result in drivers arriving at the wrong locations and therefore delivering packages late. Choice **c** is incorrect because if fuel was expensive enough, the cost of driving fast could outweigh the benefit of the 10% bonus. Choice **d** is incorrect because if drivers could earn more money at another company and therefore the majority left Potter Shipping after six months, the drivers would not remain for a year to collect the bonus, thereby eliminating the incentive.

68. **e.** Choice **e** is correct because Trikas wants to decrease air pollution in order to placate public opinion, and a significant increase in water pollution is likely the negative effect that their air pollution problem has on public opinion. Choice **a** is incorrect because cost is irrelevant to the immediate goals of Trikas listed in the prompt. Choice **b** is incorrect because the system may still significantly reduce air pollution even if it malfunctions 10% of the time. Choice **c** is incorrect because the prompt does not provide a deadline for Trikas to meet its goals. Choice **d** is incorrect because the manpower required to maintain the system is irrelevant to the immediate goals of Trikas.

69. **c.** The question asks you to identify which answer choice is LEAST important in determining whether the government's new coverage of preventative care medical services will increase senior health. Choice **c** is correct because since this program is free to seniors, the cost of the services does not matter. Choice **a** is incorrect because if the percentage of seniors who seek preventative care is very low, then the program would not improve senior health. Choice **b** is incorrect because the program would not improve senior health if the preventative services detected health conditions but early detection provided no advantage in treating those conditions. Choice **d** is incorrect because if a great percentage of seniors do not have access to preventative care, the program will not improve senior health. Choice **e** is incorrect because if only a low percentage of seniors use the government's program, then the program will not significantly impact the health of the senior population.

70. **d.** The question is asking you to identify the answer choice that would be helpful in determining whether this plan would provide an incentive to invest in start-up businesses. Choice **d** is correct because if the average start-up business did not turn a profit for the first five years, this tax break would not be advantageous for the average investor in a start-up business. Choice **a** is incorrect because the amount of capital needed does not tell us anything about the tax break. Choice **b** is incorrect because the average tax bracket of an individual investor has no impact on this proposed tax break. Choice **c** is incorrect because the type of business is irrelevant to the tax break. Choice **e** is incorrect because the number of Grow the Economy Now party candidates who would benefit from this tax break has no connection to whether the tax break would serve as an incentive to investors in general.

71. **a.** The question asks you to identify which answer choice would NOT be relevant in determining whether the free shipping offer would result in an increase in revenue. Choice **a** is correct because the price of packing materials would not matter because the prompt tells you the expected loss in profits. Only changes in this price would matter, and the answer choice does not mention changes. Choice **b** is relevant because competitors providing the same offer would not make shopping at The Lightening Tread Shoe Company particularly advantageous for customers. Choice **c** is relevant because if the average price of an order dropped by over $4.00, the company could lose money. Choice **d** is relevant because higher postal rates could mean a loss in profits greater than $4.00 in the future. Choice **e** is relevant because customers splitting their purchases into several smaller orders could result in the company losing more money without gaining in merchandise purchases.

72. **b.** The prompt does not explain whether the majority of the 35% work in buildings with more than four stories. Therefore, the additional plan should include those buildings. Choice **b** is correct because it includes the smaller commercial buildings AND it addresses the possibility that the private safety company might be doing an inadequate job in the buildings it currently covers. Choices **a** and **c** are incorrect because they do not address the possibility that the private safety company's job performance is inadequate. Choice **d** is incorrect because it does not address the possibility that commercial buildings smaller than four floors might be the source of the problem. Choice **e** is incorrect because the effectiveness of fines is unclear, especially as the answer does not provide a monetary amount for the fine. For example, a $1 fine is unlikely to provide an incentive.

73. **d.** Choice **d** is correct because it explains that citizens in the repayment plan wound up not paying off any debt because they were charging at the same rate. Choice **a** is incorrect because the current repayment plan could have enabled citizens to reduce their credit card debt no matter how many similar programs the government had offered in the past. Choice **b** is incorrect because the inconvenience of paying bills in person does not explain why people who participated in the program did not reduce their credit card debt. Choice **c** is incorrect because the need for this program does not explain why it did not succeed. Choice **e** is incorrect because the program could still be expected to reduce debt even though people were living in poverty.

74. **b.** The question is asking you to find a valid reason for the airline industry's decision to triple its flights. Choice **b** is correct because an increase in business attendance at trade shows around the nation would be a reason to expect an increase in travel. Choice **a** is incorrect because even if the percentage of retirees has increased, they will not necessarily travel more. Choices **c** and **d** are incorrect because they only state that an area of operating costs has decreased, not that there is a greater demand for air travel. Choice **e** is incorrect because there is not necessarily a correlation between a lower percentage of people who fear flying and a greater demand for air travel.

75. **d.** The question asks you to identify the answer choice that would not explain why the new 3-step process failed. Choice **d** is correct. Note that the prompt states that the 3-step process checked for "scratches and other visible defects." If the majority of the defects were visible, then the process would have caused employees to discover them. Choice **a** is a plausible explanation because it explains that the mailer envelopes are scratching the discs when the warehouse employees slide the discs into them, which would occur after the employees inspected the discs. Choices **b** and **e** would clearly explain why the process failed. Choice **c** would explain the failure because the damage to the discs would have occurred after the company mailed them out.

76. **c.** Choice **c** is correct because the strategy would increase the customer pool to include customers who are less likely to file claims for earthquake damage. Choice **a** is incorrect because since earthquakes are on the rise, customers with buildings that have not experienced earthquake damage in the past 20 years may be more likely to experience it in the future. Choice **b** is incorrect because customers who cannot obtain earthquake coverage through another provider probably cannot do so because their likelihood of experiencing earthquake damage in the future is high. Choice **d** is incorrect because people who can afford earthquake coverage will pay for it; the problem will arise when too many claims are filed in the future and the company cannot afford to pay all of them. Choice **e** is incorrect because insuring other disasters is irrelevant to the problem of maintaining coverage for earthquakes.

77. **e.** Choice **e** is correct because if people are buying higher quality clothing, they are more likely to want to preserve the dye in them. Choice **a** is incorrect because although the same cost is not an argument against the switch, it does not show that the switch will have an additional advantage. Choice **b** is incorrect because moving manufacturing overseas does not provide an additional justification regarding the switch to plant-based ingredients. Choice **c** is incorrect because a decrease in consumer spending for laundry detergent overall indicates a declining consumer demand for the product. Choice **d** is incorrect because stain remover pens are not in the scope of the prompt's discussion of the company's plan.

78. **e.** Choice **e** is correct because whether the plan will increase revenue depends on whether the ads and the ice cream's enhanced colors entice people to buy the product. Choice **a** is incorrect because natural ingredients are irrelevant to the marketing department's plan. Choices **b** and **d** are incorrect because the marketing department's plan does not have anything to do with the product's soy base. Choice **c** is incorrect because the prompt does not reveal whether the food coloring uses artificial ingredients. Assuming that it does, and even if people do not mind artificial ingredients, that fact will not motivate them to buy the product.

79. **c.** Choice **c** is correct because the university's suggested plan would require private enterprise to have a motive to conduct research in university laboratories and to offer tuition assistance to students. Choice **a** is incorrect because the size of the applicant pool is not the most relevant consideration, as private enterprise would have to first participate in the program. Choice **b** is incorrect because the suggested plan does not indicate that students have to possess great achievement levels in math and science in order to participate. Choice **d** is incorrect because the universities and the government are concerned about achievement in math and science, not necessarily in the number of majors. Choice **e** is incorrect because the type of research is not particularly relevant to whether this suggested plan would succeed.

80. **d.** Choice **d** is correct because an increase in the price of batteries could negate the savings generated by using the new drills. Choice **a** is incorrect because the number of drills that Construction Company Y would need to buy does not matter. Choice **b** is incorrect because an increase in the demand for construction work would bring Construction Company Y more business. Choice **c** is incorrect because other companies releasing a similar product at the same price would not negate the construction company's savings. Choice **e** is incorrect because a shortage of industrial-sized electrical cords would not matter since the new drills are battery operated.

81. **e.** Choice **e** is correct because the cross-training program would be disadvantageous if it resulted in slower times. Choice **a** is incorrect because it is an advantage of the program. Choice **b** is incorrect because what the team's competitors have not considered does not mean the program is not advantageous for this team. Choice **c** is incorrect because all that matters is the advantages of the runners for this team. Choice **d** is incorrect because the price of the athletic gear does not take away from the goal of the program.

82. **b.** Choice **b** is correct because the prompt stated that the plan only addresses students who are covered by the student health plan. Furthermore, the prompt stated that students would be required to have the vaccine before moving into the dormitories, which would mean that students living off campus would not be affected by the plan. Therefore, choice **a** is incorrect. Choice **c** is incorrect because it leaves out the variable of students covered by the student health plan. Choice **d** is incorrect because it does not address the issue that the vaccination plan only applies to students on the student health plan. Choice **e** is incorrect because it fails to address the issues of students on the student health plan and students who live in the dormitories.

83. **c.** Choice **c** is correct because if the wet season has not yet begun, the president of the organization does not yet have confirmation that the mosquito nets have actually reduced cases of malaria. Choice **a** is incorrect because a small need for quinine for other purposes does not negate cutting orders in half when the large public health threat that requires quinine is perceived to have abated. Choice **b** is incorrect because the perceived success of the anti-malarial mosquito nets would presumably have an effect on the 40% of the population that seeks treatment at the organization's clinics. Choice **d** is incorrect because it merely suggests that the mosquito nets' success might not be widespread, but does not give any reason to affirmatively see a failure. Choice **e** is incorrect because other clinics simply may not have known about this organization's donation of anti-malarial mosquito nets.

84. **b.** Choice **b** is correct because less time given to foreign language study for younger students will offset the benefits that are supposed to be gained by teaching students a foreign language at a younger age. Choice **a** is incorrect because students who already speak a foreign language at home do not necessarily study the same foreign language at school. Choice **c** is incorrect because a choice limited between two languages is not relevant to proficiency in a foreign language. Choice **d** is incorrect because taking instruction time away from social studies will not negatively affect proficiency in a foreign language. Choice **e** is incorrect because the superintendent's plan does not necessarily indicate that the elementary school teachers will not receive training or that they must be the ones to teach a foreign language.

85. **b.** Choice **b** is correct because the plan requires that jurors will actually find the visual aids interesting in order for the plan to succeed. Choice **a** is incorrect because the plan does not require that jurors find civil trials as interesting as criminal trials. Choice **c** is incorrect because judges allowing the visual aids is a requirement for the plan to work, not something that would actually show that jurors find the aids interesting. Choice **d** is incorrect because the litigators wanting to use the aids will not make the jurors find them interesting. Choice **e** is incorrect because what criminal litigators do is irrelevant to the plan.

86. **a.** Choice **a** is correct because it explains how the members of the ecological group will find the Burmese pythons. Choice **b** is incorrect because increased fines for releasing animals does not explain whether the ecological group's capturing procedure will succeed. Choice **c** is incorrect because other non-native snakes are not part of the group's objective. Choice **d** is incorrect because the passage already states that the procedure for capture is safe, so whether the Burmese python is venomous is not an issue. Choice **e** is incorrect because the plan is only about this ecological group, not others.

87. **d.** Note that the state's speed limit plan assumes that a speed of 70 miles per hour is safe. Choice **d** is correct because the number of drivers who were pulled over under the old speed limit would have to decrease under the new speed limit in order for the plan to work. Choice **a** is incorrect because the number of drivers who will continue to drive over 70 miles per hour has no bearing on the state's change in the speed limit; what matters is the number of drivers who were driving 70 miles per hour or less. Furthermore, the state's plan is about drivers pulled over for driving at that speed, not drivers who drove that fast in general. Choice **b** is incorrect because the state's plan has nothing to do with other reasons drivers were pulled over for besides speeding. Choice **c** is incorrect because what the voters think about the speed limit is not relevant. Choice **e** is incorrect because the passage does not provide enough information to make any associations between the density of traffic during rush hour and the speed limit.

88. **e.** Choice **e** is correct because each retailer would want to earn the $4,000 back in sales revenue for the fee to be worth paying. Choice **a** is incorrect because the percentage of mall customers who drive does not necessarily indicate a correlation between increased revenue and increased parking. Choice **b** is incorrect because the purpose of the parking plan for the retailers is to increase revenue, which could occur even if a parking shortage continued after the two new levels in the garage were built. Choice **c** is incorrect because the number of complaints about the parking shortage only indicates the problem, not how severe the problem may be. Many customers who were unable to find parking may not have bothered to complain to the mall's customer service department. Choice **d** is incorrect because the cost to the mall does not affect the retailers' decision to pay $4,000 apiece.

89. **b.** Choice **b** is correct because the municipality's plan assumes that a large cause of car accidents during the winter is snow. Choice **a** is incorrect because whether applicants will drive the snowplows for the offered wage does not address the plan's assumption that snow is the primary cause of the car accidents. Choice **c** is incorrect because the plan only addresses car accidents that occur during the winter season. Choice **d** is incorrect because the number of snowplows does not address the plan's assumption that snow is the major cause of these accidents. Choice **e** is incorrect because snow tires are out of the plan's scope.

90. **e.** Choice **e** is correct because the company's advertising plan is premised on the assumption that the savings generated will be sufficient to attract customers to this line of appliances. Choice **a** is incorrect because the advertising campaigns of competitors are not relevant. Choice **b** is incorrect because it assumes that customers will only buy these appliances if the savings will actually cancel out the cost of the appliances. Choice **c** is incorrect because the price of appliances in basic colors does not matter regarding this advertising campaign. Choice **d** is incorrect because customers would presumably still see savings in buying a matching set of these appliances.

91. b. Choice **b** is correct because the passage states that the benefit to students of the 5-year programs is job experience that employers find valuable. In a recession, this reason is even more compelling. Choice **a** is incorrect because it says that most students find their current loans to be affordable, but provides no indication that the expense of a fifth year of tuition would still be affordable. Choice **c** is incorrect because other time opportunities for internship experience are a reason that students would less likely find 5-year programs attractive. Choice **d** is incorrect because it merely provides an additional reason that students would be attracted to 5-year programs. It does not address job experience. Choice **e** is incorrect because the fact that half of undergraduate institutions plan on offering these programs does not indicate that students would necessarily enroll in all the available slots in these programs, which if true, could support an inference that students not in these programs would be at a competitive disadvantage. Even with this inference, this statement does not address the value of job experience and its relationship to the cost of the fifth year of tuition.

92. d. Choice **d** is correct because age provides a mechanism for raising premiums, and since older pets are likely to need more medical care, the premiums are more likely to cover the cost of submitted claims. Choice **a** is incorrect because capping the price of pet insurance at the cost of an annual checkup and shots simply does not make sense for either customers or the insurance company. If the insurance cost equals or is greater than the costs of the checkup and shots, customers have no reason to buy it because they might as well pay for those costs out of pocket. If the insurance cost is less than the cost of the checkup and shots, the company would lose money on the policies. Choice **b** is incorrect because the plan does not indicate that participating veterinary practices would somehow make offering the policies affordable. Choice **c** is incorrect because people who are wealthy enough to afford many veterinary services would still only buy insurance if the price provided an advantage, and they would still submit claims. Choice **e** is incorrect because the problem is that the insurance company has to insure the pets after their medical problems are revealed.

Sentence Correction

The GMAT sentence correction questions are designed to test your knowledge of correct written English, including both grammatical and stylistic components. All questions are given in multiple-choice format with five possible answers. Each question presents a sentence, of which all or part has been underlined. The test taker is then presented with five different versions of the underlined part in choices **a** through **e**. Choice **a** will always be the same version as the underlined portion that is given in the original sentence. Choices **b**, **c**, **d**, and **e** will be variants of the underlined portion. These alternate choices test a variety of aspects, ranging from grammar and sentence structure to word choice and redundancy. The correct choice must do all the following:

- utilize correct English grammar
- have correct sentence structure
- not contain any diction (word choice) mistakes
- not change the original meaning of the sentence

The questions will present problems based on two different categories: *correct expression* and *effective expression*.

Correct expression problems deal with grammar mistakes, misplaced or improperly formed modifiers, unidiomatic or inconsistent expressions, and faults in parallel construction. *Effective expression* problems deal with proper diction and syntax, redundancy, brevity, and needlessly complicated expressions. In this GMAT sentence correction practice, we have divided the practice questions into the two categories of correct expression and effective expression so test takers may easily pinpoint the types of mistakes to later recognize them on test day. Test takers will encounter, however, some slight blending of both categories in some of the questions. The real GMAT sentence correction questions will combine both categories of errors, so be sure to carefully review both sections. They complement each other and your understanding of one section will lead to a greater understanding of the other.

Remember that one question may contain multiple errors, so it is important to read all the choices before selecting your answer. Use the process of elimination whenever possible. If you get stuck on one question, look for subtle differences between the possible choices. Insert the selected part into the sentence and read it quietly to yourself. Sometimes an error will sound more obvious to the ear then it will appear on paper.

Review the material provided before you begin to tackle the questions. It has been carefully crafted to help you succeed on this practice and the real test. Good luck!

Correct Expression

The following material will help you prepare for the part of the GMAT sentence correction section that focuses on noun-verb agreement, pronouns, verb tense sequence, correctly formed and placed modifiers, idiomatic expressions, and faults in parallel construction.

Parts of Speech

In order to correctly structure a sentence, it is important to understand its basic components. Read the following parts of speech and make sure you understand their roles and limitations.

Noun: person, place, or thing; the name of anything → *dog, Disneyland, Mary, Mary's dog, etc.*

Verb: action → *run, eat, sleep, etc.*

Adjective: word used to describe a noun → *pretty, tall, incredible, surprising, good, etc.*

Adverb: word used to describe verb, adjective, other adverb, phrases; it describes *how* something is done → *quickly, carefully, patiently, well, very, etc.*

Preposition: word that shows relationship between noun/pronoun and other words in a sentence → *on, at, through, between, with, etc.*

Parts of a Sentence

Subject: It tells the reader what is being talked about. The main word of a subject is always a noun or pronoun.

Predicate: It tells the reader what is being said about the subject.

Object: It tells the reader who or what the recipient of the action (verb) is.

The teacher praised the student.

Subject: *teacher*

Predicate: *praised the student*

Object: *student*

Subject/Verb Agreement

A complete sentence must have a subject and verb. If it is missing one of these components, it is considered a fragment and is incorrect. In addition to ensuring that a sentence has both subject and verb, you must also check that the subject and verb agree with each other.

   *A singular subject requires a singular verb form, and a plural subject requires a plural verb form.

X *The development of new hybrid cars <u>have</u> been a very important step toward lessening the country's dependence on oil.*

The previous sentence is incorrect because *have* is used in the plural form to modify new hybrid cars. That is not the subject, though. The complete subject is the *development* of new hybrid cars. Therefore, the subject is singular. The correct sentence reads:

→ *The development of new hybrid cars <u>has</u> been a very important step toward lessening the country's dependence on oil.*

You will notice that the sentence correction questions try to hide the subject. Remember to capture the entire subject! It may be a phrase rather than a word, and there may be modifiers after the subject that try to confuse you!

*Beware of phrases that attempt to hide the subject.

X *The planes on the tarmac at Los Angeles International Airport <u>comes</u> and <u>leaves</u> at all hours of the night.*

The previous sentence is incorrect because the verbs *comes* and *leaves* modify a singular subject. The real subject, however, is *planes*. Try to ignore the prepositional phrases that can follow the subject (*on the tarmac, at Los Angeles International Airport*) when determining the actual subject. The correct sentence reads:

→ *The planes on the tarmac at Los Angeles International Airport <u>come</u> and <u>leave</u> at all hours of the night.*

*Beware of the difference between compound subjects and additive phrases.

X *Dr. Jones and his staff <u>goes</u> out for a Christmas dinner every December.*

X *Dr. Jones, accompanied by his staff, <u>go</u> out for a Christmas dinner every December.*

Both examples are incorrect. The first sentence features a compound subject (*Dr. Jones and his staff*). The compound subject is plural and therefore requires a plural verb formation. The second sentence, however, adds *his staff* with the phrase *accompanied by*. This different structure that uses an additive phrase does NOT change the verb formation. The correct sentences are:

→ *Dr. Jones and his staff <u>go</u> out for a Christmas dinner every December.*

→ *Dr. Jones, accompanied by his staff, <u>goes</u> out for a Christmas dinner every December.*

Common Additive Phrases
accompanied by
along with
as well as
in addition to
together with

Collective Nouns
Collective nouns are nouns that can represent a group of people or things, but they function as singular nouns. Beware of collective nouns on the sentence correction portion of the GMAT. They are used to trick you and make you believe the noun is plural. On the GMAT, collective nouns are considered to be singular. Some common ones are:

audience
band (musical)
board (of directors)
cabinet (of members)
company
committee
corporation
council
crowd
department
family
government
majority
minority
public
society
team

X *Society <u>have</u> changed over the past 20 years with the advent of technology.*

This example is incorrect because *society* is singular. Although it represents a group of people, it is a collective noun and must be treated as a singular noun. Therefore, *have* must change to *has*.

→ *Society <u>has</u> changed over the past 20 years with the advent of technology.*

Subject Phrases: Always Singular
A sentence may have a phrase or idea as its subject. This phrase is often presented with a gerund. It is always singular.

X *Having twins <u>have</u> taken a toll on Mrs. Smith's health.*

The sentence is incorrect because the real subject is *having twins*, not just *twins*. *Twins* is plural, but *having twins* is a singular concept. This is an example of a subject phrase whose corresponding verb must be singular. The correct sentence reads:

→ *Having twins <u>has</u> taken a toll on Mrs. Smith's health.*

Pronouns
A pronoun is a word that replaces a noun or noun phrase. Depending on the role of the noun or noun phrase in the sentence, a pronoun may be a subject pronoun (replacing the subject of a sentence) or an object pronoun (replacing the object of a sentence).

Subject Pronouns
I
you
he
she
it
we
they

<u>The teacher</u> praised the student. → *<u>He</u> praised the student.*

In this case, *he* has been substituted for *the teacher*. *He* is a subject pronoun.

Object Pronouns
me
you
him
her
it
us
them

The teacher praised the student. → The teacher praised her.

In this case, *her* has been substituted for *the student*. Her is an object pronoun.

Possessive Pronouns
mine
yours
his
hers
its
ours
theirs

Possessive pronouns are used to replace nouns and show ownership or possession.

Of all the excellent grades, the teacher praised Jenna's grade the most. → Of all the excellent grades, the teacher praised hers the most.

In this case, *Jenna's grade* has been replaced by *hers*. *Hers* is a possessive pronoun.

Possessive Adjectives
my
your
his
her
its
our
their

The teacher praised <u>the student's</u> efforts. → *The teacher praised <u>her</u> efforts.*

In this case, *the student's efforts* has been replaced by *her.*

Demonstrative Pronouns
this
that
these (plural of this)
those (plural of that)

The time invested by the CEO to research the project was much less than <u>the time spent</u> by his subordinates. → *The time invested by the CEO to research the project was much less than <u>that</u> spent by his subordinates.*

In this case, the second mention of *the time* has been replaced by *that.*

Pronouns are often used to avoid repeating the subject or noun they refer to in the sentence. However, because they often refer to a noun in another part of the sentence, choosing the wrong pronoun is a common mistake. Pronoun errors are very frequent on the GMAT sentence correction section. It is crucial that you check a pronoun every time you see one!

*Make sure a proper antecedent exists for a pronoun.

X *The homeowners pondered several upgrades, which would greatly raise the value of <u>it</u>.*

The previous sentence is incorrect because it does not refer to anything in the sentence. A reader might assume it refers to the home, but home is only given to modify the type of owners (*homeowners*), so *home* cannot be a logical antecedent for the pronoun *it*. The correct sentence would be:

→ *The homeowners pondered several upgrades, which would greatly raise the value of <u>the home</u>.*

*Make sure the pronoun is NOT ambiguous. It must only have ONE antecedent.

X *The dental field has developed a new series of white fillings for anterior teeth, purportedly giving <u>them</u> stronger resistance against common wear and tear.*

This sentence is incorrect because them can refer to a number of nouns in the sentence (*series of white fillings, anterior teeth*). Again, the reader can assume what *them* refers to, but more than one answer is possible. Fix this problem by rewording the sentence.

→ *The dental field has developed a new series of white fillings for anterior teeth, purportedly giving <u>teeth</u> stronger resistance against common wear and tear.*

*Make sure the pronoun and its antecedent agree.

X *Joanna's promotion to the board of directors is uncertain because she does not meet all <u>their</u> rigid standards.*

This sentence is incorrect because *their* incorrectly refers to *the board of directors*. Although *directors* is plural, the true noun is the singular *board (of directors)*. Therefore, the sentence should read:

→ *Joanna's promotion to the board of directors is uncertain because she does not meet all <u>its</u> rigid standards.*

Now that you have seen common pronoun errors, let's look at common errors with modifiers.

Modifiers

Modifiers modify or describe a part of the sentence. A noun modifier modifies a noun.

→ *John sat down in his chair, <u>worn from endless hours of pressure</u>.*

The clause *worn from endless hours of pressure* is a modifier. Upon initial glance, a reader may think that it modifies *John*. This is incorrect; in fact, it modifies *his chair*.

*A noun and its modifier should be placed next to each other.

Look at the difference in meaning when the modifier changes location.

→ *John, <u>worn from endless hours of pressure</u>, sat down in his chair.*

Be very aware of modifiers! They must be as close as possible to the noun or clause that they modify. Misplaced modifiers are a common trick on the GMAT sentence correction section. They can lead to ambiguous meaning and syntax. On some occasions, the GMAT will present a dangling modifier that does not seem to have a referent.

Dangling Modifiers

X *Forced to accept his resignation*, *sadness permeated the office.*

The clause *sadness permeated the office* is a complete, independent clause. The first part of the sentence, however, is not independent because it lacks a subject. To what does it refer? It cannot be *sadness*. *Sadness* cannot be *forced to accept his resignation*. This is illogical. Therefore, *forced to accept his resignation* is considered a dangling modifier because the noun it is trying to modify is not even in the sentence. It is incorrect and needs to be fixed. One possible correction could be:

→ *Forced to accept his resignation*, *the staff exuded a sadness that permeated the office.*

Here, *the staff* is clearly *forced to accept his resignation*. This sentence is correct.

Restrictive versus Nonrestrictive Clauses

Another important testing point on the GMAT sentence correction portion is the difference between a restrictive (essential) clause and a nonrestrictive (nonessential) clause.

*Restrictive clauses provide essential information about a subject.

→ *The dog* *that has three legs* *was adopted by a family today.*

In this example, the clause *that has three legs* is essential to identifying *which dog*. Therefore, *that* is used and there are no commas.

*Nonrestrictive clauses provide extra, or nonessential, information about a subject.

→ *The East Los Angeles Animal Shelter, <u>which was founded in 1983</u>, takes in handicapped animals and helps them find a home.*

In this example, the clause *which was founded in 1983* is not essential to identifying *the East Los Angeles Animal Shelter*. It is considered extra information and therefore set off by commas.

*Put commas between nonessential clauses and their nouns. Use *which*, NOT *that*.

*Do NOT put commas between essential clauses and their nouns. Use *that*, NOT *which*.

Active Voice versus Passive Voice

Sentences will either be in the active or passive voice. In the active voice, the subject of the sentence performs the action. In the passive voice, the subject of the sentence receives the action or has an action performed on it.

Active Voice → *The teacher <u>praised</u> the student.*

Passive Voice → *The student <u>was praised</u> by the teacher.*

Beware of intransitive verbs, which are verbs that cannot be formed in the passive voice. Intransitive verbs have no direct object. Look at the following example:

Active Voice → *Josh <u>went</u> to work on Monday morning.*

This sentence cannot be put in the passive voice, so *go* (or the past tense *went* in this example) is an intransitive verb.

The GMAT generally prefers the active voice to the passive voice. Look for more details about stylistic preferences with the active voice in the Effective Expression instructional text.

Verb Tenses and Their Uses

Review the following definitions of the different verb tenses. Make sure you have a general understanding of their different roles and limitations.

Simple Present

Uses:

- Facts or generalizations → *The Earth <u>rotates</u> around the sun.*
- Repeated or usual actions → *She always <u>forgets</u> to call her mother on Sundays.*
- Scheduled events in the near future → *The family <u>leaves</u> tonight for their vacation home.*
- Non-continuous verbs to express an action right now → *She has her train ticket in her hand.* (see Simple Present versus Present Progressive for more information on non-continuous verbs)

Present Progressive

Uses:

- Express an action that is occurring at this moment → *You <u>are</u> <u>studying</u> verb tenses.*
- Express longer actions that are in progress now → *He <u>is</u> <u>preparing</u> for his speech next month.*

*Remember that some verbs (known as non-continuous verbs) are not expressed in the gerund form.

Simple Present versus Present Progressive

Always use the simple present tense when referring to a general statement or truth.

Remember that non-continuous verbs are verbs that are almost never expressed in the gerund *-ing* form. Some of the major non-continuous verbs include the following:

To be (location) → *Ralph <u>is</u> at the store right now.* NOT *Ralph <u>is being</u> at the store right now.*

To have (possession) → *She <u>has</u> $3.00 in her hand.* NOT *She is <u>having</u> $3.00 in her hand.*

To want → *The doctor wants additional tests.* NOT *The doctor is wanting additional tests.*

Present Perfect

Uses:

- Express an action that happened at a previous unspecified time → *She has met him before.*
- Express an action that has happened various times in the past → *They have had six quizzes this semester.*

Present Perfect Progressive

Uses:

- Express an action that started in the past and continues until now, with or without reference → *She has been taking antibiotics since Tuesday. They have been behaving badly.*

Simple Past

Uses:

- Express completed action in the past → *She finished her test at noon.*
- Past facts or generalizations → *Horses were the principal means of transportation 100 years ago.*
- Express habits in the past → *He played the piano as a child.*
- Express an action that began and ended in the past → *They lived in Chile for one year.*
- Express a group of completed actions → *He checked into his room, took a shower, and met his friends for dinner.*

Past Perfect

Uses:

- Express the idea that something occurred before something else in the past → *They had visited Chile several times before they moved there.*

Past Perfect versus Simple Past

It is important to mention that the past perfect tense is not always used to indicate earlier actions. If it is obvious that the earlier event preceded the other, then the past perfect tense can be substituted for the simple past tense. Also, if the order of events is not being emphasized, the past perfect tense is not necessary.

→ *Anthony <u>drove</u> to work and <u>crashed</u> his car in the parking lot.*

→ *The family <u>checked</u> the car tires before they began the long drive home.*

Notice how the above examples mention two events in an obvious chronological order, but they don't use the past perfect tense.

Past Progressive
Uses:

- Express a longer action in the past that was interrupted → *She <u>was studying</u> for the GMAT exam when the phone rang.*
- Describe an atmosphere or situation → *The sun <u>was shining</u> and the birds <u>were chirping</u>.*

Comparing with Adjectives and Adverbs
Comparatives: to be used when comparing two things
Superlatives: to be used when comparing more than two things

Comparing with Adjectives
Adjectives, as you have already learned, describe nouns. When you want to compare two nouns with an adjective, you will need to change the adjective into its **comparative** form followed by *than* and the second object you are comparing. When you want to compare more than two things with an adjective, you will need to change the adjective into its **superlative** form.

Comparative: adjective + *-er* (for adjectives of 1 and 2 syllables)

→ *The new skyscraper is <u>taller</u> than the church.*

→ *The stained glass in the church is <u>prettier</u> than the glass on the skyscraper.*

Comparative: *more* + adjective (for longer adjectives)

→ *The new skyscraper has <u>more fascinating</u> architectural elements than the church.*

→ *The church is <u>more historical</u> than the skyscraper.*

Superlative: adjective + *-est* (for adjectives of 1 and 2 syllables)

→ *He was the <u>happiest</u> storeowner on the block.*

→ *His business was the <u>quickest</u> to succeed.*

Superlative: *the* + *most* + adjective (for longer adjectives)

→ *His restaurant had <u>the most interesting</u> dishes in the neighborhood.*

→ *His restaurant is <u>the most successful</u> on the block.*

Comparing with Adverbs

Adverbs describe adjectives, verbs, and other adverbs. The most common adverb mistakes occur when describing verbs. Watch for correct adverb use on the GMAT sentence correction portion, especially when you make a comparison. When comparing two ideas with an adverb, use the **comparative** form of the adverb, followed by *than* and the second idea you are comparing. When comparing more than two ideas with an adverb, use the **superlative** form.

Comparative: *more* + adverb + *than* (for all adverbs)

→ *A Marine is trained to react <u>more quickly than</u> a civilian in times of panic.*

→ *John received the promotion because he thinks <u>more creatively than</u> his competition does.*

Superlative: *most* + adverb (for all adverbs)

→ *Of all Robert's work references, Mr. Jacobs spoke the <u>most highly</u> of him.*

→ *She visited her parents <u>most often</u> during the summer.*

Exceptions with Comparison Words

*As with all grammar rules, there are exceptions. The following list includes some common irregular adjectives and adverbs.

Adjective/Adverb → Comparative → Superlative
good → *better* → *the best*
well → *better* → *the best*
bad → *worse* → *the worst*
badly → *worse* → *the worst*
many → *more* → *the most*
much → *more* → *the most*
little → *less* → *the least*
far → *further* → *the furthest*

It is very important on the GMAT sentence correction section for comparative and superlative forms to be correctly formed. However, the GMAT exam will go one step further and make sure that correct comparisons are made. Look for more information on logical comparisons in the Effective Expression instructional text.

Subjunctive Voice

The subjunctive voice tends to appear in two types of situations:

- Requests, desires, and suggestions that are structured with certain verbs and followed by the word *that* (known as the command subjunctive)
- Conditional sentences

Command Subjunctive

The command subjunctive form is used with certain verbs that tell people to do things or suggest that they do things. The initial verb must always be followed by *that*.

→ *The state <u>requires that</u> the school <u>be</u> prepared for an earthquake.*

Notice how the sentence begins with *requires + that*, and the second verb is in its base form. The base form of a verb is its most simple form, without *to*. This is the command subjunctive.

→ *The board <u>proposed that</u> the company <u>go</u> to career fairs to recruit younger personnel.*

Notice how *go* is in its base form following the verb *proposed + that*. There-fore, the construction of the command subjunctive is:

Command verb + *that* + subject + command subjunctive form of verb:
→ *She suggests that everyone contemplate the implications of the proposal.*

→ *They demand that the company respond with an answer by 5 P.M.*

Common verbs that require the command subjunctive:
demand, dictate, insist, mandate, propose, recommend, request, stipulate, suggest

→ *The board recommends that all employees take their time to consider their health insurance options.*

*There are, however, some verbs that seem like command verbs, but do not take the subjunctive form. Instead, they remain in the infinitive (*to* + base form of verb) form.

Common verbs that require the infinitive form:
advise, allow, forbid, persuade, want

→ *The lawyer advised his client to get his affairs in order.*

→ *He forbade her to drive after midnight.*

Other verbs can take either the subjunctive or the infinitive form. Keep in mind that the GMAT will typically prefer the subjunctive form, if a choice exists at all. Just remember to check the structure of the subjunctive clause to make sure it is formed correctly! Notice the different structures that follow with the same command verb.

Common verbs that can take the subjunctive or infinitive forms:
ask, beg, intend, order, prefer, urge, require

→ *The state requires that the school be prepared for an earthquake.* OR

→ *The state requires the school to be prepared for an earthquake.*

Remember that the *that* construction after the command verb is necessary to form the subjunctive voice!

Hypothetical Subjunctive and Conditional Sentences
Conditional sentences are also known as *if . . . then* constructions. The following examples are given with the *if* clause first. Notice in the examples following the structure that the sentence may also be inverted with the result clause first and the *if* clause second.

Used to express a general truth or statement
If + subject + present tense verb, subject + present tense verb
If you drop a ball, it falls.
A ball falls if you drop it.

Used to express the consequence of an action
If + subject + present tense verb, subject + future tense verb (or
     may/might/could + verb in base form)
If he breaks his promise, she will be disappointed.
She will be disappointed if he breaks his promise.
If she goes to London to study, her parents might be worried.
Her parents might be worried if she goes to London to study.

Used to express the consequence of an unlikely event
If + subject + past tense verb (hypothetical subjunctive voice), subject +
     would/may/might + verb in base form
If he broke his promise, she would be disappointed.
She would be disappointed if he broke his promise.
If he were here, he would know what to do.
He would know what to do if he were here.

Used to express the consequence of an action that never happened (refers to something in the past)
If + subject + *had* + past participle, subject + *would/may/might* + *have* +
     past participle
If he had broken his promise, she would have been disappointed.
She would have been disappointed if he had broken his promise.

Hypothetical Subjunctive

***The hypothetical subjunctive voice is used to express an unlikely or unreal condition. It is always the simple past form of every verb, except in the verb *to be*. With *to be*, it is always *were*, and never *was*.

→ *If I were you, I would take the risk.*
→ *If she were in your place, I would tell her to quit.*

It is common to see this structure with the verb *wish*:

→ *I wish I were finished with this test!*
→ *We wish there were more days to study for this test!*

In spoken speech, it is common to hear *I wish I was*. Although it has become accepted in everyday speech, it is grammatically incorrect, especially on the GMAT sentence correction section.

Parallelism

Parallelism, or parallel structure, improves the effectiveness of a sentence by wording multiple ideas with a similar structure. A similar structure facilitates understanding and can consist of verb and verb, noun and noun, phrase and phrase, and so on. Parallel structure is a very important aspect of GMAT sentence correction questions and in many cases, it can be the deciding factor between a right and wrong answer. You will encounter various questions that deal with parallelism. It is important to remember that other errors may exist within a question that seems to touch on parallelism, so carefully read each choice.

   Parallelism may exist in a number of instances that include:

- **List**
   → *She bought eggs, flour, sugar, pineapple, and cream for her cake.*
   X *She bought some eggs, flour, sugar, two pineapples to cut into chunks, and then some cream for her cake.*
- Notice how the first example is much easier to understand because it employs a parallel structure with simple nouns.
- **Series of Phrases**
   → *The conference speakers touched on the importance of conservation, the dangers of exploitation, and the future of ecotourism.*

X *The conference speakers talked about <u>how conservation is</u>*
<u>important</u>, <u>the dangers of exploitation</u>, and <u>what the future holds</u>
<u>for ecotourism</u>.

Notice how the first example is much more clear and succinct
because the three factors are all in noun form.

- **Compare and Contrast**

  → *It is better <u>to have loved and lost</u> than never <u>to have loved at all</u>.*

  X *It is better <u>to have loved and lost</u> than never <u>know love</u>.*

  Notice that although the parallel example that employs the
  present perfect tense in both clauses is longer, it sounds better.
  Brevity does not always indicate the best answer.

Certain expressions force the items in a sentence to be parallel. It is good
to be aware of these idiomatic expressions. When you see them, make sure
the items they refer to are structured with the same part of speech.

Parallel Indicators

And	→ *She decided to run <u>and</u> swim yesterday.*
Both . . . and	→ *She went to <u>both</u> the gym <u>and</u> the pool yesterday.*
Either . . . or	→ *She was going to <u>either</u> run <u>or</u> swim.*
From . . . to	→ *She went <u>from</u> running at the gym <u>to</u> swimming at the pool.*
Not . . . but	→ *She prefers <u>not</u> cycling, <u>but</u> running and swimming.*
Not only . . . but also	→ *She does <u>not only</u> run, <u>but also</u> swims.*
Or	→ *On most days, she runs <u>or</u> swims.*

The aforementioned examples all contain some variant of *run* and *swim*. In
each example, the ideas of *running* and *swimming* are kept in a similar structure to maintain parallelism.

Now, let us look at some additional idiomatic expressions that may
appear on the GMAT sentence correction test. You should be familiar with
them and be able to spot errors associated with their use.

Idiomatic Expressions

as many as (to be used with countable nouns)
as much as (to be used with noncountable nouns)
as (adverb/adjective) *as*
the number of (to be used with singular verbs)

a number of (to be used with plural verbs)
to consider
to regard as
x *and* y, *as well as* z

Set 5

Now it is time to answer GMAT sentence correction practice questions that have been designed to test your correct expression skills. As the questions progress, you may notice some additional concepts that are not addressed in this instructional text. These concepts are derived from the effective expression section. The real GMAT sentence correction questions will combine concepts from both sections, so pay close attention to unfamiliar ideas. They will surely be addressed in the effective expression section that follows. Good luck!

93. According to a report released by Oxfam, the most successful nations in the world <u>not only consume the bulk of the world's resources, but they are now</u> home to more than half of the world's poorest people.
    a. not only consume the bulk of the world's resources, but they are now
    b. not only consumes the bulk of the world's resources, but they are now
    c. not only consumes the bulk of the world's resources, but they are now being
    d. not only consume the bulk of the world's resources, but they have now been
    e. not only is consuming the bulk of the world's resources, but they are now

94. When it ruled that the government couldn't track an individual by attaching a GPS device to a vehicle without a warrant, the Supreme Court curtailed many covert <u>operations, setting new standards for future intelligence missions.</u>

    a. operations, setting new standards for future intelligence missions.

    b. operations, having set new standards for future intelligence missions.

    c. operations and set new standards for future intelligence missions.

    d. operations and will set new standards for future intelligence missions.

    e. operations, new standards were set for future intelligence missions.

95. One of the most important questions facing the American public in the wake of the global energy crisis <u>is if they can make the transition</u> to hybrid cars to lessen the dependence on foreign oil.

    a. is if they can make the transition

    b. are if they can make the transition

    c. is whether they can make the transition

    d. is whether it can make the transition

    e. are if it can make the transition

96. China's views of stem cell treatment, which do not place as much significance on the moral value of the embryo, differ largely from <u>the United States,</u> which views the embryo as a representation of human life.

    a. the United States

    b. that of the United States

    c. that embraced by the United States

    d. those from the United States

    e. those of the United States

97. British scientists <u>are working on preserving the world's most threatened plant species, their regeneration once they've been in frozen storage, and ways to extract their medicinal properties.</u>

    a. are working on preserving the world's most threatened plant species, their regeneration once they've been in frozen storage, and ways to extract their medicinal properties.

    b. are working on preserving the world's most threatened plant species, regenerating them after frozen storage, and extracting their medicinal properties.

    c. are working on preserving the world's most threatened plant species, to regenerate them after frozen storage, and extract their medicinal properties.

    d. are working diligent to preserve the world's most threatened plant species, regenerate them after frozen storage, and extract its medicinal properties.

    e. are working to preserve the world's more threatened plant species, regenerate them after frozen storage, and extract their medicinal properties.

98. During the bus boycott by the African American community in 1955, contemporaries <u>of Martin Luther King, Jr.'s insisted that he had had</u> the makings of a great leader.

    a. of Martin Luther King, Jr.'s insisted that he had had
    b. of Martin Luther King, Jr.'s were insisting that he has
    c. of Martin Luther King, Jr.'s insisted that he had
    d. of Martin Luther King, Jr. insisted that he has
    e. of Martin Luther King, Jr. insisted that he had

99. Floating above Earth, satellites help transmit information between newspapers and <u>printing sites, information that affects</u> society.

    a. printing sites, information that affects
    b. printing sites, with information that affects
    c. printing sites, the information affects
    d. printing sites that affect
    e. printing sites that has affected

100. If <u>there was any truth to recent findings, inactivity is as deadly than</u> smoking.

    a. there was any truth to recent findings, inactivity is as deadly than

    b. there was any truth to recent findings, inactivity is as deadly as

    c. there's been any truth to recent findings, inactivity is as deadly as

    d. there is any truth to recent findings, inactivity is as deadly as

    e. there is any truth to recent findings, inactivity is as deadly than

101. In an uncertain economy, the manufacturing sector, which includes everything <u>from automobiles, energy equipment, and medical devices, seems to be</u> making a comeback.

    a. from automobiles, energy equipment, and medical devices, seems to be

    b. from automobiles and energy equipment to medical devices, seems to be

    c. from automobiles, energy equipment, and medical devices, seems that it is

    d. from automobiles and energy equipment to medical devices, seems that it is

    e. from automobiles, energy equipment, in addition to medical devices, seems to be

102. As companies grow increasingly dependent on technology, employees <u>having mastered computer engineering become</u> more competitive in the job market.

    a. having mastered computer engineering become

    b. who mastered computer engineering became

    c. having mastered computer engineering will be becoming

    d. who master computer engineering are becoming

    e. who master computer engineering have been becoming

103. Like trees have rings to determine their age, so do growth rings on the scales of some fish.

 a. Like trees have rings to determine their age, so do growth rings on the scales of some fish.

 b. Like trees have rings to determine their age, some fish have growth rings on their scales.

 c. Trees, as some fish, have growth rings that determine their age.

 d. As trees have rings, growth rings also appear on some fish to determine their age.

 e. Some fish, like trees, have growth rings that determine their age.

104. Fossil discoveries suggest that an extinct river turtle survived the meteorite, which killed off dinosaurs 65 million years ago.

 a. meteorite, which killed off dinosaurs 65 million years ago.

 b. meteorite that had killed off dinosaurs 65 million years ago.

 c. meteorite that killed off dinosaurs 65 million years ago.

 d. meteorite, which had killed off dinosaurs 65 million years ago.

 e. meteorite killing off dinosaurs 65 million years ago.

105. Three of the most encouraging ideas to extend the life of satellites includes restoring power via a mission extension vehicle, refueling via a type of traveling service station, and to detach working parts from old satellites to attach them to new ones.

 a. includes restoring power via a mission extension vehicle, refueling via a type of traveling service station, and to detach working parts from old satellites to attach them to new ones.

 b. include restoring power via a mission extension vehicle, refueling via a type of traveling service station, and detaching working parts from old satellites to attach them to new ones.

 c. are to restore power via a mission extension vehicle, refueling via a type of traveling service station, and by detaching working parts from old satellites to attach them to new ones.

 d. includes restoring power via a mission extension vehicle, refueling via a type of traveling service station, and detaching working parts from old satellites to attach them to new ones.

 e. include restoring power via a mission extension vehicle, using a traveling service station that refuels them, and detaching working parts to attach them to new satellites from old ones.

106. Thought to be either symbolic or accurate descriptions, <u>archaeologists have debated cave paintings for some time.</u>
- **a.** archaeologists have debated cave paintings for some time.
- **b.** archaeologists have long debated the significance of cave paintings.
- **c.** much time has been devoted to debating the significance of cave paintings.
- **d.** cave paintings have been a subject of debate by archaeologists for some time.
- **e.** cave paintings have debated archaeologists for some time.

107. Some economic experts argue that <u>if government would not have intervened in the housing market, the economic crisis would have been avoided.</u>
- **a.** if government would not have intervened in the housing market, the economic crisis would have been avoided.
- **b.** the economic crisis would have been avoided if government would not have intervene in the housing market.
- **c.** if government had not intervened in the housing market, the economic crisis could have been avoided.
- **d.** the economic crisis could be avoided if government didn't intervene in the housing market.
- **e.** the economic crisis would have been avoided if government had not intervene in the housing market.

108. Easter Islanders claim that the island's ancient, famous statues walked by themselves, <u>which they allege as proof of their magical powers.</u>
- **a.** which they allege as proof of their magical powers.
- **b.** which they have alleged as proof of their magical powers.
- **c.** which they alleged as an example of evidence of its magical powers.
- **d.** which allegedly are proof of the statues' magical powers.
- **e.** which is alleged proof of the statues' magical powers.

109. Citizens often demand that a presidential candidate <u>release their tax records in order to determine how much has been taken by the government.</u>

   a. release their tax records in order to determine how much has been taken by the government.

   b. release his or her tax records in order to determine how much has been taken by the government.

   c. releases his or her tax records in order to determine how much have been taken by the government.

   d. release their tax records in order to determine how much have been taken by the government.

   e. releases his or her tax records in order to determine how much has been taken by the government.

110. Democrats' views, which favor progressive taxation and a liberal philosophy, <u>are generally deemed more revolutionary than Republicans'.</u>

   a. are generally deemed more revolutionary than Republicans'.

   b. are generally deemed more revolutionary than Republican.

   c. are generally deemed the most revolutionary over Republicans'.

   d. are generally deemed the most revolutionary in comparison to Republican's.

   e. are generally deemed more revolutionary than Republicans.

111. Figures from 2011 indicate that <u>a number of unemployed American citizens with a disability were about the same as in 2010.</u>

   a. a number of unemployed American citizens with a disability were about the same as in 2010.

   b. a number of unemployed American citizens with a disability was about the same as in 2010.

   c. the number of unemployed American citizens with a disability was about the same than in 2010.

   d. the number of unemployed American citizens with a disability were about the same than in 2010.

   e. the number of unemployed American citizens with a disability was about the same as in 2010.

112. The market forces <u>to which the movements of a stock price are subjected are</u> sufficient to surprise even the most experienced stockbrokers.

    a. to which the movements of a stock price are subjected are

    b. to which the movements of a stock price is subjected is

    c. to which the movements of a stock price are subjected is

    d. to which the movements of a stock price is subjected are

    e. subjecting the movement of a stock price is

113. A new definition for autism suggests that a new umbrella category of "autism spectrum disorder" <u>be established, and in encompassing previously separate disorders, such as Asperger's syndrome and childhood disintegrative disorder, they would achieve more accurate diagnoses and better treatment.</u>

    a. be established, and in encompassing previously separate disorders, such as Asperger's syndrome and childhood disintegrative disorder, they would achieve more accurate diagnoses and better treatment.

    b. is established, and in encompassing previously separate disorders, such as Asperger's syndrome and childhood disintegrative disorder, more accurate diagnoses and better treatment would be achieved.

    c. to be established, and in encompassing previously separate disorders, such as Asperger's syndrome and childhood disintegrative disorder, they would potentially achieve more accurate diagnoses and better treatment.

    d. be established, which would encompass previously separate disorders such as Asperger's syndrome and childhood disintegrative disorder, and lead to more accurate diagnoses and better treatment.

    e. is established, and by encompassing previously separate disorders, such as Asperger's syndrome and childhood disintegrative disorder, they would achieve more accurate diagnoses and better treatment.

114. Surveys indicate that feelings of happiness and satisfaction are relative; a poor man <u>may wish he was $1 million richer, yet a millionaire may still feel unsatisfied and wishes he had</u> $2 million more.

   a. may wish he was $1 million richer, yet a millionaire may still feel unsatisfied and wishes he had

   b. may wish he were $1 million richer, yet a millionaire may still feel unsatisfied and wish he had

   c. may wish he was $1 million richer, yet a millionaire will still feel unsatisfied and wish he had

   d. wishes he was $1 million richer, yet a millionaire still feels unsatisfied and wishes he had

   e. may wish he were $1 million richer, yet a millionaire may still feel unsatisfied and wish he has

115. A system of underground tunnels at the White <u>House were built on an impressive scale, with a complex communication network, to lead to the Deep Underground Command Center in the case a national emergency.</u>

   a. House were built on an impressive scale, with a complex communication network, to lead to the Deep Underground Command Center in the case a national emergency.

   b. House were built on an impressive scale, which has a complex communication network, leading to the Deep Underground Command Center in the event of a national emergency.

   c. House, featuring a complex communication network, was built on an impressive scale to lead to the Deep Underground Command Center in the event of a national emergency.

   d. House was built on an impressive scale with a complex communication network to lead to the Deep Underground Command Center should a national emergency occurs.

   e. House were built on an impressive scale, with a complex communication network, that lead to the Deep Underground Command Center in case of a national emergency.

116. A majority of society <u>argues that neither technology nor genetics is</u> <u>to</u> blame for rampant childhood obesity in society.
   a. argues that neither technology nor genetics is to
   b. argue that neither technology nor genetics are to
   c. argue that they cannot look at technology or genetics as the
   d. argue that not technology or genetics is to
   e. argues that not technology nor genetics is to

117. <u>Rather than waiting to die, Oregon's right-to-die law permits</u> <u>mentally stable people, which have less than six months to live,</u> <u>access to medication to accelerate their demise.</u>
   a. Rather than waiting to die, Oregon's right-to-die law permits mentally stable people, which have less than six months to live, access to medication to accelerate their demise.
   b. Rather than waiting to die, Oregon's right-to-die law permits mentally stable people that have less than six months to live to access medication to accelerate their demise.
   c. Rather than waiting to die, the demise of mentally stable people who have less than six months to live can be accelerated by Oregon's right-to-die law who permits them access to medication.
   d. Rather than waiting to die, mentally stable people who have less than six months to live are permitted access to medication by Oregon's right-to-die law to accelerate their demise.
   e. Rather then waiting to die, mentally stable people's demise can be accelerated by Oregon's right-to-die law, permitting them access to medication provided they have less than six months to live.

118. The newly established International Criminal Court brought charges against the warlord <u>for plundering villages, stealing food, and the kidnapping of children for taking as soldiers and wives.</u>

    a. for plundering villages, stealing food, and the kidnapping of children for taking as soldiers and wives.

    b. for plundering villages, to steal food, and kidnap children to take as soldiers and wives.

    c. for his plundering of villages, stealing food, and kidnapping children to be soldiers and wives.

    d. because he plundered villages, stealing food, and kidnapping children to take as soldiers and wives.

    e. for plundering villages, stealing food, and kidnapping children to take as soldiers and wives.

119. Although the Olympic athlete's mother was at home watching her son on television, the competition <u>was as exciting to her as the royal attendees sitting in the first row.</u>

    a. was as exciting to her as the royal attendees sitting in the first row

    b. was as exciting to her than the royal attendees sitting in the first row

    c. was as exciting to her as to the royal attendees sitting in the first row

    d. was as exciting to her than to the royal attendees sitting in the first row

    e. was as exciting to her then to the royal attendees sitting in the first row

120. Many <u>full veiled Muslim women are outspoken in defending their patriarchal traditions, especially when confronted with Western opposition who views them as being heavily</u> oppressed.

a. full veiled Muslim women are outspoken in defending their patriarchal traditions, especially when confronted with Western opposition who views them as being heavily

b. full veiled Muslim women are outspoken in defending her patriarchal traditions, especially when confronted with Western opposition who views her as being heavily

c. fully veiled Muslim women are outspoken in defending their patriarchal traditions, especially when confronted with Western opposition that views them as being heavy

d. fully veiled Muslim women are outspoken in defending their patriarchal traditions, especially when confronted with Western opposition that views them as being heavily

e. fully veiled Muslim women are outspoken in defending her patriarchal traditions, especially when confronted with Western opposition that views her as being heavily

121. A handful of companies offer DNA-based tests that supposedly determine how <u>well a person's natural athletic abilities are, but critics insist these tests don't reveal much more than a standard performance test.</u>

a. well a person's natural athletic abilities are, but critics insist these tests don't reveal much more than a standard performance test.

b. good a person's natural athletic abilities are, but critics insist that these tests don't reveal much more than standard performance tests do.

c. well a person's natural athletic abilities are, but critics insist these tests don't reveal much beyond a standard performance test.

d. well a person's natural athletic abilities are, but critics insist that these tests don't reveal much more than standard performance tests do.

e. good a person's natural athletic abilities are, but critics insist that standard performance tests don't reveal much less than the other tests.

122. Resigned to accept his disqualification from the Olympic trials, there was only silence in the locker room.

    a. Resigned to accept his disqualification from the Olympic trials, there was only silence in the locker room.

    b. There was only silence in the locker room, resigned to accept his disqualification from the Olympic trials.

    c. Silent in the locker room, resigned to accept his disqualification from the Olympic trials.

    d. Resigned to accept his disqualification from the Olympic trials, silence permeated the locker room.

    e. Resigned to accept his disqualification from the Olympic trials, the athlete remained silent in the locker room.

123. Latin America has no single dominant Spanish dialect: The range of Spanish encompasses many styles, speeds, and slang, with each a product of their local influences, from the fast-paced, clear Colombian variants to the more obvious, melodic Argentinian alternatives.

    a. with each a product of their

    b. each products of their

    c. each products of

    d. with each as a product of its

    e. each a product of

124. <u>In the eighteenth century, William Shakespeare was regarded as one of the greatest playwrights of all time, and not until the mid-nineteenth century was the authorship of the works attributed to Shakespeare first openly questioned by Joseph C. Hart.</u>

    a. In the eighteenth century, William Shakespeare was regarded as one of the greatest playwrights of all time, and not until the mid-nineteenth century was the authorship of the works attributed to Shakespeare first openly questioned by Joseph C. Hart.

    b. William Shakespeare was considered as one of the greatest playwrights of all time in the eighteenth century, and not until the middle of the nineteenth century did Joseph C. Hart first openly question his works.

    c. In the eighteenth century, they considered William Shakespeare as one of the greatest playwrights of all time, and not until the mid-nineteenth century did Joseph C. Hart first explicit question his authorship of Shakespeare's works.

    d. In the eighteenth century, William Shakespeare was considered to be one of the greater playwrights of all time, and not until the mid-ninteenth century did Joseph C. Hart openly question Shakespeare's authorship of the works attributed to him.

    e. In the eighteenth century, William Shakespeare was regarded to be one of the greatest playwrights of all time, and not until the middle of the ninteenth century did Joseph C. Hart first openly question Shakespeare's authorship of the works attributed to him.

125. The Happy Planet Index, <u>which ranks 151 countries, considers data like life expectancy, overall well-being, and a country's ecological footprint on calculating the happiness of a country.</u>

    a. which ranks 151 countries, considers data like life expectancy, overall well-being, and a country's ecological footprint on calculating the happiness of a country.

    b. which ranks the happiness of 151 countries, considers data like life expectancy and overall well-being and a country's ecological footprint.

    c. which ranks the happiness of 151 countries, considers data such as life expectancy and overall well-being, as well as the country's ecological footprint in its calculations.

    d. which ranks 151 countries, considers data such as life expectancy, overall well-being, as well as a country's ecological footprint when calculating the happiness of a country.

    e. which ranks 151 countries, consider data such as life expectancy, overall well-being, and a country's ecological footprint to determine the happiness of a country.

126. Results from numerous studies show that if a diabetic plans his or her diet and <u>exercised with fellow diabetics, they will regain control quicker and stick to weight goals for a longer period of time than do</u> someone who attempts to do so alone.

    a. exercised with fellow diabetics, they will regain control quicker and stick to weight goals for a longer period of time than do

    b. exercises with fellow diabetics, he or she regains control more quickly and sticks to weight goals for a longer period of time than

    c. exercises with fellow diabetics, they regain control quicker and stick to weight goals for a longer period of time than does

    d. exercised with fellow diabetics, he or she will have regained control more quickly and stuck to weight goals for a longer period of time than

    e. exercises with fellow diabetics, he or she regains control more quickly and sticks to weight goals for a longer period of time than does

127. Growing economic woes and competition could be pushing accountants to finagle their <u>clients' records; accountants can, for example, help</u> their frustrated clients write off certain luxurious purchases and justify them as business expenses.
   a. clients' records; accountants can, for example, help
   b. clients' records, as an example, they can help
   c. clients' records, like they can help
   d. clients records; which might include that they
   e. clients' records, such as to be helping

128. A series of troubling reports released by some of the top environmental organizations <u>indicates that as much as 18,000 pieces of floating plastic, which is resistant to natural biodegradation, makes up</u> every square kilometer of the ocean.
   a. indicates that as much as 18,000 pieces of floating plastic, which is resistant to natural biodegradation, makes up
   b. indicates that as much as 18,000 pieces of floating plastic, which is resistant to natural biodegradation, have made up
   c. indicate that as many as 18,000 pieces of floating plastic, which is resistant to natural biodegradation, is making up
   d. indicates that as many as 18,000 pieces of floating plastic, which are resistant to natural biodegradation, make up
   e. indicate that as many of 18,000 pieces of floating plastic, which are resistant to natural biodegradation, make up

129. Restaurateurs are well aware that the frequency of employee turnover and <u>how servers treat their customers is</u> very indicative of employee happiness on the job.
   a. how servers treat their customers is
   b. how servers treat their customers are
   c. and servers' treatment of their customers are
   d. and servers' treatment of their customers is
   e. customers' reactions to their servers are

130. The famous rivalry <u>of Coke and Pepsi may never have been if Coca-Cola hadn't seized the opportunity presented three times between 1922 and 1933 and bought</u> the bankrupt Pepsi Cola Company.

a. of Coke and Pepsi may never have been if Coca-Cola hadn't seized the opportunity presented three times between 1922 and 1933 and bought

b. of Coke and Pepsi may never have been if Coca-Cola hadn't seized the opportunity presented three times between 1922 and 1933 and hadn't bought

c. between Coke and Pepsi may never have been if Coca-Cola hadn't seized the opportunity presented three times between 1922 and 1933 and bought

d. between Coke and Pepsi would never be if Coca-Cola had seized the opportunity presented three times between 1922 and 1933 and bought

e. between Coke and Pepsi may never have been if Coca-Cola had seized the opportunity presented three times between 1922 and 1933 and bought

131. In June 2012, the Rhode Island General Assembly <u>had voted to repeal a law enacted in 1989 that made lying online a misdemeanor, citing the illogic of trying to enforce something that is so often</u> innocently violated.

a. had voted to repeal a law enacted in 1989 that made lying online a misdemeanor, citing the illogic of trying to enforce something that is so often

b. voted to repeal a law enacted in 1989 that made lying online a misdemeanor, citing the illogic of trying to enforce something that is so often

c. had voted to repeal a law enacted in 1989 that made lying online a misdemeanor, citing the illogic of the trying to enforce something that is so often

d. voted in favor of to repeal a law enacted in 1989 that has made lying online a misdemeanor, citing the illogic of attempting to enforce something that is so often

e. voted for repealing a law enacted in 1989 that had made lying online a misdemeanor, having cited the illogic of trying to enforce something that is so often

132. <u>However much United States citizens may criticize the perils of capitalism and that the democracy is corrupted,</u> it is rare to find organized national movements for a structure other than democracy.

   a. However much United States citizens may criticize the perils of capitalism and that the democracy is corrupted,

   b. Although United States citizens may agree capitalism is dangerous and democracy is corrupted,

   c. Despite criticism by United States citizens to the extent of the perils of capitalism and corruption of democracy,

   d. However much United States citizens may criticize the perils of capitalism and the corruption of democracy,

   e. However many United States citizens may criticize the perils of capitalism and corruption of democracy,

133. The private lending sector has $8 billion in student loans that are in default or at such serious risk to default <u>that it does not expect payments when it is</u> due and has consequently tightened credit standards for new student loans.

   a. that it does not expect payments when it is

   b. that payments will not be expected to be paid when

   c. that it does not expect payments to be made when they are

   d. that payments are not expected to be paid when they are going to be

   e. that they do not expect payments when it is

Effective Expression

The following material will help you prepare for the part of the GMAT sentence correction section that focuses on clarity and conciseness in sentences, effective syntax, redundancy, and proper diction.

Sentence Formation

In order to form an effective sentence, it is crucial that you understand its components. Syntax is defined as sentence structure. Syntax can make the difference between an effective and ineffective sentence. The following terms break down the different parts that make up a sentence and how their misuse can lead to confusion and ambiguity.

Independent Clause

A clause that expresses a complete sentence → *Monica walked on the grass*.

Coordinating Conjunction

A word that joins two independent and equal clauses: *and, but, so, or, for, nor, yet*

→ *Dorothy had a beautiful rose garden, and her yard was a profusion of color every summer.*

*The most common coordinating conjunction is *and*. And* can also be used in a list, such as in the following example:

→ *Dorothy has roses, lilies, and daisies in her garden.*

*When you see *and* in a sentence correction question, make sure it is used in a list (as in the aforementioned example), or as a coordinating conjunction that combines two independent clauses. Look at the following example:

X *The language test administered by the school and touched on important differences between British English and American English.*

This sentence is incorrect because *the language test administered by the school* is not an independent clause. Therefore, *and* cannot combine it with the rest of the sentence. Look at the corrected version, which changes the first part of the sentence to an independent clause by including the verb was:

→ *The language test was administered by the school and touched on important differences between British English and American English.*

Conjunctive Adverb/Transition Word

A word that introduces a relationship between two independent clauses and connects them. These words are called **conjunctive adverbs**, **transition words**, and **connecting words**. If the word is used in the middle of a sentence, a semicolon is generally used before the word. Every sentence must have at least one main clause (with a subject and verb), but many sentences will have two or more. In order to logically combine clauses in a sentence, conjunctive adverbs (or transition words) are necessary to show the relationship between clauses. Using too many or not enough conjunctive adverbs can lead to errors. Some common conjunctive adverbs and their uses are given here:

Contrast and Comparison
however, instead, nevertheless, otherwise, yet
→ *On Tuesdays, I play racquetball; <u>otherwise</u>, I would go with you.*

Cause–Effect/Consequence
as a result, consequently, hence, then, therefore, thus
→ *On Tuesdays, I play racquetball; <u>therefore</u>, I am unable to go to the meeting.*

Addition
also, as well as, furthermore, in addition (to), moreover
→ *On Tuesdays, I play racquetball; <u>furthermore</u>, I lift weights for one hour in the morning.*

*On the GMAT sentence correction section, it is important that you use the correct conjunctive adverb to connect ideas. Choose a word that logically fits into the sentence and sensibly connects the ideas. Look at the following example:

X *The children are not interested in swimming; <u>therefore</u>, swimming is their favorite Olympic sport to watch.*

The preceding sentence is incorrect because *therefore* does not logically combine the two contrasting ideas. Look at the corrected version with a different, more logical conjunctive adverb.

→ *The children are not interested in swimming; <u>however</u>, swimming is their favorite Olympic sport to watch.*

Dependent (Subordinate) Clause
A clause that does not express a complete sentence → <u>*though it was wet*</u>

→ *Monica walked on the grass, <u>though it was wet</u>.*

Subordinating Conjunction

A word that makes a clause dependent: *after, although, as, because, before, if, once, since, than, that, though, unless, until, when, whenever, where, wherever, while*

→ *The man wasn't angry, <u>though</u> he had a right to be.*

Though he had a right to be is a dependent clause because of *though*, a subordinating conjunction.

Restrictive (Essential) Clause

A dependent clause that is necessary to the basic meaning of the completed sentence. → *who are pregnant*

→ *Women <u>who are pregnant</u> can crave salty or sweet foods.* (Notice the absence of commas.)

Nonrestrictive (Nonessential) Clause

A dependent clause that is not necessary to the basic meaning of the completed sentence. → *who growls whenever the phone rings*

→ *Elmo, <u>who growls whenever the phone rings</u>, attacked the vacuum cleaner.* (Notice the commas.)

Appositive

A phrase that makes a preceding noun or pronoun clearer or more definite by explaining or identifying it → *rice pudding and fruit salad*

Candice's grandfather brought her favorite desserts, <u>rice pudding and fruit salad</u>.

Fragment

A phrase punctuated like a sentence even though it does not express a complete thought.

→ *Timothy saw the car. <u>And ran</u>.*

Correct Syntax

To obtain correct syntax, the first step in an effective sentence, a sentence must:

- Always have at least one independent clause in the sentence.
  → *Chaucer was a narrator.*
- Join two independent clauses with a comma and a <u>conjunction</u>.
  → *Chaucer was a narrator, <u>and</u> he was a pilgrim in his* Canterbury Tales.
- Not run two or more independent clauses together without punctuation; that error is called a **run-on**.
- Not separate two independent clauses with just a comma; that error is called a **comma splice**.

X *Chaucer was a narrator, he was a pilgrim in his* Canterbury Tales. The preceding example is incorrect because only a comma is separating the two independent clauses. A correct sentence would be:

→ *Chaucer was a narrator, <u>and</u> he was a pilgrim in his* Canterbury Tales.

- Do not use a **conjunctive adverb** (words such as *accordingly, besides, consequently, furthermore, hence, however, instead, moreover, nevertheless, otherwise, then, therefore, thus*) like a **conjunction**.

X *Chaucer was a narrator, <u>moreover</u> he was a pilgrim in his* Canterbury Tales.

The preceding example is incorrect because only a comma is separating the conjunctive adverb. The corrected sentence would be:

→ *Chaucer was a narrator; <u>moreover,</u> he was a pilgrim in his* Canterbury Tales.

Semicolons

Semicolons are generally used in the following two circumstances:

- Between two independent clauses
  → *Edward joined the basketball team; remarkably, the 5'4" young man excelled at the sport.*

In this example, *Edward joined the basketball team* and *the 5'4" young man excelled at the sport* are both independent clauses that have been connected by the conjunctive adverb *remarkably* and a semicolon.

- Between elements in a series that uses commas already
  → *The possible dates for the potluck dinner are Thursday, June 5; Saturday, June 7; or Monday, June 9.*

Effective Sentence Style

The GMAT sentence correction test follows some general standards to form effective sentences. Review the following points and keep them in mind as you tackle the questions.

Prefer the *That* Clause

The GMAT sentence correction test will often present sentences with a *that* clause. Review the following points to make sure you understand the role of the *that* clause in a sentence.

Reporting Verbs

Reporting verbs are verbs used to report a thought, belief, or quote. Common reporting verbs include *argue, ask, believe, claim, indicate, report, reply, respond, suggest,* and *tell*. It is important to use *that* after these verbs when another verb follows. Look at the following examples.

→ *The studies indicated <u>that</u> high school standards have risen in the past ten years.*
→ *She claimed <u>that</u> she didn't see the car approaching.*

Subjunctive Clauses

You have already learned about the subjunctive form in the correct expression section. It is crucial that you include *that* when forming a sentence with a subjunctive verb. This small difference may be the key distinction between a right answer and a wrong one on the test.

X *The state requires the school be prepared for an earthquake.*

The preceding sentence is incorrect because it did not include *that* after the verb *requires*. Look at the corrected version:

→ *The state requires <u>that</u> the school be prepared for an earthquake.*

Verbs Are Greater Than Nouns

Clarity is an important concept in the GMAT sentence correction section. Many sentences on this test will be complicated, long ideas. When possible, a *that* clause is preferred over a noun formation to achieve a clearer sentence. Look at the following example:

X *The idea <u>about change being inevitable</u> is a key message in the campaign song.*

This example is considered incorrect because it is wordy. An easy way to correct this sentence is to change the noun clause (*about change being inevitable*) to a *that* clause with a verb.

→ *The idea <u>that change is inevitable</u> is a key message in the campaign song.*

In this particular example, the number of words does not change, but the second format is preferred because it is more clear and active. Look at a few more examples:

X *Reports <u>about the violence spreading</u> in the Middle East have caused unrest at home.*
→ *Reports <u>that violence is spreading</u> in the Middle East have caused unrest at home.*
X *The discovery <u>of other planets capable of supporting life</u> has caused a stir in the world of science.*
→ *The discovery <u>that other planets are capable of supporting life</u> has caused a stir in the world of science.*

Avoiding Wordiness

Wordiness is a big issue on the GMAT sentence correction test. In addition to the aforementioned points, the following hints will help you ensure you choose the most concise sentence every time. Remember, though, that these points are to be considered in addition to any grammar problems. You may be tempted to immediately choose the sentence that fits the following criteria. However, you need to first make sure there are no grammar or clarity problems. The GMAT may try to trick you with a sentence that fits the following criteria, but has a grammar problem. Grammar will always be your first concern. If a sentence isn't grammatically correct, there is no way it can be considered a possible answer. With that in mind, review the following points and keep them in mind as you tackle the questions.

Verbs Are Greater Than Nouns, Part II

A sentence may include an action noun, a noun that expresses an action. Examples include *arrival*, *eating*, and *inspiration*. When possible, the verb form is preferred over the action noun. Look at the following examples:

> **X** *His arrival <u>was an inspiration</u> to me.*

This sentence is grammatically correct, but it could be more concise. Look at the corrected, less wordy version:

> → *His arrival <u>inspired</u> me.*
> **X** <u>*Their decision was*</u> *to continue the trip despite the bad weather forecast.*
> → <u>*They decided*</u> *to continue the trip despite the bad weather forecast.*

Verbs Are Greater Than Adjectives

When possible, try to use a verb construction over an adjective construction for a less wordy sentence.

> **X** *His arrival <u>was inspirational to</u> me.*

This sentence is grammatically correct, but it could be more concise. Look at the corrected, less wordy version:

> → *His arrival <u>inspired</u> me.*

> **X** *The solution <u>is irritating to</u> the wound.*
> → *The solution <u>irritates</u> the wound.*

Active Voice versus Passive Voice

You have already learned the difference between the active voice and passive voice in the correct expression section of this review. Although both forms are grammatically correct, the GMAT will generally prefer the active voice to the passive voice. The passive voice tends to make sentences longer and not as clear. When you notice that the passive voice form makes the sentence more confusing, look at any active voice choices (if they exist) and consider them as possible answers (provided they are grammatically sound).

The passive voice can be the correct answer. When the focus of the sentence is on the person or object receiving the action, not the doer of the action, then the passive voice is preferred. Look at the following example:

→ *The terrorist attack <u>was witnessed</u> by people all over the world.*

In this passive voice example, the focus is on *the terrorist attack*, not *the people all over the world*. The sentence is clear and concise. Consider this point when you encounter a question that uses the passive voice.

Avoiding Redundancy

The GMAT sentence correction test will test your ability to detect redundancy in a sentence. It may, however, disguise redundancy in different parts of speech. Look at the following examples and keep them in mind.

X *At least 300 workers, if not more, participated in the strike on Friday.*

This sentence is incorrect because *at least* and *if not more* convey the same idea. Therefore, one of those expressions can be eliminated. Look at a corrected version of the sentence:

→ *At least 300 workers participated in the strike on Friday.*

X *The doctors can potentially save the girl's life if they find a donor in time.*

This sentence is incorrect because *can potentially* is redundant. Both *can* and *potentially* indicate possibility, so only one of them is necessary. Look at a corrected version of the sentence.

→ *The doctors can save the girl's life if they find a donor in time.*

Also, avoid double comparatives or double superlatives. Adding the suffix *-er* or *-est* to a modifier and preceding the modifier with *more* or *most* is redundant.

X *Lindsey amazed the class with her grammatical skills; she was the most smartest person they had ever seen.*

This sentence is incorrect. Lindsey is already *the smartest*. *Most* also means smartest, so the phrase *most smartest* is redundant.

> → *Lindsey amazed the class with her grammatical skills; she was the smartest person they had ever seen.*

Avoid double negatives.

> **X** *Tom hardly did not feel tense whenever he approached grammar.*

This sentence is incorrect because *hardly* and *did not* cancel each other out. The sentence really reads: *Tom felt tense whenever approaching grammar.* The correct sentence should read:

> → *Tom hardly felt tense whenever he approached grammar.*

Beware of Eliminating Too Much
Now that you are very aware of wordiness and redundancy, you must also beware of common pitfalls that can occur when you eliminate too much.

Prepositional Phrases
A prepositional phrase is a phrase that contains a preposition and a noun. Simple phrases such as *on the bathroom floor* or *from the Dead Sea* are prepositional phrases. These will pop up on the GMAT sentence correction test. In an effort to eliminate wordiness, you may be tempted to combine these prepositional phrases with the nouns they modify, such as in the following example:

> *A planter of bricks* → *A brick planter*

Both phrases are correct. Obviously, the second example is less wordy.

*In general, it is okay to combine a prepositional phrase with its noun when the preposition is *of*, except when you have a time period, quantity, or other measurement as the initial word.

However, when the prepositional phrase involves a preposition other than *of*, it is best to avoid combining the phrase with its noun. Look at the following examples:

> *gold from the San Francisco area* instead of *San Francisco area gold*

> *dust on the bathroom floor* instead of *bathroom floor dust*

> *the amount of water* instead of *the water amount*

In these instances, it is best to keep the longer phrase to avoid confusion.

Avoiding Changes in Meaning

The GMAT sentence correction test may present two grammatically correct options, but one sentence has slightly changed the meaning of the original sentence presented as choice **a**. You must not change the original meaning. Look out for these common pitfalls:

Change in Modals

Modals such as *may*, *might*, *must*, and *should* exist to modify a verb. *I might go* is different from *I must go*, which is different from *I should go*, and so on. Be careful that a modal has not changed and altered the original message in a sentence!

Change in Verbs

In an effort to reduce wordiness, you may be tempted to change a verb and opt for one that expresses an action with fewer words. Make sure the meaning does not change in this process. For example:

> *The idea developed into a fantastic plan.*
> *The idea is a fantastic plan.*

These two sentences are not equivalent. The first one stresses the process of the idea changing into a plan, while the second sentence does not even mention it. Make sure you continue to convey any expressed process or change in an improved sentence.

Change in Syntax (Placement of Modifiers)

Changing the placement of a modifier in a sentence can greatly change the meaning of a sentence. When you review the choices for a question, pay particular attention to any modifiers and whether their location in the sentence has changed. This change could alter the meaning and help you quickly eliminate that choice as a possible answer. Some of these changes may be very subtle, and some may be more obvious. Look at the following examples:

> *Just Heather was selected to participate in the sleep study.*
> *Heather was just selected to participate in the sleep study.*

> *The dentist, a recent graduate from USC's School of Dentistry, selected his partner for his new practice.*
> *The dentist selected his partner, a recent graduate from USC's School of Dentistry, for his new practice.*

Logical Comparisons (Logical Predication)

Comparisons must make sense and compare similar things. The GMAT may try to trick you by testing for a logical comparison and conciseness. Look at the following example:

> **X** *Unlike Mark Twain's* The Adventures of Huckleberry Finn, *written in the first person, Oscar Wilde wrote his classic* The Picture of Dorian Gray *in the third person.*

Upon first look, this sentence may appear correct. It is, however, making an illogical comparison by associating *Mark Twain's* The Adventures of Huckleberry Finn (a book) with *Oscar Wilde* (an author). A book cannot be logically compared to an author. An author can be compared to another author, or a book can be compared to another book. Look at a corrected version of the sentence:

> → *Unlike Mark Twain, who wrote* The Adventures of Huckleberry Finn *in the first person, Oscar Wilde wrote his classic* The Picture of Dorian Gray *in the third person.*

This sentence logically compares the two authors. Such comparisons are a favorite topic on the GMAT sentence correction test, so pay close attention when comparisons are made!

Diction (Word Choice)

Diction is a common issue on GMAT sentence correction questions. Some of the most popular choices are explained and highlighted with examples. The GMAT sentence correction portion is also known to change words for look-alikes in the different answer choices (e.g., *practical* for *practicable*). Be sure that you read each choice carefully to make sure the meaning has not changed.

Study these issues and keep them in mind as you tackle the sentence correction questions.

According to versus In accordance with

According to is used to attribute information to a source:

> → *According to nutritionists, protein is a crucial part of our diet.*

In accordance with is used to indicate compliance:

> → *Every day I eat protein in accordance with my nutritionist's instructions.*

The correct use of *in accordance with* is restricted to *following rules*, *conventions*, or *established patterns*. An actual rule or convention needs to be stated.

Amount of versus Number of

Amount of refers to an uncountable noun (a noun that cannot be counted, such as *information*)

> → *The amount of information on the Internet is overwhelming.*

Number of refers to a countable noun (a noun that can be counted, such as *websites*)

> → *The number of websites dedicated to beauty products is overwhelming.*

Because of versus Due to

Because of answers the question *why?* It is an adverbial phrase that modifies a verb.

> → *He won because of his persistence and drive.*

Due to is an adjectival phrase that modifies a noun. It commonly follows a form of the verb *to be*.

→ *His win was <u>due to</u> his persistence and drive.*

Between versus Among
Between is used when referring to two concepts, and before the word *each*.

→ *He placed second <u>between</u> John and Rachel.*
→ *They have 10 minutes to rest <u>between</u> each event.*

Among is used when referring to three or more concepts.

→ *He divided his property <u>among</u> his four children.*

Farther versus Further
Farther is the comparative form of *far*, which is used to refer to distance.

→ *She drove <u>farther</u> today than she did yesterday.*

Further is also the comparative form of far, but it can be used to refer to distances and figurative distance.

→ *She took the idea one step <u>further</u> than what we had anticipated.*

Few versus Little
Few is used to refer to a countable noun (a noun that can be counted, such as *websites*)

→ *There are <u>few</u> beauty websites that are not trying to sell a product.*

Little is used to refer to an uncountable noun (a noun that cannot be counted, such as *information*)

→ *There is <u>little</u> information in this pamphlet that I consider trustworthy.*

Fewer versus Less

Fewer is the comparative form of *few*, used to refer to a countable noun (such as *websites*)

→ *There are <u>fewer</u> websites in Spanish than there are in English.*

Less is the comparative form of *little*, used to refer to an uncountable noun (such as *information*)

→ *There is <u>less</u> information on the Internet in Spanish than there is in English.*

For + Gerund versus To + Verb (Infinitive)

The **for + gerund** form is used to express the function of a thing or object.

→ *This machine is used <u>for counting</u> coins.*

The **to + verb (infinitive)** form is used to express the purpose of a thing/object, but also of a person.

→ *This machine is used <u>to count</u> coins.*
→ *She went to the store <u>to buy</u> eggs.*

Like versus As

Like is used to compare only nouns, and therefore should be followed by only a noun, pronoun, or noun phrase.

→ *<u>Like</u> her sister, Alice loves to paint.*

As is used to compare clauses, and therefore should be followed by a clause.

→ *<u>As</u> her sister does, Alice loves to paint.*

Like versus Such as

Like is used to express the idea *similar to.*

→ *<u>Like</u> soccer, football is a very competitive sport.*

Such as is used to list examples.

> → *There are many competitive sports, <u>such as</u> football and soccer.*

Much versus Many
Much is used to describe an uncountable noun (a noun that cannot be counted, such as *information*)

> → *There is too <u>much</u> information on the Internet.*

Many is used to describe a countable noun (a noun that can be counted, such as *sources*)

> → *Joshua backed up his research with <u>many</u> different sources.*

Native of versus Native to
Native of is used only when referring to people.

> → *Jacob was born and raised in Washington, so he is a <u>native of</u> Washington.*

Native to is used when referring to species, crops, and so on.

> → *Corn is <u>native to</u> North America.*

Rather than versus Instead of
Rather than shows preference, and can be followed by a clause.

> → *They invested in land <u>rather than</u> machinery.*
> → *<u>Rather than</u> invest in machinery, they invested in land.*

Instead of shows replacement, but not necessarily preference. Also, it must be followed by a noun or noun clause because of the preposition *of*. It cannot be followed by a clause like *rather than*.

> → *He drank coffee <u>instead of</u> tea.*
> → *They invested in land <u>instead of</u> machinery.*

That versus Which

That is used in a restrictive or essential clause to introduce information that is necessary to a sentence. It directly follows the noun that it modifies.

→ *She avoids animals that appear dangerous.* (In this example, she only avoids those animals that appear dangerous, not all animals.)

Which is used in a nonrestrictive or nonessential clause to introduce additional information that is not necessary to the meaning of a sentence. A comma is used between the noun it modifies and *which*.

→ *She avoids animals, which appear dangerous.* (In this example, she avoids all animals because they appear dangerous.)

Set 6

Now it is time to answer 41 GMAT Sentence Correction practice questions that have been designed to test your effective expression skills. Since you have already been exposed to the correct expression skills and questions, you may encounter some concepts from the Correct Expression portion. This has been done to prepare you for the real test, which will combine concepts from both sections. Good luck!

134. <u>Having been accused of polluting huge areas of the Ecuadorian Amazon from its oil operations there in the 1970s and 1980s,</u> Chevron is currently involved in the biggest environmental lawsuit the world has ever seen.
   a. Having been accused of polluting huge areas of the Ecuadorian Amazon from its oil operations there in the 1970s and 1980s
   b. Being accused of polluting huge Ecuadorian Amazon areas from its oil operations there in the 1970s and 1980s
   c. Accused of polluting huge areas of the Ecuadorian Amazon from its oil operations there in the 1970s and 1980s
   d. Having been accused of polluting huge Ecuadorian Amazon areas from their oil operations there in the 1970s and 1980s
   e. Due to being accused of polluting huge areas of the Ecuadorian Amazon from its oil operations there in the 1970s and 1980s

135. <u>Inspired by the success of Disneyland Paris, one French politician wants to create France's very own theme park devoted to Napoleon Bonaparte, with construction slated to begin in 2014 provided enough funds are raised.</u>

   a. Inspired by the success of Disneyland Paris, one French politician wants to create France's very own theme park devoted to Napoleon Bonaparte, with construction slated to begin in 2014 provided enough funds are raised.

   b. Inspired by the success of Disneyland Paris with construction slated to begin in 2014, one French politician wants to create France's very own theme park devoted to Napoleon Bonaparte, provided enough funds are raised.

   c. One French politician wants to create France's very own theme park devoted to Napoleon Bonaparte, inspired by the success of Disneyland Paris with construction slated to begin in 2014 provided enough funds are raised.

   d. One French politician, inspired by the success of Disneyland Paris, wants to create France's very own theme park devoted to Napoleon Bonaparte, with construction slated to begin, provided enough funds are raised, in 2014.

   e. With construction slated to begin in 2014, provided enough funds are raised, one French politician wants to create France's very own theme park inspired by the success of Disneyland Paris devoted to Napoleon Bonaparte.

136. <u>Yellow saddle goatfish in the Red Sea have the capability to hunt in groups, groups with designated members who spread out to cut off the escape routes of the prey.</u>

  a. Yellow saddle goatfish in the Red Sea have the capability to hunt in groups, groups with designated members who spread out to cut off the escape routes of the prey.

  b. Red Sea yellow saddle goatfish are capable of hunting in groups, groups with designated members who spread out to cut off the prey's escape routes.

  c. Red Sea yellow saddle goatfish have the capability to hunt in groups with designated chosen members who spread out to cut off the prey's escape routes.

  d. Yellow saddle goatfish in the Red Sea are capable of hunting in groups with designated members who spread out to cut off the prey's escape routes.

  e. Red Sea yellow saddle goatfish possess the capability to hunt in groups, groups with designated chosen members who spread out to cut off the escape routes of the prey.

137. <u>The hypothesis about the coevolution of species, such as a predator and prey, adapting to each other's evolutionary changes, is fascinating.</u>

  a. The hypothesis about the coevolution of species, such as a predator and prey, adapting to each other's evolutionary changes, is fascinating.

  b. The hypothesis that species, such as a predator and prey, coevolve to adapt to each other's evolutionary changes is fascinating.

  c. Coevolution, where species like a predator and prey adapt to each other's evolutionary changes, is a hypothesis that is fascinating.

  d. The hypothesis regarding coevolution, like a predator and prey adapting to each other's evolutionary changes, fascinates.

  e. The hypothesis that species, like a predator and prey, coevolve to adapt to each other's evolutionary changes is fascinating.

138. <u>The belief that whales were terrestrial mammals that transitioned into the ocean is supported by evidence of whale fossils with legs and knees.</u>

    a. The belief that whales were terrestrial mammals that transitioned into the ocean is supported by evidence of whale fossils with legs and knees.

    b. The belief about whales being terrestrial mammals which transitioned into the ocean was supported by whale fossils having legs and knees.

    c. The belief about whales as terrestrial mammals transitioning into the ocean have been supported by evidence of whale fossils with legs and knees.

    d. The belief that whales were terrestrial mammals that made the transition into the ocean is supported by evidence of whale fossils with legs and knees.

    e. Whale fossils with legs and knees is evidence supporting the belief of whales as once being terrestrial mammals.

139. A new study found <u>that the representation of global migrants on a world scale is overpowered by Christians, who overrepresent a high 49%.</u>

    a. that the representation of global migrants on a world scale is overpowered by Christians, who overrepresent a high 49%.

    b. that Christians overrepresent a high 49% of the world scale of global migrants.

    c. that Christians are overrepresented by an elevated 49% on the world scale of global migrants.

    d. that Christians represent an overwhelming 49% of global migrants on a world scale.

    e. that 49% of global migrants are represented overwhelmingly high by Christians.

140. <u>New workforce trends suggest that a large number of working wives will outearn their husbands within a generation.</u>

    a. New workforce trends suggest that a large number of working wives will outearn their husbands within a generation.

    b. According to new workforce trends, a majority of working wives will be outearning their husbands with greater wages within the next generation.

    c. New workforce trends within a generation suggest an outearning of a large number of working wives by their husbands.

    d. Within a generation, a large number of husbands will be outearned by their working wives, according to new workforce trends.

    e. New workforce trends suggest an outearning of husbands by a majority of their working wives within the next generation.

141. An article revealed <u>one language dies every 14 days because of communities abandoning native tongues in favor of more common ones.</u>

    a. one language dies every 14 days because of communities abandoning native tongues in favor of more common ones.

    b. that one language dies every 14 days due to communities abandoning native tongues in favor of more common ones.

    c. that one language dies every 14 days because communities abandon native tongues in favor of more common ones.

    d. one language dies every 14 days because communities abandon native tongues in favor of more common ones.

    e. the death of one language every 14 days because communities are favoring more common tongues.

142. With initial deployment scheduled in the San Joaquin and Sacramento valleys, the Picarro is the first of <u>many analyzers that is part of a long-term effort of subjecting carbon dioxide, methane, and other greenhouse gas emissions</u> to statewide scrutiny and investigation.

    a. many analyzers that is part of a long-term effort of subjecting carbon dioxide, methane, and other greenhouse gas emissions
    b. many analyzers, which is a part of a long-term effort to subject how carbon dioxide, methane, and other greenhouse gases emit
    c. many analyzers, part of a long-term effort of subjecting how carbon dioxide, methane, and other greenhouse gases are emitting
    d. many analyzers that are part of an effort in the long term that has subjected the carbon dioxide, methane, and other greenhouse gas emissions
    e. many analyzers that are part of a long-term effort to subject carbon dioxide, methane, and other greenhouse gas emissions

143. Scientists have observed large cracks that go on for miles in <u>gigantic Antarctica icebergs, which are consistent with the predictions of global warming.</u>

    a. gigantic Antarctica icebergs, which are consistent with the predictions of global warming.
    b. gigantic icebergs in Antarctica, findings consistent with the predictions of global warming.
    c. gigantic icebergs in Antarctica, consistent with the predictions of global warming.
    d. gigantic Antarctica icebergs, where the predictions of global warming agree with these findings.
    e. gigantic Antarctica icebergs, findings consistent with the global warming predictions.

144. <u>However ten European nations have approved the installation of cobblestones bearing the names of Nazi victims peppered throughout their cities, regardless some municipalities argue that enough</u> exist and the idea is inappropriate.

    a. However ten European nations have approved the installation of cobblestones bearing the names of Nazi victims peppered throughout their cities, regardless some municipalities argue that enough

    b. In spite of ten European nations having approved installing cobblestones bearing Nazi victims' names peppered throughout their cities, regardless some municipalities argue that enough Holocaust memorials

    c. Ten European nations have approved the cobblestone installation bearing the names of Nazi victims peppered throughout their cities, but some municipalities argue that enough

    d. Although ten European nations have approved the installation of cobblestones bearing the names of Nazi victims to be peppered throughout their cities, some municipalities argue that enough Holocaust memorials

    e. Despite ten European nations approving cobblestone installation bearing Nazi victims' names peppered throughout their cities, some municipalities argue that enough Holocaust memorials

145. An entrepreneur seeking a loan from a financial institution will find it difficult to persuade a lender <u>if there is a lacking concrete business plan to prove</u> his or her potential for success.

    a. if there is a lacking concrete business plan to prove

    b. unless there will be a concrete business plan to prove

    c. if there is an absence of a concrete business plan to prove

    d. without a concrete business plan that proves

    e. in the case there is not a business plan proving

146. Very little <u>has the ability to grow in the Andean highlands of Peru</u> <u>due</u> to the thin air, scarce water supply, and rocky terrain.
   a. has the ability to grow in the Andean highlands of Peru due to
   b. is able of growing in the Andean highlands of Peru caused by
   c. can grow in the Andean highlands of Peru because
   d. can grow in the Andean highlands of Peru due to
   e. can grow in the Andean highlands of Peru because of

147. New shifts in <u>the organization of Mexico's hydrocarbon industry</u> <u>are expected to build its increasing competitiveness in the market</u> <u>of international energy.</u>
   a. the organization of Mexico's hydrocarbon industry are expected to build its increasing competitiveness in the market of international energy.
   b. Mexico's hydrocarbon industry organization are expected to build its competitiveness in the international energy market.
   c. the organization of Mexico's hydrocarbon industry are expected to increase its competitiveness in the international energy market.
   d. Mexico's hydrocarbon industry organization predict growth in its surging competitiveness within the international energy market.
   e. the organization of Mexico's hydrocarbon industry are predicted to increase its surging competitiveness in the international energy market.

148. The <u>mountain climber's decision to abandon his friend on the</u> <u>slope to find help would change the lives of both men.</u>
   a. mountain climber's decision to abandon his friend on the slope to find help would change the lives of both men.
   b. decision from the mountain climber that led to him abandoning his friend on the slope to find help would change both men's lives.
   c. decision made by the mountain climber on the slope of abandoning his friend to find help would be life-changing for both men.
   d. mountain climber's decision of abandoning his friend on the slope to find help would change the lives of both men.
   e. mountain climber's decision to abandon his friend to find help on the slope would change the lives of both men.

149. The UN's High Commission for Refugees (UNHCR) indicates that while there was a slight decrease in the number of refugees at the end of 2009, <u>the number of internally displaced people within their own countries rose up to 27.5 million people at the end of 2010.</u>

    a. the number of internally displaced people within their own countries rose up to 27.5 million people at the end of 2010.

    b. the number of internally displaced people rose to 27.5 million people at the end of 2010.

    c. the number of internally displaced people increased to an amplified 27.5 million people at the end of 2010.

    d. the number of displaced people within their own countries rose to 27.5 million people at the end of 2010.

    e. the number of internally displayed people increased to 27.5 million people at the end of 2010.

150. Unlike the Washington Monument, <u>the structure of the San Jacinto Memorial Monument is not comprised entirely of stone, in spite of being taller.</u>

    a. the structure of the San Jacinto Memorial Monument is not comprised entirely of stone, in spite of being taller.

    b. the San Jacinto Memorial Monument's structure is not comprised entirely of stone, despite being taller.

    c. the San Jacinto Memorial Monument is not comprised entirely of stone, although it is taller.

    d. the structure of the San Jacinto Memorial Monument is not comprised entirely of stone, although it is taller.

    e. the San Jacinto Memorial Monument is not comprised entirely of stone, in addition to being taller.

151. <u>Revolutionary 3-D printers are evidence that far-fetched *Star Trek*</u> <u>ideas have become a reality, as users are allowed to create physical</u> <u>items from digital blueprints.</u>

   a. Revolutionary 3-D printers are evidence that far-fetched *Star Trek* ideas have become a reality, as users are allowed to create physical items from digital blueprints.

   b. Revolutionary 3-D printers, which allow users to create physical items from digital blueprints, are evidence of far-fetched *Star Trek* ideas being a modern reality.

   c. The idea that far-fetched *Star Trek* ideas have become a reality is supported by the invention of revolutionary 3-D printers, which allow users to create physical items from digital blueprints.

   d. Proving that far-fetched *Star Trek* ideas have become a reality, revolutionary 3-D printers allow users to create physical items from digital blueprints.

   e. As proof of far-fetched *Star Trek* ideas being a reality, revolutionary 3-D printers allow users to create physical items from digital blueprints.

152. According to the American Red Cross, <u>approximately 300,000</u> <u>homes were damaged or destroyed by Hurricane Katrina, the</u> <u>worst natural disaster in United States history.</u>

   a. approximately 300,000 homes were damaged or destroyed by Hurricane Katrina, the worst natural disaster in United States history.

   b. Hurricane Katrina, the worst natural disaster in United States history, was responsible for the damage and destruction of approximately 300,000 homes.

   c. approximately 300,000 homes were damaged or destroyed by Hurricane Katrina, which is considered as the worst natural disaster in United States history.

   d. approximately 300,000 homes were damaged and destroyed thanks to Hurricane Katrina, considered the worst natural disaster in United States history.

   e. Hurricane Katrina, the worst natural disaster in United States history, was responsible for damaging or destroying exactly 300,000 homes.

153. In contrast to older automobiles that primarily used steel for its durability and cost, <u>carmakers are now turning to aluminum to meet new fuel efficiency standards, remaining</u> competitive in the ever-changing market.

   a. carmakers are now turning to aluminum to meet new fuel efficiency standards, remaining

   b. aluminum is now being used by carmakers to meet new fuel efficiency standards, thereby remaining

   c. newer automobiles are now using aluminum to meet new fuel efficiency standards and remain

   d. newer automobiles are now using aluminum to meet new fuel efficiency standards, remaining

   e. new fuel efficiency standards have forced carmakers to turn to aluminum and remain

154. China's population control methods, <u>which included a one-child policy imposed in 1979, helped slow the fast annual rate of population growth per year, though</u> many denounced the policy as an abuse of human rights.

   a. which included a one-child policy imposed in 1979, helped slow the fast annual rate of population growth per year, though

   b. which included a one-child policy imposed in 1979, helped slow the high annual rate of population growth, though

   c. which included a one-child policy imposed in 1979, helped slow the fast rate of population growth per year, in addition

   d. which included a one-child policy imposed in 1979, helped decrease the quick annual rate of population growth, moreover

   e. which included a one-child policy imposed in 1979, helped slow the high annual rate of population growth per year; however,

155. Tasmanian devils, <u>native of the island of Tasmania close to Australia, arc endangered because of a cancer called Devil Facial Tumor Disease.</u>

    a. native of the island of Tasmania close to Australia, are endangered because of a cancer called Devil Facial Tumor Disease.

    b. native of the island of Tasmania close to Australia, are endangered because of a Devil Facial Tumor Disease cancer.

    c. native of the Tasmania Island close to Australia, are endangered due to a cancer called Devil Facial Tumor Disease.

    d. native to the island of Tasmania close to Australia, are endangered due to a Devil Facial Tumor Disease cancer.

    e. native to the island of Tasmania close to Australia, are endangered because of a cancer called Devil Facial Tumor Disease.

156. <u>Instead of viewing their money as a way to alleviate poverty, microfinance is now seen by some donors as primarily an investment opportunity.</u>

    a. Instead of viewing their money as a way to alleviate poverty, microfinance is now seen by some donors as primarily an investment opportunity.

    b. Instead of viewing their money as a way to alleviate poverty, microfinance is now currently being seen by some donors as primarily an investment opportunity.

    c. Rather than view their money as a way to alleviate poverty, some donors are now primarily seeing microfinance as an investment opportunity in today's world.

    d. Rather than view their money as a way to alleviate poverty, some donors now see microfinance as primarily an investment opportunity.

    e. Instead of view their money as a way to alleviate poverty, some donors now see microfinance as an investment opportunity in today's world.

157. Experts <u>have differences over how tarantulas make silk come out of</u> <u>their feet for maintaining a grip on</u> steep, slippery surfaces.

    a. have differences over how tarantulas make silk come out of their feet for maintaining a grip on

    b. have differing opinions as to how tarantulas make silk come out of their feet for maintaining a grip on

    c. differ as to how tarantulas are able to create silk with their feet in order to maintain a grip on

    d. differ over how tarantulas emit silk from their feet in order to maintain a grip on

    e. disagree over the abilities of tarantulas to emit silk from their feet for maintaining a grip on

158. <u>The federal legislation mandated the right to have their leases</u> <u>honored to tenants in the event of a foreclosure of the land being</u> <u>rented.</u>

    a. The federal legislation mandated the right to have their leases honored for tenants in the event of a foreclosure of the property being rented.

    b. Tenant leases were required to be honored in the case of a foreclosure of the property the tenant is renting, according to federal legislation.

    c. The federal legislation made mandatory for tenants to have their leases honored in the event of a foreclosed rental property.

    d. The federal legislation made mandatory that existing tenant leases have to be honored if a rental property is foreclosed.

    e. The federal legislation mandated that tenant leases be honored in the event of a foreclosed rental property.

159. <u>Enthusiastic about the upcoming reception lunch approaching, Mrs. Brown hastily phoned her committee members to</u> assign tasks and delegate responsibilities.

   a. Enthusiastic about the upcoming reception lunch approaching, Mrs. Brown hastily phoned her committee members to

   b. Being enthusiastic about the upcoming reception lunch approaching, Mrs. Brown phoned her committee members in a hastily manner to

   c. Feeling enthusiastic about the upcoming reception lunch, Mrs. Brown hastily phoned her committee members to

   d. Enthusiastic with regards to the reception lunch approaching, the committee members were hastily phoned to

   e. Enthusiastic about the upcoming reception lunch, Mrs. Brown hastily phoned her committee members in a rushed effort to

160. In an effort to understand climate change and rising sea levels, <u>scientists studied and researched samples of coral and discovered that the ocean level rose by an increase of 46 to 60 feet 14,650 years ago.</u>

   a. scientists studied and researched samples of coral and discovered that the ocean level rose by an increase of 46 to 60 feet 14,650 years ago.

   b. scientists studied samples of coral and discovered that the ocean level increased 46 to 60 feet 14,650 years ago.

   c. scientists studied coral samples, discovering that the growth of the ocean level went up 46 to 60 feet 14,650 years ago.

   d. scientists studied samples of coral, thereby discovering the rise of the ocean level by an increased 46 to 60 feet 14,650 years ago.

   e. samples of coral were studied and researched by scientists, who discovered that the ocean level rose by 46 to 60 more feet 14,650 years ago.

161. It is possible that <u>more than half of the babies in the wealthiest</u> <u>nations of today may reach to live to 100 years, with greater</u> <u>chances increasing if they're wealthy or slim.</u>

    a. more than half of the babies in the wealthiest nations of today may reach to live to 100 years, with greater chances increasing if they're wealthy or slim.

    b. more than half of today's wealthiest nations' babies, if they're wealthy or slim, will live to be 100 years old.

    c. more than half of the babies in today's wealthiest nations will live to 100 years, with greater chances if they're wealthy or slim.

    d. with greater chances increasing if he or she is wealthy or slim, more than half of the babies who are from the wealthiest nations of today might live to 100 years.

    e. more than half of today's wealthiest nations' babies may live to be 100 years old if they're wealthy or slim.

162. Efforts to stabilize the political and social climate of Colombia have resulted in <u>large-scale rescues of kidnapping victims,</u> <u>internationally coordinated arrests of drug traffickers, pivotal</u> <u>captures of left-wing terrorist groups, and renewed confidence in</u> <u>the nation's politicians.</u>

    a. large-scale rescues of kidnapping victims, internationally coordinated arrests of drug traffickers, pivotal captures of left-wing terrorist groups, and renewed confidence in the nation's politicians.

    b. sweeping rescuing of kidnapping victims, internationally coordinated arrests of drug traffickers, pivotal capturing of left-wing terrorist groups, and a renewed sense of confidence in the nation's politicians.

    c. sweeping rescuing of kidnapping victims, internationally coordinated arresting of drug traffickers, pivotal capturing of left-wing terrorist groups, and renewed feelings of confidence in the nation's politicians.

    d. large-scale rescues of kidnapping victims, internationally coordinated arrests of drug traffickers, pivotal captures of terrorist groups who are progressive in their ideals, and renewed confidence in the nation's politicians.

    e. sweeping rescues of kidnapping victims, internationally coordinated arrests of drug traffickers, pivotal captures of idealistically progressive terrorist groups, and renovated confidence in the nation's politicians.

163. A judge in New York recently ruled <u>that the 613 victims of one of the most noteworthy Ponzi schemes should be in total paid out a sum of $6.2 million, coming from personal and business assets that were seized after an undercover investigation that was directed by the U.S. Postal Service and the IRS.</u>

    a. that the 613 victims of one of the most noteworthy Ponzi schemes should be in total paid out a sum of $6.2 million, coming from personal and business assets that were seized after an undercover investigation that was directed by the U.S. Postal Service and the IRS.

    b. that the 613 victims of one of the most noteworthy Ponzi schemes be paid out a total of $6.2 million, which was seized in personal and business assets following an undercover investigation by the U.S. Postal Service and the IRS.

    c. that the state must pay out $6.2 million to the 613 victims of one of the most noteworthy Ponzi schemes, with the money having come from the sale of personal and business assets, which were seized after an undercover investigation that was directed by the U.S. Postal Service and the IRS.

    d. that the 613 victims of one of the most noteworthy Ponzi schemes ought to be paid out a total of $6.2 million, which were from selling the personal and business assets that were seized following an undercover investigation led by the U.S. Postal Service and the IRS.

    e. that the state must pay out to the 613 victims of one of the most noteworthy Ponzi schemes a total of $6.2 million, derived from the sale of personal and business assets that were seized following a joint U.S. Postal Service and IRS investigation.

164. A harsh new tobacco law in Australia has encountered massive resistance from big tobacco companies that <u>argue the new rules abuse intellectual property rights and diminish the value of their trademarks.</u>

    a. argue the new rules abuse intellectual property rights and diminish the value of their trademarks.

    b. argue on the grounds of intellectual property rights being violated or trademark values being diminished by the new rules.

    c. argue that the new rules intellectually abuse property rights and devalue their trademarks.

    d. argue that the new rules abuse intellectual property rights and devalue their trademarks.

    e. argue that the new rules abuse property rights intellectually or devalue their trademarks.

165. Video game enthusiasts emphasize that a handful of deaths from extended gaming are an inadequate means of predicting long-term effects of video gaming and underscore that experts remain divided <u>on whether the overall health of gamers will suffer in the long term and what impact their compromised health would have on society.</u>

    a. on whether the overall health of gamers will suffer in the long term and what impact their compromised health would have on society.

    b. on whether compromised health will be suffered among gamers in the long term and what impact society would feel.

    c. if gamers' health will suffer in the long term or not and what impact their compromised health would have on society.

    d. over whether gamers will become not as healthy or the impact their compromised health will have on society.

    e. as to whether fewer gamers will be healthy or the impact their health would have on society if they were.

166. Alaska is feeling the impact of global warming more than its fellow states as average temperatures in Alaska have risen <u>greater than twice the national average, according to data released by the U.S. Global Change Research Program that was compiled over the past 50 years.</u>

    a. greater than twice the national average, according to data released by the U.S. Global Change Research Program that was compiled over the past 50 years.

    b. over twice the national average, in keeping with data compiled during the past 50 years released by the U.S. Global Change Research Program.

    c. more than twice the national average, in accordance with data compiled over the past 50 years and released by the U.S. Global Change Research Program.

    d. more than twice the national average, according to 50-year-old data released by the U.S. Global Change Research Program.

    e. more than twice the national average, according to data compiled over the past 50 years and released by the U.S. Global Change Research Program.

167. One of the most pressing concerns facing lawyers who have just graduated from law school <u>is the amount of fellow graduates who currently outnumber the amount of available job openings.</u>

    a. is the amount of fellow graduates who currently outnumber the amount of available job openings.

    b. is the amount of fellow graduates that currently outnumbers the amount of available job openings.

    c. is the number of fellow graduates that currently exceeds the number of job openings.

    d. is the number of fellow graduates who currently exceed the number of available job openings.

    e. is the number of fellow graduates that currently exceed a number of job openings.

168. Since its opening in 1869, <u>the Suez Canal has made transportation by water among Europe and Asia easier by providing a connection between the Mediterranean Sea and the Red Sea.</u>

    a. the Suez Canal has made transportation by water among Europe and Asia easier by providing a connection between the Mediterranean Sea and the Red Sea.

    b. the Suez Canal has eased transportation between Europe and Asia by water to a greater degree by providing a connection between the Mediterranean Sea and the Red Sea.

    c. the Suez Canal has facilitated maritime transportation between Europe and Asia by connecting the Mediterranean Sea and the Red Sea.

    d. transportation between Europe and Asia has been facilitated by the Suez Canal, which connects the Mediterranean Sea to the Red Sea.

    e. Europe and Asia transportation has been relieved thanks to the Suez Canal, a connection between the Mediterranean Sea and the Red Sea.

169. The success of sailboat racing as a television sport <u>largely depends on the technology in the helicopters that fly above to a great deal, technology so advanced that it makes the insertion of a first-down line during the broadcast of a football game seem insignificant.</u>

a. largely depends on the technology in the helicopters that fly above to a great deal, technology so advanced that it makes the insertion of a first-down line during the broadcast of a football game seem insignificant.

b. to a great deal depends on the helicopter technology that flies above, technology so advanced that it makes the insertion of a first-down line during the broadcast of a football game seem insignificant.

c. to a great deal depends on the helicopter technology that fly above, technology so advanced that it makes the first-down line during a football game seem insignificant.

d. largely depends on the technology in the helicopters that fly above, technology so advanced that it makes the insertion of a first-down line during a football game broadcast seem insignificant.

e. largely depends on the advanced technology in the helicopters flying above that make the insertion of a first-down line during a football game broadcast seem insignificant.

170. Hans <u>Krasa had only begun to emerge as a celebrated composer, having written the short fairy tale opera *Brundibar*, when the grips of Nazism took their hold and rendered his additional developing as a composer</u> impossible.

a. Krasa had only begun to emerge as a celebrated composer, having written the short fairy tale opera *Brundibar*, when the grips of Nazism took their hold and rendered his additional developing as a composer

b. Krasa had only hardly begun to emerge as a celebrated composer, having written a short fairy tale opera by the name of *Brundibar*, when the grips of Nazism took their hold and rendered his farther professional development

c. Krasa had not hardly begun to emerge as a celebrated composer, having written a short fairy tale opera by the name of *Brundibar*, when the grips of Nazism took their hold and rendered his developing into a better composer

d. Krasa who wrote the short fairy tale opera *Brundibar* had not hardly begun to emerge as a celebratory composer when he was taken hold by the grips of Nazism and his further professional development was rendered

e. Krasa, who wrote the short fairy tale opera *Brundibar*, had only begun to emerge as a celebrated composer when the grips of Nazism took their hold and rendered his further professional development

171. In order to transfer media across a home from a computer to a television, three items are needed: a media source, or server, <u>that contains all the media like pictures, music, and videos, a receiver that supports the DLNA standard, which new "smart" TVs often do; and a translator, which will convert files to a readable format.</u>

   a. that contains all the media like pictures, music, and videos, a receiver that supports the DLNA standard, which new "smart" TVs often do; and a translator, which will convert files to a readable format.

   b. that contains all the media such as pictures, music, and videos; a receiver that supports the DLNA standard, which new "smart" TVs often do; and a translator, which will convert files to a readable format.

   c. which contains all the media like pictures, music, and videos, a receiver that supports the DLNA standard, which new "smart" TVs often do; and a translator, which will convert files to a readable format.

   d. which contains all the media like pictures, music, and videos; a receiver that supports the DLNA standard, that new "smart" TVs often do; and a translator, which will convert files to a readable format.

   e. that contains all the media such as pictures, music, and videos, a receiver that supports the DLNA standard, which new "smart" TVs do, and a translator, which will convert files to a readable format.

172. <u>Certain flea control methods can become ineffective if used repeatedly on an animal; one reason is suggested by evidence that fleas, like cockroaches, adapt to their environment and become increasingly immune to popular flea medicine with each generation.</u>

   a. Certain flea control methods can become ineffective if used repeatedly on an animal; one reason is suggested by evidence that fleas, like cockroaches, adapt to their environment and become increasingly immune to popular flea medicine with each generation.

   b. If used repeatedly on an animal, one reason that certain flea control methods can become ineffective is suggested by evidence that fleas, like cockroaches, increasingly adapt to their environment and become more immune to popular flea medicine with each generation.

   c. If used repeatedly on an animal, one reason certain flea control methods can become ineffective is suggested by evidence that there are fleas, like cockroaches, that increasingly adapt to their environment and become more immune to popular flea medicine with each generation.

   d. Certain flea control methods can become ineffective if they are used repeatedly on an animal; one reason, which derives from evidence, suggests that fleas, like cockroaches, adapt to their environment and become immune to increasingly popular flea medicine with each generation.

   e. The evidence that fleas, like cockroaches, adapt to their environment and become increasingly immune to popular flea medicine with each generation is suggestive of one reason, if used repeatedly on an animal, certain flea control methods can become ineffective.

173. <u>Oscar Arias, who won the Nobel Peace Prize for these efforts in 1987, submitted a peace plan for a series of disputes which led to the Esquipulas Peace Agreement among multiple nations of Central America, namely El Salvador, Guatemala, Nicaragua, Honduras, and Panama, at a time when various armed conflicts were threatening the stability of the Central American region.</u>

a. Oscar Arias, who won the Nobel Peace Prize for these efforts in 1987, submitted a peace plan for a series of disputes which led to the Esquipulas Peace Agreement among multiple nations of Central America, namely El Salvador, Guatemala, Nicaragua, Honduras, and Panama, at a time when various armed conflicts were threatening the stability of the Central American region.

b. Oscar Arias submitted a peace plan, which was for a series of disputes leading to the Esquipulas Peace Agreement among multiple nations of Central America, namely El Salvador, Guatemala, Nicaragua, Honduras, and Panama, at a time when various armed conflicts were threatening the stability of the Central American region, earning him the Nobel Peace Prize in 1987.

c. Being the receptor of the Nobel Peace Prize for his efforts in 1987, Oscar Arias submitted a peace plan for a series of various armed conflicts that were threatening the stability of the Central American region which led to the Esquipulas Peace Agreement between El Salvador, Guatemala, Nicaragua, Honduras, and Panama.

d. At a time when various armed conflicts were threatening the stability of the Central American region, Oscar Arias submitted a peace plan which led to the Esquipulas Peace Agreement being signed between El Salvador, Guatemala, Nicaragua, Honduras, and Panama; his contribution earned him the Nobel Peace Prize in 1987.

e. At a time when various armed conflicts were threatening the stability of the Central American region, Oscar Arias submitted a peace plan that led to the Esquipulas Peace Agreement among El Salvador, Guatemala, Nicaragua, Honduras, and Panama; his contribution earned him the Nobel Peace Prize in 1987.

174. Studies over the past decade <u>indicate people working at home or outside the office as tending to work longer hours, contrary to</u> employers' initial fears.

    a. indicate people working at home or outside the office as tending to work longer hours, contrary to

    b. indicate people who work at home or outside the office as tending to work longer hours, in contradiction of

    c. indicate that people who work at home or outside the office tend to work longer hours, contrary to

    d. have indicated longer hours of work by people who work at home or outside the office, contrary to

    e. indicate that home-working people tend to work longer hours, contrary to

Answers

Set 5

93. **a.** The verb *consume* is correct in the plural form to agree with the plural subject *the most successful nations in the world*. Choice **b** is incorrect because it conjugates the verb as *consumes*, which is only correct if the subject is singular. Choice **c** also incorrectly conjugates the verb as *consumes* to agree with a singular subject, and it changes the simple present verb tense *are* to the present progressive *are being*, which is incorrect for a general statement that uses the verb *to be*. Choice **d** changes the verb tense *are* to *have been*, which changes the original idea and implies the most successful nations have already been home to the world's poorest people for a certain amount of time. This information cannot be assumed. Choice **e** is incorrect because the phrase *not only is consuming* does not agree with the plural subject *the most successful nations in the world*.

94. **c.** The past tense *set* maintains a parallel structure among all the verbs in the sentence (*ruled*, *curtailed*, *set*) and makes choice **c** the clearest sentence. Choice **a** is incorrect because *setting* is the present progressive tense. The sentence already uses *curtailed* in the simple past, so it is best to keep this verb in the simple past as well. Remember, parallelism is preferred. Choice **b** is incorrect for the same reason; *having set* is not the best verb tense to maintain unity and a parallel structure among all the actions presented. Choice **d** is incorrect because it represents the future tense; this sentence refers to actions that already happened, so the future tense is wrong. Choice **e** is incorrect because it is an independent clause. An independent clause cannot be joined to another independent clause with just a comma. This is comma splicing and it is incorrect.

95. **d.** Although *public* is a collective noun referring to many people, it is singular and so the pronoun *it* must be used. *Is*, not *are*, is correct because it refers to *one of the most important questions*, which is singular. Choice **a** is incorrect because it uses *they* to refer to the singular noun *public*. Choice **b** is incorrect because it uses the plural verb *are* for the singular subject *one of the most important questions*; it also uses the plural pronoun *they* to represent the singular noun *public*. Choice **c** is incorrect because it also uses the plural pronoun *they* to refer to *public*. Choice **e** is incorrect because it uses *are* as the verb for the singular subject *one of the most important questions*.

96. **e.** In order to make a logical comparison, two similar ideas must be compared. In this sentence, the views of China are compared with the views (*those*) of the United States. Choice **a** is incorrect because it compares China's views with the United States. A country's views cannot be logically compared with a country. Choice **b** is incorrect because it uses the singular *that* to refer to the plural subject *views*. Choice **c** is incorrect because it also uses the singular *that* to refer to *views*. Choice **d** is incorrect because the ideas compared (*the views of China* compared to the *views from the United States*) are not parallel.

97. **b.** Choice **b** maintains a parallel structure by keeping all the verbs in the gerund form; this makes for an easy and clear read. Choice **a** is incorrect because the work of the scientists is not presented in a parallel form: *preserving* is in the gerund form, *their regeneration* is a noun, and *ways to extract* is also a noun. Choice **c** is incorrect because the three aspects are not structured in a parallel form: *working* is in the gerund form, but *regenerate* and *extract* are in their infinitive forms. Choice **d** is incorrect because it adds the adjective *diligent*, which would be considered an altered meaning; this also is incorrect because it modifies the verb *working* and needs to be in adverb form as *diligently*. Also, the possessive pronoun *its* to define *medicinal properties* is incorrect because it is singular to refer to the plural noun *the world's most threatened plant species*. Choice **e** is incorrect because it uses the comparative form *more* instead of *the most* when describing the *threatened plant species*. The sentence refers to many different plant species, so the superlative form *the most* must be used.

98. **e.** The apostrophe is correctly omitted from *Jr.* since the placement of *of* before *Martin* already indicates possession. The verbs *insisted* and *had* are correctly formed in the past tense. Choice **a** is incorrect because *of Martin Luther King, Jr.'s* is redundant: It has both *of* and the apostrophe to indicate possession. *Of Martin Luther King, Jr.* or *Martin Luther King, Jr.'s* is correct, but not a combination of the two forms. Also, in choice **a**, the verb tense *had had* is incorrect because it implies that Martin Luther King, Jr. had the makings of a great leader before the boycott and before his contemporaries insisted about it, but not during (see Correct Expression notes on the past perfect tense). This is illogical since he had the makings of a great leader at the time of the boycott and when his contemporaries insisted. Choice **b** is incorrect because it uses the apostrophe in *Jr.'s* and because it combines both the past progressive and simple present tense to describe two events that happened in the past. Choice **c** is incorrect because it incorrectly uses the apostrophe in *Jr.'s*. Choice **d** is incorrect because *has* is in the simple present form. It must be in the simple past.

99. **a.** The information after the comma adequately expands on the type of *information*; it is an appositive. Choice **b** is incorrect because the prepositional phrase *with information . . .* has no clear phrase or idea to attach to. Choice **c** would form two independent clauses separated by a comma. This would be a comma splice, which is incorrect. Choice **d**, without the comma, implies that the newspapers and printing sites affect society. While this may be true, it changes the original meaning. Choice **e** incorrectly employs the present perfect verb tense for a general statement that is better expressed in the simple present tense. It is incorrect because *that has affected* needs to be closer to what it modifies, which is *information*. Placing it at the end of the sentence makes the sentence unclear.

100. **d.** The phrase *recent findings* suggests the present time. The correct idiomatic expression is *as . . . as* to compare two ideas or things. Choice **a** is incorrect because the verb *was* is in the past and *deadly* must be followed by *as* to form the correct idiomatic expression. Choice **b** is incorrect because the verb should be in the present tense, not the past (*there was*). Choice **c** is incorrect because it uses the present perfect form (*there's been*), which sounds awkward when referring to *truth*, a general statement that needs to be expressed in the simple present form. Choice **e** is incorrect because it uses *as . . . than*, not the correct idiomatic expression *as . . . as* to compare two ideas or things.

101. **b.** Choice **b** correctly uses the idiomatic expression *from . . . to* to describe the range of industries within the manufacturing sector. Choice **a** is incorrect because it does not finish the idiomatic expression *from . . . to* with *to*. Choice **c** is incorrect because it also fails to finish the idiomatic expression with *to*; also, *seems that it is* sounds awkward and is not as concise as *seems to be*. Choice **d** is also incorrect because it uses *seems that it is* over *seems to be*, a better option. Choice **e** is incorrect because it does not use the complete expression *from . . . to* to describe the range of industries within the manufacturing sector; instead, it incorrectly starts with *from* and finishes with *in addition to*.

102. **d.** The dependent clause (*as companies grow . . .*) indicates the sentence is in the present tense. The verbs in the main clause should also use the present tense. *Having mastered* in choice **a** is an awkward past participle, and *become* (the simple present) sounds awkward. Choice **b** uses verbs in the past tense, which is incorrect since the first part of the sentence is in the present tense. Choice **c** is incorrect because *will be becoming* is the future present progressive. The sentence is in the present, not the future. Choice **e** is incorrect because the present perfect progressive (*have been becoming*) is awkward in this context that has already used the simple present; the present progressive is preferred.

103.   **e.** In choice **e**, *like* is correctly followed by a noun to form a parallel comparison between the rings of both fish and trees. Choice **a** is incorrect because *like* is followed by a clause and the comparison is not formed with two parallel clauses to make sense. Choice **b** is incorrect because *like* is followed by a clause, not a simple noun. Choice **c** is incorrect because *as* should be replaced by *like*. Also, the main topic is *fish* in all the other sentences; in choice **c**, *trees* seem to be the focus over *fish*. Choice **d** is incorrect because the second clause after the comma is not formed in a parallel fashion to agree with the first clause (*as trees have rings*) and form a correct comparison.

104.   **c.** The information *that killed off dinosaurs 65 million years ago* is essential to understanding and identifying the meteorite. Therefore, the sentence must use *that*, not *which*, and omit the comma. Choice **a** is incorrect because it uses a comma and *which*, which are used when extra information is given that is not necessary to understanding the sentence; that is not the case with this sentence. Choice **b** is incorrect because it changes *killed* to the past perfect *had killed*. The past perfect is used when one event happens before another; in this example, the turtle survived the meteorite and the dinosaurs died at the same time. The past perfect cannot be used in this example. For that same reason, choice **d** is also incorrect. Choice **d** also makes the mistake of including the comma and using *which* instead of *that*. Choice **e** is incorrect because the gerund *killing* should be changed into a *that* clause, *that killed*.

105. **b.** The ideas are all correctly structured in the gerund form to provide a clear, comprehensible sentence. Choice **a** is incorrect because the verb *includes* should be *include* to agree with the plural subject *three of the most encouraging ideas*. Also, the ideas are not structured in the same way; *to detach* should be *detaching* so the three ideas are expressed in a parallel structure. Choice **c** is incorrect because *to restore* is presented in the infinitive form, not the gerund form. It should be in the gerund form to agree with the structure of the other ideas; also, *by* should be eliminated before *detaching*. Choice **d** is incorrect because *includes* needs to be *include* to agree with the plural subject *three of the most encouraging ideas*. Choice **e** is incorrect because the second idea (*using a traveling service station that refuels them*) is wordy and it is unclear what *them* refers to; also, *detaching working parts to attach them to new satellites from old ones* is wordy and could be phrased better. *From old ones* should directly follow what it modifies: *working parts*.

106. **d.** The first part of the sentence (not subject to change) is a modifier. What it modifies must be placed directly afterward so it is clear to what *thought to be either symbolic or accurate descriptions* refers. Choice **d** successfully does this with a clear, succinct clause. Choice **a** is incorrect because it implies the first part of the sentence is describing *archaeologists* since *archaeologists* is the first word of the independent clause. This is incorrect and as a result, the first part of the sentence becomes a dangling modifier without any clear referent. The same mistake is made in choice **b**. Choice **c** is incorrect because the complete sentence would also result in a dangling modifier; the independent clause (the answer) begins with *much time*, thereby implying that *much time* was *thought to be either symbolic or accurate descriptions*. This is illogical; *much time* cannot begin the independent clause. Choice **e** is incorrect because it says that *cave paintings have debated archaeologists*. This idea is illogical; cave paintings cannot debate.

107. **c.** Choice **c** presents the sentence in the correct conditional sentence form. Choice **a** is incorrect because the *if* clause employs the structure *would not have intervened*; this is incorrect as the *would have + past participle* structure is only correct for the result clause. Choice **b** is incorrect because it also uses the *would not have* structure in the *if* clause (in this sentence, the *if* clause comes second). Also, the past participle is missing the final *d* to make it a past participle (*intervened*) and not just the verb (*intervene*). Choice **d** is incorrect because it changes the time reference of the entire sentence. It implies that the economic crisis could still be avoided if government didn't intervene. This is illogical since the economic crisis already happened and this choice changes the original meaning. It does not represent the best choice. Choice **e** is incorrect because the past participle *intervene* in the *if* clause is missing the final *d* (*intervened*).

108. **e.** Choice **e** eliminates any possibility of ambiguity regarding the antecedents of the pronouns *they* and *its*. Choice **a** is incorrect because *they* and *their* have ambiguous antecedents; either pronoun *could refer to Easter Islanders* or *statues*. Choice **b** is incorrect for the same reason; only the verb tense has been changed, which does not change the underlying problem of ambiguous antecedents. Choice **c** is incorrect because it is unclear what *its* refers to; though it could refer to the island, the choice is wordy and not very clear. Choice **d** is incorrect because *are* should be *is*, as *which* refers to the singular idea that *the island's ancient, famous statues walked by themselves.*

109. **b.** Choice **b** correctly keeps *release* in the subjunctive form (required because of *demand + that*), and *his or her* is used to correctly refer to *a presidential candidate*. Choice **a** is incorrect because *their* is incorrectly used to refer to a singular *presidential candidate*. Choice **c** is incorrect because *releases* should be in the subjunctive form *release* as required by *demand + that*. Also, *have been taken* should be *has been taken* to agree with the singular subject *how much*. Choice **d** is incorrect because *their* should be *his or her*, and *have been taken* should be *has been taken*. Choice **e** is incorrect because *releases* should be *release*.

110. **a.** Choice **a** is correct because it keeps the comparisons parallel; the sentence compares Democrats' views to Republicans' views. To keep the comparison logical, *Republicans'* must be possessive like *Democrats'*. Choice **b** is incorrect because the comparison is not parallel with *Republican*; it must be phrased in the same possessive way as *Democrats'*. Choice **c** is incorrect because the superlative form (*the most revolutionary*) is used when the comparative form must be used; only two different groups are being compared. Choice **d** also incorrectly uses the superlative form instead of the comparative form; also, *Republican's* is in singular possessive form when it should be in plural possessive form with the apostrophe after the *s*. Choice **e** is missing the apostrophe after *Republicans* to make the comparison parallel with *Democrats'*.

111. **e.** Choice **e** correctly uses *the number of* (to indicate a specific statistic) with the singular verb *was* and the idiom *about the same as*. Choice **a** is incorrect because it uses the expression *a number of* instead of *the number of*. The use of the expression *a number of* (meaning *some* or *many*) in this sentence is illogical. Choice **b** is incorrect because it also uses the expression *a number of*, which is incorrect in this context. Also, the subject *a number of unemployed Americans* requires a plural subject; in choice **b**, a singular subject is incorrectly used. Choice **c** is incorrect because it uses the expression *about the same than*; the correct expression is *about the same as*. Choice **d** is incorrect because it uses the plural verb *were* instead of *was*, and the incorrect expression *about the same than* instead of *about the same as*.

112. **a.** Choice **a** uses the correct verbs to agree with the plural subjects *market forces* and *movements of a stock price*. Choice **b** is incorrect because the plural subjects require the verbs *are* and *are*, not *is* and *is*. Choice **c** is incorrect because the second verb *is* should be *are* to agree with *market forces*. Choice **d** is incorrect because the first verb *is* should be *are* to agree with *movements of a stock price*. Choice **e** is incorrect because *subjecting* does not make sense in this context.

113. **d.** Choice **d** is grammatically correct because it uses the subjunctive voice *be established* (required by the preceding clause *suggests that*) and proper verb forms and sentence structure to avoid any ambiguous pronoun references. The subjunctive voice is used because this sentence is implying that a potential new standard *should* be established by using the verb *suggest*. Choice **a** is incorrect because *they* has no logical referent. Choice **b** is incorrect because *is established* is wrong; the subjunctive voice is needed after *suggests that*. Choice **c** is incorrect because *to be established* needs to change to *be established* (without *to*), and *they* has no logical referent. Choice **e** is incorrect because *is established* needs to change to *be established*, and *they* has no logical pronoun referent.

114. **b.** Choice **b** correctly uses the conditional tenses *were* and *had* required after the verb *wish*. Choice **a** is incorrect because *was* is used instead of the correct *were*, and *wishes* is used instead of *wish* to go after the modal *may* and to agree with *feel*. Choice **c** is incorrect because *was* is used instead of *were*, and *will* has replaced *may*, which is incorrect because it changes meaning. Choice **d** is incorrect because *may wish* has been changed to *wishes*, and *may still feel* has been changed to *still feels*; both changes alter meaning. Also, choice **d** uses *was* instead of *were*. Choice **e** is incorrect because *has* should be *had*.

115. **c.** Choice **c** uses correct subject-verb agreement and appropriate idiomatic expressions to form a grammatically correct sentence. Choice **a** is incorrect because *were* should be *was* to agree with the singular subject *a system of underground tunnels*; also, *in the case a national emergency* is not a correct idiomatic expression. The placement of the modifier *with a complex communication network* after *were built on an impressive scale* is confusing because it's unclear whether the building of the system has a *complex communication network* or whether the system itself does. Choice **b** is incorrect because *were* should be *was* to define *a system . . .* ; also, the clause *which has a complex communication network* is incorrect. The *which* must always refer to the noun immediately before it; in this case, that would be *scale* when it needs to be *a system of underground tunnels*. That entire clause needs to be reworded. Also, the dependent clause *leading to . . .* could be worded better. Choice **d** is incorrect because *occurs* needs to change to *occur* in the clause *should a national emergency occurs*. Choice **e** is incorrect because *were* needs to change to *was*, and *lead* needs to change to *leads* to agree with the singular subject.

116. **a.** Choice **a** correctly utilizes the idiomatic expression *neither . . . nor* with the appropriate subject-verb agreement. Choice **b** is incorrect because *argue* should be *argues* to agree with the singular noun *a majority of society*, and *are* should be *is* to agree with the expression *neither . . . nor*. Choice **c** is incorrect because *argue* should be *argues*; also, *they* has no clear referent since *a majority of society* is singular. Choice **d** is incorrect because *not . . . or* is not a correct idiomatic expression; also, *argue* should be *argues*. Choice **e** is incorrect because *not . . . nor* is not a correct idiomatic expression. The correct expression is *neither . . . nor*.

117. **d.** Choice **d** represents the most logical, grammatically correct sentence. Choice **a** is incorrect because the clause *rather than waiting to die* should modify what directly follows it. In this case, it is *Oregon's right-to-die law*, which is illogical. Choice **b** makes the same mistake. Choice **a** is also incorrect because the clause *which have less than six months to live* is set off by commas as a nonessential clause (also called a nonrestrictive clause). This is incorrect because the information between the commas is essential to describing what kind of *mentally stable people*. The commas imply that mentally stable people have access to medication to accelerate their demise, and the fact that they have less than six months to live is extra information. This is incorrect since that information is essential to the definition and meaning of the sentence. Choice **c** is incorrect because *rather than waiting to die* is immediately followed by *the demise*, not *mentally stable people*. It modifies *mentally stable people*, so *mentally stable people* must follow the comma. Also, *who permits them access to medication* should be worded as *that permits them access to medication* since it refers to the law (a concept, not a person). Choice **e** is incorrect because it also has *the demise* as the subject, instead of *mentally stable people*, following the clause *rather than waiting to die*. In addition, the sentence is not as clear or succinct as choice **d**.

118. **e.** Choice **e** presents the three ideas in a parallel verb form that results in a clear, grammatically correct sentence. Choice **a** is incorrect because *the kidnapping of children* does not maintain the same gerund verb form as the other factors presented; using *the* in front of *kidnapping* changes its structure and it loses its parallelism with the rest of the sentence. Also, *for taking as* is incorrect to express purpose; the infinitive form (*to take as*) must be used in this context. Choice **b** is incorrect because the first verb is in the gerund form and the second and third verbs are in the infinitive form. This does not maintain a parallel structure among all elements. Choice **c** is incorrect because the first element (*his plundering of villages*) is presented as a noun, and the rest are presented as simple gerunds. Once again, a parallel structure among all the elements is not achieved. Choice **d** is incorrect for the same lack of parallel structure; the first element is presented in the past tense (*he plundered*) and the other two elements are presented in the gerund form. Consistency among the verbs is essential to achieve parallelism.

119. **c.** Choice **c** correctly uses the expression *as . . . as* and
appropriately compares the excitement of the competition between
the two parties with *to* inserted after the second *as*. Choice **a** is
incorrect because it fails to insert *to* after the second *as* to form a
grammatically correct comparison. Choice **b** is incorrect because the
correct expression *as . . . as* is inappropriately changed to *as . . . than*
and the *to* is also missing to form a correct comparison. Choice **d** is
incorrect because the second *as* has been changed to *than*. Choice **e**
is incorrect because *then* is used instead of *as*.

120. **d.** Choice **d** is a grammatically correct sentence that corrects all
pronoun and adverb errors. Choice **a** is incorrect because *full veiled*
should be *fully veiled* since *veiled* is an adjective and *fully* acts as an
adverb; also, *who* is incorrect to refer to *Western opposition*; *that* is
the correct word. Choice **b** is incorrect because *full* should be *fully*,
her should be *their* (twice in the sentence) to agree with the plural
subject *women*, and *who* should be *that* in reference to Western
opposition. Choice **c** is incorrect because the adjective *heavy*
should be *heavily* as it's an adverb that describes the adjective
oppressed. Choice **e** is incorrect because *her* should be *their* in two
instances to agree with the plural subject *women*.

121. **b.** Choice **b** is the best grammatically correct sentence. Choice **a** is
incorrect because *well* should be *good*; *good* describes *athletic abilities*,
so it is an adjective. Also, the second clause of the sentence is
missing a final *does* at the end to appropriately compare *DNA-based*
tests to *a standard performance test*. Choice **c** is incorrect because
well must be *good*, and *much beyond a standard performance test*
should read *much beyond what a standard performance test does* to
appropriately compare the two types of tests. Choice **d** is incorrect
because *well* needs to be *good*. Choice **e** is incorrect because even
though the comparison is inverted in the second part of the
sentence and still maintains the original meaning, a *do* is missing at
the very end to appropriately compare the two types of tests.

122. **e.** Choice **e** fixes the problem of the dangling modifier *resigned to accept his disqualification from the Olympic trials* by starting the independent clause with *the athlete*. Choice **a** is incorrect because there is no subject in the sentence to which the modifier *resigned to accept his disqualification from the Olympic trials* can attach. Choice **b** is incorrect for the same reason, despite having inverted the clauses in the sentence. Choice **c** is incorrect because it is missing both a subject and a verb. Choice **d** is incorrect because it suggests that *silence resigned to accept his disqualifications*; this is illogical. A reasonable noun needs to be inserted.

123. **e.** Choice **e** is the correct option. Choice **a** is incorrect because the preposition *with* is unnecessary and *each* is singular, so it needs to be followed by *its*, not *their*. Choice **b** is incorrect because *each products* is illogical; *each* is singular so it cannot be followed by a plural noun. The same logic can be applied to choice **c**. It would also need an article before the singular *product*. Choice **d** is incorrect because *with* and *as* are unnecessary. The resulting expression is not idiomatic.

124. **a.** Choice **a** is grammatically correct with no ambiguous pronoun references. Choice **b** is incorrect because *considered as* is not a correct idiomatic expression. The *as* is incorrect. Also, it is unclear whether the referent of *his* in *his works* refers to *Joseph C. Hart* or *William Shakespeare*. Choice **c** is incorrect because *they* has no logical referent, and *considered as* is not an idiomatic expression. *Explicit* must be *explicitly* to define the verb *question*, and *his authorship of Shakespeare's works* is misleading to imply *Hart's authorship of Shakespeare's works*, which is illogical. Choice **d** is incorrect because *considered to be* is unidiomatic, and *the greater playwrights* must be changed to *the greatest playwrights* since more than two playwrights are being compared. The *him* in choice **d** is also ambiguous, as it could possibly refer to *Shakespeare* or *Joseph C. Hart*. Choice **e** is incorrect because *regarded to be* is not a correct idiomatic expression, and it is unclear exactly to whom *him* refers at the end of the sentence.

125. **c.** Choice **c** is a grammatically correct and concise sentence that appropriately uses the expression *x and y, as well as z*. Choice **a** is incorrect because the preposition *on* is not appropriate; it could be substituted by *in* or *when*. Also, *like* cannot be given to list examples; the correct expression is *such as*. Choice **b** is incorrect because the expression *x and y and z* is not idiomatic. Also, *like* needs to be substituted by *such as*. Choice **d** is incorrect because the expression *x, y, as well as z* is not idiomatic; *x* and *y* require *and* between them. Choice **e** is incorrect because the verb *consider* should be *considers* to match its singular subject *the Happy Planet Index*.

126. **b.** Choice **b** conjugates all the verbs in the correct tense and uses *more quickly* to describe the verb *control*. Choice **a** is incorrect because *exercised* is in the past tense, which does not agree with the first verb *plans* in the simple present tense, and the pronouns *they* and *their* are used, despite the singular subject *a diabetic*. *Quicker* (comparative adjective) is also incorrect because it defines the verb *control*, which requires an adverb (*more quickly*). *Do* must be omitted from the comparison between two types of diabetics. Choice **c** is incorrect because the pronoun *they* is used for a singular subject, *quicker* is used instead of *more quickly*, and *does* needs to be omitted from the comparison. Choice **d** is incorrect because *exercised, will have regained*, and *stuck* must be in the present tense. Choice **e** is incorrect because *does* must be omitted from the comparison.

127. **a.** Choice **a** correctly uses the semicolon to join two independent clauses that have similar meanings. Choice **b** is incorrect because two independent clauses (the first ending with *records*, the second beginning with *as an example*) are joined by a comma. This is incorrect and constitutes a comma splice. Choice **c** is incorrect because *like* must be used to compare two nouns (which does not happen in this sentence). Choice **d** is incorrect because the clause starting with *which* does not represent an independent clause. Therefore, a semicolon cannot be used to separate the first clause from the second. Also, *which* technically refers to *records*, which is illogical. In addition, the wording is awkward. Choice **e** is incorrect because *such as to be helping* is awkward and wordy. It would sound more idiomatic if *to be* were omitted.

128. **d.** Choice **d** uses the correct verb forms to agree with its subjects. Choice **a** is incorrect because *as much as* must be *as many as* to agree with the countable noun *pieces of floating plastic*, *is* must be *are* to agree with the plural subject *pieces of floating plastic*, and *makes up* must be *make up* to agree with the plural subject. Choice **b** is incorrect because *as much as* must change to *as many as*, *is* must change to *are* to agree with *pieces of floating plastic*, and the present perfect tense *have made up* must change to the simple present tense to agree with the rest of the sentence. Choice **c** is incorrect because *indicate* must change to *indicates*, *is* must change to *are*, and *is making up* must be changed to the simple present *make up* since this is a general statement. Choice **e** is incorrect because *indicate* must change to *indicates* and *as many of* is not a correct idiomatic expression. It must be changed to *as many as*.

129. **c.** Choice **c** is correct because both clauses *the frequency of employee turnover* and *servers' treatment of their customers* are parallel as nouns. Choice **a** does not offer a parallel clause to the first clause in the sentence, nor is the singular verb *is* correct. It should be *are* to agree with the compound subject. Choice **b** is incorrect because it is a clause, not a noun that is parallel to *the frequency of employee turnover*. Choice **d** is incorrect because *is* must be *are* to agree with the compound subject. Choice **e**, though phrased as a noun in a fashion parallel to *the frequency of employee turnover*, does not make sense when inserted into the sentence as *customers' reactions to their servers*. This changes the original meaning.

130. **e.** Choice **e** uses the correct idiomatic expression *rivalry between x and y* and the correct positive conditional verb forms to form a logical, grammatically correct sentence. Choice **a** is incorrect because *of* must be *between* to form the idiomatic expression *rivalry between x and y*, and *hadn't* must be *had* to make logical sense. Coca-Cola didn't buy Pepsi. *If it had bought it, the rivalry may never have been.* Choice **b** makes the same mistake using *of* instead of *between*, and it also incorrectly uses *hadn't seized* and *hadn't bought* when both instances must be positive to make logical sense. Choice **c** is incorrect because it too uses *hadn't* instead of *had*. Choice **d** is incorrect because the result clause is not conjugated correctly and the modal of possibility *may* has been changed to a more concrete *would*: *Would never be* must be changed to *would never have been*, and in order to preserve the original implied possibility, *would* must be changed to *may*.

131. **b.** Choice **b** uses correct verb tense and subject-verb agreement to convey a clear, sound sentence. Choice **a** is incorrect because *had voted* needs to be *voted*. The past perfect would only be used if something else in the sentence happened afterward (see Explanation of past perfect tense in Instructional Text). Choice **c** is incorrect because *had voted* must be *voted*, and *the trying of* is not idiomatic; *the* should be eliminated to make the sentence read more naturally in English. Choice **d** is incorrect because *in favor of* + *infinitive* is not an idiomatic expression; *to repeal* needs to be *repealing* in order for the expression to be correct. Choice **e** is incorrect because the *for* + *gerund form* (*for repealing*) needs to change to the infinitive form (*to repeal*) in order to express purpose.

132. **d.** Choice **d** successfully makes the two clauses parallel for an effective sentence. Choice **a** is incorrect because the ideas are not parallel: *the perils of capitalism* is expressed as a noun phrase, and *that the democracy is corrupted* is expressed as a *that* clause with a subject and verb. Choice **b** is incorrect because *that* is missing after *agree*. It also changes the meaning by omitting any mention of *criticism*. Choice **c** is incorrect because the notion of possibility (originally conveyed with *may*) is missing, which changes the meaning, and the expression *to the extent of the perils* is awkward. Choice **e** is incorrect because the correct idiomatic expression is *however much*, not *however many* to describe the extent of the United States citizens' criticism (an uncountable noun).

133. **c.** Choice **c** correctly uses *it* to agree with the singular subject *the private lending sector*. Also, adding the phrase *to be made* helps clarify the sentence meaning. Choice **a** is incorrect because *it is* must be *they are* to agree with the plural subject *payments*. Choice **b** is incorrect because the active voice is preferred over the passive voice; the passive voice in this sentence makes it unclear who does not expect payments to be made. Also, *will not be expected to be paid* suggests some control over the expectations, which is awkward and changes meaning. Choice **d** is incorrect because the passive voice is less clear, and the expression *payments . . . to be paid* is redundant. The future tense *are going to be* is awkward in this choice as well. Choice **e** is incorrect because *they* must be *it* to agree with the singular subject *the private lending sector*, and *it is* must be *they are* to agree with the plural subject *payments*.

Set 6

134. **c.** Starting the sentence with *Accused of* is the most concise and effective way to present the information. Choice **a** is not the best answer because *having been* at the beginning of the sentence is not necessary and is best omitted. Choice **b** is incorrect because *being accused* is not the most concise way to express the idea. The *being* is confusing and is best omitted. Also, combining *huge areas of the Ecuadorian Amazon* to read *huge Ecuadorian Amazon areas* is unclear. The phrase is best left as it originally appears with the *of*. Choice **d** is incorrect for the same unclear *huge Ecuadorian Amazon areas* and because *having been* at the beginning of the sentence is unnecessary. Choice **e** is too wordy; *due to being* at the beginning of the sentence is incorrect.

135. **a.** This choice provides the clearest sentence with the most logically placed modifiers. Choice **b** is incorrect because the modifier *with construction slated to begin in 2014* is placed after *Disneyland Paris*; this placement is confusing because it implies the construction of Disneyland Paris is slated to begin in 2014. Choice **c** is incorrect because the placement of the modifiers results in a confusing sentence. *With construction slated to begin in 2014 provided enough funds are raised* should be placed closer to *France's very own theme park devoted to Napoleon Bonaparte*, not directly after the mention of Disneyland Paris. It is unclear whether Disneyland Paris or France's theme park devoted to Napoleon Bonaparte is slated to begin construction in 2014. Choice **d** is not the best option presented; it has many commas that cut off the flow and cohesion of the sentence. Choice **e** is incorrect due to syntax. The placement of *devoted to Napoleon Bonaparte* at the end of the sentence after *Disneyland Paris* makes it seem as though Disneyland Paris is devoted to Napoleon Bonaparte. This is incorrect.

136. **d.** The phrase *yellow saddle goatfish in the Red Sea* is best left as is without collapsing it into a noun-adjective phrase (*Red Sea yellow saddle goatfish*). Choice **d** effectively eliminates the comma by combining the appositive (*groups with designated members*) with the rest of the sentence. Choice **a** is incorrect because *have the capability to hunt in groups* is understandable, but it is not the most effective way to express the goatfish's abilities. Choice **b** better phrases this part of the sentence with *are capable of hunting in groups*. However, choice **b** describes the goatfish as Red Sea yellow saddle goatfish. This is incorrect because it is not known whether the yellow saddle goatfish are exclusively from the Red Sea; they are best left with the location placed afterward following *in*. Choice **c** is incorrect for the same noun-adjective error (*Red Sea yellow saddle goatfish*) and because *have the capability to hunt in groups* is not the most effective wording. It also uses the phrase *designated chosen members*, which is redundant. Choice **e** makes the same mistake with the *Red Sea yellow saddle goatfish* combination and by placing *designated* and *chosen* next to each other. Furthermore, *possess the capability to hunt in groups* is wordy.

137. **b.** This sentence effectively and concisely describes the idea with a *that* clause that changes the idea into an active verb. Choice **a**, while understandable, is wordier because it uses more nouns than active verbs. Choice **c**, while one of the shortest options presented, incorrectly uses *like* where it should use *such as*. Choice **d**, like choice **a**, uses more nouns than action verbs; furthermore, the verb *fascinates* at the end of the sentence is awkward as it doesn't specify who is fascinated. The idea seems to be cut off. Choice **e**, while it correctly changes the structure of the sentence to include a *that* clause, it incorrectly uses *like* instead of *such as*.

138. **a.** This sentence effectively uses the *that* clause and active verbs. Choice **b** is incorrect because *the belief about whales being terrestrial mammals* is wordy and confusing. *Which* is incorrect and should be replaced by *that*; also, *was supported* is unclear because the evidence still supports the belief; therefore, *was supported* needs to be in the present tense as *is supported*. Choice **c** avoids the *that* clause, which leads to excessive nouns and not enough action verbs. Furthermore, *have been supported* is incorrectly structured in the plural tense and does not agree with the singular subject *the belief*. It should read *has been supported*. Choice **d**, while one of the best options presented, fails in comparison to choice **a** because *made the transition* is not as succinct as *transitioned*. Choice **e** is awkwardly structured and does not represent the best sentence. *The belief of whales as once being terrestrial mammals* can be phrased much better as *the belief that whales were once terrestrial mammals*. Also, *is* must change to *are* to agree with the plural subject *whale fossils*.

139. **d.** Choice **d** is the most concise sentence that doesn't repeat any information. Choice **a** is extremely wordy and redundant; the high numbers of Christians on the scale is overemphasized with the words *overpowered*, *overrepresent*, and *high*. Choice **b**, while less wordy than choice **a**, is still redundant with *overrepresent* and *high*; also, the original phrase *a world scale* has been changed to *the world scale*. This change in article from *a* to *the* changes meaning and implies there is only one scale. Choice **c** changes the wording to the passive voice, a style that is generally not preferred on this test. It is redundant with *overrepresented* and *elevated*. Like choice **b**, it also changes the article *a* before *world scale* to *the* to imply there is only one supposed world scale. This cannot be assumed from the information given. Choice **e** is in the passive voice; generally speaking, the active voice is preferred on this test. It also leaves out the information *on a world scale*.

140. **a.** Choice **a** is the best sentence because it is in the active voice (done using the *that* clause) and it is clear. Choice **b** is redundant with the phrase *will be outearning their husbands with greater wages*. *With greater wages* is superfluous since the verb *outearn* already conveys this information. Also, *within the next generation* is wordier than *within a generation*. Choice **c** is unclear due to the placement of *within a generation* directly after *new workforce trends*. This placement implies *within a generation* defines *new workforce trends*, not when wives will outearn their husbands. The sentence is awkward and confusing as it also seems to imply that husbands will outearn their working wives; this is not the same idea expressed in the original sentence. Choice **d** is worded in the passive voice, which results in an awkward and wordier sentence that does not represent the best option. Choice **e** is incorrect because it uses more noun clauses instead of active verbs.

141. **c.** *That* needs to be included after *revealed* in this sentence. Choice **c** also maintains the second part of the sentence (*because communities abandon . . .*) in the active voice, which makes for the clearest, most succinct sentence. Choice **a** is incorrect because *that* is omitted after the reporting verb *revealed*, and the noun phrase *because of communities abandoning* is not as clear or efficient as the active verb choice *because communities abandon* in choice **c**. Choice **b** is incorrect because it uses *due to*; *because of* would be the correct phrase, but the sentence can be worded even better as the explanation for choice **a** suggests. Choice **d** is missing *that* at the beginning of its answer. Choice **e** is incorrect because the article does not reveal *the death of one language every 14 days*. Such a sentence would imply that the article spanned various 14-day periods to reveal the death of a different language. This choice greatly changes the information presented in the original sentence.

142. **e.** Choice **e** correctly uses the *that* clause followed by *are* since *that* refers to *many analyzers*. Choice **a** is incorrect because *is* should be *are* to agree with the plural *many analyzers*. *Effort* + infinitive (*effort to subject*) is preferred over *effort* + *of* + gerund (*effort of subjecting*). Choice **b** is incorrect because *is* should be the plural *are* after which to agree with *many analyzers*. Also, the entire phrase does not flow well with the remaining part of the sentence *to statewide scrutiny and investigation*; it implies that the gases are emitting to statewide scrutiny, which does not make sense. Choice **c** is incorrect for the same nonsensical reason as choice **b**; it implies that the efforts are to subject how the gases are emitting to scrutiny, which does not make sense. Choice **d** is incorrect because *effort in the long term* is best phrased as *long-term effort*; also, the two relative clauses beginning with *that* right after each other result in a confusing and wordy sentence.

143. **b.** This sentence is logical. *Findings* refers back to the observations of the scientists, and the icebergs are best described as *gigantic icebergs in Antarctica*, not *gigantic Antarctica icebergs*. Choice **a** is incorrect because it names the icebergs as *Antarctica icebergs*, and because *which*, in this context, refers to *Antarctica icebergs* (since *which* must always refer to the noun immediately before it). This is incorrect because the second clause refers to *large cracks observed*, not the icebergs themselves as the structure of choice **a** suggests. Choice **c** is incorrect because it is unclear what the phrase *consistent with the predictions of global warming* refers to. Choice **d** is incorrect because *where* cannot logically refer to *Antarctica icebergs*. Choice **e** is incorrect because the icebergs are named *Antarctica icebergs* versus the correct *icebergs in Antarctica*. Remember that the shortest idea isn't always the best!

144. **d.** Choice **d** correctly utilizes the transition word *although* at the beginning of its sentence to introduce a contrasting idea. Choice **a** is incorrect because it suggests the wrong transition word (*however* is illogical at the beginning) and an additional transition word *regardless*, which is incorrect. It also does not define the referent of *enough*. *Enough* stands alone in the sentence and its referent is unclear. Choice **b** is incorrect because the wording *having approved installing cobblestones* sounds awkward. Although it is shorter than other choices, the repeated gerund form sounds awkward. In addition, choice **b** offers a superfluous transition word *regardless* after the comma. Having two transition words for one sentence is unnecessary. Choice **c** correctly uses *but* after the comma, but there is no referent for *enough* and the wording *cobblestone installation bearing the names of Nazi victims* implies the installation bears the names of the victims, not the cobblestones. Choice **e** commits the same mistake with the wording *cobblestone installation*. . . .

145. **d.** Choice **d** effectively presents the idea in the clearest way with the fewest words. Choice **a** is incorrect because it is wordy and the phrase *if there is a lacking concrete business plan* is awkward; action verbs are preferred over nouns. Choice **b** is incorrect because the expression *x will happen unless y happens first* calls for the present tense after *unless*; in this choice, the future tense is employed. Choice **c** is incorrect because the clause is wordy and awkward. Choice **e** is incorrect because it does not represent the clearest option.

146. **e.** Choice **e** represents the most concise and clearest sentence of all the options presented. Choice **a** is incorrect because *has the ability to grow* can be phrased with fewer words and *due to* needs to be replaced by *because of*. Choice **b** is incorrect because *is able of growing* is not a correct expression (*is able* needs to be followed by an infinitive), and *caused by* is inappropriate in the sentence. Choice **c** is incorrect because *because* needs to be followed by a clause with a verb, not just a noun (*the thin air . . .*) as the choice suggests. Choice **d** is incorrect because *due to* needs to be replaced by *because of*.

147. **c.** Choice **c** makes for a clear and concise sentence that represents the best option. Choice **a** is incorrect because the language is redundant (*build its increasing*) and *the market of international energy* can be reworded to be more concise. Choice **b** is incorrect because *Mexico's hydrocarbon industry organization* cannot be combined without making the idea unclear; the phrase is best left as *the organization of Mexico's hydrocarbon industry*. Choice **d** is incorrect because the phrasing *Mexico's hydrocarbon industry organization* is incorrect, and it is redundant to use both *growth* and *surging*. Choice **e** is incorrect because it is also redundant (*increase its surging competitiveness*).

148. **a.** This sentence is clear and concise. Choice **b** is incorrect because *decision from the mountain climber* is improperly worded; *from* should be *of*. Also, *that led to him abandoning his friend*, while comprehensible, is a bit wordy. Choice **c** is incorrect due to its wordiness. *Of abandoning his friend* is better phrased *to abandon his friend*, and the adjective phrase *would be life-changing for* is more concise as a verb phrase *would change the lives of*. Choice **d** is not the best choice because *of abandoning his friend* is better worded as *to abandon his friend*. Choice **e** is not the best choice because the phrase *on the slope* is placed after *to find help*, which implies that the mountain climber went to find help on the slope and did not abandon his friend there. This placement changes the idea presented in the original sentence.

149. **b.** The sentence is concise and clear without any redundant phrases. Choice **a** is incorrect because *internally displaced people within their own countries* is redundant. *Internally displaced* already implies they are displaced within their own countries. Choice **c** is incorrect because *increased to an amplified 27.5 million people* is redundant; amplified is superfluous in the sentence. Choice **d**, while grammatically correct, changes the expression *internally displaced people* to a wordier *displaced people within their own countries*. Therefore, it is not the best option. Choice **e** is incorrect because the correct adjective is *displaced*, not *displayed*.

150. **c.** Choice **c** correctly compares the Washington Monument to the San Jacinto Memorial Monument with the correct contrast word *although* followed by a dependent clause. Choice **a** is incorrect because the Washington Monument is compared to the *structure* of the San Jacinto Memorial Monument; this is not an equal comparison. Either the two monuments are compared, or the structures of the two monuments are compared, but not one of each. Choice **b** is incorrect because it also wrongly compares the Washington Monument to the San Jacinto Memorial Monument's structure, an unequal comparison. Choice **d** is incorrect for the same unequal comparison. Choice **e** is incorrect because the wrong transition word (*in addition to*) is used, when in fact a contrasting transition word should be used.

151. **d.** Choice **d** represents the clearest and most concise sentence. Choice **a** is not the best sentence because it uses noun clauses (*are evidence*) and the passive voice (*users are allowed*) over active verbs (like *proving* and *allow users* in choice **d**). The sentence is comprehensible, but it is wordier and more passive than choice **d**. Choice **b** is incorrect due to its wordiness in the last clause after the second comma (*are evidence of far-fetched* Star Trek *ideas being a modern reality*); furthermore, choice **b** changes the meaning from *have become* to *being a modern reality*. This change in verb from *become* to *being* changes the meaning and progression of transformation implied in the initial sentence. Choice **c** is incorrect because it is in the passive voice, which makes the sentence wordier and not as clear. Choice **e** is incorrect because it also changes *have become a reality* to *being a reality*, which is a change in meaning. Also, the phrase *as proof of far-fetched* Star Trek *ideas being a reality* could be more succinctly worded.

152. **a.** Choice **a** represents the best sentence for its succinctness and clarity. Choice **b** is incorrect because homes cannot be *damaged* and *destroyed* at the same time; it is either one or the other. Choice **c** is incorrect because *considered as* is incorrect. Choice **d** is incorrect because *damaged and destroyed* needs to be *damaged or destroyed*; also, the word choice *thanks to* is inappropriate in this context; *thanks to* is typically used for a positive situation, not one of suffering and destruction. Choice **e** is incorrect because *approximately* has been changed to *exactly*; this change in word choice is inappropriate because it changes the meaning.

153. **c.** In this choice, *older automobiles* are clearly contrasted with *newer automobiles*, and *to meet* is parallel with *remain* (the *to* is implied). Choice **a** is incorrect because *older automobiles* cannot be contrasted with *carmakers*; also, *remaining* is not structured in the infinitive form (*remain*) to agree with *to meet*. Choice **b** is incorrect because *automobiles* cannot be contrasted with *aluminum*. Choice **d** is incorrect because *remaining* is best phrased in the infinitive form to be parallel with *to meet*. Choice **e** is incorrect because *older automobiles* cannot be contrasted with *new fuel efficiency standards*.

154. **b.** Choice **b** is a grammatically correct sentence that uses accurate idiomatic expressions without being redundant. Choice **a** is incorrect because a rate is *high*, not *fast*, and it is redundant to have *annual* and *per year* in a sentence to describe the same thing. Choice **c** is incorrect because *fast* should be replaced by *high*, and *in addition* is not the correct word to introduce a contrasting idea. Choice **d** is incorrect because *a quick rate* is not a good phrase choice, and *moreover* is not the correct word to introduce a contrasting idea. Choice **e** is incorrect because *annual rate per year* is redundant.

155. **e.** Choice **e** is correct because it uses the correct expression *native to* to describe the origin of a species and it correctly uses *because of*. Choice **a** is incorrect because *native of* should be replaced by *native to*. Choice **b** is incorrect because *native of* needs to be replaced by *native to*, and *a Devil Facial Tumor Disease cancer* is best phrased as *a cancer called Devil Facial Tumor Disease*. Choice **c** is incorrect because *native of* needs to be replaced by *native to*, and *due to* needs to be replaced by *because of*. Choice **d** is incorrect because *due to* should be *because of*, and *a Devil Facial Tumor Disease cancer* is best worded as *a cancer called Devil Facial Tumor Disease*.

156. **d.** Choice **d** is the most effective, succinct sentence. Choice **a** is incorrect because the first dependent clause before the comma is a dangling modifier with no logical referent. It implies that *microfinance views their money as a way to alleviate poverty*, which is illogical. Also, *rather than* would be preferred in this sentence because *rather than* implies preference, whereas *instead of* is more of a replacement, not a preference. Choice **b** is incorrect because the first clause continues to be a dangling modifier with no logical referent, and *now currently* is redundant and wordy. Also, *rather than* is a better option in this sentence. Choice **c** is incorrect because *now . . . seeing . . . in today's world* is redundant; *in today's world* is best omitted from the sentence since the time frame of the present is already conveyed. Also, the sentence would be more effective if both clauses utilized the same verb tense. Choice **e** is incorrect because *view* must be *viewing* if it is to follow *instead of*. Also, *now . . . in today's world* is redundant.

157.   **d.** Choice **d** represents the most concise and effective sentence. Choice **a** is incorrect because *have differences* is better worded as *differ*, and *for maintaining*, when it describes a purpose, needs to be expressed in the infinitive form (*to maintain*). Choice **b** is incorrect because *have differing opinions as to* is wordy and awkward, and *for maintaining* needs to be in the infinitive form (*to maintain*) since it describes purpose. Choice **c** is incorrect because the expression *create silk with their feet* is misleading and can imply something different from the original idea of *making silk come out of their feet or emit silk from their feet*; the expression is also wordier than *emit silk from their feet* as suggested by choice **d**. Choice **e** is incorrect because *disagree over the abilities of* is wordy, and *for maintaining* needs to be in the infinitive form.

158.   **e.** Choice **e** is the best option because it is succinct and clear. Choice **a** is incorrect because it is wordy and awkward: *mandated the right to have their leases honored for tenants* is comprehensible, but wordy and awkward. Choice **b** is incorrect because it is very wordy; also, the use of the passive voice makes the message awkward and changes the focus. Choice **c** is incorrect because the subjunctive form (*made mandatory that tenants have*) is preferred over the wordier infinitive form (*made mandatory for tenants to have*). Choice **e** successfully uses the subjunctive form. Choice **d** is incorrect because it is redundant; in the phrase *made mandatory that existing tenant leases have to be honored*, both *made mandatory* and *have to be honored* convey obligation. *Have to* is superfluous in the sentence. Also, *made mandatory* is better expressed as a single verb *mandated*.

159. **c.** Choice **c** represents the most succinct option. Choice **a** is redundant because it includes both *upcoming* and *approaching*. *Upcoming* already indicates the immediacy of the lunch. Choice **b** is incorrect because *being*, *approaching*, and *in a hastily manner* are superfluous: *being* can easily be omitted, *approaching* is redundant after *upcoming*, and *in a hastily manner* can be reworded with *hastily* before the verb *phoned* for a more concise sentence. Choice **d** is incorrect because *with regards to* is incorrect; the correct expression is *with regard to* or *regarding*. Also, the second phrase must not be in the passive voice with *the committee members* beginning it as this implies that *the committee members are enthusiastic about the upcoming reception lunch*, not Mrs. Brown, as the original sentence indicates. Mrs. Brown is not even mentioned in choice **d**, so this choice must be eliminated as a possible answer. Choice **e** is incorrect because *in a rushed effort* is redundant; *hastily* already conveys the hurriedness of Mrs. Brown.

160. **b.** Choice **b** is a grammatically correct, clear sentence. Choice **a** is incorrect because it is redundant: the phrase *studied and researched* is unnecessary since *studied* and *researched* convey the same idea; the same is true with *rose by an increase of*. Choice **c** is incorrect because *the growth of the ocean level went up* is redundant; both *went up* and *growth* indicate an upward movement. Also, parallel structure is preferred on the GMAT, so the verb *discovering* would best be expressed as *discovered* to mirror the other verb *studied*. The same can be said for choice **d**; *thereby discovering* is better phrased as *and thereby discovered* to maintain parallel structure. Also, *rise* and *increased* are redundant since they both express an upward movement; only one of those words is needed. Choice **e** is incorrect because *studied and researched* together are redundant, and *more* before *feet* changes the original meaning and implies the ocean level had already risen. Also, the first clause *samples of coral were studied and researched by scientists* is in the passive voice, which is generally less preferred than the active voice.

161. **c.** Choice **c** correctly conveys the same idea as the original sentence, yet it eliminates any redundancy and wordiness. Choice **a** is incorrect because it is redundant. Both *it is possible* and *may* convey possibility so *may* needs to be eliminated and replaced by *will*. In choice **b**, *today's wealthiest nations' babies* is awkward; the phrase is best left with *the babies* placed before the rest of the expression. Choice **d** is incorrect because if the answer is plugged into the rest of the sentence, it reads *it is possible with greater chances increasing*; half of the sentence needs to be read before the reader even knows what is being discussed. This results in an unclear sentence. Also, the wrong pronouns *he or she* are used to refer to the plural subject *more than half of the babies*. The sentence is also wordy. In addition, the use of the modal *might* results in a repetitive sentence, since both *it is possible* and *might* imply possibility. Choice **e** is incorrect because the phrase *today's wealthiest nations' babies* is awkward and best left with *babies* beginning the expression to avoid confusion. Also, *may* must change to *will* since possibility is already conveyed with *it is possible*.

162. **a.** Choice **a** is the most succinct and effective sentence. Choice **b** is incorrect because two of the ideas (*rescuing* and *capturing*) have been changed into the gerund form, which causes the sentence to lose its flow and parallel structure. Furthermore, *a renewed sense of confidence* is wordier than *renewed confidence* without adding any more substance. Although all the results are in the same part of speech in choice **c**, the gerund form (*sweeping rescuing, arresting, capturing, feelings*) does not read as well or succinctly as the noun form (*rescues, arrests, captures, confidence*); the sentence is wordier and less effective. Choice **d** does use the more effective noun form for its list, but the clause *who are progressive in their ideals* is wordier than choice **a**'s adjective *left-wing*. Choice **e** is incorrect because *idealistically progressive* is not as succinct as *left-wing*, and *renovated* has been used instead of *renewed*; the latter substitution changes meaning and renders the choice incorrect.

163. **b.** Choice **b** is the most effective and concise sentence. Choice **a** is incorrect because *should* is an incorrect modal to describe the ruling of a judge; *should* is used to describe a moral obligation, not a judge's ruling. Also, choice **a** is redundant with its wording of *in total* and *a sum of*; both expressions convey the same meaning. The rest of the sentence, though grammatically correct, involves two different *that* clauses that result in a wordy, drawn-out sentence. Choice **c** is not the best option because it is wordier without offering any additional information. Notice the difference of *with the money having come from the sale of personal and business assets, which were seized after an undercover investigation* versus *which was seized in personal and business assets following an undercover investigation* in choice **b**. Choice **b** is much more succinct. Also, choice **c** adds additional information of *the state* paying out the money that is not present in the original sentence. This information cannot be concluded from what is given in the original sentence. Therefore, it inappropriately alters the meaning. Choice **d** is incorrect because the modal *ought to* is inappropriate for a judge's ruling. *Ought to* suggests a moral obligation. Also, *which were from selling* is awkward, and the verb *were* does not agree with the singular subject *a total of $6.2 million*. Choice **e** is incorrect because, like choice **c**, it suggests that the judge ruled that the *state* must pay out the money; this information constitutes an assumption, not a fact, and it is therefore inappropriate. It also places the direct object *a total of $6.2 million* after the indirect object *to the 613 victims*; the resulting sentence is awkward and the direct and indirect objects are best reversed to achieve the most clarity.

164. **d.** Choice **d** correctly uses the *that* clause after *argue* with an effective, concise structure and word choice. Choice **a** is incorrect because *that* is missing after *argue*; also, *diminish the value* is not as succinct as *devalue*. Choice **b** is incorrect because the passive structure makes the sentence wordier without adding any additional information, and *or* is used instead of *and*, which changes the meaning. Choice **c** changes the meaning from *abuse intellectual property rights* to *intellectually abuse property rights*. Choice **e** is incorrect because *intellectually* now functions as an adverb instead of an adjective and *or* is used instead of *and*, both of which change the meaning of the clause.

165. **a.** Choice **a** is a clear, grammatically correct sentence. Choice **b** is not the best choice because it is in the passive voice for the first part (*on whether compromised health will be suffered among gamers in the long term*) and in the active voice for the second (*what impact society would feel*). This creates confusion and makes the sentence not as clear. Choice **c** is not the best choice because *if . . . or not* is redundant; *whether* is best (without *or not*). Choice **d** is incorrect because the wording alters the meaning from the original sentence: *whether the overall health of gamers will suffer in the long term* is more serious than *whether gamers will become not as healthy. And* is changed to *or* in the sentence, which changes the meaning. Also, the modal *would* has been changed to *will* (*the impact their compromised health will have on society*), which changes the meaning. Choice **e** is incorrect because the wording once again changes the meaning. *Whether fewer gamers will be healthy* is quite different from *whether the overall health of gamers will suffer in the long term.* Also, *and* has been changed to *or*, and the final clause *or the impact their health would have on society if they were* is illogical. It would make more sense if were changed to *weren't*.

166. **e.** Choice **e** is correct because it correctly chooses *more than* before *twice the national average. More than* is used when a quantity is involved. Furthermore, it represents the most concise and effective sentence. Choice **a** is incorrect because *greater than* must not be used before *twice the national average* to describe the rising of temperatures. *Greater than* can be used to compare numbers, but not the rising of the numbers/temperatures. Choice **b,** *in keeping with*, although a correct expression, is not as preferred stylistically as *according to.* The sentence would also be more clear if *and* were placed after *years* and before *released.* Choice **c** is incorrect because *in accordance with* is inappropriate in this sentence. *In accordance with* is correctly used with rules, conventions, or established patterns. *Data* is not considered one of the aforementioned. Choice **d** is incorrect because *50-year-old data* is not the same as *data that was compiled over the past 50 years.* The change in wording changes the meaning entirely.

167. **c.** Choice **c** correctly uses *the number of* before the two countable nouns *fellow graduates* and *job openings* without any redundancy or wordiness. Choice **a** is incorrect because *the amount of* must be used only before uncountable nouns. *Fellow graduates* and *available job openings* are countable nouns. *Who* must be substituted by *that* since the word refers to *the amount of graduates*, not the graduates themselves. Because *the amount of* is singular, *outnumber* must be *outnumbers* to agree with a singular subject (if *the amount of* were correct, which it isn't). Furthermore, *available job openings* is redundant since the word *opening* already indicates availability. Choice **b** is incorrect because *the amount of* must be replaced by *the number of* in both cases, and *available job openings* is redundant. Choice **d** is incorrect because *who* must be replaced by *that* to agree with the subject *the number of*, *exceed* must change to *exceeds* to agree with the singular subject *the number of fellow graduates*, and *available job openings* is redundant. Choice **e** is incorrect because *exceed* needs to be *exceeds* to agree with the singular subject *the number of*, and *a number of job openings* must be *the number of job openings*.

168. **c.** Choice **c** is the correct answer because it is the most succinct, effective sentence. Choice **a** is incorrect because *among* must be *between*. Choice **b** is incorrect because *eased . . . to a greater degree* is redundant and *transportation* is separated from its modifier *by water*. To achieve the most clarity, the modifier needs to be placed directly next to what it defines. Choice **d** is incorrect because it is in the passive voice, which results in an ambiguous dependent clause because *since its opening in 1869* doesn't refer to anything. In addition, any reference to *water* has been omitted, thereby changing the meaning of the sentence. Choice **e** is incorrect because the reference to *water* has also been omitted. It also poses the same problem as choice **d** in that the first clause of the sentence has no logical referent.

169. **d.** Choice **d** is a concise and clear sentence. Choice **a** is incorrect because *largely . . . to a great deal* is redundant. Choice **b** is incorrect because *helicopter technology* is different from *technology in the helicopters*; in this case, shortening the expression changes the meaning. Also, *helicopter technology* cannot fly, so the idea is nonsensical. Choice **c** is incorrect because *helicopter technology* cannot fly, only helicopters can. Also, key elements have been omitted from the clause after the comma; namely, *insertion* and *broadcast*, which serve to indicate that first-down lines in broadcast games are being referenced, not first-down lines at regular games, the latter of which are irrelevant to the technology being discussed. Choice **e** is incorrect because *makes* is conjugated in the plural *make* to refer to *helicopters*. Helicopters do not make the insertion of a first-down line during a football game broadcast seem insignificant; it is the technology that does. Therefore, this sentence is incorrect.

170. **e.** Choice **e** correctly uses commas to set off the nonrestrictive clause *who wrote the short fairy tale opera* Brundibar and uses concise, efficient language. Choice **a**, though grammatically sound, is incorrect because *his additional developing as a composer* is awkward; *developing* sounds better as *development*. Choice **b** is incorrect because *only hardly* is redundant and *farther* is not the correct choice. *Farther* is used when referring to distance; *further* means *to a greater extent*. Choice **c** is incorrect because *not hardly* is incorrect; the two words cannot be used next to each other. Also, *his developing into a better composer* is an awkward phrase; *developing* must be changed to *development* and the selection of *better* implies that Krasa may have needed improvement. Choice **d** is incorrect because a comma is missing after *Krasa* and *Brundibar* to set off the information between those two words as a nonrestrictive clause. Also, *not hardly* is not a correct expression and *celebratory* does not mean the same thing as *celebrated*. The sentence is also phrased in the passive voice, which results in a wordier and more confusing sentence.

171. **b.** Choice **b** correctly sets off the three items with semicolons and uses *such as* before a list. Choice **a** is incorrect because *like pictures, music, and videos* needs to be replaced with *such as pictures, music, and videos*; also, a semicolon is needed before *a receiver that supports the DLNA standard*, not a comma. Choice **c** is incorrect because the first *which* must be *that* to begin a restrictive clause; *like* needs to change to *such as*, and the comma needs to change to a semicolon before *a receiver that supports*. Choice **d** is incorrect because *which* needs to change to *that* for a restrictive clause (it is essential that the *media source* or *server* contain *all the media such as pictures, music, and videos*); also, *that* before *new "smart" TVs* needs to change to *which* for a nonrestrictive clause (*which new "smart" TVs often do* is extra information about the translator, not essential information). Choice **e** is incorrect because only commas are used. Semicolons need to separate the three items that are needed to *transfer media across a home*; that is, semicolons are needed after *videos* and before *a receiver*, and after *do* and before *and a translator*.

172. **a.** Choice **a** is correctly constructed to result in a clear, comprehensible sentence. Choice **b** is incorrect because *if used repeatedly on an animal* is placed in such a way that it defines *one reason*. The syntax is wrong and the modifier needs to be moved. Choice **c** commits the same error with *if used repeatedly on an animal*. It also becomes wordier by adding *there are fleas, like cockroaches, that. . . . There are* does not add any value to the sentence; rather, it only makes it wordier and more confusing. Choice **d** is incorrect because *increasingly* has been moved to modify *popular flea medicine*; this is incorrect since it changes the meaning. Choice **e** is incorrect because *if used repeatedly on an animal* is placed so it defines *one reason*. The sentence structure results in an illogical sentence.

173. **e.** Choice **e** is a concise and clear sentence that includes a semicolon to logically show the sequence of events in the sentence. Choice **a** is incorrect because *which* should be *that* since the clause is restrictive. Choice **b** is incorrect because the clause following *which* should be restrictive without commas and with *that* instead of *which*. Also, the appositive *earning him the Nobel Peace Prize in 1987* seems to have been tacked on to the end of the sentence; this confusing structure makes the sentence awkward. Choice **c** is incorrect because its structure implies that Oscar Arias submitted a peace plan because he received the Nobel Peace Prize. Also, *between* needs to change to *among*. Choice **d** is incorrect because *which* needs to be *that*, *being signed* is superfluous, and *between* needs to be changed to *among*.

174. **c.** Choice **c** correctly uses the *that* clause to create a clear, active sentence. Choice **a** is incorrect because the noun formation (*people working*) is less preferred than the active *that* clause formation. Choice **b** is incorrect because the latter part of its suggested variation (*as tending to work longer hours, in contradiction of*) is wordier than choice **c**. Choice **d** is incorrect because the verb tense unnecessarily changes to *have indicated*, the meaning changes by excluding *tending to*, and the noun clause (*longer hours of work by*) is less preferred than an active verb clause. Choice **e** is incorrect because *home-working people* is not idiomatic and the modifier *outside the office* has been omitted.

4

Reading Comprehension

Reading comprehension questions on the GMAT tend to be intimidating and even feared, but they don't need to be with strategizing and planning. The subject matter might include unfamiliar subjects with complicated jargon, but knowing how to read the passages and what to look for is critical to succeeding. This kind of reading is probably already familiar in your life; it's only a matter of accessing and employing that skill set as you take the GMAT. Everyone skims when reading, which helps zero in on important or necessary information. We do this constantly in life—skimming articles for juicy tidbits, breezing through ingredients to find the one that's missing, looking at a map and zeroing in on where to be directed and so on. It's eliminating the stress and fear of the test while asserting these skills that will get you through this section.

The GMAT reading comprehension passages are approximately 350 words in length and will be followed by four or so questions. The passages vary in structure depending on the subject matter and the author's purpose. The questions will cover subjects in science, social science, and business.

There are four primary question types on the GMAT:

- understanding words and statements
- understanding the logical relationships between significant points and concepts

- drawing inferences from facts and statements
- understanding quantitative concepts in verbal material

There is no telling which question type will be on your test, but identifying each question type will help you to know what to look for.

Reading Strategies

Developing a strategy on how you will read these passages is your best defense against this GMAT section. This will help you to avoid wasting time looking for the answers after you've read the passage.

Skim the passage quickly to get an overall sense of it. Is it objective or subjective? Is the author presenting an argument or hypothesis or relaying knowledge on a subject? Is there a specific tone of the passage, for instance, is it criticizing? Or is it imploring the reader to change an opinion? What is the overall subject matter and what is being addressed? Briefly assessing these things will help to generally understand the passage.

Next, read the first question and then read the passage again, this time reading more closely. Look for transitional words and phrases, such as *however*, *although*, or *that being said*. Many times these phrases introduce the main idea or present the argument of the passage. By reading the first question before getting started on your closer reading, you are multitasking—you are looking closely at the passage and hunting for the answer to the first question at the same time.

Understanding Words and Statements

The ability to determine the meaning of unfamiliar words from their context is an essential skill for reading comprehension. Sometimes, there will be unfamiliar words whose meaning you can't determine without a dictionary. But more often than not, a careful look at the context will give you enough clues to meaning. Larger words can be broken down to their roots, or can be deciphered by looking at the prefix or suffix.

The general tone or theme of the text can also help you figure out the meaning of an unfamiliar word. Titles can also provide clues about the tone of a story and the type of vocabulary words that are likely to be found in the text. Tone questions are prevalent on the GMAT; a question might ask you to identify the slant of the author or the motivation for writing the passage.

If you are unfamiliar with a particular word, use context clues to try to figure out its meaning. Draw on the important clues in the sentences that appear directly before and after the unfamiliar word or passage.

Punctuation can also help you decipher unfamiliar words. Parentheses are often used to highlight or explain words or phrases and elaborate on the words that precede them.

Understanding the Structure between Significant Points and Concepts

On the GMAT, some questions require you to understand the different points and concepts being presented in a passage. Identifying the author's main idea and the secondary, or supporting, ideas is key to answering these types of questions.

Main idea questions are prevalent on the GMAT. They test your ability to assess the passage as a whole and identify a summation of it. The trick is to know the difference between supporting ideas that support the main idea and the main idea itself. Many times, in a main idea question, the answer choices are filled with supporting ideas that are true, but they are not the central theme. Identifying the difference early will help you weed out incorrect answer choices. Main idea questions are often presented in the first paragraph of a passage. Sometimes, the main idea is reiterated in the last paragraph. This is where to best look for your answer to a main idea question.

Supporting idea questions are also prevalent on the GMAT. The answers always draw on facts given in the passage, not on assumptions you can make after reading the passage. The answers are often an exact paraphrase of the facts given in the passage.

There may be a few questions that require you to apply information. These questions are a blend of structure and main idea/secondary idea questions. You may be asked to identify basic passage structure and significant relationships or scenarios, and then asked to apply that information to a completely different set of circumstances. You are looking for the similarities of the structure, rather than the similarities of the subject, when answering these questions.

Drawing Inference from Facts and Statements

There will be several inference questions on the GMAT. In these questions, information is not simply stated; however, specific clues, structure, and language will lead to a conclusion. Identifying the inference requires the application of all the facts of the passage, then drawing a reasonable assumption.

Some questions may ask you to determine an implied main idea. Finding an implied main idea is a lot like finding the stated main idea. A main idea is defined as an assertion about the subject that controls or holds together all the ideas in the passage. Therefore, the main idea must be general enough to encompass all the ideas in the passage. Much like a net, it holds everything in the passage together. Implied main ideas are the same; they are just an invisible net.

GMAT questions are not likely to make wild inferences. They are generally modest and logical, with very little emotion. Eliminate your personal opinion at all times; it will lead you in the wrong direction. Utilize logic instead. Keep the tone of the passage in mind when you're answering these questions, as well. Tone and inference cannot contradict one another, so any answer choices that are not parallel with the tone can be eliminated.

Physical or Biological Science Passages

Physical or biological sciences are one of three different general subjects explored on the GMAT. Generally, these passages will deal with fieldwork or a study in progress and its subsequent report. That being said, an angle or subjectivity can often be found in these passages, either refuting or supporting the main idea. Focus on finding the central idea at once; it's likely a hypothesis of some kind.

The topics will range a wide variety of scientific areas, but will generally stay current. A scientific breakthrough in 1987 isn't relevant unless the findings support a study in progress today.

Set 7

Now it is time to answer GMAT reading comprehension practice questions that have been designed to test your physical or biological science skills. Read the passages and answer the questions that follow. Good luck!

Antibiotics and similar drugs, together called antimicrobial agents, have been used for the last 70 years to treat patients who have infectious diseases. Since the 1940s, these drugs have greatly reduced illness and death from infectious diseases. Antibiotics have been beneficial and, when prescribed and taken correctly, their value in patient care is enormous. However, these drugs have been used so widely and for so long that the infectious organisms the antibiotics are designed to kill have adapted to them, making the drugs less effective. Many fungi, viruses, and parasites have done the same. Some microorganisms may develop resistance to a single antimicrobial agent (or related class of agent), while others develop resistance to several antimicrobial agents or classes. These organisms are often referred to as multidrug-resistant or MDR strains. In some cases, the microorganisms have become so resistant that no available antibiotics are effective against them.

Antimicrobial drug resistance occurs everywhere in the world and is not limited to industrialized nations. Hospitals and other healthcare settings are battling drug-resistant organisms that spread inside these institutions. Drug-resistant infections also spread in the community at large. Examples include drug-resistant pneumonias, sexually transmitted diseases (STDs), and skin and soft tissue infections.

People infected with drug-resistant organisms are more likely to have longer and more expensive hospital stays, and may be more likely to die as a result of the infection. When the drug of choice for treating their infection doesn't work, they require treatment with second- or third-choice drugs that may be less effective, more toxic, and more expensive. This means that patients with an antimicrobial-resistant infection may suffer more and pay more for treatment.

175. Which of the following would the author be most likely to recommend regarding this passage?

    a. A stronger focus in research should be implemented to combat multidrug-resistant strains.

    b. An increase in funding should be given to third world countries in an effort to both treat and research new MDR strains.

    c. Staph and MRSA should be listed as deadly diseases.

    d. Safe sex education should be reprioritized as paramount, as it's a controllable variable whereas the spreading of soft tissue infections isn't.

    e. Healthcare professionals should lower their fees for people who suffer from MDR strains.

176. Which of the following best expresses the main idea of the passage?

   a. Drug-resistant infections are causing an increase in hospital and medical fees.

   b. Drug-resistant pneumonia and fierce STDs are on their way to becoming a global epidemic unless preparedness action is aggressively taken.

   c. The longtime use of certain antibiotics has rendered them ineffective against the ever-adapting viruses they combat.

   d. The value of antibiotics has been underestimated; hence, its continuing development has been neglected.

   e. Antibiotics are frequently not taken correctly, weakening the immune system against MDR strains.

177. Of the following situations, which most resembles the information regarding antibiotics in the passage?

   a. a superhero who has lost his invisibility powers

   b. a cucumber in a salt solution halfway on a course to being a pickle

   c. a sixteenth-century castle surrounded by a giant moat hosting a kingdom that is being attacked by a rival empire that has canoes

   d. two apple pies entered in a bake-off, one made with Granny Smith apples and one made with Red Delicious

   e. Buying tickets to a sold-out show on the street outside the venue rather than on the Internet through an overinflated third-party source

178. What is most likely the structural purpose of the fourth sentence?

   a. to report more data regarding the author's interest in the study

   b. to begin a comparison between two different ideas

   c. to introduce a rebuttal to a widely accepted opinion

   d. to vehemently denounce an institution's stance

   e. to appeal to the reader's sense of compassion

179. Based on the information in the passage, which of these statements is true?

    a. As infectious organisms evolve, less effective and more expensive drugs will have to be used for treatment.

    b. Hospitals are the only institutions that benefit from the inefficacy of antibiotics since they're likely to reap more capital with increased hospital stays.

    c. People who live in industrialized areas are more prone to contracting an MDR strain.

    d. If antibiotics were taken as prescribed more often, the viruses being fought would never have had the chance to adapt to them.

    e. We can expect a rise in sexually transmitted diseases in our society since we've lost the power to treat them.

180. The tone of this passage could be described as:

    a. critical

    b. sarcastic

    c. admonishing

    d. infuriated

    e. resentful

Biotechnology can be broadly defined as "using living organisms or their products for commercial purposes." As such, biotechnology has been practiced since the beginning of recorded history in such activities as baking bread, brewing alcoholic beverages, or breeding food crops or domestic animals.

A narrower and more specific definition of biotechnology is "the commercial application of living organisms or their products, which involves the deliberate manipulation of their DNA molecules." This definition implies a set of laboratory techniques developed within the last 20 years that have been responsible for the tremendous scientific and commercial interest in biotechnology, the founding of many new companies, and the redirection of research efforts and financial resources among established companies and universities.

Combining DNA from different existing organisms (plants, animals, insects, bacteria, etc.) results in modified organisms with a combination of traits from the parents. The sharing of DNA information takes place naturally through sexual reproduction and has been exploited in plant and animal breeding programs for many years.

However, sexual reproduction can occur only between plants and animals of the same species. A Holstein cow can be mated with a Hereford bull because the two animals are different breeds of the same species, cattle. But trying to mate a cow with a horse, a different species of animal, would not be successful.

What's new since 1972 is that scientists have been able to identify the specific DNA genes for many desirable traits and transfer only those genes, usually carried on a plasmid or virus, into another organism. This provides a method to transfer DNA between any living cells (plant, animal, insect, bacterial, etc.). Virtually any desirable trait found in nature can, in principle, be transferred into any chosen organism. An organism modified by genetic engineering is called transgenic.

Specific applications of genetic engineering are abundant and increasing rapidly in number. Genetic engineering is being used in the production of pharmaceuticals, gene therapy, and the development of transgenic plants and animals.

181. Which of the following best describes the tone of the passage?
   a. ambivalent
   b. critical
   c. defensive
   d. enthusiastic
   e. objective

182. Based on what's been said thus far, what is the next paragraph most likely to discuss?
   a. the effects of what would happen if a cow and horse were mated
   b. the specific examples of biotechnology and its benefits to science
   c. what happened in 1972 and which scientists were involved
   d. who opposes the use of biotechnology
   e. how the production of beer is not so different from the production of pharmaceuticals

183. The outcome of the mating of a Holstein cow and a Hereford bull would be called:
a. an abomination
b. transgenic
c. improbable
d. manipulation
e. transference

184. The relationship between transgenic plants and biotechnology is most like the relationship between:
a. a graham cracker crust and apple pie
b. hardwood floors and a shag carpet
c. an airline pilot and a jet plane
d. opiate abuse and addiction
e. sheet music and a grand piano

185. According to the passage, all the following are products of biotechnology EXCEPT:
a. new lines of pharmaceuticals
b. the breeding of transgenic animals
c. the production of alcoholic beverages
d. the development of viral warfare
e. the transferring of DNA between different organisms

186. Which of the following best summarizes the main idea of the passage?
a. The sweeping changes in the use of biotechnology since 1972 have redefined its necessity to mankind.
b. Although still in its fledgling stages, biotechnology shows promise to help benefit our society one day.
c. As the science of biotechnology continues to broaden and strengthen, the fruits of its applications become more powerful and abundant.
d. The swapping of DNA could sometimes yield beneficial results, but on the whole is too risky to undertake.
e. The development of transgenic plants is paramount to the development of better pharmaceuticals.

Men with high risk for heart disease had lower blood pressure after drinking nonalcoholic red wine every day for 4 weeks, according to a new study in the American Heart Association journal *Circulation Research*.

Nonalcoholic red wine increased participants' levels of nitric oxide, which helped decrease both systolic and diastolic blood pressure, researchers said. Nitric oxide is a molecule in the body that helps blood vessels relax and allows more blood to reach your heart and organs.

Researchers studied 67 men with diabetes or three or more cardio-vascular risk factors, who ate a common diet plus one of the following drinks: about 10 ounces of red wine, nonalcoholic red wine, or about 3 ounces of gin. All the men tried each diet/beverage combination for 4 weeks.

The red wine and nonalcoholic wine contained equal amounts of polyphenols, an antioxidant that decreases blood pressure.

During the red wine phase, the men had very little reduction in blood pressure and there was no change while drinking gin. However, after drinking nonalcoholic red wine, blood pressure decreased by about 6 mmHg in systolic and 2 mmHg in diastolic blood pressure—possibly reducing the risk of heart disease by 14% and stroke by as much as 20%.

Researchers concluded that the alcohol in red wine weakens its ability to lower blood pressure. But polyphenols—still present after alcohol is removed from wine—are likely the beneficial element in wine.

187. The study in the passage would best conclude that
   a. alcohol has no effect on blood pressure.
   b. alcoholics are the most likely to suffer strokes.
   c. the antioxidants present in red wine that are beneficial to health concerns are negated by alcohol.
   d. polyphenols are detrimental to health.
   e. drinking gin is a useless endeavor.

188. Based on the information in the passage, nonalcoholic red wine will have a better impact on combating
   a. neither heart disease nor stroke.
   b. stroke.
   c. heart disease.
   d. stroke and heart disease.
   e. nitric oxide.

189. It can be inferred from the passage that diabetic men
   a. have a propensity for eating and drinking beyond the point of average human consumption.
   b. are susceptible to having a negative reaction to nitric oxide.
   c. are at higher risk than the average male for developing heart disease.
   d. have a physiological reaction to red wine.
   e. have blood pressure that's anywhere from 14% to 20% higher than the average male's.

190. According to the information in the passage, which of the following best expresses the main idea?
   a. The consumption of alcoholic beverages is constantly proving to be detrimental to health.
   b. Polyphenols are of great value to the human body.
   c. The alcohol in red wine negates the positive effects the consumption of polyphenols can achieve.
   d. Nitric oxide helps blood vessels to relax, allowing more blood flow to the heart and brain.
   e. The risk of heart disease can be reduced by drinking red wine

191. The purpose of paragraph 5 is to
   a. introduce the variables that will support a thesis.
   b. present the counterpoint to the passage.
   c. include the support of additional peripheral expertise.
   d. present the findings for the conclusion of a study.
   e. defend an opinion.

192. The two different wines mentioned in the passage most resemble:
   a. a Labrador retriever and a Labradoodle
   b. whole milk and lactose-free milk
   c. Granny Smith apples and Fuji apples
   d. a gas oven and a microwave oven
   e. a Big Wheel and a bicycle

Widespread media coverage tells us today of a new drug that "halts" Alzheimer's symptoms "for three years." The news is based on a press release issued yesterday that highlighted positive early results of research into the use of intravenous immunoglobulin to treat Alzheimer's disease.

Intravenous immunoglobulin (IVIG) is a medication made by harvesting antibodies from donated blood. It is currently used to treat severe forms of infection and a number of autoimmune conditions (where the immune system attacks healthy tissue).

The idea behind using IVIG to treat Alzheimer's disease is that it could encourage the immune system to "attack" abnormal clumps of protein (amyloid plaques) that can develop in the brains of people with Alzheimer's disease.

Some media coverage of the press release was inaccurate. The *Daily Express* tells us there is a "pill to beat Alzheimer's" when IVIG is actually given by injection into a blood vessel. The *Daily Mail* describes it as a "new vaccine," which is technically incorrect as it implies only one injection needs to be given when in fact IVIG was injected every two weeks.

Once past the somewhat misleading headlines, most coverage does mention that it may be 10 years before this drug can be available, if it passes further scrutiny. IVIG can also be very expensive to manufacture, so this may limit its availability through the national health service.

Limited conclusions can be drawn from this research as it is in its early stage, was conducted on a small number of people, and was not peer-reviewed. Larger studies that compare IVIG to other existing treatments for Alzheimer's disease are required to determine how safe and effective the drug is.

193. Which of the following would be the most fitting title to this passage?

    a. New Drug to Combat Alzheimer's to Be Released on the Market

    b. Alzheimer's Cure a Complete Fabrication

    c. Miracle Pill for Alzheimer's Has Patients Hopeful

    d. Weakened Immune Systems of Patients to Blame for Alzheimer's

    e. Reports of Potential Breakthrough Alzheimer's Treatment Both Premature and Misinformed

194. The author's attitude about the medication being studied to treat Alzheimer's would be best described as:

    a. skeptical

    b. ambivalent

    c. stoic

    d. enthusiastic

    e. cantankerous

195. According to the passage, all of the following are true about IVIG EXCEPT:

    a. IVIG will be administered by injection.

    b. IVIG will encourage the immune system to fight proteins in the brain.

    c. IVIG can be defined as a vaccine.

    d. IVIG may not be available for 10 years or more.

    e. IVIG may not be cost-efficient to produce.

196. Which of the following would best describe the purpose of the fourth paragraph?

    a. It refutes an argument presented by others in the medical field.

    b. It provides an objective approach that has been expounded upon by many.

    c. It serves to introduce the author's misgivings about the media.

    d. It denounces the accuracy of a study.

    e. It combines the background information with the opinions of different medical professionals.

197. Which of the following statements is the author most likely to agree with?
   a. Exciting new medical breakthroughs regarding the treatment of Alzheimer's could be around the corner, but it is unknown how long the road ahead is.
   b. The use of IVIG should be introduced to senile mice before it is used to treat people.
   c. Research dedicated to a drug that doesn't attack abnormal clumps but rather coaxes them should be paramount for any scientists involved in this study.
   d. The media have a tendency to deliver misleading information to the public because sensationalism sells.
   e. A national healthcare system could introduce medications to people with Alzheimer's who couldn't afford it otherwise.

Even the smallest quantity of salmonella may, in the future, be easily detected with a technology known as SERS, short for "surface-enhanced Raman scattering." U.S. Department of Agriculture (USDA) scientist Bosoon Park at Athens, GA, is leading exploratory studies of this analytical technique's potential for quick, easy, and reliable detection of salmonella and other foodborne pathogens.

According to the U.S. Centers for Disease Control and Prevention, salmonella causes more than one million cases of illness in the United States every year.

If SERS proves successful for cornering salmonella, the technique might be used at public health laboratories around the nation to rapidly identify this or other pathogens responsible for outbreaks of foodborne illness, according to Park, an agricultural engineer. What's more, tomorrow's food makers might use SERS at their in-house quality control labs.

The Agricultural Research Service is the USDA's chief intramural scientific research agency. Park's research supports the USDA priority of enhancing food safety.

In a SERS analysis, a specimen is placed on a surface, such as a stainless steel plate, that has been "enhanced," or changed from smooth to rough. For some of their research, Park's team enhanced the surface of stainless steel plates by coating them with tiny spheres, made up of a biopolymer encapsulated with nanoparticles of silver.

Rough surfaces, and colloidal metals such as silver, can enhance the scattering of light that occurs when a specimen, placed on this nanosubstrate, is scanned with the Raman spectrometer's laser beam.

The scattered light that comes back to the spectroscope forms a distinct spectral pattern known as a Raman spectral signature, or Raman scattered signal. Researchers expect to prove the concept that all molecules, such as those that make up salmonella, have their own unique Raman spectral signature.

The idea of using a substrate of silver nanoparticles for Raman spectroscopy is not new. But in SERS studies to detect foodborne pathogens, the use of a surface enhanced with biopolymers coated with silver nanoparticles is apparently novel.

In work with comparatively large concentrations of two different kinds, or serotypes, of salmonella enterica—enteritidis and typhimurium—Park's tests showed, apparently for the first time, that SERS can differentiate these two serotypes. With further research, SERS may prove superior for finding very small quantities of bacteria in a complex, real-world background, such as a food or beverage sample, Park notes.

198. Which of the following is NOT like the rest of the answer choices?
  a. foodborne pathogens
  b. salmonella
  c. typhimurium
  d. clemteritidis
  e. biopolymers

199. Which of the following most accurately expresses the main idea of the passage?
  a. Colloidal metals such as silver can enhance the scattering of light that occurs when a specimen is placed under a Raman laser.
  b. Scientists are close to finding a way to detect salmonella and other foodborne illnesses with the development of a surface-enhanced Raman scattering laser.
  c. The U.S. Department of Agriculture has been diligently looking for an effective way to detect foodborne illness earlier.
  d. The idea of using a substrate of silver nanoparticles is revolutionary and SERS is one way of illustrating that.
  e. According to the Centers for Disease Control and Prevention, salmonella causes a great number of health problems that the general public is not aware of.

200. According to the passage, a nanosubstrate is
   a. a laser beam that can detect salmonella.
   b. tiny spheres made of a colloidal metal.
   c. an enhanced surface that the specimen being tested will be placed on.
   d. the scattered light that comes back to the spectroscope after using SERS.
   e. a foodborne pathogen.

201. The enhanced surface described in the passage most resembles which of the following?
   a. a stripped screw that no drill bit can reckon with
   b. a peach's skin as opposed to an apple's skin
   c. a skinned knee after a few days
   d. a cat's reaction to a red laser beam light
   e. an old tire's tread

202. The author's inclusion of the information in the second paragraph is most likely intended to
   a. criticize the work of the United States Centers for Disease Control.
   b. support the research of Park for the SERS project.
   c. alienate the specific problems salmonella can produce.
   d. emphasize the importance of the research being conducted.
   e. reiterate the main idea of the article.

Social Science Passages

The second type of passage found on the GMAT deals with the social sciences. These passages might touch on history, geography, and politics. They may cover current social topics. These passages are probably the easiest to read; they are unlikely to contain scientific jargon and business language. They are, however, most likely to be accompanied by inference questions, so read carefully. Try not to jump to conclusions based on your opinions and judgments.

Set 8

Now it is time to answer GMAT reading comprehension practice questions that have been designed to test your social science skills. Read the passages and answer the questions that follow. Good luck!

In 1891, the federal government assumed responsibility from the states for regulating immigration through the Immigration Act of 1891, which established the Office of Immigration (later the Bureau of Immigration) to administer immigration affairs. The government also appropriated money to build a new immigrant inspection station on Ellis Island. The Immigration Act assigned the Marine Hospital Service (later the Public Health Service) the responsibility of examining the health of immigrants entering the United States.

Before construction of Ellis Island's first immigration depot began, the island was doubled in size with landfill. A ferry slip was dredged and a dock installed next to the main building site. A number of older buildings from the island's time as a military post were adapted for reuse. Ellis Island's first immigration building, constructed of Georgia pine, opened on January 1, 1892.

Due to the economic depression at the time, immigration was light and Ellis Island inspectors had no difficulty processing the fewer than 20,000 immigrants who arrived annually. On June 15, 1897, a fire destroyed the complex of wooden buildings. Although 140 immigrants and numerous employees were on the island, no one was killed.

The government announced almost immediately that Ellis Island would be rebuilt with fireproof buildings. The New York architectural firm of Boring and Tilton was awarded the contract after a competition entered by five outstanding firms, including McKim, Mead & White.

The first building to be built was the new main immigration building, which opened on December 17, 1900. Following its completion, the kitchen and laundry and powerhouse buildings were erected in 1901 and the island was enlarged by landfill to make room for a hospital complex. In March of 1902, the main hospital building opened. The hospital had the space and equipment to care for 125 patients but it was still not enough—the hospital was overwhelmed with patients diagnosed with trachoma, favus, and other contagious illnesses that warranted exclusion. Over the next seven years, additional buildings were added to the hospital complex, including the Hospital Addition / Administration building, the New Hospital Extension, and the Psychopathic Ward. The island was also enlarged once more using landfill, which allowed for the construction of a contagious disease hospital and isolation wards, as well as additional support buildings.

203. Which of the following statements best summarizes the passage?
    a. Architecture on Ellis Island set a precedent on how immigrants were treated, and was used as a means of segregation.
    b. Immigrants were forced to stay in hospitals if they were not well enough to help build new buildings on the island before they were admitted to the United States.
    c. Ellis Island had a health epidemic due to disease and illness brought by immigrants that led the government to build large extensions on the existing hospital and surrounding grounds.
    d. The island had to be enlarged through the use of landfill to add many isolation wards for the mentally ill who were to be deported.
    e. Due to a large fire, thousands of immigrants were deported until the island was completely demolished and rebuilt after the Great Depression.

204. What role did the federal government play in regulating immigration on Ellis Island?
    a. The government consulted an award-winning architecture firm that was hired to design buildings that had only small capacity, thus forcing overflow to be deported.
    b. They oversaw the employment of every physically able immigrant to work on construction sites before they were accepted into the United States.
    c. The government set up mandates such as one requiring that all immigrants be tested for literacy upon entering the United States.
    d. Certain age groups were not allowed to enter the United States.
    e. The government oversaw the physical and mental inspection of all people trying to enter the United States.

205. Which of the following statements presented in paragraph 2 helps to further the passage the most?
a. The island was doubled in size with landfill.
b. Immigration was light due to an economic depression.
c. Older buildings already on the island were repurposed to function for immigration.
d. The buildings were constructed of Georgia pine.
e. The first immigration building was opened on January 1, 1892.

206. Based on the information provided, the author of the passage would most likely agree with which of the following statements?
a. If the buildings had been made with fire-safe materials the first time around, a lot of energy could have been spared rebuilding the island.
b. It would have been advantageous to have built the hospital before any of the other buildings on the island.
c. An economic depression spared the island from being overwhelmed much sooner than it was.
d. The island was enlarged by landfill to accommodate people as more responsibilities for them presented themselves.
e. The creation of competition to erect the buildings on Ellis Island helped to keep the architects at their very best when drafting plans for expansion.

207. What was constructed after the completion of the third landfill?
a. the main house constructed of Georgia pine
b. the laundry room
c. a psychopathic ward
d. a contagious disease ward
e. the main hospital building

Almost 12 million immigrants were processed through the immigration station on Ellis Island between 1892 and 1954 when the station closed. By 1924, however, the number of immigrants being processed at Ellis Island had been significantly reduced by anti-immigration legislation designed to establish quotas by nationality. This legislation dramatically reduced the number of immigrants allowed to enter the United States.

The Emergency Quota Act, passed in 1921, ended the United States' open door immigration policy. The law significantly reduced the number of admissions by setting quotas according to nationality. The number of people of each nationality that could be admitted to the United States was limited to 3% of that nationality's representation in the U.S. census of 1910. The law created havoc for those on Ellis Island and thousands of immigrants were stranded on the island awaiting deportation. The island sometimes became so overcrowded that officials had to admit excess-quota immigrants.

The First Quota Act was replaced with the even more restrictive Immigration Act of 1924. This act further limited admissions of each nationality to the United States to 2% of that nationality's representation in the 1890 census. The act sought not only to limit admissions to the United States, but also to curtail immigration of southern and eastern Europeans, who by the 1900s comprised over 50% of the immigrant flow. Additionally, the Immigration Act of 1924 allowed prospective immigrants to undergo inspection before they left their homeland, making the trip to Ellis Island unnecessary.

Anti-immigration legislation passed in the 1920s, as well as the Great Depression, kept immigration at an all-time low. For the first time in Ellis Island's history, deportation far outnumbered admissions. In view of this situation, the Ellis Island Advisory Committee (a committee appointed by the Department of Labor under Franklin D. Roosevelt's New Deal program) advised that new buildings be erected for detained immigrants to separate them from deportees, who were often criminals. This final surge of construction included the new immigration building, the new ferry house, and the new recreation building and recreation shelters.

208. According to the passage, what was the main reason that immigration numbers fell during the 1920s?
   a. the enactment of anti-immigration legislation
   b. the Great Depression
   c. overcrowding at Ellis Island
   d. overwhelming disease
   e. None of these are accurate.

209. Which best represents the main idea of the passage?
  a. Quota legislation was designed to control the number of immigrants based on their nationality.
  b. Due to criminality, a series of quotas were designed and implemented.
  c. The Emergency Quota was enacted to ostensibly shut the door on the United States' open door policy until after the Great Depression.
  d. The enactment of quotas only allowed 1% of one nationality that was currently represented in the United States in at a time.
  e. The threat of deportation caused widespread panic on Ellis Island during the 1920s.

210. The tone of the passage would be best described as:
  a. restrained
  b. nostalgic
  c. inflammatory
  d. informative
  e. contemptuous

211. The Immigration Act of 1924 would most likely negatively affect which of the following groups of people?
  a. the Ellis Island Advisory Committee
  b. citizens of Greece wishing to emigrate
  c. citizens of Great Britain wishing to emigrate
  d. the Lower East Side of New York City
  e. citizens of Italy and Great Britain wishing to emigrate

212. What is the purpose of the fourth paragraph?
  a. to support a theory previously expanded on
  b. to paraphrase the information already given and reach a general conclusion
  c. to refute the facts provided
  d. to pinpoint specific problems with the outcome of previous paragraphs
  e. to criticize an institution

The intense preparation required for the law school admission test (LSAT) changes the structure of the brain, resulting in stronger connections between areas of the brain that play an important role in reasoning.

That's the finding of University of California, Berkeley, neuroscientists who used diffusion tensor imaging to analyze the brains of 24 college students or recent graduates before and after 100 hours of LSAT training over three months.

The findings suggest that training people in reasoning skills can reinforce brain circuits involved in thinking and reasoning and might even help increase a person's IQ scores, the researchers said.

"The fact that performance on the LSAT can be improved with practice is not new. People know that they can do better on the LSAT, which is why preparation courses exist," study leader Allyson Mackey, a graduate student in UC Berkeley's Helen Wills Neuroscience Institute, said in a university news release.

"What we were interested in is whether and how the brain changes as a result of LSAT preparation, which we think is, fundamentally, reasoning training. We wanted to show that the ability to reason is malleable in adults," she explained.

The U.S. National Institute of Neurological Disorders and Stroke funded the study, along with Blueprint Test Preparation, the release noted.

The study was published recently in the journal *Frontiers in Neuroanatomy*.

"A lot of people still believe that you are either smart or you are not, and sure, you can practice for a test, but you are not fundamentally changing your brain," senior author Silvia Bunge, an associate professor in the UC Berkeley department of psychology and the Helen Wills Neuroscience Institute, said in the news release.

"Our research provides a more positive message. How you perform on one of these tests is not necessarily predictive of your future success, it merely reflects your prior history of cognitive engagement, and potentially how prepared you are at this time to enter a graduate program or a law school, as opposed to how prepared you could ever be," Bunge noted.

Another expert, John Gabrieli, a professor of cognitive neuroscience at the Massachusetts Institute of Technology, agreed.

"I think this is an exciting discovery," Gabrieli, who was not involved in the study, said in the news release. "It shows, with rigorous analysis, that brain pathways important for thinking and reasoning remain plastic in adulthood, and that intensive, real-life educational experience that trains reasoning also alters the brain pathways that support reasoning ability," he explained.

213. Which of the following best describes the tone of this passage?
   a. passionate
   b. despondent
   c. articulate
   d. opinionated
   e. arrogant

214. All the following institutions were included in the study EXCEPT:
   a. University of California at Berkeley
   b. Helen Wills Neuroscience Institute
   c. Massachusetts Institute of Technology
   d. The U.S. National Institute of Neurological Disorders and Stroke
   e. Blueprint Test Preparation

215. The purpose of paragraph 3 is best described by which of the following?
   a. to present more cumulative data
   b. to introduce an argument that defies a theory
   c. to introduce the comparative study of two different theories
   d. to paraphrase the hypothesis
   e. none of the above

216. This passage suggests:
   a. insight to how test takers will score in the future
   b. humans have pliable minds capable of change despite how smart we are.
   c. people are born with little or no ability to reason.
   d. lawyers are more likely to have heightened reasoning skills.
   e. 100 hours is enough time to affect a person's ability to reason.

217. Which of the following best describes the main idea of the passage?

   a. An increase in IQ is possible through training that will strengthen brain circuits used for reasoning and thinking.

   b. The U.S. National Institute of Neurological Disorders and Stroke funded the study because of the inferred link between a brain in atrophy and stroke.

   c. Merely practicing for a test can make your brain fundamentally change chemically.

   d. Preparedness can predict your future success and reflect your prior cognitive engagement.

   e. Preparing for law school will inadvertently shift an individual's IQ upward.

218. According to the passage, all of the following are true EXCEPT:

   a. Possible improvement on the LSAT with training and preparation is old news.

   b. Even after preparation, a score of a test is only predictive of your brain function at the time of taking the test and not of how you could score in the future.

   c. Brain function specific to reasoning is malleable through adulthood.

   d. Intensive, real-life educational experience that trains reasoning cannot alter the brain pathways that support reasoning ability.

   e. The LSAT fundamentally amounts to reasoning training.

Thirty percent of health spending in the United States in 2009—about $750 billion—was wasted on unnecessary services, excessive administration costs, fraud, and other problems, a government advisory panel said Thursday.

The report from the Institute of Medicine urges that changes be made to the United States healthcare system to reduce costs and improve care.

Institute of Medicine experts added, however, that inefficiency, a vast amount of data, and other economic and quality issues obstruct efforts to improve health and threaten the nation's economic stability and global competitiveness, the document warned.

Numerous inefficiencies caused needless suffering. One estimate indicates that about 75,000 deaths might have been prevented in 2005 if every state had delivered healthcare at the level of the best-performing state.

Gradual upgrades and changes by individual hospitals or healthcare providers are inadequate to solve the problems, the report committee said.

"Achieving higher-quality care at lower cost will require an across-the-board commitment to transform the U.S. health system into a 'learning' system that continuously improves by systematically capturing and broadly disseminating lessons from every care experience and new research discovery," according to an Institute of Medicine news release.

Solutions include greater use of electronic health records, promoting patient and family involvement in healthcare decision making, and quicker adoption of medical breakthroughs.

"It will necessitate embracing new technologies to collect and tap clinical data at the point of care, engaging patients and their families as partners, and establishing greater teamwork and transparency within healthcare organizations," according to the news release. "Also, incentives and payment systems should emphasize the value and outcomes of care."

"The nation has the knowledge and tools to improve the health system so it can provide better quality care at lower cost," the report authors said.

"The threats to Americans' health and economic security are clear and compelling, and it's time to get all hands on deck," report committee chairman Mark Smith, president and CEO of California Health-Care Foundation, said in the news release.

219. This passage is primarily concerned with
    a. the advancement of technology to better aid the healthcare system.
    b. the pain and suffering current patients are living with due to an incompetent system.
    c. the paramount necessity to lower spending while boosting care quality within the medical field.
    d. the ill effects of poorly appropriated budget and its inadvertent consequences.
    e. the inevitable decline in our healthcare due to fraud, theft, and shoddy products.

220. Which of the following is NOT being suggested to change our healthcare system?

    a. gradual upgrades and changes by individual hospitals

    b. the implementation of an ever-evolving healthcare system

    c. encouraging families to get involved with sick relatives' prognosis and treatment

    d. using the knowledge and resources already available to make substantial headway

    e. digitalizing our record system

221. The author of the passage would be most likely to agree with which of the following statements?

    a. Obamacare should be implemented at once.

    b. The U.S. healthcare system has the wherewithal to be much better than it is, but due to human error it remains redundant and ineffective.

    c. This country is in desperate need of a universal healthcare system.

    d. In spite of its ineffectiveness, the United States still has one of the strongest healthcare systems.

    e. Insurance companies that do not process individuals' claims because of legal loopholes should be disenfranchised.

222. The author's attitude toward the U.S. healthcare system could be best described as:

    a. irrational

    b. critical

    c. impartial

    d. moralistic

    e. sardonic

223. The report being discussed in the passage would be of interest to which of the following individuals?

    a. healthcare professionals

    b. people without insurance

    c. insurance companies

    d. data entry specialists

    e. Americans

224. The basic structure of this passage is
   a. to present a point and its counterpoint.
   b. to state a hypothesis and evidence to support said theory.
   c. to deliver data supporting an idea and a recommended agenda.
   d. to contrast two opposing theories.
   e. to attack an opposing theory.

In 1977, an international tobacco industry trade group, including representatives of all major cigarette companies, noted in a document on the social acceptability of smoking that "cigarette smoking is becoming a downscale social activity." As the disease effects of smoking became better understood, more affluent and educated people were the most likely to quit. Cigarette companies thus increasingly marketed toward lower-income, less educated, and minority segments of the U.S. population. A marketing study done for R.J. Reynolds (RJR) noted in a downscale market profile that this demographic was "more impressionable to marketing/advertising . . . they're more susceptible. They're less formed intellectually . . . more malleable."

In addition to general marketing efforts directed toward downscale consumers, by the early 1990s the homeless had become one of the sub-populations specifically targeted by major cigarette companies. For example, RJR included direct targeting to the homeless as part of an urban marketing plan in the 1990s, focused on the advertising of "value" brands to "street people." In 1990, American Tobacco paid for product placement and supplied cigarettes for the movie *Robocop 3*, which showed homeless activists smoking Pall Malls and Lucky Strikes. In addition to advertising, tobacco companies gave away cigarette brand logo products to the homeless; for example, in 1994 Philip Morris (PM) apparently distributed 7,000 Merit cigarette brand labeled blankets to New York homeless shelters and homeless individuals. By the late 1990s, the ties between homelessness and smoking had grown so overt that a major marketing periodical characterized the target market of Brown and Williamson's GPC brand as "Homeless Man."

Offering free samples is a well-established strategy by which tobacco companies recruit new smokers, and cigarette samples were distributed to homeless shelters, mental hospitals, and homeless service organizations. In 1988 alone, Lorillard Tobacco Company spent over $570,000 on cigarette donations, though not all of these were distributed to marginalized populations. Internal company documents show that in a single month in 1990, however, Lorillard distributed over 100 sample packs apiece to a homeless shelter, a soup kitchen, and a mental health association. Similar donations were logged regularly from 1983 to at least 1993.

225. According to the passage, what other demographics will likely be targeted by the tobacco industry?
   a. senior citizens
   b. adolescent children
   c. the homeless
   d. the affluent
   e. actors

226. The author implies that the motivation of RJR to distribute Merit cigarette brand labeled blankets to homeless shelters in New York City was to
   a. elevate public opinion of the tobacco industry.
   b. give back to the community it was receiving business from.
   c. illustrate compassion for humanitarian concerns in the face of scrutiny from the medical field.
   d. target homeless people as a marketing strategy.
   e. achieve recognition as a charitable organization.

227. Taken in context with the passage, *malleable* most nearly means:
   a. breakable
   b. refractory
   c. pliable
   d. malicious
   e. intractable

228. Which of the following best represents the main idea of the passage?

   a. The tobacco industry gives out free cigarettes to the less fortunate population in an effort to stimulate more popularity among them.

   b. As the awareness of the ill effects of cigarettes increases, the affluent and more educated start stubbing out their cigarettes.

   c. The homeless and other downscale consumers became a main target for tobacco marketing.

   d. Merit, Pall Mall, and Lucky Strike are the most popular cigarettes within the homeless demographic of cigarette smokers.

   e. R.J. Reynolds is a despicable company that lacks both tact and shame in its approach to selling cigarettes.

229. Which of the following best describes the author's tone?

   a. poignant objectivity

   b. critical and informative

   c. impartial and somber

   d. restrained scorn

   e. cold anger

230. Based on the information in the passage, which of the following is the author most likely to be affiliated with?

   a. R.J. Reynolds

   b. New York City homeless shelters

   c. an antismoking campaign

   d. the board of health

   e. a homeless activist group

Business Passages

The final type of GMAT passage involves business-related topics. Business passages can be challenging to read; they will contain unique vocabulary and "business-speak." Read slowly and try to identify root words if you encounter an unfamiliar term. It is also helpful to identify the author of these types of passages or determine whether a passage deals with a specific business or industry. This will help you classify the tone, specifically whether a passage will be subjective or objective in nature.

Set 9

Now it is time to answer GMAT Reading Comprehension practice questions that have been designed to test your business skills. Read the passages and answer the questions that follow. Good luck!

A gene that keeps switchgrass forever young could have far-reaching implications for the development of the plant as a biofuel crop, according to U.S. Department of Agriculture (USDA) scientists.

Inserting a specific gene called *corngrass* from corn into switchgrass essentially keeps the perennial grass in its juvenile form—a plant that doesn't flower, doesn't produce seeds, and doesn't have a dormant growth phase. Because of these changes, the sugars making up the plant starch are more readily available for conversion into cellulosic ethanol.

According to Agricultural Research Service (ARS) geneticist Sarah Hake, the starch in these transgenic plants stays inside the stem because it isn't needed elsewhere for nourishing flower buds and blossoms. As a result, starch levels can increase as much as 250%, which increases the sugars that can be fermented into ethanol.

Hake, director of the ARS Plant Gene Expression Center in Albany, CA, teamed with University of California–Berkeley plant geneticist George Chuck to conduct this investigation. ARS is the USDA's chief intramural scientific research agency, and this work supports the USDA priority of developing new sources of bioenergy.

The scientists observed that the leaves in the transgenic switchgrass are not nearly as stiff as leaves in switchgrass cultivars that haven't been modified. In addition, they determined that leaf lignin is slightly different in the transgenic switchgrass than leaf lignin in other plants. This could lead to new findings on how to break down the sturdy lignin and release sugars for fermentation, a development that will be essential to the commercial production of cellulosic ethanol.

The researchers are now introducing DNA segments called genetic promoters that would "turn on" the expression of the corngrass gene in aboveground switchgrass shoots. This could help increase root mass development that otherwise would be inhibited by the gene. Hake and Chuck also suggest that developing nonflowering switchgrass varieties would eliminate the possibility of cross-pollination between transgenic switchgrass cultivars and other switchgrass cultivars.

231. The following are all side effects of the modified switchgrass EXCEPT:
     a. stiffer leaves
     b. infertility
     c. dormant growth
     d. inability to flower
     e. higher sugar levels

232. The passage suggests that the development of transgenic switchgrass will
     a. eliminate the need to farm corn.
     b. support the USDA's priority of finding alternative fuel sources.
     c. strengthen the plant lignin.
     d. introduce new DNA segments.
     e. pit the Department of Agriculture against the Plant Gene Expression Center.

233. The passage's primary function is to
     a. criticize the work of an institution.
     b. compare two possible solutions when only one is needed.
     c. provide the outcome of a finished study.
     d. optimistically deliver the findings of a study in progress.
     e. eliminate assumptions that are not critical to the findings.

234. Geneticist Sarah Hake heads the
     a. U.S. Department of Agriculture.
     b. University of California–Berkeley.
     c. corngrass study.
     d. Plant Gene Expression Center.
     e. Agricultural Research Center.

235. Which of the following would be most interested in the study?
     a. corn farmers
     b. Orville Redenbacher
     c. alternative energy car manufacturers
     d. the president of the United States
     e. DNA specialists

236. Which of the following inferences can be drawn based on the information provided in the passage?

    a. The USDA has previously neglected its duty to prioritize the development of biofuels.

    b. Our society is becoming more open to the idea of widespread use of genetically engineered products.

    c. We will inevitably drain all our fuel sources, forcing the prioritization of the USDA to produce more.

    d. The development of switchgrass can lead to a lot of promising uses from different avenues.

    e. The cross-pollination of different variants of switchgrass is a little problem that could have devastating effects.

Natural gas use for power generation rose this summer because of hot weather-driven electricity demand for air conditioning coupled with low natural gas prices. According to Bentek Energy, estimated daily natural gas use to produce electric power (also called power burn) averaged 26.3 billion cubic feet per day (Bcf/d) so far in 2012 (Jan 1–Aug 15), up 24% compared to the same period for 2011. Bentek Energy, which has been estimating power burn since January 2005, said that 17 of the 25 highest days of power burn since 2005 occurred this summer between June 28 and August 9. The two main drivers of the increased use of natural gas at power plants this year are weather and a structural shift toward generating more electricity from natural gas-fired power plants.

    The National Oceanic and Atmospheric Administration reported the warmest first half of the year since 1895 in 28 states, and that heat continued in July and August. U.S. population-weighted cooling degree days (CDDs), a measure of cooling requirements, averaged 26% higher than the 30-year average from January 1 through August 15, and has been consistently above average for most of the year. Regionally, CDDs in the Midwest, where hot, dry weather was particularly severe, were 59% above their 30-year average, with the Northeast, South, and West at 43%, 18%, and 14%, respectively, above their corresponding averages.

In April 2012, the Energy Information Administration (EIA) reported that monthly shares of coal- and natural gas-fired generation were equal for the first time. This is a result of several factors, including:

- lower natural gas prices, the result of new drilling technologies, growing production, a large increase in proved reserves, and robust natural gas infrastructure additions over the last several years
- power plant efficiencies, with newer natural gas units more efficient than older coal units and rising capacity factors of natural gas-fired units
- Coal unit retirements, expecting almost 9,000 MW of coal-fired capacity to be retired in 2012, with additional retirements in subsequent years

237. Which of the following most accurately summarizes the main point of the passage?
   a. It is clear by how much energy we are burning that the earth's weather patterns are becoming increasingly warmer.
   b. Coal units are not as efficient or cost-effective as natural gas sources.
   c. The Northeast and Midwest are going to become warmer and warmer each year.
   d. Due to weather and lower natural gas prices, power plants are using natural gas more than ever as an energy source.
   e. The earth is running out of efficient ways to produce electricity as it gets warmer and warmer, creating a precarious predicament.

238. According to the passage, Bentek Energy is responsible for
   a. an alliance with National Oceanic and Atmospheric Administration to strategize what to do about the energy crisis.
   b. gathering and collecting data that will assess the use of natural gases.
   c. newer natural gas units that are more efficient than older coal units.
   d. the leveling of the playing field between coal and natural gas.
   e. bringing up public consciousness about the amount of power being used.

239. Based on the passage, which of the following statements can be inferred regarding the earth's future weather patterns?

a. Eventually all life will either adapt to hotter conditions or become extinct.

b. There will not be enough energy left on the planet to accommodate the drastic differences in weather.

c. If it continues to grow warmer, a parallel rise in energy use will occur, accounted for by air conditioning.

d. The West is the best region to live in for moderate weather conditions.

e. Hurricanes and typhoons will become more devastating and increase in occurrence.

240. The purpose of the last sentence of the first paragraph is to

a. refute the facts that Bentek Energy keeps delivering.

b. emphasize the central idea of the passage.

c. present a new point of view to be discussed.

d. segue into a new discussion of more interest to the author.

e. deliver a hopeful message regarding the increased use of power.

241. Based on the information provided by the passage, which would most likely reflect the author's attitude regarding natural gas usage?

a. dreamy

b. objective

c. hollow

d. complimentary

e. elegiac

242. Which of the following pairs most resembles the relationship between coal and natural gas as presented in the passage?

a. a hard-wired chandelier and a table lamp

b. a kick drum and a drum machine

c. a video rental store and a streaming video system

d. an electrical outlet and a generator

e. a bicycle and a skateboard

Our flagship market is focused on building strong brands, translating brand value into customer value, and strengthening system capabilities to sustain and repeat success. We delivered solid results in a challenging environment, including 2% organic volume growth, as we continued our integration efforts following the largest acquisition in our company's history, creating synergy savings to reinvest in our brands and capabilities. Strong consumer and customer programs included ABC Soda, which generated more than 2.1 billion consumer impressions, and continued successful marketing partnerships between ABC Soda and XYZ Drinks. Effective execution of our occasion-based, brand, package, price, and channel strategies delivered volume and value share gains across beverage categories. ABC Soda achieved its sixth consecutive year of double-digit volume growth; XYZ Drinks all grew triple digits.

The Europe Group overcame an uncertain economic environment to deliver 5% operating income growth and 4% unit case volume growth. The 130th anniversary of ABC Soda was activated with passion and creativity, driving brand love on a massive scale. Other marketing highlights included ABC Soda & Meals, driving sales with imaginative partnerships and cross promotions. We scored with summer music campaigns and built momentum for the London 2012 Olympic Games. A key strategic success was strengthening ties with bottling partners and driving growth with key customers. We spent more time in the marketplace, using the insights to act with greater flexibility and get closer to consumers with an adapted brand, package, and price architecture.

In 2011, we continued to execute the strategies of the Bottling Investments Group. Our core focus on top-line growth and aggressive cost management, combined with marketplace execution, operational excellence, and productivity, generated strong performance. We grew unit case volume 3% on a comparable basis after adjusting for the impact of the sale of our Norway and Sweden bottling operations. However, on a reported basis, unit case volume was even with the prior year. We continued to focus on prudent capital planning to ensure we have the capacity to meet sales growth. Our focus on improving environmental metrics has resulted in significant positive changes, especially in energy and water usage. In addition, we opened more than

450,000 new outlets, placed an incremental 150,000 new coolers, and continued building market segmentation capabilities to ensure consumers continue to have access to our brands for all occasions, in the right packages, at the right price. We remained focused on the implementation of QRS Colas, our end-to-end bottler operating system that enables the development of standard tools, data, and systems geared toward enhancing sales force effectiveness.

243. What business strategies led to the generation of double-digit volume growth?
   a. brand value lead to repeat success while using "old school door-to-door" advertising
   b. longer time spent asking the opinions of longtime consumers
   c. strengthening ties with bottling partners and driving growth with key customers
   d. targeting larger areas and other countries
   e. aggressive media marketing

244. Based on the information provided, what is the tone of this passage?
   a. factual ambivalence
   b. enthusiastic pride
   c. objective reporting
   d. inconclusiveness
   e. critical

245. Which of these situations most resembles the situation described in this passage?
   a. a mutant strain of super ants that recolonizes so efficiently that they become the strongest ants in their habitat, nearly exterminating other species
   b. a blockbuster film that becomes a miniseries on TV
   c. a car dealership that changes its business plan to exclude imported cars
   d. a lamp company formerly specializing in all lighting limiting itself to chandeliers
   e. None of these are true.

246. Which best describes the basic structure of this passage?
- **a.** comparing different strategies
- **b.** accumulating data to support a conclusion
- **c.** different theories leading to the same conclusion
- **d.** disproving an existing hypothesis
- **e.** compiling facts to sway an opinion

A hedge fund is an investment fund that can undertake a wider range of investment and trading activities than other funds, but is generally only open to certain types of investors specified by regulators. These investors are typically institutions, such as pension funds, university endowments and foundations, or high-net-worth individuals who are considered to have the knowledge or resources to understand the nature of the funds. As a class, hedge funds invest in a diverse range of assets, but they most commonly trade liquid securities on public markets. They also employ a wide variety of investment strategies, and make use of techniques such as short selling and leverage.

Hedge funds are typically open-ended, meaning that investors can invest and withdraw money at regular, specified intervals. The value of an investment in a hedge fund is calculated as a share of the fund's net asset value, meaning that increases and decreases in the value of the fund's investment assets (and fund expenses) are directly reflected in the amount an investor can later withdraw.

Most hedge fund investment strategies aim to achieve a positive return on investment whether markets are rising or falling. Hedge fund managers typically invest their own money in the fund they manage, which serves to align their interests with those of investors in the fund. A hedge fund typically pays its investment manager a management fee that is a percentage of the assets of the fund, and a performance fee if the fund's net asset value increases during the year. Some hedge funds have a net asset value of several billion dollars. As of 2009, hedge funds represented 1.1% of the total funds and assets held by financial institutions. As of April 2012, the estimated size of the global hedge fund industry was US$2.13 trillion.

Because hedge funds are not sold to the public or retail investors, the funds and their managers have historically not been subject to the same restrictions that govern other funds and investment fund managers with regard to how the fund may be structured and how strategies and techniques are employed. Regulations passed in the United States and Europe after the 2008 credit crisis are intended to increase government oversight of hedge funds and eliminate certain regulatory gaps.

247. According to the passage, the relationship between Bank of America and a hedge fund is most like:
    a. an iPad and a plasma television
    b. Prospect Park and a private Long Island country club
    c. a Mack truck and a motorcycle
    d. a state hospital and a chiropractor's clinic
    e. Domino's Pizza and a local pizzeria

248. According to the information in the passage, which of the following is NOT true of hedge funds?
    a. Withdrawal from hedge funds can be made based on the value of the fund at the time.
    b. The people who manage hedge funds typically invest their own money, helping to form solidarity with the original investors' interests.
    c. High-net-worth individuals can invest in hedge funds.
    d. Hedge funds typically maintain a positive return, unless the market is doing considerably poorly.
    e. The 2008 credit crisis affected the strategies previously employed by hedge fund specialists.

249. Based on the information in the passage, "liquid securities" most likely refers to:
    a. difficult to access funds, swimming in a sea of paperwork before they can be accessed
    b. stock in alcoholic beverages
    c. funds that are easy to trade and don't change value while changing hands
    d. savings bonds
    e. the stock market's private cache

250. This passage would best be described as:
   a. didactic
   b. sententious
   c. indignant
   d. irreverent
   e. detached

251. Based on the information provided in the last paragraph, which of the following can be reasonably inferred regarding hedge funds?
   a. Hedge funds relentlessly manipulate money to their advantage even when an economic crisis ensues.
   b. If hedge funds were made available to the general public, they wouldn't be as lucrative based on inexperience.
   c. While hedge funds may represent trillions of dollars, other institutions have a far greater percentage of the world's capital.
   d. Prior to the credit crisis of 2008, hedge funds were likely to be circumventing regulatory conditions that most others are subject to.
   e. A hedge fund is an unscrupulous means of creating money among the wealthiest citizens.

The Penelope Royalty Trust is a United States oil and natural gas royalty trust based in Waco, Texas. With a market capitalization of US $620,040,000, and an average daily trading volume of about 237,000 shares at the end of 2007, it is one of the largest royalty trusts in the United States. Its source of revenue is oil and gas pumped from the geologic formation at the Land of Penelope, as well as a few locations in other parts of the country.

Most of the trust's properties are on Jeepers Ranch in Curr County, Texas, where it owns a 75% net overriding royalty interest in the fee mineral interests (in this case, oil and natural gas). Other properties of the trust are in 32 other Texas counties, most of which are in the western portion of the state, on the High Plains; the trust owns a 95% net overriding royalty interest in all its properties outside of the Jeepers Ranch.

The principal productive zones for oil on Jeepers Ranch are in two geologic units, the Grayburg and the San Andreas, at a depth of from 2,800 to 3,400 feet (1,000 m) below ground surface; however there are a total of 12 producing zones on the ranch, including one at a depth of

10,600 feet (3,200 m). As of the end of 2006, there were a total of 620 operational and productive oil wells and 142 natural gas wells on the Jeepers Ranch in the trust. On December 31, 2006, the trust claimed a lifetime of approximately 8.3 years for all mineral reserves of the trust.

Penelope Royalty Trust came into being in November 1980, with an agreement between Brickabrack Royalty Company and the Nations Star Bank of Fort Worth. As is the case with U.S. royalty trusts, the trust cannot function as a business, and has no employees; all operations and maintenance are carried out by the trustee and its subcontractors. Currently, the assets of the trust are managed by Barnaby and Boom, Inc., which acquired Melenial oil, the previous operator.

The trust pays a relatively high dividend, yielding an annual rate of 12.4% in early 2008; in addition, it pays out monthly, a relative rarity for U.S. stocks. However, its distribution is dependent on the prices of oil and gas; thus, unlike traditional stocks (that, when declaring a dividend, usually maintain it at the same amount for each quarter of the year), the dividend payout will differ each month.

Since the trust's assets are considered a depletable resource, its dividend payments are not taxed at the regular dividend rate, but rather as return of capital instead of return on investment; this is an additional tax advantage in the United States, and applies to all royalty trusts.

252. Which of the following best expresses the main idea of the passage?
   a. The principal production zones for oil of Penelope Royalty Trust are in two different zones.
   b. The Texas-based gas trust Penelope Royalty has grown considerably since its 1980 beginning.
   c. The Penelope Royalty Trust's dealings with oil give it the advantage of different tax laws because its product is considered a depletable resource.
   d. The Jeepers Ranch has turned out to be a very lucrative place for Penelope Royalty Trust.
   e. The land of Penelope is rich with oil and inspired a trust to be developed; thus, it bears its name.

253. According to the passage, who currently controls the assets of the Penelope Royalty Trust?
   a. Penelope Royalty Trust
   b. Melenial Oil
   c. Barnaby and Boom, Inc.
   d. Jeepers Ranch
   e. Brickabrack Royalty Company and Nations Star Bank

254. What is the author of this passage primarily concerned with?
   a. the Penelope Royalty Trust's contribution to the gas industry and its proposal to preserve its resources for the future
   b. the Penelope Royalty Trust's history and its current standing in the economic divisions of energy and finance
   c. the growing crisis of oil depletion, with a renewed sense of hope because of domestic oil discoveries, specifically those of the Penelope Trust
   d. the unfair advantage oil producers have regarding tax breaks
   e. a depiction of how many companies can be involved in one primary interest

255. Where does most of the production of oil take place for the Penelope Royalty Trust?
   a. in the High Plains
   b. in the western part of Texas
   c. at a depth of 10,600 feet
   d. at the Grayburg and the San Andreas on Jeepers Ranch
   e. at 142 natural gas wells

256. For what purpose does the author include the fifth paragraph?
   a. to cite how and why oil and gas differ from other stocks
   b. to show the unfair advantages oil companies receive
   c. to negate any disdainful opinion of oil companies
   d. to explain dividends and returns to laymen
   e. to show how odd the U.S. economic system can be

Answers

Set 7

175. **a.** The author's concern is clearly stated: Although antibiotics have been useful to date, new illnesses have developed that will not be combated by this treatment approach. The author never implies that funding be given to third world countries, therefore the answer is not choice **b**. It is never implied that staph and MRSA should be listed as deadly diseases, therefore choice **c** is incorrect. Sexually transmitted diseases are not the main concern of the author, so the answer is not choice **d**. It is not implied that fees will be lowered for patients in spite of having to pay more, so the answer is not choice **e**.

176. **c.** The main idea of the passage is stated after the word *however*, a usually telling transitional word. "However, these drugs have been used so widely and for so long that the infectious organisms the antibiotics are designed to kill have adapted to them, making the drugs less effective." The fact that drug-resistant infections are becoming more problematic is a supporting idea, so choice **a** is incorrect. There is no implication that an epidemic will ensue, so the answer is not choice **b**. The development of antibiotics has not been neglected, so choice **d** is incorrect. Choice **e** is not true according to the passage.

177. **c.** The antibiotics used to work to combat illness, but have lost their efficiency as the illnesses have adapted to their defenses, just as a moat may have been effective to protect a kingdom until enemies found a way to get across the water. A superhero losing any power wouldn't speak to the evil attacking it or why it needed to be invisible to begin with, so choice **a** is incorrect. Choice **b** is incorrect because a cucumber in a salt solution becoming a pickle is similar to viruses changing, but doesn't resemble this situation as there is no parallel to the antibiotics stagnation. Two pies of different flavors in a bake-off isn't anything like the antibiotics situation, and neither is buying tickets to a show anywhere, so choices **d** and **e** are incorrect.

178. **c.** The first three lines of the passage state already accepted, studied, and proven information. The fourth line introduces new findings on the subject, suggesting a rebuttal of the previously widely believed information. The author isn't reporting data that matches what has already been stated, therefore choice **a** is incorrect. Choice **b** is incorrect because the passage does not compare two different ideas. The initial information given is not an idea but proven material. There is nothing so drastic as vehemence suggested in the passage, and the author doesn't seem to be begging for the reader's compassion, so choices **d** and **e** are incorrect.

179. **a.** As infectious organisms evolve, a wider variety of drugs will have to be used if the first treatment prescribed isn't effective. This can be costly, and second choice drugs will have to be used as an option as well, as stated in the last paragraph. Hospitals may incur higher fees, but it is never suggested there is anything beneficial about this study, so choice **b** is incorrect. The passage states that not only industrialized nations will feel the brunt of this development, contrary to choice **c**. It is never suggested that antibiotics weren't taken as prescribed, so choice **d** is incorrect. It is never stated that an increase in STDs is expected, just that they are in fact drug-resistant infections that could spread in the community at large, so choice **e** is incorrect.

180. **c.** *Admonishing* is defined as warning or cautioning, which is suggestive of the author's intent. The drug's previous successes are mentioned, but the passage suggests that further study is needed or there could be potentially hazardous consequences such as a rise in illness and the upset of inflated drugs. The author is somewhat *critical* (choice **a**) of the current usefulness of antibiotics, but isn't critical as a whole against any specific institution, only suggestive that further action is required. The author's tone is not *sarcastic* (choice **b**) at all. The adjectives in choices **d** and **e** suggest emotional response, which the author does not imply.

181. **d.** The author cites the benefits and leaping bounds science has been able to make since the discovery. The tone of the article is one of excitement, using adjectives such as "tremendous" and citing examples of its efficacy. Ambivalence is contrary to the tone, so choice **a** is incorrect. The answer is not choice **b** because the author doesn't criticize anything but rather supports the findings. The answer is not choice **c**; although the author seems to be defending the legitimacy of the use of biotechnology, it is never suggested that anyone else has attacked it. Objectivity (choice **e**) would imply that no emotion is involved in the findings, and the author has a clear interest in the further development of biotechnology.

182. **b.** The last line in the last paragraph cites nonspecific examples of where genetic engineering has been used with benefit. It is implied that the author will continue to articulate the strides made with the use of genetic engineering by more specifically citing its contribution. The answer is not choice **a**. The reference made to mating a cow and a horse was made to cite an example of what couldn't work prior to new scientific findings. There is never implication that a cow and a horse should swap DNA for any reason. Although reference can be made eventually to the advancements made in 1972, this segue would be clumsy if made here, and therefore choice **c** is incorrect. The answer is not choice **d**. There is never any reference to opponents of biotechnology. The answer is not choice **e**. There is never any additional implied link between beer and pharmaceuticals.

183. **b.** The end of the fifth paragraph states, "An organism modified by genetic engineering is called transgenic." Although any individual may have the opinion that DNA swapping is an abomination, it's not called that technically, so choice **a** is incorrect. The answer is not choice **c**. It is stated that manipulating the DNA between these two animals of the same breed has been possible for years. Although it is a manipulation, this is not what it is definitively called, so choice **d** is incorrect. This is not what transference means, so choice **e** is incorrect.

184. **d.** Transgenic plants are both a product of and an example of biotechnology just as opiate abuse could be the product of addiction and an example of a specific addiction. None of the other relationships between the things listed share the same kind of relationship.

185. **d.** The passage references transmitting DNA through viruses, yet never suggests using the viruses in an act of war or as a weapon. All of the rest of the answers are mentioned in the passage as examples of biotechnology.

186. **c.** The passage explores the uses of biotechnology since inception, which predates its study, up until its present, and how more recent findings continue to broaden the horizon of its advantages. Choice **a** is certainly a supporting idea of the passage, but would not qualify as the main idea. The answer is not choice **b** since the benefits of biotechnology are documented throughout the passage. The author clearly supports the continuance of this study, and never mentions risks or concerns, therefore choice **d** is incorrect. Choice **e** could also be inferred as true, but is a less significant point of the passage.

187. **c.** This statement would best describe the main idea of this passage. Alcohol negates the benefits of the polyphenols that decrease blood pressure. Its other effects aren't discussed; therefore, choice **a** is incorrect. There is no correlation made between alcoholics and strokes, so choice **b** is incorrect. Polyphenols are the antioxidant known to decrease blood pressure, so choice **d** is incorrect. Gin may not decrease blood pressure, but whether drinking it is useless is subjective, so choice **e** is incorrect.

188. **d.** The passage states that drinking nonalcoholic red wine can potentially reduce the risk of heart disease by 14% and stroke by as much as 20%. All of the other answer choices are contrary to the facts given in the passage.

189. **c.** It is implied that men with diabetes are at higher risk to develop heart disease than the average male. Choice **a** is a complete fabrication, so it is therefore incorrect. It is never stated or understated that men will respond poorly to nitric oxide, so choice **b** is incorrect. No physiological reaction is ever reported, so choice **d** is incorrect. There is no evidence in the passage to support choice **e**.

190. **c.** The study discussed in the passage was based on proving that the removal of alcohol from red wine would yield greater results. Neither choice **a** or **b** was implied at any point in the passage. Choices **d** and **e** were both stated at one point, but could not be concluded as the main idea as they weren't discussed enough to qualify as main ideas.

191. **d.** The offered data supports the conclusion of the study, unlike choice **a**, which states that data is being introduced. This is incorrect because the study has already been described and therefore isn't being introduced. Choice **b** is incorrect because there isn't a counterpoint. Choice **c** is incorrect because there aren't any outside sources being accessed. The paragraph produces facts from a study, not opinions, making choice **e** incorrect.

192. **b.** Lactose-free milk will have started out as whole milk before the lactose was removed from it, just like nonalcoholic red wine would have alcohol in it until removed. A Labradoodle is genetically engineered from a Labrador retriever's DNA, but the dog can't be a Labrador first and then a Labradoodle. Granny Smith and Fuji apples are two different kinds, but they are never the same product. A gas oven and a microwave are just two different kinds of ovens, not at all the same relationship, and the same goes for the Big Wheel and a bicycle.

193. **e.** The author concedes that the treatment looks positive and could make incredible strides for the treatment of Alzheimer's. However, this article points out inconsistencies in the findings of the report versus the articles being printed about it. The article points out that the treatment may not be available for 10 years, so choice **a** is incorrect. While the author remains skeptical about the advancement, there have been legitimate findings that would render the drug credible. Therefore, choice **b** is incorrect. The answer is not choice **c** since the drug is to be administered intravenously. The title in choice **d** does not match any of the information in the article, so it is incorrect.

194. **a.** The author reports that although the drug is being researched, the research is in its early stages, and since it hasn't been peer reviewed, it can hardly be justified. The answer is not choice **b**. The author has too much of an opinion to be considered ambivalent or choice **c**, stoic. Enthusiasm generally denotes positivity, and if the author is enthusiastic at all it is to criticize, so choice **d** is incorrect. Whether the author seems cantankerous has no bearing on the passage, so choice **e** is incorrect.

195. **c.** In the fourth paragraph the author states that although a news source called it one, a vaccine would technically only be administered once, and this drug will need to be delivered every two weeks. The drug will be administered by injection, so choice **a** is incorrect. The answer is not choice **b**. The author reports that IVIG will encourage the immune system to fight proteins in the brain of Alzheimer's patients. The answer is not choice **d**. The author reports that IVIG may not be available for 10 or more years. The answer is not choice **e**. The author states that IVIG may be expensive to manufacture.

196. **c.** The first two paragraphs present the background information about the drug, but the fourth paragraph introduces the point the author was trying to make by writing it. Until now there has been no mention of misleading information. Yet from now until the end of the article, the author cites ways in which the media presented false or misleading information regarding the drug's legitimacy. The author argues that the media acted with haste to publish the medical field's findings, but is not arguing a point presented by anyone who made such findings, so choice **a** is incorrect. The fourth paragraph is contrary to objectivity, so choice **b** is incorrect. The study isn't being denounced, it is only suggested that it needs more research before a conclusion can be reached, so choice **d** is incorrect. This paragraph does not compare the opinions of medical professionals, so choice **e** is incorrect.

197. **a.** The author acknowledges that medical advances have been made regarding the treatment of Alzheimer's, but shows disdain for the media's inaccurate and premature conclusions. The advancements are surely exciting, but when IVIG will be available is unknown. Although the author states that more research is needed regarding IVIG, there is never any mention of testing on mice, so choice **b** is incorrect. The answer is not choice **c**. There is never mention of coercing abnormal clumps rather than attacking them. The answer is not choice **d**. The author never suggests why the media presented misleading information, but only that it was done. The author hasn't made reference to a national healthcare system, so choice **e** is incorrect.

198. **e.** All the other choices are foodborne illnesses or conditions that will lead to a foodborne illness.

199. **b.** The passage is about the development and implementation of SERS, how it works, where it will work, and how that will affect tracking foodborne illness. This is clearly the main idea. The facts regarding colloidal metals is a supporting idea of this passage, not the main idea, rendering choice **a** incorrect. Choices **c** and **d** are both supporting ideas as well, so they are both incorrect. There is no evidence to back choice **e**, so it is incorrect.

200. **c.** The sixth paragraph states that a specimen will be placed on this enhanced surface, a nanosubstrate. According to the passage, a nanosubstrate is not a laser beam, so choice **a** is incorrect. The surface can be enhanced by tiny spheres of colloidal metal, but that's not a defining characteristic, making choice **b** incorrect. A nanosubstrate is not described as the scattering of light, so choice **d** is incorrect. A nanosubstrate is not a foodborne pathogen, so choice **e** is incorrect.

201. **c.** The surface in the passage is described as changing from smooth to rough, just as the surface of a knee would change from smooth to rough while it was scabbing over and healing. A stripped screw would be an example of a surface changing its shape, but not from smooth to rough, so choice **a** is incorrect. Peaches and apples are different fruits with different surfaces, unlike the one surface that changes, making choice **b** incorrect. A cat's reaction to a laser has nothing to do with the enhanced surface, so choice **d** is incorrect. An old tire's tread would go from grooved to smooth, so choice **e** is incorrect.

202. **d.** Including how many people are affected by salmonella in the United States yearly further emphasizes how useful the development of the SERS will be after its completion. The author never criticizes the work of any institution, so choice **a** is incorrect. The author clearly supports the SERS project, but the second paragraph does not mention Parks' research, so choice **b** is incorrect. The second paragraph does call attention to the problems salmonella creates, but its purpose is beneath the surface of the obvious, so choice **c** is incorrect. The second paragraph does not contain the main idea of the article, so choice **e** is incorrect.

Set 8

203. **c.** The government and affiliates of the island wanted to keep the number of health epidemics low by expanding the hospital grounds to accommodate ailing immigrants, as well as those scheduled for deportation. There was no mention of segregation in the passage, so choice **a** is incorrect. Immigrants were not forced to build any new buildings in order to be admitted into the United States, so choice **b** is incorrect. There was no specific evidence in the passage to support the statement of choice **d**. The fire did not do enough damage to warrant the demolition to the entire island, so choice **e** is incorrect.

204. **e.** When the government assumed responsibility of the island, the welfare of the people entering the country also became their charge. The architecture firm was hired to build because of the overflow, not for aesthetics, so choice **a** is incorrect. There was no mention of anyone being forced to work for entry, so choice **b** is incorrect. Neither literacy nor age discrimination was mentioned in the passage, so choices **c** and **d** are also incorrect.

205. **d.** The fact that houses were constructed of Georgia pine becomes relevant when the information is presented that a fire destroyed all the buildings, and the subsequent necessity to rebuild with fire-safe materials. Choice **a** does not help to further the passage structurally, as relevant as the information is. Inclusion of the economy's impact on immigration isn't brought up until paragraph 3, so choice **b** is incorrect. Choices **c** and **e** are both true and a part of paragraph 2, but the facts stand alone.

206. **d.** This passage is told completely from a historical point of view free of opinion and bias. Choice **d** is the only choice that eliminates opinion and is true. The author never insinuates that the buildings were built with shoddy materials, so choice **a** is incorrect. The author never inserts advice on what would have been better, so choice **b** is incorrect. The depression is never given credit for the island's initial emptiness, so choice **c** is incorrect. The author never implies that the spirit of competition aided the island's structural integrity, so choice **e** is incorrect.

207. **d.** The third landfill would be the last landfill mentioned, and directly following it the contagious disease ward was constructed. All the other choices were constructed before the last landfill was completed.

208. **e.** The answer includes both the enactment of anti-immigration legislation and the Great Depression, so choice **e**, none of these are accurate, is correct. Choices **c** and **d** were not mentioned as factors for the decreased numbers.

209. **a.** Limited percentages of each nationality were allowed in order to curb the flow of immigration to the United States. Criminal activity was never linked to the enforcement of quota, so choice **b** is incorrect. The numbers were reduced, but not completely stopped during the Great Depression; choice **c** is incorrect. The percentages were either 2% or 3%, not 1%, so choice **d** is incorrect. There was never any mention of panic on the island as choice **e** would indicate.

210. **d.** *Informative* best matches the author's tone. This passage presents from a historical vantage point, refraining from interjection of opinion or emotion. *Restrained* would insinuate the holding back of emotion, which was not found. *Nostalgic* also implies an emotional response to the past, which is not present. *Inflammatory* does not describe the tone; there is no presence of anger or opinion. *Contemptuous* is incorrect as well, as it too suggests the show of emotion.

211. **b.** The act would restrict immigrants to 2% of their nationality currently living in the United States. The passage continues to inform that more than 50% of the immigrants were from southern and eastern Europe; Greece is in Southeast Europe. The Ellis Island Advisory Committee would not be gravely affected by the 1924 act. Citizens of Great Britain are in northern Europe, so they would have had a greater chance to immigrate. The Lower East Side of New York City is never mentioned in the passage.

212. **b.** The fourth paragraph provides a summation of the other three paragraphs and includes some outcomes of said information, so choice **b** is the most logical answer. There is no theorizing evident, so choice **a** is incorrect. No argument or counterpoint is ever addressed, making choices **c**, **d**, and **e** incorrect.

213. **a.** Although the author never states an opinion, the enthusiasm about the scientists' findings can only be regarded as passionate. Nowhere in the passage does the tone reflect despondency, making choice **b** incorrect. Articulation is not an adjective describing tone, making choice **c** incorrect. The article is not opinionated and the tone is not arrogant, making choices **d** and **e** incorrect.

214. **c.** The Massachusetts Institute of Technology commented on the study, but was not directly involved in it. The study was conducted at the Helen Wills Neuroscience Institute located at the University of California at Berkeley, making choices **a** and **b** incorrect. Both the U.S. Institute of Neurological Disorders and Stroke and Blueprint Test Preparation funded the study, making choices **d** and **e** incorrect.

215. **d.** The third paragraph is a good paraphrase of the first paragraph, both of which could be seen as the hypothesis, so the answer cannot be choice **e**. Choice **a** is incorrect because no cumulative data is presented in paragraph 3. The third paragraph does not present an argument, making choice **b** incorrect. Two different theories are not being presented here, only one, making choice **c** incorrect.

216. **b.** This point is made in two different statements that can be joined. Choice **a** is not the answer because there is no such insight. The passage states that people are born with reason and that it can be developed, so choice **c** is incorrect. The test in question is the LSAT, but is never mentioned that only lawyers can benefit from reasoning training, so choice **d** is incorrect. Choice **e** is just not true.

217. **a.** The main idea of the passage is mentioned in the first paragraph, and then reiterated and paraphrased in the third paragraph, "that training people in reasoning skills can reinforce brain circuits involved in thinking and reasoning and might even help increase a person's IQ scores." There is no mention of why the U.S. National Institute of Neurological Disorders and Stroke funded the study, rendering choice **b** incorrect. Although practicing for the LSAT is stated to change the brain, it never says it will do so chemically, making choice **c** false. The passage states that preparedness can NOT predict your future success, making choice **d** incorrect. The statement in choice **e** may be true, but it is sure to be subjective for each individual and would not be labeled as a main idea.

218. **d.** The last paragraph states "that intensive, real-life educational experience that trains reasoning also alters the brain pathways that support reasoning ability." It is stated that improving on the LSAT after preparation is not a new idea, making choice **a** true. The statement of choice **b** is mentioned in the third to last paragraph. The passage states that brain function specific to reasoning is plastic, or malleable, through adulthood, so choice **c** is true. It is stated in the passage that among other things, the LSAT is reasoning training, making choice **e** true.

219. **c.** The first line of the second paragraph states that the report the passage concerns urges changes be made to our healthcare system to lower cost while improving healthcare quality. The advancement of technology is a supporting idea, but isn't mentioned enough to be the primary concern. An increase in pain and suffering is an outcome of the main idea. A poorly appropriated budget is also a supporting idea, as is the inevitable decline of healthcare for various reasons.

220. **a.** Gradual upgrades and changes are cited as inadequate and part of the problem. Choice **b** is incorrect; it is suggested that a learning system be implemented. The seventh paragraph references encouraging family involvement in patient care, so choice **c** is incorrect. The second-to-last paragraph suggests that we already have the know-how and technology, so choice **d** is incorrect. The eighth paragraph states the intent of electronic health records, so choice **e** is incorrect.

221. **b.** The passage provides examples of a number of human errors involved in the healthcare system, such as fraud, excessive cost, and unnecessary spending. A diligent recommitment by people involved is recommended to fix the healthcare system. Neither Obamacare nor a universal healthcare system is ever mentioned, rendering choices **a** and **c** incorrect. The United States ranking among worldwide healthcare systems is never mentioned, so choice **d** is incorrect. Insurance companies are arguably part of the problem, but the conclusion in choice **e** cannot be drawn with no reference to them.

222. **b.** The author cites what is wrong with the state of the current healthcare system and what could be done to fix it. Whether the author is irrational would be an opinion of the material presented, but not the author's voice. The passage draws too many references to fault, rendering it very partial. There is no information to support a moral platform. The passage refrains from both mocking sneering, never intonating sardonicism.

223. **e.** All Americans are affected by the healthcare system provided they live in the country. Therefore, it could not be limited to any of the other choices, as it would be all-inclusive.

224. **c.** The author reports the Institute of Medicine findings after much research in the first half of the passage and then delivers the possible solutions in the second half. There is no counterpoint, so the answer is not choice **a**. The Institute of Medicine isn't presenting a hypothesis, making choice **b** incorrect. There isn't a comparison being drawn, so choice **d** is incorrect. Attacking denotes violence, an emotional response far more drastic than this passage ever suggests, rendering choice **e** incorrect.

225. **c.** The passage reports that smoking is becoming a "downscale social activity." The homeless are the only answer here that would be specific to downscale and social. Neither senior citizens nor adolescent children were mentioned as a target. The affluent were mentioned as a group likely to quit smoking right now, and actors weren't mentioned at all.

226. **d.** The passage states "Cigarette companies thus increasingly marketed toward lower-income, less educated, and minority segments of the U.S. population." Distribution of blankets is one of the marketing tools employed. The tobacco industry did not seek better public opinion, so choice **a** is incorrect. Although the industry may have been thanking the homeless for doing their part to keep them in business, this wasn't the motivation, so choice **b** is incorrect. There is no mention of seeking compassion from anyone, so choice **c** is incorrect. The author does not imply that seeking to be seen as charitable is any sort of motivation, so choice **e** is incorrect.

227. **c.** A tobacco industry representative stated that this demographic would be more susceptible to marketing and therefore more easily moldable or *pliable* to suit the needs of the company. The tobacco industry wouldn't benefit from a *breakable* new demographic; a stubborn, or *refractory*, demographic wouldn't be ideal so choices **a** and **b** are incorrect. The answer is not choice **d** because it would not make any sense. The answer is not choice **e**. *Intractable* is synonymous with stubborn, so again, this wouldn't be ideal.

228. **c.** The passage cites several examples of the ways in which the tobacco industry has targeted homeless people as its most likely demographic to continue smoking. The answer is not choice **a** because giving out cigarettes is just one example of how the marketing is done, and not the central point of the passage. Choice **b** is also a supporting idea, as the affluent are only mentioned once in the beginning of the passage. There is no evidence to support the insinuation of choice **d**. Choice **e** is incorrect because it is an opinion, and although this may be the opinion of the author, it is not stated.

229. **b.** The passage delivers the information, but there is definitely a critical attitude toward the tobacco industry. Pointing out all the industry's dirty tricks without using angry adjectives keeps the tone at critical rather than angry. The answer is not choice **a** because the author is not objective, nor is it choice **c** because although it is somber it is not impartial. There is never an indication that the author is holding back anything, so choice **d** is incorrect. Cold anger (choice **e**) would be too harsh a description for this article.

230. **c.** The author is bringing to light the unethical tactics of the tobacco industry, making an anti-tobacco movement the most likely of all the answers. The answer would not be choice **a** as R.J. Reynolds is a tobacco company, and such crude evidence wouldn't be offered from within. Choice **b** is a completely arbitrary choice. Although the author could be involved with the board of health, this passage concentrates on smoking rather than a full spectrum of health issues, making **c** rather than **d** the better choice. It is never implied that the author is in league with a homeless activist group, so choice **e** is incorrect.

Set 9

231. **a.** The passage states that the scientists observed that the leaves in the transgenic switchgrass are not nearly as stiff. The answer is not choice **b** because it is noted that the modified plant will not produce seeds. It is noted that the plants will not have a dormant growth phase, so choice **c** is incorrect. In the second paragraph, it is said that the modified plant will not be able to flower, so choice **d** is incorrect. The answer is not choice **e**. In the third paragraph, it is said the modified plant will have 250% more starch, and as a result will yield more sugar.

232. **b.** The end of the fourth paragraph states that "the work supports the USDA priority of developing new sources of bioenergy." Choice **a** is incorrect because the passage never suggests anything about the cessation of corn production. Choice **c** is incorrect; it is stated only that the plant lignin will be different; if anything, it can be inferred that it may be weaker. Choice **d** is incorrect because researchers are introducing new DNA segments, not the plant. Nowhere in the passage is any kind of dispute mentioned between the Department of Agriculture and the Plant Gene Expression Center, so choice **e** is incorrect.

233. **d.** The passage delivers the facts of the study thus far and highlights the hopes of the scientists involved. Choice **a** is incorrect because there is no criticism to be found in this passage. There is no comparison in this passage, so choice **b** is incorrect. The passage reports the finding of a study in progress, so choice **c** is incorrect. Coice **e** is incorrect because nothing is eliminated.

234. **d.** The first line of the fourth paragraph states that Hake is the director of the Plant Gene Expression Center. The center is a part of the ARS, but it never stated that she is the director of it. She may be leading the corngrass study as well, but this is also never stated. It is never mentioned that she has anything to do with the Department of Agriculture.

235. **c.** The manufacturers of cars that run on alternative energy would be the most interested to hear the findings of the study since their product relies on the continual growth of biofuels. Corn farmers will probably not be planting very many genetically engineered plants, and will likely stick to corn. Switchgrass and popcorn have no relationship to each other, therefore Orville Redenbacher will probably not have very much interest. Although the president may find the data fascinating, its results certainly won't further any of his more pressing agendas. DNA specialists will also be interested in the findings, but not as much as people dependent on switchgrass production for their products to be useful.

236. **d.** The researchers express enthusiasm for the development of the study because its production could have a multitude of positive effects for developing products. There is no mention in the passage of the USDA dropping the ball on the development of biofuels, making choice **a** incorrect. Nowhere in the passage is the attitude of American society toward genetically engineered products implied. Choices **b** and **c** can be tricky since they are both ideas taken from pop culture, but not from the information provided in the passage. Choice **e** is incorrect because there is no evidence that the cross-pollination of switchgrass could lead to devastating effects.

237. **d.** This statement is made once in the first paragraph, as the first line of the passage, and then again in the second paragraph. Although data was collected to suggest the earth's weather patterns are getting warmer, it is not the central idea of the passage, so choice **a** is incorrect. There is no specific citation of the efficiency of coal versus natural gas, so choice **b** is incorrect. The Northeast and Midwest are only mentioned once in the passage, so choice **c** is incorrect. There is no reference to the depletion of energy sources, so choice **e** is incorrect.

238. **b.** The author states in the first paragraph that Bentek Energy has been estimating power burn since January 2005. There is no alliance mentioned between the National Oceanic and Atmospheric Administration and Bentek Energy, so choice **a** is incorrect. It is never implied that Bentek Energy created new gas units as choice **c** would indicate, so it's incorrect. The answer is not choice **d** because no playing field is mentioned. There is also no mention of an agenda to raise public awareness, so choice **e** is incorrect.

239. **c.** The two points made regarding the use of natural gas are symbiotic. It can be reasonably inferred that if the weather continues to get warmer, the use of energy-gobbling air conditioning will continue to rise. There is no tone of impending doom with looming extinction articulated, so choice **a** is incorrect. There is no reference to a dwindling gas resource, so there is no need to assume how much energy there is from the facts in this article, so choice **b** is incorrect. Although the West's weather conditions are mentioned to have changed the least, this cannot be inferred as being favorable since this is a subjective matter, so choice **d** is incorrect. Based on the information in the passage, there is no reason to conclude that there will be an increase in devastating storms, so choice **e** is incorrect.

240. **b.** This sentence reiterates the central idea of the passage. The passage never presents an argument, so choice **a** is incorrect. A new point of view is never presented, so choice **c** is incorrect. Choice **d** is incorrect since the author writes with objectivity, presenting data that's been collected. There is no way to tell what would be of most interest to him. There is never an intimation of hope in the passage, so choice **e** is incorrect.

241. **d.** The author cites from a *complimentary* standpoint the effects of weather and other variables on the use of natural gas, and noting that old, less effective agents are being replaced implies the author views natural gas in a favorable light. Whereas the author seems to be positive, he never comes off as *dreamy*, so choice **a** is incorrect. The author's tone is slightly biased, ruling out *objective* (choice **b**) as the correct answer. The passage provides facts to back the findings, so the tone cannot be *hollow* (choice **c**). The passage is far from *elegiac*, which would be lamenting or sad, so choice **e** is incorrect.

242. **c.** The movie rental store and streaming video are both vessels that supply the consumer with access to movies. Renting movies was a primary way of watching releases at home for a long time. Like natural gases, as streaming video gained popularity, numbers of movie rental stores began to dwindle, with huge franchises going out of business due to a lack of demand, just as coal will. A chandelier and a table lamp are both sources of light, but the relationship doesn't resemble that between coal and natural gas. A kick drum and a drum machine are two forms of percussion, and one is new and the other is old, but the drum machine will not replace the kick drum. An electrical outlet and a generator are two different sources of power. A bicycle and a skateboard are two modes of transportation, but one is not likely to replace the other.

243. **c.** Choice **a** is incorrect because it was not only brand value, but the translation into customer value that led to strengthening the system capabilities leading to repeat success. Although consumers were targeted through promotions and other programs, the passage does not mention formal opinion surveys of consumers, making choice **b** incorrect. Choice **c** is the correct answer, making choices **d** and **e** incorrect.

244. **b.** This passage is written from the first-person perspective boasting the company's successes and ambitions. Choice **b** is the only available option. Choice **a** is incorrect because although this claims to be a factual report, it is by no means ambivalent. Choice **c** is incorrect because a first-person account is hardly ever anything but subjective. There is no hypothesis present and nothing to conclude, so choice **d** is incorrect. Choice **e** is incorrect because there is no trace of criticism.

245. **a.** Just as XYZ Cola did, the mutant ants become the strongest most capable ants in their species. XYZ leveled the competition. Choice **b** is incorrect because a blockbuster film is much larger than a miniseries, which is generally less successful. Choice **c** is incorrect because we read that ABC Soda has expanded to include other types of beverages; choice **d** is incorrect for the same reason.

246. **b.** The passage seeks to show the accomplishments of the company over time, relating all its feats. There were no comparisons noted, so choice **a** is incorrect. There weren't different theories presented, so choice **c** is incorrect. No hypothesis is ever noted, so choice **d** is incorrect. The compiling of facts is presented factually without an intonation of persuasion, so choice **e** is incorrect.

247. **b.** Prospect Park is a large public park and Bank of America is a large bank open to anyone who qualifies; a private country club is also a park but only members are allowed in to use it, just as a hedge fund is a form of a bank but is not open to the general public. An iPad and a plasma television have no relationship to each other aside from both having the capability to play motion pictures, so choice **a** is incorrect. A motorcycle and a Mack truck are two forms of transportation, but their relationship does not resemble the one in question, so choice **c** is incorrect. A state hospital and a chiropractor's clinic would both treat any patient, so choice **d** is incorrect. The two pizza places have no relationship to each other except for making pizza, so choice **e** is incorrect.

248. **d.** The first line of the third paragraph states that hedge funds will typically always maintain a positive return regardless of how the market is doing. The second paragraph justifies choice **a**. The second line of paragraph three proves choice **b** to be true. The first paragraph states that high net individuals can invest in hedge funds, so choice **c** is true. The last paragraph states that the credit crisis of 2008 affected hedge fund strategies, so choice **e** is incorrect.

249. **c.** Based on the information provided in the passage, it can be easily inferred that hedge funds are designed by capitalists and economists to benefit those at the top of the finance food chain, insinuating that those involved would reap the most benefit. If the hedge funds lost money per transaction and were difficult to access, this wouldn't benefit those involved with the fund, and high-net-worth people and institutions would not have so much of an interest in being involved with it, making choice **a** incorrect. There is never any mention of alcohol, so choice **b** is incorrect. There is never any mention of savings bonds, so choice **d** is incorrect. There is no evidence to support choice **e**.

250. **a.** *Didactic* is defined as designed or intended to teach. Choice **b**, *sententious*, would also regard teaching, but from a moralistic standpoint, which this passage lacks. The author speaks from an objective standpoint, so none of the other answer choices would be possible, including *detached*, because in order for one to detach, there is an implication of a previous attachment.

251. **d.** The last paragraph states that after the crisis of 2008, hedge funds were regulated more, implying that prior to that, without supervision, liberties were taken. Choice **a** is a similar statement with far too negative a connotation. There is no evidence to support choice **b**. It is stated that hedge funds represent 1.1% of the total funds, but it is not implied who has the rest of the funds, so choice **c** is incorrect. Choice **e** is slanted and opinionated, so it is incorrect.

252. **b.** This is the only answer that supports all the other ideas in the passage. All the other answer choices are true, but they cannot envelop the other points mentioned in the passage.

253. **c.** The fourth paragraph states that Barnaby and Boom, Inc. currently controls the company's assets. All the other options are incorrect based on this statement.

254. **b.** The passage is written objectively and, over the course of the material, details the facts surrounding the business of the Penelope Royalty Trust. The passage never mentions the preservation of resources, so choice **a** is incorrect. There is no evidence to support an interest in possible oil depletion, so choice **c** is incorrect. Tax breaks are mentioned without an indication of subjectivity, so choice **d** is incorrect. The number of companies involved with Penelope Royalty Trust is an arbitrary fact, so choice **e** is incorrect.

255. **d.** The first line of the third paragraph states that the principal productive wells on Jeepers Ranch are at these two geologic units, and it is previously revealed that Jeepers Ranch is the chief producer for oil for the trust. This makes all the other choices incorrect.

256. **a.** The fifth paragraph breaks down why oil and gas stocks differ from others and why they would pay out at a different rate. Choice **b** is incorrect because there is no hint of criticism noted in the author's tone. Choice **c** is incorrect for the same reason. Choice **d** is incorrect because it isn't implied that the author doesn't already know what the stock differences are. Choice **e** is incorrect because this opinion is not stated.

SECTION 3

GMAT Integrated Reasoning Section

In today's business world, you will often be tasked with making sound decisions, determining patterns, and using both verbal and quantitative skills to solve problems. The GMAT integrated reasoning section measures these skills.

The integrated reasoning section is composed of four different question formats. These questions are intended to test your ability to problem solve when given an array of different types of data—a skill necessary in today's business world.

Graphics Interpretation

Graphics interpretation questions are one question type you'll see in the integrated reasoning section of the GMAT. With graphics interpretation questions, you will be asked to analyze a graphic and use the graphic to make well-reasoned deductions. Some of the graphics you will find are Venn diagrams, line graphs, bar graphs, scatterplots, and scientific diagrams. With each graphics interpretation question, you will be asked to correctly fill in the blank of two statements using drop-down menus. The correct answers are deductions best supported by the details in the graphics.

Test-Taking Tips

When working on the graphics interpretation questions of the GMAT, there are a few techniques to keep in mind that can help you improve your score. Practice using the following techniques when answering the graphics interpretation questions in this book.

How Should I Work on Graphics Interpretation Questions?

- Begin by reading the question and the graphic carefully.
  Be sure to read both of the statements you will need to complete—this will help you know what information to look for in the graphic.
- Read all the answer choices in the drop-down menus.
  Reading the answer choices will help you know the type of information you need to find in the graphic. Additionally, reading the answer choices will help you know the degree of specificity the answers need to be in. For example, a question may ask you about the slope of a graphed line. Yet the question is not asking you to calculate the slope; the question may simply be asking you to determine whether the slope is positive or negative.
- Eliminate any clearly incorrect answer choices.
  You may be able to spot a clearly incorrect answer immediately once you've seen the answer choices provided. If so, focus on the remaining answer choices.

What Do I Do If I Don't Know the Answer?

- Try to make an educated guess.
  Use the information you know and understand to choose the best answer that you can.
- Do not skip the question unless you are sure you do not know the answer.
  With the computerized GMAT, you will be unable to return to the question later.
- Make sure you understand the question and the graphic.
  Take a moment to reread the statements and to review the graphic. You may have misunderstood the question or missed a key word (such as "not" or "only"). Once you are sure you clearly understand what the question is asking, try to answer it again.
- Give yourself another minute or two to answer the question, but do not take too long.
  You want to be sure to answer the question correctly. But you also want to have enough time to answer all the questions on the test. So be sure to keep a calm, even pace as you work on the question. And try to avoid wasting time

General GMAT Tips and Techniques

- Use scrap paper.

  Scrap paper is a key tool on the GMAT. You can write down answer choices that you've eliminated. You can also write down key pieces of information from the questions and the graphics. Also, be sure to do any calculations on graph paper instead of in your head in order to avoid careless mistakes.

- Pace yourself.

  Give yourself enough time to read and comprehend the question, but be conscientious about your time. Managing your time wisely will help you have enough time to finish the test—or complete as many questions as possible.

- Be sure you have everything you need before you begin the test.

  Be sure you have pencils, paper, and anything else you need before beginning the test.

- Try to answer all the questions on the test.

  Answering all the questions on the test is a way to shoot for a higher score. Of course, you may encounter questions you do not know how to answer. While you do not want to wildly guess at the answers, you do want to try to make educated guesses. Even if you can eliminate one answer choice as incorrect, you have improved your chances of picking the correct answer for that question. So try to answer all the questions, or as many questions as possible.

Set 10

Now it is time to answer GMAT graphics interpretation practice questions that have been designed to test your integrated reasoning skills. Good luck!

257.

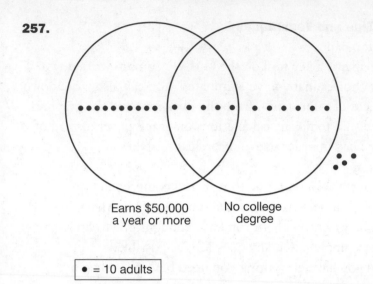

Earns $50,000
a year or more

No college
degree

• = 10 adults

Refer to the pictograph of a survey of adults. Each symbol represents 10 adults in a survey of 250 total adults. Complete each statement according to the information presented in the diagram.

If one adult is randomly selected from the 250 surveyed, the chance that the adult will make less than $50,000 a year or have a college degree or both is:
a. 1 out of 5
b. 1 out of 2
c. 1 out of 10
d. 4 out of 5

If one adult is randomly selected from the 250 surveyed, the chance that the adult will both make less than $50,000 a year and have a college degree is:
a. 4 out of 25
b. 1 out of 2
c. 1 out of 10
d. 4 out of 5

258.

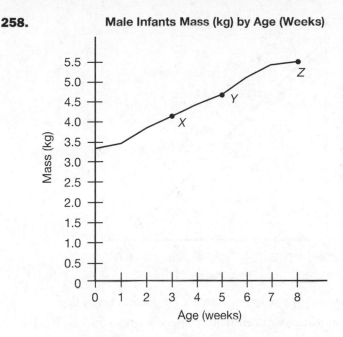

Male Infants Mass (kg) by Age (Weeks)

The line graph models the mass, in kilograms, of an average male infant up to 8 weeks of age. Points *X*, *Y*, and *Z* represent the masses for the male infant at ages 0.5, 2, and 8 weeks, respectively, according to the model. For each question, select the option that creates the most accurate statement based on the information provided.

For integer values of the age from 0.5 weeks to 2 weeks, the average (arithmetic mean) mass falls approximately between _____ kilograms.
a. 3 and 3.5
b. 3.5 and 3.8
c. 3.5 and 4.2

The change in mass from age 0.5 weeks to 2 weeks is approximately _____ the change in mass from age 2 weeks to 8 weeks.
a. equal to
b. one third
c. one eighth

259.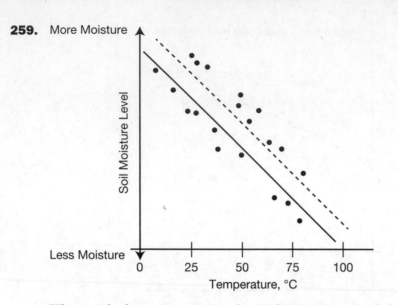

The graph shown is a scatterplot with 20 points. Each line represents soil samples taken from a specific area of land. Each point represents a sample of soil. Each sample of soil was tested for moisture level. Fill in the blanks in each of the following statements based on the information given by the graph.

The relationship between the temperature of the soil and the moisture level is:
a. positive
b. negative
c. zero

The slope of the solid line is ___ the slope of the dashed line.
a. less than
b. greater than
c. equal to

260.

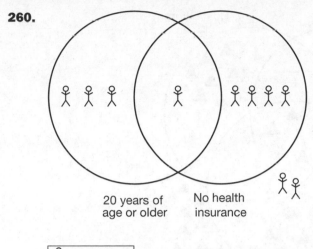

20 years of age or older   No health insurance

= 20 people

Refer to the Venn diagram of a survey. Each symbol represents 20 people in a sample of 200. Complete each statement according to the information presented in the diagram.

If one person is selected at random from the 200 surveyed, the chance that the person will be under 20 or have health insurance or both is:

a. 1 out of 10

b. 2 out of 10

c. 1 out of 5

d. 9 out of 10

If one person is selected at random from the 200 surveyed, the chance that the person will be both under 20 and have health insurance is:

a. 1 out of 10

b. 2 out of 10

c. 1 out of 5

d. 4 out of 5

261.

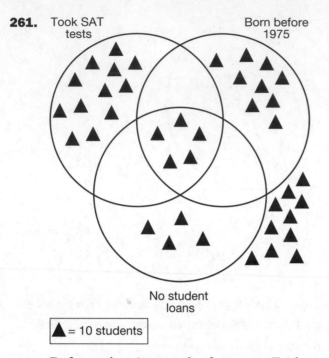

Took SAT tests

Born before 1975

No student loans

▲ = 10 students

Refer to the pictograph of a survey. Each symbol represents 10 students in a sample of 400. Complete each statement according to the information presented in the diagram.

If one student is selected at random from the 400 surveyed, the chance that the student will have not taken the SAT tests, received student loans, be born after 1975, or all of these is:

a. 1 out of 8
b. 1 out of 5
c. 3 out of 10
d. 7 out of 8

If one student is selected at random from the 400 surveyed, the chance that the student will have not taken the SAT tests, received student loans, and be born after 1975 is:

a. 1 out of 20
b. 1 out of 4
c. 3 out of 10
d. 7 out of 8

262.

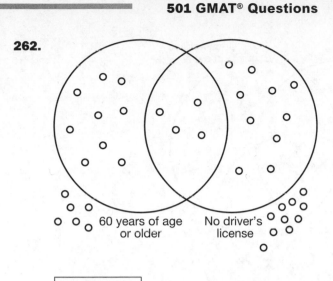

60 years of age or older   No driver's license

☉ = 5 people

Refer to the pictograph of a survey. Each symbol represents 5 people in a sample of 200. Complete each statement according to the information presented in the diagram.

If one person is selected at random from the 200 surveyed, the chance that the person will be under 60 or have a driver's license or both is:

a. 1 out of 8
b. 3 out of 20
c. 7 out of 8
d. 9 out of 10

If one person is selected at random from the 200 surveyed, the chance that the person will both be under 60 and have a driver's license is:

a. 1 out of 8
b. 2 out of 5
c. 9 out of 40
d. 5 out of 8

263.

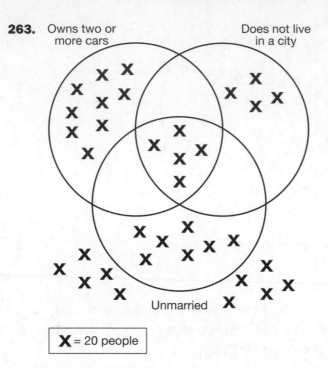

Owns two or more cars

Does not live in a city

Unmarried

$\mathbf{X}$ = 20 people

Refer to the pictograph of a survey. Each symbol represents 20 people in a sample of 700. Complete each statement according to the information presented in the diagram.

If one person is selected at random from the 700 surveyed, the chance that the person will own less than two cars, live in a city, be married, or all of these is:

a. 1 out of 14
b. 2 out of 7
c. 3 out of 7
d. 6 out of 7

If one person is selected at random from the 700 surveyed, the chance that the person will own less than two cars, live in a city, and be married is:

a. 1 out of 14
b. 1 out of 7
c. 3 out of 7
d. 5 out of 7

264.

Mass Garbage Produced by City over Time

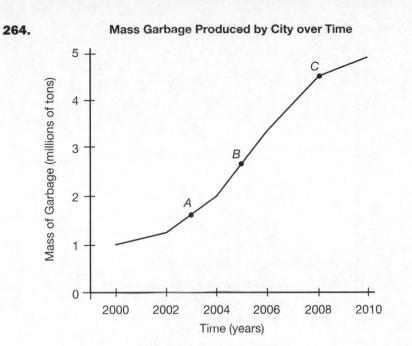

The graph models the mass, in millions of tons, of the garbage produced annually by a city over a decade. Points *A*, *B*, and *C* represent the masses of garbage produced in 2003, 2005, and 2008, respectively, according to the model. Select the option that creates the most accurate statement based on the information provided.

For values from years 2003 to 2010, the average (arithmetic mean) mass of garbage falls approximately between
a. 1 million tons and 1.5 million tons.
b. 2 million tons and 2.5 million tons.
c. 3 million tons and 4 million tons.

The change in mass of garbage from 2003 to 2005 is approximately ___ the change in mass of garbage from 2005 to 2008.
a. less than
b. equal to
c. greater than

265. **Customer Product Reviews Posted Online over Time**

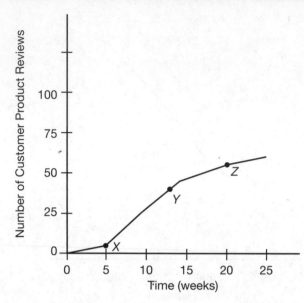

The line graph models the number of product reviews customers wrote online regarding a product up to 25 weeks after the product was posted online. Points *X*, *Y*, and *Z* represent the number of product reviews posted at 5 weeks, 13 weeks, and 20 weeks, respectively, according to the model. Select the option that creates the most accurate statement based on the information provided.

For values from 5 weeks to 25 weeks, the average (arithmetic mean) number of product reviews falls approximately between
a. 5 and 10 reviews.
b. 10 and 20 reviews.
c. 30 and 55 reviews.

The change in number of product reviews from 5 weeks to 13 weeks is approximately _____ the change in number of product reviews from 13 weeks to 20 weeks.
a. equal to
b. 2 times
c. 4 times

266.

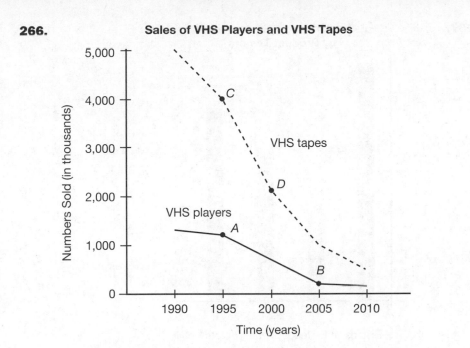

Sales of VHS Players and VHS Tapes

The line graph models the number of VHS players and VHS tapes sold at a given electronics store over time. Points *A* and *B* represent the number of VHS players sold in 1995 and 2005, respectively. Points *C* and *D* represent the number of VHS tapes sold in 1995 and 2000, respectively. Select the option that creates the most accurate statement based on the information provided.

From 1995 to 2005 the average (arithmetic mean) number of VHS players sold falls approximately between
a. 1300 and 1200.
b. 800 and 600.
c. 400 and 200.

The percent change in the number of VHS player sales from 1995 to 2005 is approximately _____ the percent change in the number of VHS tape sales from 1995 to 2000.
a. equal to
b. half of
c. two-thirds of

267.

E-Readers and Tablets Scored by Product Testers

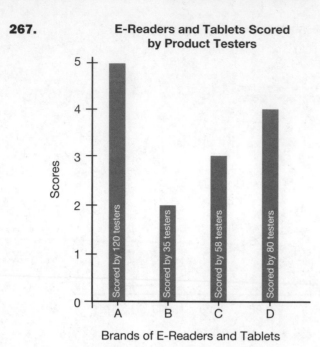

Brands of E-Readers and Tablets

The graph portrays the results of product testers regarding competing brands of e-readers and tablets. Bars *A*, *B*, *C*, and *D* represent different brands of e-readers and tablets, according to the model. Select the option that creates the most accurate statement based on the information provided.

The score that resulted in the statistical mode was achieved by _____.
a. Product A
b. Product B
c. Product C
d. Product D

The average (arithmetic mean) review on all e-readers and tablets falls approximately between
a. 1 and 2.
b. 2 and 3.
c. 3 and 4.
d. 4 and 5.

268.

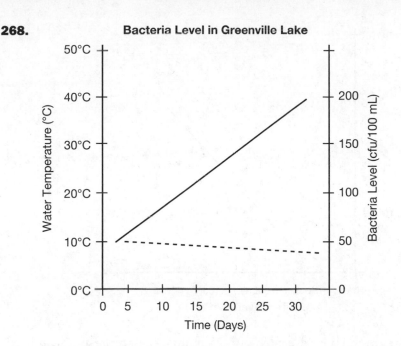

Bacteria Level in Greenville Lake

The graph depicts measurements of water temperature and bacteria levels of Greenville Lake. Both the water temperature and bacteria levels were measured every day at noon for 30 days in a row. The solid line represents the change in water temperature over time, and the dashed line represents the change in bacteria levels over time. Select the option that creates the most accurate statement based on the information given by the graph.

The relationship between the water temperature of the lake and the bacteria level is

a. positive.
b. negative.
c. zero.

The slope of the line representing the change in water temperature is _____ the slope of the line representing the change in bacteria levels.

a. less than
b. greater than
c. equal to

269.

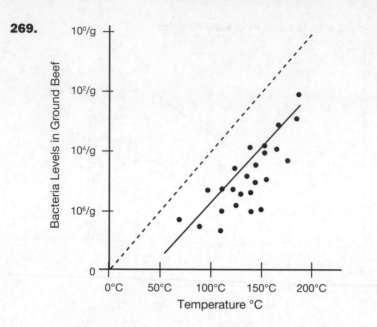

The graph is a scatterplot with 25 points, each representing a beef tested for bacteria levels. Each beef sample was heated to a certain temperature, and the bacterial level in the sample was then measured. The solid line is the regression line and the dashed line is the line through points $(10^8/g, 0°C)$ and $(10^0/g, 200°C)$. Fill in the blanks in each of the following statements based on the information given by the graph.

The relationship between the temperature of the beef sample and the bacterial level is

a. positive.

b. negative.

c. zero.

The slope of the regression line is _____ the slope of the dashed line.

a. less negative than

b. more negative than

c. equal to

270.

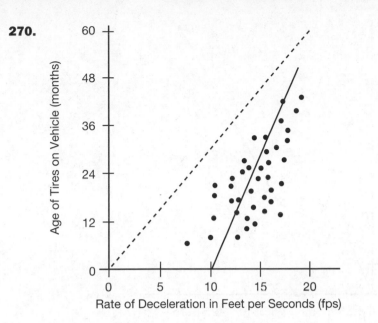

The graph is a scatterplot with 40 points, each representing the results of a test conducted on a vehicle. During each test, the same vehicle and same set of tires was driven to a speed of 60 mph, and then the vehicle decelerated to a stop. The rate of deceleration for each test was measured. The solid line is the regression line and the dashed line is the line through points (0/0 fps) to point (60/20 fps). Fill in the blanks in each of the following statements based on the information given by the graph.

The relationship between the age of the tires on the vehicle and the rate of deceleration is
a. positive.
b. negative.
c. zero.

The slope of the regression line is _____ the slope of the dashed line.
a. less than
b. greater than
c. equal to

271.

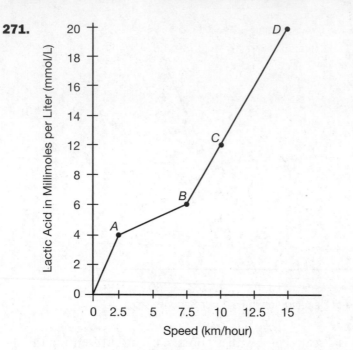

The graph is a line graph depicting the lactic acid levels in the muscles of a jogger on a laboratory treadmill. The speed of the jogger was recorded along with the lactic acid levels every five minutes. Fill in the blanks in each of the following statements based on the information given by the graph.

The relationship between the running speed and the lactic acid levels is
a. positive.
b. negative.
c. zero.

The slope of the line between Point *A* and Point *B* is _____ the slope of the line between Point *C* and Point *D*.
a. less than
b. greater than
c. equal to

272.

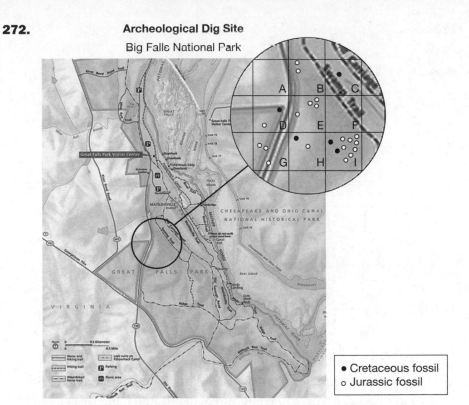

Archeological Dig Site
Big Falls National Park

● Cretaceous fossil
○ Jurassic fossil

The map shows an archeological dig site occurring in a section of Big Falls National Park, along with markers for the locations of fossils found. Fill in each blank using the drop-down menus to create the most accurate statement on the basis of the information provided.

Cretaceous fossils make up approximately _____ of the fossils found in the archeological dig.

a. 20%
b. 25%
c. 80%

According to the map, _____ of all Jurassic fossils were found in Section I.

a. about one quarter
b. about one half
c. about three quarters

273.

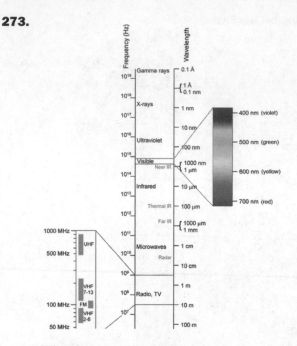

The diagram shows, in three columns, different sections of the electromagnetic spectrum. The far left column shows the radio and television waves portion of the electromagnetic spectrum. The central column shows all the types of waves in the electromagnetic spectrum. The far right column shows the visible portion of the electromagnetic spectrum.

Fill in each blank using the drop-down menus to create the most accurate statement on the basis of the information provided.

The color green spans closest to _____ of the visible light spectrum.
a. 5%
b. 25%
c. 45%

According to the diagram, the color _____ marks the beginning of light with a 10^{15} Hz frequency and the beginning of the visible spectrum.
a. violet
b. green
c. white
d. red

274.

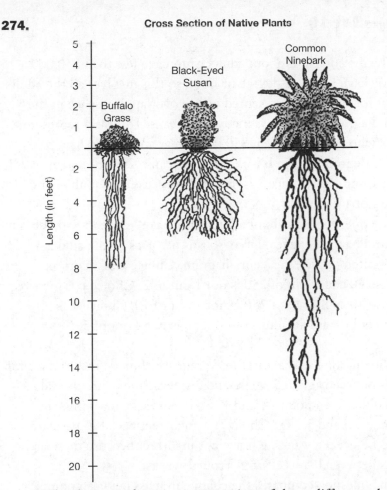

Cross Section of Native Plants

The diagram shows a cross section of three different plants, providing information regarding the plants' height and length of roots. Fill in each blank using the drop-down menus to create the most accurate statement on the basis of the information provided.

The roots of the buffalo grass are approximately _____ the length of the roots of the common ninebark.
a. 20%
b. 30%
c. 50%

According to the diagram, the roots of the Black-Eyed Susan are approximately _____ of the total length of the entire common ninebark plant.
a. one tenth
b. one third
c. one half

Answers—Set 10

257.   d. The question asks about adults who make less than $50,000 a year or have a college degree or both, so this involves all the adults except for the ones represented by the overlapping space in the Venn diagram. Choice **a** is incorrect because this ratio represents adults who earn more than $50,000 a year and do not have a college degree. Choice **b** is incorrect because 200 adults out of 250 is not 1 out of 2. Choice **c** is incorrect because 200 adults out of 250 is not 1 out of 10.

   a. The question asks about adults who make less than $50,000 a year and have a college degree, so this involves all the adults represented outside the Venn diagram. Choice **b** is incorrect because 40 adults out of 250 is not 1 out of 2. Choice **c** is incorrect because 40 adults out of 250 is not 1 out of 10. Choice **d** is incorrect because 40 adults out of 250 is not 4 out of 5.

258.   b. The question asks about the average (arithmetic mean) mass for values between ages 0.5 weeks and 2 weeks. These are the values that fall between points X and Y. So the average mass must be between 3.5 and 3.8 kg. Choice **a** is incorrect because these are values before 0.5 weeks. Choice **c** is incorrect because these are values between 0.5 weeks and about 3 weeks.

   b. The question compares the change in mass between points X and Y with the change in mass between points Y and Z. The mass changes less than 0.5 kilograms between points X and Y and changes about 1.5 kilograms between points Y and Z, so the correct answer is choice **b.** Choice **a** is incorrect because the mass changes about three times as much between points Y and Z as it changes between points X and Y. Choice **c** is incorrect because the mass changes about three times as much between points Y and Z as it changes between points X and Y.

259. **b.** The question asks about the relationship between the temperature of the soil sample and the moisture level. According to the scatterplot, moisture levels decrease as the temperature increases. Therefore, this is a negative relationship. Choice **a** is incorrect because both factors would have to increase in order to have a positive relationship. Choice **c** is incorrect because there is a correlation between soil temperature and moisture levels.

c. The question compares the slope of the lines. Both lines have the same slope. Therefore, choice **a** is incorrect because the slope of the solid line is not less than the slope of the dashed line. Choice **b** is incorrect because the slop of the solid line is not greater than the slope of the dashed line.

260. **d.** The question asks about people who are under 20 years old or have health insurance or both, so this involves all the people except for the ones represented by the overlapping space in the Venn diagram. Therefore, this means nine stick figures, or 180 people out of a total of 200 people surveyed. Choice **a** is incorrect because 180 people out of a total of 200 people is not 1 out of 10. Choice **b** is incorrect because 180 people out of a total of 200 people is not 2 out of 10. Choice **c** is incorrect because 180 people out of a total of 200 people is not 1 out of 5.

c. The question asks about people who are under 20 years old and have health insurance, so this involves all the people represented outside the Venn diagram. Therefore, this means two stick figures, or 40 people out of a total of 200 people surveyed (or 1 out of 5). Choice **a** is incorrect because 40 people out of 200 is not 1 out of 10. Choice **b** is incorrect because 40 people out of 200 is not 2 out of 10. Choice **d** is incorrect because 40 people out of 200 is not 4 out of 5.

261. **d.** The question asks about students who have not taken the SAT tests or received student loans or were born after 1975, or all these factors. So this involves all the students except for the ones represented by the overlapping space in the Venn diagram. Therefore, this number is represented by 35 symbols out of 40 symbols in the Venn diagram, or 7 out of 8. Choice **a** is incorrect because 350 students out of 400 is not 1 out of 8. Choice **b** is incorrect because 350 students out of 400 is not 1 out of 5. Choice **c** is incorrect because 350 students out of 400 is not 3 out of 10.
b. The question asks about students who have not taken the SAT tests, received student loans, and were born after 1975. So this involves all the students represented outside the Venn diagram, or 100 students out of 400 students (or 1 out of 4). Choice **a** is incorrect because 100 students out of 400 is not 1 out of 20. Choice **c** is incorrect because 100 students out of 400 is not 3 out of 10. Choice **d** is incorrect because 100 students out of 400 is not 7 out of 8.

262. **c.** The question asks about people who are under 60 or have a driver's license, or both. So this involves all the people represented by the Venn diagram, except for the ones represented by the overlapping space. Therefore, the correct answer is 175 people out of 200, or 7 out of 8. Choice **a** is incorrect because 175 people out of 200 is not 1 out of 8. Choice **b** is incorrect because 175 people out of 200 is not 3 out of 20. Choice **d** is incorrect because 175 people out of 200 is not 9 out of 10.
b. The question asks about people who are under 60 and have a driver's license. So this involves all the people represented outside the Venn diagram, or 80 out of 200 (or 2 out of 5). Choice **a** is incorrect because 80 people out of 200 is not 1 out of 8. Choice **c** is incorrect because 80 people out of 200 is not 9 out of 40. Choice **d** is incorrect because 80 people out of 200 is not 5 out of 8.

263. **d.** The question asks about people who own less than two cars or live in a city or are married, or all these factors. So this involves all the people represented in the Venn diagram, except for the ones represented by the overlapping space. Therefore, the correct answer is 600 people out of 700, or 6 out of 7. Choice **a** is incorrect because 600 people out of 700 is not 1 out of 14. Choice **b** is incorrect because 600 people out of 700 is not 2 out of 7. Choice **c** is incorrect because 600 people out of 700 is not 3 out of 7.

b. The question asks about people who own less than two cars, live in a city, and are married. So this involves all the people represented outside the Venn diagram, or 100 people out of 700 (1 out of 7). Choice **a** is incorrect because 100 people out of 700 is not 1 out of 14. Choice **c** is incorrect because 100 people out of 700 is not 3 out of 7. Choice **d** is incorrect because 100 people out of 700 is not 5 out of 7.

264. **c.** The question asks about the average (arithmetic mean) mass for values between 2003 and 2010. These are the values that fall between point A and the end of the graphed line. So the average mass must be between 1.5 and 5.0 millions of tons. Choice **a** is incorrect because these are values before 2003. Choice **b** is incorrect because most of the values represented by the line are greater than 2.5 million tons, so this can't be the average.

a. The question compares the change in mass between points A and B with the change in mass between points B and C. The mass changes about 1 million tons between points A and B and changes about 2 million tons between points B and C, so the correct answer is choice **a**. Choices **b** and **c** are incorrect because the mass changes less between points A and B than it changes between points B and C.

265. **c.** The question asks about the average (arithmetic mean) number of product reviews for values between 5 weeks and 25 weeks. These are the values that fall between points X and Z on the graphed line. The correct answer is choice **c** because most of the values graphed by the line fall between 30 and 55 reviews. Choice **a** is incorrect because these are the very values represented by the line. Choice **b** is incorrect because these are the very values represented by the line and most of the values represented by the line are for 20 reviews or more.

b. The question compares the change in the number of product reviews between points X and Y with the change in the number of product reviews between points Y and Z. The change in the number of product reviews between points X and Y is about 35 reviews. The change in the number of product reviews between points Y and Z is about 15 reviews. So the correct answer is choice **b**. Choice **a** is incorrect because the change is not equal. Choice **c** is incorrect because the change between points X and Y is not four times the change between points Y and Z.

266. **b.** The question asks about the average (arithmetic mean) number of VHS players sold between 1995 and 2005. These are the values that fall between points A and B, so the average must be between 200 and 1200 VHS players sold. Choice **a** is incorrect because these values do not fall between 1995 and 2005. Choice **c** is incorrect because most of the values graphed between points A and B are greater than 400, so the average is likely greater than 400.

c. The question compares the percent change in the number of VHS player sales from 1995 to 2005 with the percent change in the number of VHS tape sales from 1995 to 2000. There was a change of 1,000 in the number of VHS players sold over 10 years (or 200 sales per year) and a change of 1,500 in the number of VHS tapes sold over 5 years (or 300 sales per year). So, the percent change in VHS player sales is about two-thirds the percent change in VHS tape sales. Choice **a** is incorrect because the percent change in the number of VHS player sales from 1995 to 2005 and the percent change in the number of VHS tape sales from 1995 to 2000 are not equal. Choice **b** is incorrect because the percent change in the number of VHS player sales from 1995 to 2005 is more than half of the percent change in the number of VHS tape sales from 1995 to 2000.

267. **a.** The question asks about the product with the score that is the statistical mode. Product A had the most testers give it the same score (a score of 5), therefore this is the mode. Choice **b** is incorrect because only 35 testers gave Product B a score of 2. Choice **c** is incorrect because only 58 testers gave Product C a score of 3. Choice **d** is incorrect because only 80 testers gave Product D a score of 4.

d. The question asks for the average score on all e-readers and tablets. Because a majority of the scores were 4 and 5, the average is most likely between 4 and 5. Choice **a** is incorrect because no products scored a 1 and only Product B scored a 2 thirty-five times. Choice **b** is incorrect; less than half of the scores were in this range. Choice **c** is incorrect; less than half of the scores were in this range.

268. **a.** The question asks about the relationship between the water temperature of the lake and the bacteria level. The graph shows that as the water temperature increases, the bacteria level increases, which is a positive relationship. Choice **b** is incorrect because one factor would have to increase while the other factor decreases in order to have a negative relationship. Choice **c** is incorrect because there is a correlation between water temperature values and bacteria levels.

b. The question compares the slope of the line representing the change in water temperature with the slope of the line representing the change in bacteria levels. The line graphed to represent the change in water temperature has a positive slope, and the line graphed to represent the change in bacteria levels has a less positive slope. Choice **a** is incorrect because the slope of the line representing the change in water temperatures if greater than the slope of the line representing bacteria levels. Choice **c** is incorrect because the slopes of the lines are not equal.

269. **b.** The question asks about the relationship between the temperature of the beef sample and the bacterial level. According to the scatterplot, bacteria levels decrease as the temperature increases. Therefore, this is a negative relationship. Choice **a** is incorrect because both factors would have to increase in order to have a positive relationship. Choice **c** is incorrect because there is a correlation between beef temperature and bacteria levels.

a. The question compares the slope of the lines. The regression line has a negative slope, and the dashed line has a very negative slope. Therefore, choice **b** is incorrect because the regression line has a less negative slope than the dashed line. Choice **c** is incorrect because the slopes of the lines are not equal.

270. **a.** The question asks about the relationship between the age of the tires on a vehicle and the rate of deceleration. According to the scatterplot, the rate of deceleration increases as the tires increase in age. Therefore, this is a positive relationship. Choice **b** is incorrect because one factor would have to increase while the other factor decreases in order to have a negative relationship. Choice **c** is incorrect because there is a correlation between the age of the tires on a vehicle and the rate of deceleration.

a. The question compares the slope of the lines. The regression line has a positive slope, and the dashed line has a very positive slope. Choice **b** is incorrect because the slope of the regression line is not greater than the slope of the dashed line. Choice **c** is incorrect because the slopes of the lines are not equal.

271. **a.** The question asks about the relationship between the running speed and the lactic acid levels. According to the graph, as the speed of the runner increases, the lactic acid levels in the runner increase. Therefore, the relationship is positive. Choice **b** is incorrect because one factor would have to increase while the other decreases in order to have a negative relationship. Choice **c** is incorrect because there is a correlation between the running speed and the lactic acid levels.

a. The question compares the slope of the line between Point *A* and Point *B* with the slope of the line between Point *C* and Point *D*. The slope of the line between Point *A* and Point *B* is 2/5, whereas the slope of the line between Point *C* and Point *D* is 8/5. Therefore, the slope of the line between Point *A* and Point *B* is less than the slope of the line between Point *C* and Point *D*. Choice **b** is incorrect because the slope of the line between Point *A* and Point *B* is not greater than the slope of the line between Point *C* and Point *D*. Choice **c** is incorrect because the slopes of the lines are not equal.

272. **a.** The question asks about percentage of the fossils that are Cretaceous. According to the map, there are 5 Cretaceous fossils and 20 Jurassic fossils found in the dig. Therefore, there are 5 Cretaceous fossils out of a total of 25 fossils, so 20% of the fossils found are Cretaceous fossils. Choice **b** is incorrect because there are 5 Cretaceous fossils out of a total of 25 fossils, not 5 Cretaceous fossils out of a total of 20 fossils. Choice **c** is incorrect because there are 5 Cretaceous fossils out of a total of 25 fossils, not 20 Cretaceous fossils out of a total of 25 fossils.

b. The question asks about the portion of all Jurassic fossils that were found in Section I of the map. According to the map, a total of 20 Jurassic fossils were found, and 8 of them were found in Section I. Therefore, 8 out of 20, or about one half, of all Jurassic fossils were found in Section I. Choice **a** is incorrect because more than 5 Jurassic fossils were found in Section I. Choice **c** is incorrect because 8 out of 20 of all Jurassic fossils were found in Section I, not 15 out of 20.

273. **b.** The question asks the percent that the color green takes up in the spectrum of visible light. According to the diagram, green takes up roughly one quarter, or 25%, of the visible light spectrum. Choice **a** is incorrect because green takes up about 25% of the visible light spectrum; violet takes up about 5% of the visible light spectrum. Choice **c** is incorrect because no colors take up nearly half of the visible light spectrum.

a. The question asks about the color that both begins the visible light spectrum and additionally begins the light in the spectrum that has a 10^{15} Hz frequency. According to the diagram, the visible light spectrum begins at 10^{15} Hz frequency, and the color that begins at this frequency is violet. Choice **b** is incorrect because green has a lower frequency than 10^{15} Hz frequency. Choice **c** is incorrect because white is not a color in the visible light spectrum on the diagram. Choice **d** is incorrect because red does not begin the visible light spectrum and has a frequency closer to $10^{14.5}$ Hz.

274. **c.** The question asks the percent of the length of the roots of the common ninebark that are taken up by the roots of the buffalo grass. According to the diagram, the roots of the buffalo grass are 8 feet long, and the roots of the common ninebark are 15 feet long. Therefore, the roots of the buffalo grass are about 50% the length of the roots of the common ninebark. Choice **a** is incorrect because the roots of the buffalo grass are 8 feet long, not 3 feet long. Choice **b** is incorrect because the roots of the buffalo grass are 8 feet long, not 5 feet long.

b. The question asks the fraction of the length of the entire common ninebark plant that are taken up by the roots of the Black-Eyed Susan. According to the diagram, the common ninebark plant is 4 feet tall with 15-foot roots. So its total length is 19 feet. The roots of the Black-Eyed Susan are 6 feet long. Therefore, the roots of the Black-Eyed Susan are about a third of the length of the entire common ninebark plant. Choice **a** is incorrect because the roots of the Black-Eyed Susan are 6 feet long, not 1.9 feet long. Choice **c** is incorrect because the roots of the Black-Eyed Susan are 6 feet long, not 9.5 feet long.

Two-Part Analysis

Two-part analysis questions are one question type you'll see in the integrated reasoning section of the GMAT. With two-part analysis questions, you will be asked questions that have two-part solutions. The solutions will be provided in a table with several columns. In order to answer these questions, you must choose correct answers from column 3. The correct answers are deductions best supported by the details in the text or by provided formulas and information.

Test-Taking Tips

When working on the two-part analysis questions of the GMAT, there are a few techniques to keep in mind that can help you improve your score. Practice using the following techniques when answering the two-part analysis questions in this book.

How Should I Work on Two-Part Analysis Questions?

- Begin by reading the question carefully.
  Be sure to read the entire question, including any text and formulas provided.
- Read all the answer choices in the columns.
  The answer choices often provide important information that you will need to solve the problem. So, read all the answer choices carefully. For example, a question may ask you to determine which answer choice fits a series of requirements. To answer the question correctly, you will need to assess each of the answer choices.
- Eliminate any clearly incorrect answer choices.
  You may be able to spot a clearly incorrect answer immediately once you've seen the answer choices provided. If so, focus on the remaining answer choices.

What Do I Do if I Don't Know the Answer?

- Try to make an educated guess.
  Use the information you know and understand to choose the best answer that you can.
- Do not skip the question unless you are sure you do not know the answer.
  With the computerized GMAT, you will be unable to return to the question later.
- Make sure you understand the question and the answer choices.
  Take a moment to reread the statements and to review the answer choices. You may have misunderstood the question or missed a key word (such as "not" or "only"). Once you are sure you clearly understand what the question is asking, try to answer it again.
- Give yourself another minute or two to answer the question, but do not take too long.
  You want to be sure to answer the question correctly, but you also want to have enough time to answer all the questions on the test. Be sure to maintain a calm, even pace as you work on the question, and try to avoid wasting time

General GMAT Tips and Techniques

- Use scrap paper.

  Scrap paper is a key tool on the GMAT. You can write down answer choices that you've eliminated. You can also write down key pieces of information from the questions and the answer choices.

- Pace yourself.

  Give yourself enough time to read and comprehend the question, but be conscientious about your time. Managing your time wisely will help you have enough time to finish the test—or complete as many questions as possible.

- Be sure you have everything you need before you begin the test. Be sure you have pencils, paper, and anything else you need before beginning the test.

- Try to answer all the questions on the test.

  Answering all the questions on the test is a way to shoot for a higher score. Of course, you may encounter questions you do not know how to answer. While you do not want to wildly guess at the answers, you do want to try to make educated guesses. Even if you can eliminate one answer choice as incorrect, you have improved your chances of picking the correct answer for that question. So try to answer all the questions, or as many questions as possible.

Set 11

Now it is time to answer GMAT Two-Part Analysis practice questions that have been designed to test your integrated reasoning skills. Good luck!

275. The XP Racer is a new electric scooter. When driving on smooth city roads, the XP Racer's energy efficiency is X kilometers per joule (X km/J) when traveling at a constant speed of Y kilometers per hour (Y km/h).

In terms of the variables X and Y, select the expression that best represents the number of joules of electricity used in one hour of traveling on smooth city roads at a constant speed of Y. Then, select the expression that represents the number of joules of electricity used in a 100 km drive traveling on smooth city roads at a constant speed of Y. Make only two selections, one in each column.

Joules of electricity in 1 hour	Joules of electricity in 100 kilometers	
		Y/X
		X/Y
		$100/X$
		$100/Y$
		$X/100$
		$Y/100$

276. At a hot dog eating contest, one contestant ate at a constant rate of H hot dogs per minute (H hot dogs/min.). The contestant had burned calories from activity during the contest and taken in calories from eating the hot dogs for an overall caloric intake of C calories per hot dog (C calories/hot dog).

In terms of the variables H and C, select the expression that best represents the number of calories taken in during one minute of eating at a constant rate. Then, select the expression that represents the number of calories taken in if the contestant had eaten 100 hot dogs at a constant rate of H. Make only two selections, one in each column.

Calories taken in during 1 minute	Calories taken in if the contestant ate 100 hot dogs	
		C/H
		H/C
		C^2
		H^2
		$(C)(H)$
		$(C)(100)$

277. A survival instructor teaches a class how to survive when lost in the wild. The survival instructor takes the class hiking through the woods and makes sure to keep his water loss through sweat at around W meters per liter of water lost (W m/L) when hiking at a constant speed of S meters per hour (S m/h).

In terms of the variables W and S, select the expression that best represents the number of liters of water lost in one hour of hiking in the woods at a constant speed of S. Then, select the expression that represents the number of liters of water lost in a 1,000 m hike traveling at a constant speed of S. Make only two selections, one in each column.

Liters of water in 1 hour	Liters of water in 1,000 meters	
		W/S
		S/W
		$1{,}000/W$
		$1{,}000/S$
		$W/1{,}000$
		$S/1{,}000$

278. A marathon runner's energy efficiency is C meters per calorie (C m/cal) when running at a rate of M meters per second (M m/s).

In terms of the variables C and M, select the expression that best represents the number of calories used in one hour of running at a constant rate of M. Then, select the expression that represents the number of calories used in a 500-meter race while running at a constant rate of M. Make only two selections, one in each column.

Calories used in 1 hour	Calories used in a 500-meter race	
		500/C
		500/M
		C/500
		M/500
		C/M
		M/C

279. The following excerpt from a fictitious science news report discusses a fictitious type of pollutant called *tritans*.

> For years, scientists have studied the effects of tritans on birds' eggs, but recently scientists have also discovered that tritans affect other egg-laying species. Tritans were known to cause birds to lay their eggs too early and also weaken the shell of eggs. As a result, embryos in the eggs have less of a chance to survive. Fewer eggs resulted in live offspring, and the numbers of these species of birds diminished. Now, scientists recently discovered that the decreasing numbers of certain species of lizards has also been caused by tritans. These species of lizards tend to bury their eggs in sand nests, whereas the birds had nests in trees. Scientists are now researching the source of the tritans in order to limit tritans pollution in the environment.

Based on the definition of the imaginary word *tritans* that can be inferred from the previous paragraph, which of the following traits of a pollutant must be true for that pollutant to be tritans and which must NOT be true for that pollutant to be tritans? Make only two selections, one in each column.

Must be true	Must not be true	*Traits of a pollutant*
		Decrease the number of eggs laid
		Comes from the water supply
		Increases the number of embryos that die
		Builds up in animals' bodies
		Thickens the shell of eggs

280. The following excerpt from a fictitious economics news article focuses on a type of financial exchange called an *M.T.B.*

> After the recent banking collapse, new regulations have forced larger banks to acknowledge all M.T.B. exchanges that exceed $250,000. Banks that do not disclose this information to the government will risk losing all federal bailout monies. In addition, all M.T.B.s involving IPOs must be disclosed to all shareholders on a quarterly basis. While the long-term effects of this new regulation cannot be predicted, the goal of this regulation is to limit the number of annual M.T.B. exchanges that larger banks conduct.

Based on the definition of the imaginary word *M.T.B.* that can be inferred from the previous paragraph, which of the following traits of a financial exchange must be true for that financial exchange to be an M.T.B. and which must NOT be true for that financial exchange to be an M.T.B.? Make only two selections, one in each column.

Must be true to be an *M.T.B.*	Must not be true to be an *M.T.B.*	*Traits of a financial exchange*
		Must be disclosed to shareholders of IPOs
		Not regulated by the government
		Involving more than $250,000
		Occurring every three months
		Happens at all banks

281. The following excerpt from a fictitious veterinary textbook discusses a fictitious type of disease called *spurnit*.

> The diagnosis of spurnit in dogs can be difficult as symptoms do not always manifest until the disease has progressed. Unlike other illnesses that cause an increase in swelling in the glands, spurnit does not, making early detection difficult. Nonetheless, early symptoms include a slightly swollen tongue and/or an elevated level of white blood cells. Early detection is key because the treatment of spurnit varies depending on the duration the dog has carried the disease. Early treatments can involve a simple course of antibiotics and then a year-long daily regimen of probiotics. Later stages of the disease often tend to resist all treatments, but daily blood transfusions have been shown to ease symptoms in certain cases.

Based on the definition of the imaginary word *spurnit* that can be inferred from the previous paragraph, which of the following are definitely traits of spurnit and which of the following are definitely NOT spurnit? Make only two selections, one in each column.

Trait of spurnit	NOT trait of spurnit	
		Only affects dogs
		Causes glands to swell
		Can be detected in a basic exam
		Causes more white blood cells
		Transmitted by the mouth

282. The following excerpt from a fictitious camping guidebook focuses on a fictitious type of plant called *poison senity*.

> Poison senity thrives only in a limited region of the Pacific Northwest. The oily coating and sap from the poison senity, known as urushiol, can cause itching, burning, and severe blistering on the skin. Notable features of poison senity include its five almond-shaped leaflets and its aroma. While being similar to poison ivy and poison oak, the injuries caused by the urushiol produced by poison senity can be much more severe because poison senity's urushiol can take a longer time to have an effect. As a result, sufferers do not realize that they have the oils on their skin and can transfer the poisonous oils to more places on their body. Typical places are the hands, legs, mouth, neck, and eyes. A person exposed to poison senity's urushiol should wash the area with soap and warm water immediately and seek medical help.

Based on the definition of the imaginary plant *poison senity* that can be inferred from the previous paragraph, which of the following characteristics of a plant must be true for that plant to be a poison senity, and which must NOT be true for that plant to be a poison senity? Make only two selections, one in each column.

Must be true	Must not be true	*Traits of a plant*
		Causes high fevers
		Common through parts of the United States
		Grows best in damp climates
		Poisonous oil spreads easily
		Can be fatal if swallowed

283. The following excerpt from a fictitious advertisement discusses a fictitious type of acne treatment called *Clarens*.

> Clarens users have reported a dramatic improvement in their acne and skin irritations. Most users prefer Clarens to other acne treatments. That is because Clarens is specially formulated to fight acne in all its forms: whiteheads, blackheads, regular pimples, and the scars that can form from acne as it heals. The Clarens treatment comes in three parts. First, a simple tea tree oil facial wash to rid the pores of dirt. Second, a benzoyl peroxide ointment that can be spread over the whole face or dabbed on problem areas. Unlike other acne treatments, the Clarens ointment contains a stronger dosage of benzoyl peroxide than other brands, but Clarens doesn't irritate the skin. Lastly, the Clarens treatment includes to-go washes that contains salicylic acid. No other brand on the market offers these special washes.

Based on the definition of the imaginary brand *Clarens* that can be inferred from the previous paragraph, which of the following describes an acne treatment that must be Clarens and which of the following describes an acne treatment that is NOT Clarens? Make only two selections, one in each column.

Must be Clarens	Must NOT be Clarens	
		Can be used to wash the face
		A form of salicylic acid that can be used outside the home
		A strict face regimen that must be adhered to
		Free of dyes, perfumes, and chemicals
		Gentle on the skin

284. Country A presently produces 4 billion tons of carbon emissions each year. Country B presently produces 5 billion tons of carbon emissions each year. The carbon emissions produced by both countries is increasing yearly, each at its own constant rate. Scientists predict that both countries will maintain their constant yearly increase in carbon emissions. In addition, scientists predict that Country A and Country B will produce the same carbon emissions in 10 years, and Country A will produce more carbon emissions than Country B after 10 years.

In the following table, identify the rate of increase in carbon emissions per year for both countries that support the scientists' predictions. Make only one selection in each column.

Country A	Country B	Rate of Carbon Emission Increase (billions of tons each year)
		0.05
		0.15
		0.50
		1
		5
		15

285. During a period of time when the price of gas is on the rise, Gas Station X charges $3.40 a gallon and Gas Station Y charges $4.00 a gallon. Both gas stations are increasing the cost they charge for gas each week, each at its own constant rate. If both gas stations continue to increase their costs at their constant rates, they will be charging the same price for gas four weeks from now, and Gas Station Y will charge more than Gas Station X in subsequent weeks.

In the following table, identify the rate of increase per week for the cost of gas for both gas stations that supports the predictions stated in the paragraph. Make only one selection in each column.

Gas Station X	Gas Station Y	Rate of Cost of Gas Increase (each week)
		$0.01
		$0.05
		$0.10
		$0.15
		$0.20
		$0.45

286. University A currently has 20,000 students enrolled. University B currently has 22,500 students enrolled. The number of students enrolling in University A and the number of students enrolling in University B increases each year, each at its own constant rate. The deans of the universities project that if each university maintains its constant rate of student enrollment increase, five years from now they will both have the same number of students enrolled, and University A will have more students enrolled than University B in subsequent years.

In the following table, identify the rate of increase, in student enrollment per year, for University A and the rate of increase, in student enrollment per year, for University B that are both consistent with the deans' projections. Make only one selection in each column.

University A	University B	*Rate of Increase (students enrolled per year)*
		400
		1,000
		1,500
		1,800
		2,200
		2,600

287. Environmental scientists studying endangered species in a given region have observed that there are presently 800 members of Species X in the region and 600 members of Species Y in the region. The number of each species is decreasing annually, each at its own constant rate. Environmental scientists predict that both species will maintain their constant yearly decrease in numbers. In addition, environmental scientists predict that if both species maintain their constant rate of decrease, 10 years from now they will for the first time have the same number of members, and in subsequent years there will be fewer Species X than Species Y.

In the following table, identify the rate of decrease in the numbers of each species per year that supports the environmental scientists' predictions. Make only one selection in each column.

Species X	Species Y	Rate of Decrease of Species (in number of members per year)
		20
		40
		50
		200
		400
		500

288. Athlete A currently trains 180 minutes each week. Athlete B currently trains 250 minutes each week. Both athletes A and B are increasing the number of minutes spent training each week, both at a different constant rate. If both athletes keep to their constant rate of training increase, in seven weeks from now, they will be training for the same number of minutes each week, and in subsequent weeks, athlete A will train more each week than athlete B.

In the following table, identify the rate of increase in number of training minutes each week for both athletes that support the predictions stated in the last paragraph. Make only one selection in each column.

Athlete A	Athlete B	Rate of Training Increase (number of minutes per week)
		3
		5
		15
		25
		30
		50

289. A caterer offers two menus for large events, such as weddings and conferences. To show the variety of foods the caterer can prepare, one of the menus has entirely meat-free and vegetarian options and the other menu includes two fish options. Neither menu should have more than two hot options. The caterer has already decided on three out of the four options for both menus. Those menus are shown here.

Menu 1	*Menu 2*
Spanish gazpacho (appetizer, vegetarian, cold)	Thai shrimp soup (appetizer, hot)
Curried tofu (entree, vegetarian, hot)	Salmon tacos (entree, hot)
Bananas flambé (dessert, vegetarian, hot)	Chocolate mousse (dessert, vegetarian, cold)

Select an option that could be added to both menus. Then, select an option that could NOT be added to either menu. Make only two selections, one in each column.

Both menus	Neither menu	*Option*
		Sesame carrot salad (salad, vegetarian, cold)
		Whitefish and tomato salad (salad, cold)
		Hot bread pudding (dessert, vegetarian, hot)
		Beef spring rolls (entree, cold)
		Spinach and wild rice (salad, vegetarian, hot)
		Lobster ravioli (entree, hot)

290. The staff at the Botanical Garden is planning the garden's yearly two-day spring festival intended to celebrate the blooming of the cherry trees. Five events will be offered each day. To celebrate the blooming cherry trees, the majority of events scheduled for at least one day will be located in the Cherry Tree Esplanade in the park. On the other day of the spring festival, at least four of the events can be for children or allow children. Neither day should have more than two events that are just for seniors. The Botanical Garden staff has already agreed on a festival schedule for eight of the ten events. That schedule is shown here.

Day 1	Day 2
Children's Flower Parade (in Cherry Esplanade, ages 0–12)	Face Painting (in Cherry Esplanade, ages 0–12)
Using Blossoms in Paintings (in Cherry Esplanade, ages 5–12)	Yoga for Senior Citizens (in Cherry Esplanade, seniors)
Jazz and Cocktails (seniors only)	Singles Mingle with Music (ages 21 and up)
String Quartet Playing Mozart (ages 0 and up)	Dancing among Blossoms: Learn to Waltz (all ages)

Select an event that could be added to the schedule for either day. Then, select an event that could be added to the schedule for neither day. Make only two selections, one in each column.

Either day	Neither day	Event
		Lecture on the History of the Gardens (ages 21 and up)
		Creating Your Own Garden (all ages)
		Making Cherry Ice Cream (in Cherry Esplanade, all ages)
		Blossoms: Puppet Show (Main Theater, ages 0–12)
		Senior Walking Tour (in Cherry Esplanade, seniors)

291. The American Arts department at a small museum is organizing an exhibit focused on Georgia O'Keeffe. Her work will be featured in two rooms of the museum. Both rooms have space to accommodate five of her paintings. The museum wants a majority of the paintings in one room to be O'Keeffe paintings that include skulls or bones. In the other room, the museum wants at least four of the paintings to be from 1935 or later. Neither room should have more than two O'Keeffe paintings of buildings of any sort. The museum has already decided on eight of the paintings for these two rooms. The plan is shown here.

Room 1	Room 2
"Cow's Skull: Red, White, and Blue," 1931	"Red Hills with Flowers," 1937
"Church Steeple," 1930	"Ram's Head, Blue Morning Glory," 1938
"Ranchos Church," 1930	"Ram's Head with Holly-hock," 1935
"Cow's Skull with Calico Roses," 1931	"Horse's Skull with White Rose," 1931

Select a painting that could work for both rooms. Then, select a painting that could NOT work in either room. Make only two selections, one in each column.

Both rooms	Neither room	*Paintings*
		"Calla Lillies on Red," 1928
		"Sky Above Clouds," 1965
		"White Rose," 1927
		"Church Bell, Ward Colorado," 1917
		"Deer's Skull with Pedernal," 1936

292. A nonprofit literary group in the United States is organizing a day-long poetry event for the community. Five poets will read in the morning, and another five poets will read in the afternoon. To make sure that the poets engage a young audience, the literary group wants a majority of poets in one part of the event to be born after 1970. The other part of the event should have at least four women poets. Neither part of the event should have more than two poets from other countries. The literary group has already agreed on a plan for eight of the ten poets. That plan, showing names along with each poet's birth year and country of origin, is shown here.

Morning	Afternoon
Matthew Dickman (male, born 1975, USA)	Tracy K. Smith (female, born 1972, USA)
Kwame Dawes (male, born 1962, Ghana)	Jo Shapcott (female, born 1953, England)
Erika Metiner (female, born 1975, USA)	Coral Bracho (female, born 1951, Mexico)
Aimee Nezhukumatathiln (female, born 1974, USA)	Amiri Baraka (male, born 1934, USA)

Select a poet who could be added to either the morning or the afternoon. Then, select a poet who could NOT be added to either the morning or the afternoon. Make only two selections, one in each column.

Both morning and afternoon	Neither morning nor afternoon	*Poet*
		Rita Dove (female, born 1952, USA)
		Claribel Alegria (female, born 1924, Nicaragua)
		Camille Dungy (female, born 1972, USA)
		Natasha Trethewey (female, born 1966, USA)
		Kazim Ali (male, born 1971, USA)

Answers—Set 11

275. **Column 1, line 1.** The question asks about using two variables to determine the number of joules of electricity used in one hour of driving in certain circumstances. For column 1, line 2 (X/Y) is incorrect because the result would be in terms of the number of hours, not the number of joules. Line 3 ($100/X$) is incorrect because this determines the amount of electricity used when driving 100 kilometers. Line 4 ($100/Y$) is incorrect because the answer would be in terms of the number of hours. Line 5 ($X/100$) is incorrect because this simply divides the energy efficiency by 100 and does not show the number of joules used in one hour of driving. Line 6 ($Y/100$) is incorrect because this divides the speed by 100 and does not show the number of joules used in one hour of driving.

 Column 2, line 3. The question asks about using two variables to determine the number of joules of electricity used when driving 100 kilometers in certain circumstances. For column 2, line 1 (Y/X) is incorrect because dividing speed by energy efficiency doesn't determine the amount of energy used in 100 kilometers. Line 2 (X/Y) is incorrect because dividing energy efficiency by speed doesn't determine the amount of energy used in 100 kilometers. Line 4 ($100/Y$) is incorrect because the answer would be in terms of the number of hours, not number of joules. Line 5 ($X/100$) is incorrect because dividing the energy efficiency by 100 does not show the number of joules used when driving 100 kilometers. Line 6 ($Y/100$) is incorrect because dividing the speed by 100 does not show the number of joules used when driving 100 kilometers.

276. Column 1, line 5. The question asks about using two variables to determine the number of calories taken in during one minute of eating hot dogs at a constant rate. For column 1, line 1 (C/H) is incorrect because dividing the number of calories per hot dog by the rate at which the contestant ate hot dogs does not result in finding out the number of calories taken in during one minute. Line 2 (H/C) is incorrect because dividing the rate at which the contestant ate hot dogs by the number of calories per hot dog does not result in finding out the number of calories taken in during one minute. Line 3 (C^2) is incorrect because this only involves the number of calories per hot dog and does not involve a unit of time. Line 4 (H^2) is incorrect because this only involves the number of hot dogs eaten over time and does not involve finding out the caloric intake. Line 6 (C)(100) is incorrect because this does not involve time.

Column 2, line 6. The question asks about using two variables to determine the number of calories taken in if the contestant ate 100 hot dogs at a constant rate. For column 2, line 1 (C/H) is incorrect because dividing the number of calories per hot dog by the rate at which the contestant ate hot dogs does not result in finding out the number of calories taken in from eating 100 hot dogs. Line 2 (H/C) is incorrect because dividing the rate at which the contestant ate hot dogs by the number of calories per hot dog does not result in finding out the number of calories taken in from eating 100 hot dogs. Line 3 (C^2) is incorrect because this only involves the number of calories per hot dog and does not involve a specific number of hot dogs. Line 4 (H^2) is incorrect because this only involves the number of hot dogs eaten over time and does not involve finding out the caloric intake. Line 5 (C)(H) is incorrect because it results in finding out the number of calories taken in from one minute of eating, not the number of calories taken in from eating 100 hot dogs.

277. **Column 1, line 2.** The question asks about using two variables to determine the number of liters of water lost in one hour of hiking in the woods at a constant speed. For column 1, line 1 (W/S) is incorrect because dividing the number of meters walked per liter of water lost by the hiking speed does not result in finding out the number of liters of water lost. Line 3 ($1,000/W$) is incorrect because dividing 1,000 by the rate at which water is lost does not involve a unit of time. Line 4 ($1,000/S$) is incorrect because this only involves the hiking speed and does not involve a unit of time. Line 5 ($W/1,000$) is incorrect because dividing the rate at which the water is lost by 1,000 diminishes the rate and does not result in finding out the amount of water lost in one hour. Line 6 (S)($1,000$) is incorrect because dividing the speed by 1,000 diminishes the speed and does not result in finding out the amount of water lost in one hour.

Column 2, line 3. The question asks about using two variables to determine the number of liters of water lost hiking 1,000 meters in the woods at a constant speed. For column 2, line 1 (W/S) is incorrect because dividing the number of meters walked per liter of water lost by the hiking speed does not result in finding out the number of liters of water lost. Line 2 (S/W) is incorrect because dividing the hiking speed by the number of meters walked per liter of water lost does not involve 1,000 meters. Line 4 ($1,000/S$) is incorrect because dividing the distance by the hiking speed doesn't result in the number of liters of water lost. Line 5 ($W/1,000$) is incorrect because dividing the rate at which the water is lost by 1,000 diminishes the rate and does not result in finding out the amount of water lost when walking 1,000 meters. Line 6 (S)($1,000$) is incorrect because dividing the speed by 1,000 diminishes the speed and does not result in finding out the amount of water lost when walking 1,000 meters.

278. Column 1, line 6. The question asks about using two variables to determine the number of calories used when a marathon runner runs for one hour at a constant rate. Column 1, line 1 (500/*C*) is incorrect because the question asks about the calories burned in one hour, not when running 500 meters. Line 2 (500/*M*) is incorrect because the question asks about the calories burned in one hour, not when running 500 meters. Line 3 (*C*/500) is incorrect because the question asks about the calories burned in one hour, not when running 500 meters. Line 4 (*M*/500) is incorrect because the question asks about the calories burned in one hour, not when running 500 meters. Line 5 (*C*/*M*) is incorrect because dividing the energy efficiency by the rate does not result in finding out the number of calories used in one hour.

Column 2, line 1. The question asks about using two variables to determine the number of calories used when a marathon runner runs a 500-meter race at a constant rate. For column 2, line 2 (500/*M*) is incorrect because the question asks about the number of calories. Therefore, the distance must be divided by the energy efficiency, not by the running rate. Line 3 (*C*/500) is incorrect because the question asks about the number of calories. Therefore, the distance must be divided by the energy efficiency, not the energy efficiency divided by the distance. Line 4 (*M*/500) is incorrect because this would result in a number of seconds, not a number of calories. Line 5 (*C*/*M*) is incorrect because dividing the energy efficiency by the rate does not result in finding out the number of calories used when running 500 meters. Line 6 (*M*/*C*) is incorrect because dividing the rate by the energy efficiency does not result in finding out the number of calories used when running 500 meters.

279. Column 1, line 3. The question asks about determining a trait that the imaginary pollution tritans has based on the details in the paragraph. For column 1, line 1 is incorrect because there are no details to suggest that tritans decrease the number of eggs laid. Line 2 is incorrect because the paragraph states that scientists are "researching the source of the tritans," so this does not support the idea that tritans come from the water supply. Line 4 is incorrect because the paragraph is focused on the effects on eggs, not animals' bodies. Line 5 is incorrect because the paragraph states that tritans "weaken the shell of eggs," not thicken the eggshells.

Column 2, line 5. The question asks about determining a trait that the imaginary pollution tritans must NOT have based on the details in the paragraph. For column 2, line 1 is incorrect because there are no details in the paragraph to suggest that tritans do or do not decrease the number of eggs laid. Line 2 is incorrect because the paragraph states that scientists are "researching the source of the tritans," so tritans could come from the water supply. Line 3 is incorrect because the paragraph states that fewer eggs survive, so this is a trait of titans. Line 4 is incorrect because there are no details about this in the paragraph, so it could be a trait of titans.

280. **Column 1, line 1.** The question asks about a trait that an imaginary type of financial exchange called an *M.T.B.* must have based on the details in the paragraph. For column 1, line 2 is incorrect because the paragraph states that there are new regulations. Line 3 is incorrect because, while M.T.B. exchanges greater than $250,000 must be acknowledged, being greater than $250,000 is not necessarily a trait of M.T.B.s. Line 4 is incorrect because, while M.T.B.s involving IPOs must be disclosed quarterly (or every three months), this does not necessarily mean that all M.T.B.s happen every three months. Line 5 is incorrect because there are no details in the paragraph to suggest that all banks conduct this type of exchange.

Column 2, line 2. The question asks about a trait that must NOT describe the imaginary type of financial exchange called an *M.T.B.* For column 2, line 1 is incorrect because the paragraph states that certain types of M.T.B.s "must be disclosed to all shareholders." Line 3 is incorrect because the paragraph states that some M.T.B. exchanges are greater than $250,000. Line 4 is incorrect because there are no details to determine whether M.T.B. exchanges happen every three months. Line 5 is incorrect because there are no details in the paragraph to determine whether all banks conduct this type of exchange.

281. **Column 1, line 4.** The question asks about an imaginary type of disease called *spurnit* and a trait that spurnit definitely has. For column 1, line 1 is incorrect because, while the paragraph focuses on diagnosing the disease in dogs, the paragraph never states that the disease only occurs in dogs. Line 2 is incorrect because the paragraph states that spurnit is unlike diseases that "cause an increase in swelling in the glands." Line 3 is incorrect because the paragraph states that detection "can be difficult." Line 5 is incorrect because, while the paragraph states that the disease affects the tongue, the paragraph never describes the transmission of the disease.

Column 2, line 2. The question asks about an imaginary type of disease called *spurnit* and a trait that spurnit definitely does NOT have. For column 2, line 1 is incorrect because the paragraph describes diagnosing the disease in dogs. Line 3 is incorrect because, while the paragraph states that detection "can be difficult," it also states that symptoms can manifest and be detected early. Line 4 is incorrect because the paragraph states that the disease results in an "elevated level of white blood cells." Line 5 is incorrect because, while the paragraph states that the disease affects the tongue, the paragraph never describes the transmission of the disease.

282. **Column 1, line 4.** The question asks about an imaginary type of plant called *poison senity* and a characteristic that poison senity definitely has. For column 1, line 1 is incorrect because the paragraph never states that poison senity causes fevers. Line 2 is incorrect because the paragraph states that poison senity "thrives only in a limited region of the Pacific Northwest." Line 3 is incorrect because, while the paragraph states poison senity thrives in the Pacific Northwest, which tends to be damp, the paragraph never states that poison senity grows best in damp climates. Line 5 is incorrect because no information is provided in the paragraph about what happens if poison senity is swallowed.

Column 2, line 2. The question asks about an imaginary type of plant called *poison senity* and a characteristic that does NOT describe poison senity. For column 2, line 1 is incorrect because poison senity could cause fevers; this information is not provided in the paragraph. Line 3 is incorrect because poison senity could thrive in damp climates, but no information specifically regarding dampness is provided in the paragraph. Line 4 is incorrect because the paragraph states that the oils from poison senity can transfer to "more places" on the body, which suggests that the oils transfer easily. Line 5 is incorrect because poison senity could be fatal if swallowed, but no information about this is provided in the paragraph.

283. **Column 1, line 2.** The question asks about an imaginary type of acne treatment called *Clarens* and a description that only pertains to Clarens. For column 1, line 1 is incorrect because the other acne treatments or soaps could be used to wash the face, not just Clarens. Line 3 is incorrect because, while the paragraph suggests that there is a regimen involved using Clarens, there is no information to support the idea that Clarens is the only product that involves a regimen. Line 4 is incorrect because there is no information about "dyes, perfumes, and chemicals" in the paragraph. Line 5 is incorrect because, while the paragraph states that Clarens doesn't irritate the skin and so could be assumed to be gentle, there is no information to suggest that other brands are not also gentle on the skin.
Column 2, line 4. The question asks about an imaginary type of acne treatment called *Clarens* and a description that does NOT pertain to Clarens. For column 2, line 1 is incorrect because Clarens includes a "simple tea tree oil facial wash," so it could be used to wash the face. Line 2 is incorrect because Clarens has "to-go washes that contains salicylic acid," so this form of salicylic acid can be used outside the home. Line 3 is incorrect because the paragraph states that Clarens comes in three parts, which suggests that there is a regimen. Line 5 is incorrect because the paragraph states that Clarens doesn't irritate the skin, which suggests that it is gentle on the skin.

284. **Column 1, line 2.** The question asks about the rate of increase in carbon emissions for Country A that would cause Country A's carbon emissions to be the same as Country B's carbon emissions in 10 years and greater than Country B's carbon emissions after 10 years. For column 1, line 1 is incorrect because this would cause Country A's carbon emissions to increase by only 0.5 billion tons in 10 years, resulting in Country A's carbon emissions reaching only 4.5 billion tons. This is not equal to Country B's carbon emissions. Line 3 is incorrect because this would cause Country A's carbon emissions to increase by 5 billion tons in 10 years, resulting in Country A's carbon emissions reaching 9 billion tons. There are no rates provided for Country B that would cause it to reach 9 billion tons of carbon emissions in 10 years. Line 4 is incorrect because this would cause Country A to produce 14 billion tons of carbon emissions in 10 years. In order for the countries to produce equal carbon emissions, Country B would have to produce 9 billion tons

more in 10 years, and there are no rates that support that increase for Country B. Line 5 is incorrect because this would cause Country A to produce 54 billion tons of carbon emissions in 10 years. In order for the countries to produce equal carbon emissions, Country B would have to produce 49 billion tons more in 10 years, and there are no rates that support that increase for Country B. Line 6 is incorrect because this would cause Country A to produce 154 billion tons of carbon emissions in 10 years. In order for the countries to produce equal carbon emissions, Country B would have to produce 159 billion tons more in 10 years, and there are no rates that support that increase for Country B.

Column 2, line 1. The question asks about the rate of increase in carbon emissions for Country B that would cause Country B's carbon emissions to be the same as Country A's carbon emissions in 10 years and less than Country A's carbon emissions after 10 years. For column 2, line 2 is incorrect because this would cause Country B's carbon emissions to increase by 1.5 billion tons in 10 years, resulting in Country B's carbon emissions reaching 6.5 billion tons. There are no rates in column 2 for Country A that would cause it to increase by 2.5 billion tons in 10 years. Line 3 is incorrect because this would cause Country B's carbon emissions to increase by 5 billion tons in 10 years, resulting in Country B's carbon emissions reaching 10 billion tons. There are no rates in column 2 for Country A that would cause it to reach 10 billion tons of carbon emissions in 10 years. Line 4 is incorrect because this would cause Country B to produce 15 billion tons of carbon emissions in 10 years. In order for the countries to produce equal carbon emissions, Country A would have to produce 11 billion tons more in 10 years, and there are no rates that support that increase for Country A. Line 5 is incorrect because this would cause Country B to produce 55 billion tons of carbon emissions in 10 years. In order for the countries to produce equal carbon emissions, Country A would have to produce 51 billion tons more in 10 years, and there are no rates that support that increase for Country A. Line 6 is incorrect because this would cause Country B to produce 155 billion tons of carbon emissions in 10 years. In order for the countries to produce equal carbon emissions, Country A would have to produce 151 billion tons more in 10 years, and there are no rates that support that increase for Country A.

285. Column 1, line 5. The question asks about the rate of increase in the cost of gas for Gas Station X that would cause Gas Station X's price for gas to be the same as Gas Station Y's price for gas in four weeks and less than Gas Station Y's price for gas after four weeks. For column 1, line 1 is incorrect because this would cause Gas Station X's price for gas to increase by only $0.04 in 4 weeks, resulting in Gas Station X's price for gas being less than Gas Station Y's price for gas (even if Gas Station Y's price for gas didn't increase). Line 2 is incorrect because this would cause Gas Station X's price for gas to increase by only $0.20 in 4 weeks, resulting in Gas Station X's price for gas being less than Gas Station Y's price for gas (even if Gas Station Y's price for gas didn't increase). Line 3 is incorrect because this would cause Gas Station X's price for gas to increase by only $0.40 in 4 weeks, resulting in Gas Station X's price for gas being less than Gas Station Y's price for gas (even if Gas Station Y's price for gas didn't increase). Line 4 is incorrect because this would cause Gas Station X's price for gas to increase by $0.60, which would cause it to be equal to Gas Station Y's prices if Gas Station Y did not increase its prices over four weeks. Line 6 is incorrect because this would cause Gas Station X's price of gas to increase by $1.80. In order for both the gas stations to be charging the same price in 4 weeks, Gas Station Y's price of gas would have to increase by $1.20 in four weeks, and there are no rates that support that increase. **Column 2, line 2.** The question asks about the rate of increase in the cost of gas for Gas Station Y that would cause Gas Station Y's price for gas to be the same as Gas Station X's price for gas in four weeks and greater than Gas Station X's price for gas after four weeks. For column 2, line 1 is incorrect because this would cause Gas Station Y's price for gas to increase by $0.04 in 4 weeks, resulting in Gas Station Y's price for gas being $4.04. Gas Station X's price of gas would have to increase by $0.64 in four weeks, and there are no rates that support that increase. Line 3 is incorrect because this would cause Gas Station Y's price for gas to increase by $0.40 in 4 weeks, resulting in Gas Station Y's price for gas being $4.40. Gas Station X's price of gas would have to increase by $1.00 in four weeks, and there are no rates that support that increase. Line 4 is incorrect because this would cause Gas Station

Y's price for gas to increase by $0.60 in 4 weeks, resulting in Gas Station Y's price for gas being $4.60. Gas Station X's price of gas would have to increase by $1.20 in four weeks, and there are no rates that support that increase. Line 5 is incorrect because this would cause Gas Station Y's price for gas to increase by $0.80 in 4 weeks, resulting in Gas Station Y's price for gas being $4.80. Gas Station X's price of gas would have to increase by $1.40 in four weeks, and there are no rates that support that increase. Line 6 is incorrect because this would cause Gas Station Y's price for gas to increase by $1.80 in 4 weeks, resulting in Gas Station Y's price for gas being $5.80. Gas Station X's price of gas would have to increase by $1.40 in four weeks, and there are no rates that support that increase.

286. **Column 1, line 3.** The question asks about the rate of increase in student enrollment per year for University A that would cause University A and University B to have the same number of enrolled students in 5 years and for University A to have more enrolled students than University B after five years. For column 1, line 1 is incorrect because this would cause University A's student enrollment to increase by 2,000 students, resulting in 22,000 students enrolled at University A. This will not equal University B's enrollment. Line 2 is incorrect because this would cause University A's student enrollment to increase by 5,000, resulting in 25,000 students enrolled in University A. There are no rates that would cause University B to also have 25,000 students in five years. Line 4 is incorrect because this would cause University A's student enrollment to increase by 9,000, resulting in 29,000 students enrolled in University A. There are no rates that would cause University B to also have 29,000 students in five years. Line 5 is incorrect because this would cause University A's student enrollment to increase by 11,000, resulting in 31,000 students enrolled in University A. There are no rates that would cause University B to also have 31,000 students in five years. Line 6 is incorrect because this would cause University A's student enrollment to increase by 13,000, resulting in 33,000 students enrolled in University A. There are no rates that would cause University B to also have 33,000 students in five years.

Column 2, line 2. The question asks about the rate of increase in student enrollment per year for University B that would cause University A and University B to have the same number of enrolled students in 5 years and for University B to have fewer enrolled students than University A after five years. For column 2, line 1 is incorrect because this would cause University B's student enrollment to increase by 2,000 students, resulting in 24,500 students enrolled at University B. There are no rates to cause University A to have 24,500 students in five years. Line 3 is incorrect because this would cause University B's student enrollment to increase by 7,500, resulting in 30,000 students enrolled in University B. There are no rates that would cause University A's enrollment to increase by 10,000 students in five years. Line 4 is incorrect because this would cause University B's student enrollment to increase by 9,000, resulting in 31,500 students enrolled in University B. There are no rates that would cause University A's enrollment to increase by 11,500 students in five years. Line 5 is incorrect because this would cause University B's student enrollment to increase by 11,000, resulting in 33,500 students enrolled in University B. There are no rates that would cause University A's enrollment to increase by 13,500 students in five years. Line 6 is incorrect because this would cause University B's student enrollment to increase by 13,000, resulting in 35,500 students enrolled in University B. There are no rates that would cause University A's enrollment to increase by 15,500 students in five years.

287. Column 1, line 2. The question asks about the rate of decrease in the numbers of Species X that would cause there to be the same number of members of Species X and Species Y in 10 years and for there to be fewer members of Species X than Species Y in subsequent years. For column 1, line 1 is incorrect because this would cause Species X to decrease by 200 members in 10 years, which would equal the number of member of Species Y only if Species Y did not decrease. Line 3 is incorrect because this would cause Species X to decrease by 500 members in 10 years, which would result in there being 300 members of Species X. Species Y would have to decrease by 300 members in 10 years, and there is no rate that supports this. Line 4 is incorrect because this would cause Species X to decrease by 2,000 members in 10 years, which would result in a negative number and so is not possible. Line 5 is incorrect because this would cause Species X to decrease by 4,000 members in 10 years, which would result in a negative number and so is not possible. Line 6 is incorrect because this would cause Species X to decrease by 5,000 members in 10 years, which would result in a negative number and so is not possible.

Column 2, line 1. The question asks about the rate of decrease in the numbers of Species Y that would cause there to be the same number of members of Species X and Species Y in 10 years and for there to be more members of Species Y than Species X in subsequent years. For column 2, line 2 is incorrect because this would cause Species Y to decrease by 400 members in 10 years, leaving 200 members of Species Y. There are no rates that would result in there being 200 members of Species X in ten years. Line 3 is incorrect because this would cause Species Y to decrease by 500 members in 10 years, which would result in there being 100 members of Species Y. Species X would have to decrease by 700 members in 10 years, and there is no rate that supports this. Line 4 is incorrect because this would cause Species Y to decrease by 2,000 members in 10 years, which would result in a negative number and so is not possible. Line 5 is incorrect because this would cause Species Y to decrease by 4,000 members in 10 years, which would result in a negative number and so is not possible. Line 6 is incorrect because this would cause Species Y to decrease by 5,000 members in 10 years, which would result in a negative number and so is not possible.

288. **Column 1, line 3.** The question asks about the rate of increase in the number of minutes athlete A trains each week that would cause athletes A and B to train the same number of minutes in seven weeks and for athlete A to train more than athlete B in subsequent weeks. For column 1, line 1 is incorrect because this would cause athlete A's training to increase by only 21 minutes in 7 weeks, resulting in athlete A training for 201 minutes. This is not equal to athlete B's training minutes (even if the number of minutes athlete B trains does not increase). Line 2 is incorrect because this would cause athlete A's training to increase by only 35 minutes in 7 weeks, resulting in athlete A training for 215 minutes. This is not equal to athlete B's training minutes (even if the number of minutes athlete B trains does not increase). Line 4 is incorrect because this would cause athlete A's training to increase to a total of 355 minutes by 7 weeks. There are no rates that would cause athlete B to also train 355 minutes per week by 7 weeks. Line 5 is incorrect because this would cause athlete A's training to increase to a total of 390 minutes by 7 weeks. There are no rates that would cause Athlete B to also train 390 minutes per week by 7 weeks. Line 6 is incorrect because this would cause athlete A's training to increase to a total of 530 minutes by 7 weeks. There are no rates that would cause athlete B to also train 530 minutes per week by 7 weeks.

Column 2, line 2. The question asks about the rate of increase in the number of minutes athlete B trains each week that would cause athletes A and B to train the same number of minutes in seven weeks and for athlete B to train for fewer minutes than athlete A in subsequent weeks. For column 2, line 1 is incorrect because this would cause athlete B's training to increase by only 21 minutes in 7 weeks, resulting in athlete B training for 271 minutes. There are no rates that would cause athlete A to train for 271 minutes per week after 7 weeks. Line 3 is incorrect because this would cause athlete B's training to increase by only 105 minutes in 7 weeks, resulting in athlete B training for 355 minutes. There are no rates that would cause athlete A to train for 355 minutes by 7 weeks. Line 4 is incorrect because this would cause athlete B's training to increase to a total of 425 minutes by 7 weeks. There are no rates that would cause athlete A to also train 425 minutes per week by 7 weeks. Line 5 is incorrect because this would cause athlete B's training to increase to a total of 460 minutes by 7 weeks. There are no rates that would cause athlete A to also train 460 minutes per week by 7 weeks. Line 6 is incorrect because this would cause athlete B's training to increase to a total of 600 minutes by 7 weeks. There are no rates that would cause athlete A to also train 600 minutes per week by 7 weeks.

289. **Column 1, line 1.** The question asks about the meal option that could be added to both menus and fulfill the menu requirements. For column 1, lines 2 and 4 are incorrect because these would result in neither menu being vegetarian. Lines 3 and 5 are incorrect because these would result in both menus having more than two hot options. Line 6 is incorrect because this would result in neither menu being vegetarian and both menus having more than two hot options.
Column 2, line 6. The question asks about the meal option that could NOT be added to either menu in order to fulfill the menu requirements. For column 2, line 1 could be added, so this is incorrect. Lines 2 and 4 would result in Menu 1 not being vegetarian, but they could be added to Menu 2. Lines 3 and 5 would result in Menu 2 having too many hot options, but they could be added to Menu 1.

290. **Column 1, line 3.** The question asks about an event that could be added to either day of the spring festival schedule and meet the requirements for the festival. For column 1, lines 1, 2, and 5 are incorrect because these events would result in neither day having four events for children. Line 4 is incorrect because this would result in neither day having a majority of events located in the Cherry Esplanade.
Column 2, line 1. The question asks about an event that could NOT be added to either day of the festival schedule as it would not meet the requirements for the festival. For column 2, line 2 is incorrect because this event could be added to Day 1 in order to have four events for children. Line 3 is incorrect because this would cause both days to have a majority of events in the Cherry Esplanade. Line 4 is incorrect because this event could be added to Day 1 in order to have four events for children. Line 5 is incorrect because this would cause both days to have a majority of events in the Cherry Esplanade.

291. **Column 1, line 5.** The question asks about the painting that could be added to either room that would allow the room to meet the museum's requirements. For column 1, lines 1, 2, and 3 are incorrect because, if any of these paintings were placed in Room 1, then Room 1 would not have a majority of paintings include skulls or bones and would not have four paintings from 1935 or later. Line 4 is incorrect because, if used in Room 1, then Room 1 would have too many paintings about buildings.
Column 2, line 4. The question asks about the painting that could NOT work for both rooms and meet the museum's requirements. For column 2, lines 1 and 3 are incorrect because these paintings could be added to Room 2 and a majority of the paintings in Room 2 would still include skulls and bones. Line 2 is incorrect because it could be added to Room 2 and Room 2 would have four paintings from 1935 or later. Line 5 is incorrect because it could be added to Room 1 and a majority of the paintings in Room 1 would include skulls and bones. Also, it could be added to Room 2 and Room 2 would contain four paintings from 1935 or later.

292. **Column 1, line 3.** The question asks about the poet who could be added to the event's schedule for either morning or afternoon and fulfill the requirements. For column 1, lines 1, 2, and 4 are incorrect because if any of these poets were included in the morning or afternoon sections, then the morning section would not have four women poets or a majority of poets born after 1970. Line 5 is incorrect because if this poet were included, then the morning and afternoon sections would not have four women poets.
Column 2, line 2. The question asks about the poet who could NOT be added to the event's schedule for either morning or afternoon and fulfill the requirements. For column 2, lines 1, 3, and 4 are incorrect because any of these poets could be added to the afternoon in order for the afternoon to have four women poets. Line 5 is incorrect because this poet could be added to the morning in order for the morning to have a majority of poets born after 1970.

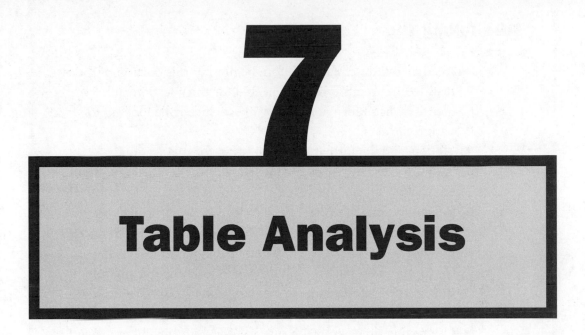

Table Analysis

The table analysis questions in the integrated reasoning portion of the GMAT will require you to analyze and interpret information from multiple sources, and to use and apply the data in a variety of ways. The data displayed in tables will be used to draw conclusions, make inferences, and identify statements that support or refute the information and relationships that exist between different sets of information. Specific content knowledge is not needed; however, being able to identify relationships between, make inferences, and determine when certain conditions are met based on information in a table will be tested in this section. Use of a calculator is permitted on this section of the test.

Test-Taking Tips

- Read directions carefully before beginning this portion of the text. Read through what is expected for the question and identify what information you will specifically be looking for within the data.
- Understand the format of the question for this section. Although content-specific knowledge is not necessary, you will be making conclusions based on information given to you.
- Read questions thoroughly and carefully. Read through the entire question so you are aware of what is necessary to choose the best option. Be aware of whether the question is asking you to choose an option that supports or refutes the information in the table, or whether the question is asking you to choose the statement that says EXCEPT.
- Use testing time wisely. Be sure to pace yourself and not spend too much time on an individual question. It is often helpful to eliminate choices before committing to one.
- Look for trends in data. The trends that exist in the data will assist you in making inferences and choosing the best options for the question.

Set 12

Now it is time to answer GMAT table analysis practice questions that have been designed to test your integrated reasoning skills. Good luck!

293. The following table shows the total number of fast-food restaurants and Type-2 diabetes statistics for six cities in the United States with similar square mileage and population size. Which of the following CANNOT be inferred by the data represented in the table below?

Fast-Food Restaurants and Population of Type-2 Diabetics			
Town	Number of fast-food restaurants	% of reported children diagnosed with Type-2 diabetes under the age of 16	Overall % of population with Type-2 diabetes
Rockville	24	8	15
Medford	29	15	19
Pittsfield	21	5	7
Beaver Creek	37	19	23
Greene	40	20	25
Lewistown	28	7	7

a. The city with the most fast-food restaurants will also have the highest overall occurrence of diabetes.
b. The city with the highest percentage of children with Type-2 diabetes also has the highest number of adults with Type-2 diabetes.
c. The more fast-food restaurants in a city, the more childhood diabetics it will have.
d. Other factors besides fast-food restaurants, such as culture and economy, may influence a city's diabetic population.

294. Scientists wanted to analyze risk factors for a certain lung ailment. Some scientists argue that the presence of a certain gene (labeled gene *Lfac*) is responsible for a person's chance of developing the disease, while others from the group claim the pollution from a ten-year-old factory in the region is more to blame. The following table shows 10 patients who have the disease, their level of toxin exposure based on distance of their homes from the factory, and whether they have the *Lfac* gene. Which of the statements can be supported by the information in the table?

Environmental and Genetic Information on Patients with Lung Disease		
Patient	Toxin exposure (%)	Gene *Lfac* present?
1	20	Yes
2	45	No
3	84	No
4	34	Yes
5	62	Yes
6	31	Yes
7	75	No
8	33	Yes
9	77	No
10	58	No

a. The greater the toxin exposure the more likely a person is to get the disease, whether they have the *LFac* gene or not.
b. The disease is caused only by genetic factors.
c. The closer a person lives to the factory, the more likely he or she is to acquire the disease.
d. It is not possible to determine whether genetics or toxin exposure increase a person's chances of developing the disease.

295. In 2011, 10 different companies reported sales for products they advertised for on two social media websites. Data was collected for online sales of products and was determined by customer surveys. Which of the following statements is true, according to the data in the table?

Change in Sales of Products 1 and 2, for Companies 1–10 (percent)				
	Social Media Site #1		Social Media Site #2	
Company	Product 1	Product 2	Product 1	Product 2
1	+2.0	+1.7	+3.0	+2.7
2	+2.3	−0.3	+2.5	+1.0
3	−4.6	−2.0	−4.0	−2.1
4	+3.0	+3.2	+2.0	−1.5
5	−2.9	+1.0	−3.6	+0.5
6	−5.0	−2.1	+2.5	+2.5
7	+3.1	−2.0	+1.0	+1.7
8	−0.3	−1.2	+6.2	+4.7
9	+1.0	−1.0	−3.0	−2.2
10	−1.0	−2.5	+4.3	+4.3

  a. Product 2 had a higher sales increase than Product 1 on both websites.
  b. Company 1 was not honest when reporting sales of both products.
  c. Overall, the second social media site was more effective for increasing sales of both products.
  d. Company 2 was not honest when reporting sales of both products.

296. The data presented in the following table shows the population of snakes and the population of rabbits in a meadow ecosystem for a 10-year time period. What can be inferred from the data in the table?

Rabbit and Snake Populations in a Meadow Ecosystem, 2000–2008		
Year	Snake population	Rabbit population
2000	100	250
2001	120	210
2002	160	185
2003	130	170
2004	110	190
2005	95	215
2006	85	230
2007	90	245
2008	100	235

a. The population of snakes is influenced by the population of available rabbits.

b. New sources of prey were found by the snakes between 2000 and 2008.

c. There was an increase in other predators of rabbits from 2001 to 2002.

d. If the rabbit population were to double in 2009, the snake population would double as well.

297. A team of botanists wanted to figure out what sort of conditions were best for growing a type of flowering plant. The following table shows the variables that were tested and the results of the experiment. All other conditions were kept the same, and the plants came from the same package of seeds. What can we infer are the best conditions from the data in the table?

Effects of Temperature and Water on Plant Blossoms			
Plant	Temperature (°F)	Amount of water (mL)	# of blossoms
1	60	25.0	2
2	60	50.0	2
3	60	75.0	0
4	65	25.0	3
5	65	50.0	4
6	65	75.0	1
7	70	25.0	8
8	70	50.0	10
9	70	75.0	2
10	75	25.0	13
11	75	50.0	10
12	75	75.0	9
13	80	25.0	16
14	80	50.0	12
15	80	75.0	10

a. The plant prefers cool, damp growing conditions.
b. The plant prefers cool, dry growing conditions.
c. The plant prefers warm, damp growing conditions.
d. The plant prefers warm, dry growing conditions.

298. Five private universities released statistics on the top three college
majors at their schools, graduation rates for each major, and
graduates who reported having a degree-related job in their field
within 12 months of graduation. The following table represents
the information that was released. Which of the following
statements CANNOT be inferred from the data in the table?

Top Three Majors, Graduation Rates, and Graduates with a Degree-Related Job			
University	Top three majors	Four-year graduation rate within each major (%)	Graduates with a degree-related job (%)
Abracadabra University	Biology	82.5	75.0
	Chemistry	83.0	80.0
	Zoology	87.0	80.0
Crescent Moon College	Liberal Arts	90.0	70.0
	Finance	91.5	80.0
	Business Administration	90.0	75.0
Westfield University	Women's Studies	92.0	50.0
	Biology	93.5	89.0
	Liberal Arts	95.0	70.0
Letterbox University	Chemistry	95.0	90.0
	Mathematics	97.0	91.0
	Business Administration	95.0	80.0
Cranberry College	Botany	85.0	95.0
	Biology	85.0	96.0
	Zoology	83.0	88.0

a. Crescent Moon College has the most successful networking and job placement of the universities listed.

b. In the current economic conditions, it is probably more challenging to get a job in the liberal arts than it is in a science-related field.

c. Students who require more than four years to graduate will likely have a harder time finding a job post-college.

d. Those who graduate from Westfield University with degrees that are not ranked in the table will probably have more success finding a job within 12 months of graduation.

299. The following table shows the top ten United States imports and exports for the year 2008. The data in the table supports which of the following statements?

a. The United States is self-sufficient for many facets of its transportation industry.

b. Passenger cars make up a higher percentage of exports than imports for the United States.

c. Other nations are dependent on the United States for civilian aircraft.

d. The United States has little demand for foreign-made clothing.

Top Ten Imports and Exports for the United States, 2008					
Imports			Exports		
Rank	Product	% of total imports	Rank	Product	% of total exports
1	Crude oil	16.3	2	Semiconductors	3.9
8	Cotton apparel	2.4	5	Automotive accessories	3.1
3	Medicinal preparations	3.8	9	Telecommunications equipment	2.6
4	Automotive accessories	3.1	7	Fuel oil	2.7
5	Other household goods	2.9	6	Other industrial machines	3.0
2	Passenger cars	6.0	1	Civilian aircraft	5.7
6	Computer accessories	2.8	10	Plastic materials	2.5
10	Video equipment	1.9	4	Pharmaceutical preparations	3.1
7	Petroleum products	2.5	3	Passenger cars	3.9
9	Telecommunications equipment	2.1	8	Organic chemicals	2.6

300. A school district in Maryland integrated a state-funded reading program into its curriculum for four years. The same program was integrated in a school district in Virginia. The passing rates for elementary (K–5), middle (6–8), and high school (9–12) are shown in the following table. Which statement is true about the implementation of the reading program?

Passing test rates for Virginia and Maryland school districts, before and after state-funded reading program (percent)								
	Grade Level							
	K–3		4–6		7–9		10–12	
State	Before program	After program	Before program	After program	Before program	After program	Before program	After program
Virginia	85	78	75	65	82	87	82	89
Maryland	80	78	84	75	79	80	82	85

    a. As grade level increased, so did passing rate, both prior to and after the reading program.
    b. The program was unsuccessful in Virginia.
    c. The program was unsuccessful in Maryland.
    d. The reading program was more effective for older students.

301. The following table shows the percent of commuters and the type of transportation they primarily use, for six countries. Which of the statements that follows can be supported by the data in the table?

Common Modes of Transportation for Commuters				
	Transportation Type (percent)			
Country	Bus	Walk/ Bicycle	Train	Automobile
Brazil	30	50	10	10
Argentina	40	30	15	15
Germany	30	20	25	25
United Kingdom	30	10	40	20
France	20	30	35	15
United States	20	10	10	60

a. Of all the listed countries, pollution is probably lowest in Brazil.
b. South Americans commute with the automobile more frequently than Europeans.
c. Mass transit is the most common way to commute in the United States.
d. Mass transit is the most common way to commute for the majority of the countries listed.

302. A school in New York State has experienced a decrease in graduation rate for the past six years. The school wants to determine some of the outside factors that could be playing a role in the decreasing rates. Behavior reports and juvenile arrests of students enrolled at the school were the focus of the study. Which of the following statements can be made, based on the information in the table?

Graduation Rates, Behavior Reports, and Juvenile Arrests, 2002–2011			
Year	Graduation rate (%)	Behavior reports (total)	Juvenile arrests (total)
2002	54	416	5
2003	55	419	5
2004	55	415	4
2005	57	400	4
2006	52	436	8
2007	49	482	11
2008	45	510	16
2009	41	540	20
2010	37	593	25
2011	34	704	31

a. As the total number of behavior reports increases, so do graduation rates.

b. As graduation rates decrease, behavior reports do the same, but juvenile arrests increase.

c. Juvenile arrests and behavior reports have been steadily increasing since 2006, and the graduation rate has been steadily decreasing.

d. Students who do not have behavior issues both in and out of school make up most of the graduating class each year.

303. The following table shows four different cable providers and the change in their rates for the 2012 subscription year. All four of the companies have experienced a change in their clientele based on renewal subscriptions, also shown in the table. What is a reasonable conclusion based on the information given?

Changes in Cable and Internet Costs for Cable Providers A, B, C, and D			
Cable provider	% change in cost of wireless Internet	% change in cost of cable	% of customers who re-signed contract for 2012 service year
A	+2.0	+5.0	70%
B	+4.0	+5.0	65%
C	+5.0	+3.0	85%
D	+6.0	+2.0	90%

a. The rising cost of cable has more of an influence over whether a customer will re-sign than the cost of the Internet.
b. The rising cost of Internet service has more of an influence over whether a customer will re-sign than the cost of cable.
c. Changing Internet and cable costs have little effect on whether a customer decides to re-sign with the company.
d. Customers are not likely to renew a subscription for a year of service if the wireless Internet price increases.

304. The rate of magazine versus tablet or other device subscription for three magazines is shown in the following table. Which of the following statements CANNOT be supported by the information in the table?

Tablet and Print Magazine Subscriptions for Three Magazines, 2009–2012 (thousands)						
	Fashion Forward		*Sports Weekly*		*Classy Cooking*	
Year	Print	Tablet	Print	Tablet	Print	Tablet
2009	25	4	15	2	20	5
2010	28	10	15	4	22	10
2011	32	14	13	7	21	15
2012	35	18	10	10	20	29

a. All three of the magazines have seen an increase in tablet subscriptions for the past four years.
b. People interested in fashion are more likely to get their information from a tablet than those interested in cooking.
c. People interested in sports are less likely to have a print subscription than those interested in fashion.
d. People interested in cooking are more likely to have a tablet subscription than people interested in sports

305. The number of new hires for the year 2011 is displayed in the following table, for four various industries within a county in Ohio. Which statement is true about the data in the table?

New Hires, Mason County Ohio, 2011		
Industry	Number of new hires	Change in new hire employment from year prior
Education	173	+5%
Civil Service	200	+5%
Service Industry	210	+10%
Health Care	205	+5%

a. The healthcare industry hired more new employees for the year 2011 then the civil service industry.
b. There was an increased demand for teachers in 2011.
c. As new hires and employment increase, there is an increased demand for employees in the service industry.
d. There were more people hired in the service industry and healthcare than in education and civil service.

306. A survey was conducted with groups of people between the ages of 14 and 17 in different states in the United States, measuring how young people typically spent their time outside of school. The results of the surveys that were given are displayed in the following table. Which of the following statements is a reasonable inference based on the survey results?

How Teenagers Spent Their Free Time, 2010						
	Activities					
State	Television	Computer/Internet use	Sports or time outside	Books and magazines	Work	Other
Florida	25%	30%	10%	10%	20%	5%
Vermont	15%	15%	30%	15%	20%	5%
Minnesota	20%	25%	20%	10%	15%	10%
Oregon	15%	15%	25%	15%	25%	5%
Louisiana	20%	30%	20%	5%	15%	10%
Utah	5%	10%	30%	15%	35%	5%

a. Teenagers in northern regions tend to spend more time outside than teenagers in southern regions.
b. Teenagers in southern states are most likely than teenagers in northern states to spend time on the Internet in their spare time.
c. Most people in Vermont get their first job as a teenager.
d. More teenagers spend time watching television than using the Internet.

307. A study was conducted to see whether people who drove red cars were more likely to be written a speeding ticket. The number of speeding tickets written between 2005 and 2009 for red, black, and silver cars is displayed in the following table. Which of the following conclusions can be made, based on the data in the table?

Speeding Tickets Given by Car Color, Monroe County, 2005–2009			
Year	Tickets given to red cars	Tickets given to black cars	Tickets given to silver cars
2005	600	500	550
2006	700	400	500
2007	640	450	600
2008	800	600	700
2009	750	550	600
Total tickets written	3,490	2,500	2,950

a. People driving silver cars are most likely to be given a speeding ticket.

b. People who drove black cars in 2009 were written the most speeding tickets.

c. The police wrote more total speeding tickets in 2007 than any of the other years.

d. People who drive red cars are more likely to get a speeding ticket in Monroe County than those in black and silver cars.

308. A laboratory conducted a study on how certain antioxidants regulate cell division in a variety of groups of the same specimen. The purpose of the study was to see whether certain antioxidants can be directly linked to uncontrolled cell division (cancer) in living organisms, when exposed to cancer-causing agents. The results of the study are displayed in the following table. What is a possible inference based on the data the scientists gathered?

Effects of Various Antioxidants on Uncontrolled Cell Division			
Antioxidant	Primary food source	% of specimens who had uncontrolled cell division (control)	% of specimens who had uncontrolled cell division (experimental)
Alpha-carotene	Tomatoes, squash	20.0	12.0
Beta-carotene	Squash, sweet potatoes	20.0	11.0
Lutein	Spinach, kale	20.0	4.0
Lycopene	Cooked red tomatoes	20.0	13.0
Zeaxanthin	Kale, collard greens	20.0	4.5

a. Lutein and lycopene are the antioxidants that showed the most beneficial impact on the specimens, so a diet rich in them would mean a decreased cancer risk.
b. Diets rich in dark green vegetables could mean a decreased cancer risk.
c. Diets rich in alpha-carotene and beta-carotene will increase the risk of cancer if exposed to cancer-causing agents.
d. Red and orange vegetables are an excellent source of zeaxanthin.

309. The total number of medals for the seven countries who won the most gold medals at the 2012 Summer Olympic Games is shown in the following table. Which statement is true about the data in the table?

Medal Count for the 2012 Summer Olympic Games				
Country	Gold	Silver	Bronze	Total
United States	46	29	29	104
China	38	27	23	88
Great Britain	29	17	19	65
Russia	24	26	32	82
Korea	13	8	7	28
Germany	11	19	14	44
France	7	11	12	34

a. The country with the most total medals won also had the highest medal count for gold, silver, and bronze.
b. The country with the fifth highest gold medal count also had the fifth highest total medal count.
c. France had the least number of gold medals as well as the lowest total medal count.
d. Russia had the fourth highest gold and bronze medal counts.

310. A certain pheromone produced by the female monarch butterfly has been identified as responsible for their reproductive success. The same pheromone has been tied to other species of butterflies but they do not emit it as much as monarchs do, and their reproductive rates are also significantly lower. Scientists want to see if increased exposure to the pheromone will be effective in encouraging mating among an endangered species of butterfly. Six test groups, with 50 male and 50 female butterflies, were separated and exposed to different amounts of the pheromone to see if it increased the mating activity between them. Which of the following can be inferred from the data in the table?

Mating among Butterflies, Various Pheromone Exposure		
Test group	Amount of pheromone exposure (%) times normal amount	Number of butterflies who mated during exposure
1	0	0
2	20	12
3	40	36
4	60	74
5	80	94
6	100	90

a. The butterflies would probably mate the most when exposed to 50% pheromone levels.
b. Controlling the amount of pheromone exposure would be an effective way for scientists to promote reproduction among these butterflies.
c. An increase in pheromone exposure always leads to increased mating activity between butterflies.
d. Exposure to controlled levels of pheromones would not encourage mating between the endangered butterflies.

Answers—Set 12

293. **c.** The city of Lewistown has 28 fast-food restaurants, which is four more than Rockville, but has 1% fewer diabetics under the age of 16, and 8% fewer overall diabetics. Choice **a** is incorrect because Greene, the city with the most fast-food restaurants, does have the highest total occurrence of diabetes. Choice **b** is incorrect because Greene, the city with the highest percentage of children with Type-2 diabetes also has the highest total population with diabetes. Choice **d** is incorrect because other factors may contribute to diabetes, as shown by Lewistown not having the least number of fast-food restaurants but having the lowest occurrence of diabetes.

294. **d.** Since all the patients have the lung disease, and all have some degree of toxin exposure, and only some have the gene, it is not possible to tell which one is responsible using this data. Choice **a** is incorrect because only some of the patients have the gene, but all are sick. Choice **b** is incorrect because the data does not show conclusive evidence of what causes the disease. Choice **c** is incorrect because all of the patients had some degree of exposure.

295. **c.** For both products, social media site 2 had higher overall sales. Choice **a** is incorrect because Product 1 had a higher sales increase than Product 2 for both websites. Choice **b** is incorrect because based on the data, that inference cannot be made. Choice **d** is incorrect because based on the data in the table, that inference cannot be made.

296. **a.** As the rabbit population increases or decreases, the snake population shows an opposite trend. Choice **b** cannot be supported because there is no data that can support the definite presence of other prey. Choice **c** is incorrect because there is no data in the table that can support the definite presence of other predators. Choice **d** is incorrect because the populations do not exactly mimic each other.

297. **d.** The plant had the most blossoms at the highest temperature with the least amount of water. Choice **a** is incorrect because the plant had fewer blossoms at the lower temperatures. Choice **b** is incorrect because the plant had no blossoms at the lowest temperature when given the most amount of water. Choice **c** is incorrect because the plant had the fewest blossoms under the wettest conditions for the warmest temperatures.

298. **b.** The data shows both of the universities that have liberal arts as a top-three major have 12-month job placement at 70.0%. This is the lowest percent of job placement besides women's studies. Choice **a** is incorrect because some of the other universities have higher job placement rates for their top three majors. Choice **c** is incorrect because there is no evidence in the table that could lead to an inference about students who take more than four years to graduate. Choice **d** is incorrect because there is no data in the table that provides any information about unlisted majors; therefore, an inference about other majors cannot be made based on the given data.

299. **c.** Civilian aircraft is the United States' highest-ranking export. Choice **a** is incorrect because the United States' top export is crude oil and its second top import is passenger cars. Choice **b** is incorrect because passenger cars make up a higher percentage of imports (6.0%) than exports (3.9%). Choice **d** is incorrect because cotton apparel is one of the top imports, at rank number eight.

300. **d.** Students in the 7–9 and 10–12 groups showed an increase in reading scores for both states. Choice **a** is incorrect because fewer students in the 4–6 age group passed in Virginia than the K–3 group both prior to and after the program was implemented. Choice **b** is incorrect because some student groups in Virginia showed an increase in passing rate after the reading program was implemented. Choice **c** is incorrect because some student groups in Maryland showed an increase in passing rate after the reading program was implemented.

301. **d.** Except for Brazil and the United States, over 50% of commuters from the other four countries rely on the bus and/or train. Choice **a** is incorrect because it is an inference that cannot be directly supported with the evidence in the table. Choice **b** is incorrect because the European countries have an overall higher percentage of commuters using the automobile. Choice **c** is incorrect because the majority of Americans (60%) commute by automobile.

302. **c.** The graduation rate decreases from 52% to 34% between 2006 and 2011. The behavior reports increase from 436 to 704 and the juvenile arrests increase from 8 to 31. Choice **a** is incorrect because as behavior reports increase, graduation rates decrease. Choice **b** is incorrect because as graduation rates decrease, both behavior reports and juvenile arrests decrease. Choice **d** is incorrect because none of the data in the table accounts for factors besides behavior problems in school and juvenile arrests.

303. **a.** Although cable provider D increased Internet cost by 6.0% (the highest) they increased the cost of cable by 2.0% (the lowest) and they also had the highest percent of customers who re-signed their contract. Choice **b** is incorrect because although cable provider A only increased their Internet service by 2.0%, they increased their cable cost by 5.0%, but only had 70% of people renew for 2012. Choice **c** is incorrect because none of the companies had a 100% renewal rate for 2012. Choice **d** is incorrect because all the companies raised their Internet prices, and all experienced renewal of contracts.

304. **b.** *Fashion Forward* magazine has 18,000 tablet subscriptions, but *Classy Cooking* has 29,000. Choice **a** is incorrect because tablet subscriptions for the four years given increased for all the magazines. Choice **c** is incorrect because *Fashion Forward* had 35,000 print subscriptions, which is almost twice as many as their tablet subscriptions. *Sports Weekly* has an equal number of tablet and print magazine subscriptions. Choice **d** is incorrect because 29,000 people have a tablet subscription, while 10,000 have one for *Sports Weekly*.

305. **d.** There were 415 total people hired for healthcare and the service industry, which is more than the 373 hired in the education and civil service fields. Choice **a** is incorrect because the healthcare field hired 205 new employees, and the civil service field hired 200. Choice **b** is incorrect because the education field does not specify teachers only. Choice **c** is incorrect because it is not possible to determine whether there is a correlation between service industry hires and employment in other fields.

306. **b.** Based on the results of the survey, 30% of teenagers from Florida and Louisiana spent time on the Internet, compared to 15% in Vermont and 15% in Oregon, and 25% in Minnesota. Choice **a** is incorrect because teenagers in Utah spend the same amount of time outside as those in Vermont. Choice **c** is incorrect because the data in the table does not account for first jobs of older people in the state. Choice **d** is incorrect because for all the states the percentage of teenagers who spend time on the computer is equal to or higher than the percentage who spend time with television.

307. **d.** According to the total number of speeding tickets for each color of car, red cars had the most tickets written. Choice **a** is incorrect because there were 2,950 tickets written to silver cars for the time period, but 3,490 were written for red cars. Choice **b** is incorrect because black cars were written a total of 550 tickets in 2009, behind both silver and red cars. Choice **c** is incorrect because police wrote 1,690 tickets in 2007 but 2,100 in 2008.

308. **b.** The data shows that green vegetables—kale, spinach, and collard greens—had the least number of specimens that had uncontrolled cell division. Choice **a** is incorrect because the specimens exposed to lycopene showed a 13.0% likelihood of acquiring cancer, which is higher than that of zeaxanthin, which showed a 4.5% cancer occurrence. Choice **c** is incorrect because the experimental groups for alpha-carotene and beta-carotene showed a decrease in uncontrolled cell division when compared to the control group. Choice **d** is incorrect because the primary sources of zeaxanthin are dark green vegetables.

309. **a.** The United States had 46 gold medals, and 104 medals total, which is the highest for the data given. Choice **b** is incorrect because Korea had the fifth highest number of gold medals, but was seventh in total medal count. Choice **c** is incorrect because France had a total medal count of 34, which is more than Korea and therefore not the least. Choice **d** is incorrect because Russia had the highest number of bronze medals, not the fourth.

310. **b.** Mating activity increased between the butterflies as the amount of pheromone exposure increased, except when they were exposed to 100% of the pheromone, where four less butterflies mated. However, there was a steady increase in the mating activity between the butterflies as the amount of exposure increased. Choice **a** is incorrect because if the data follows the trend in the table, a 50% exposure would lead to somewhere between 36 and 74 butterflies mating, and this is less than when they were exposed to even higher levels. Choice **c** is incorrect because when the butterflies were exposed to 100% of the pheromone levels, four fewer butterflies mated than at 80% exposure. Choice **d** is incorrect because more, not less, butterflies mated as the pheromone levels increased.

8

Multisource Reasoning

The multisource reasoning section of the GMAT is a test of your ability to synthesize information from a variety of sources (usually two or three) to arrive at reasonable inferences and logical conclusions. In today's information-rich environment, we are often called on to connect pieces of data that we receive across a variety of communication types—e-mail, letters, text messages, editorials, manifests and contracts, and so on—as well as to draw and support suppositions about the ways in which those data might interact in a wide array of circumstances. To be able to create an inferential link between such sources and to draw empirically valid conclusions from them is a valuable skill in today's detail-oriented business environment.

This section presents information broken into segments that are typically 300 words or fewer. Skim through the paragraphs to review the exchange of information and then assess the questions and answers according to the presented data. Be sure to read the question stems carefully. A few will require a single response (e.g., multiple-choice questions), but the majority will require that you select one of two or three possible responses for each part of the question (e.g., "Yes or No" responses to three- or four-question segments). To be credited with a correct response for this latter type, you must answer all the parts correctly. Please note that questions are independent of one another, so that you will not be asked to answer one correctly to correctly answer another. Once you have submitted a response to a given question, you cannot return to it, so select your responses with care.

Test-Taking Tips

Maybe the most important thing to keep in mind about the multisource reasoning section of the GMAT is that the material is loaded with information that you will never be asked questions about. Much like the reading comprehension component, multisource reasoning questions are designed to lure test takers into becoming bogged down in extraneous data and information. Remember always that you are not being tested on your ability to memorize information! Keeping this in mind will help you to formulate and enact an effective and efficient approach to the section.

Step One: See the Big Picture

As with the reading comprehension section, a sensible strategy for tackling multisource reasoning questions is to first skim through the passages to get a broad sense of the information contained therein. It's enough at this point to be able to say, "This is an exchange of offers for the possible acquisition of a new online business," or "These are e-mails between a manager and her human resources officer concerning employee productivity." You may want to break the tabs down into very simple statements to help you to keep track of the flow of information. For example: "Para 1: The manager thinks her staff is underproducing. Para 2: The HR officer tries to prove otherwise. Para 3: The manager presents more data to the contrary." Or even: "Para 1: Offer. Para 2: Counteroffer. Para 3: Response to counteroffer." Keep it simple.

You'll want to keep it simple because, at least for now, getting bogged down in the fine details (i.e., the nature and specifics of the data presented)—or, worse, trying to memorize those details—is a waste of your valuable time. Much, and perhaps most, of the presented information may prove to be irrelevant. You will not be asked questions about it. More, you should keep in mind that you will have to return to the passages in order to answer the questions anyway (and you should never try to answer them from memory), thus doubling the time you spend engaging the information in the tabs. See the big picture.

Step Two: Assess the Stem

Now that we have some sense of what the tabs contain, it's time to carefully read the question stem to determine exactly what task it is directing us to do. A few question stems will ask for a single response (e.g., "If Gillian receives her anticipated yearly bonus, her salary for the month will be . . ."). Most, however, require multiple responses (e.g., "Does the information in the articles support each of the following inferences as they appear here? YES or NO."). To this end, you will have to read and carefully consider a number of segments, answering each of them before moving on to the next question stem. Look for key words in the question stems and answer segments (e.g., "The *manager* apparently believes that . . . ," "The data from *September* suggest that . . .") and let those guide you back to specific details and data in the multisource reasoning tabs.

Step Three: What Is the Answer?

The best way to answer a question on the GMAT (or, for that matter, any standardized test) is to find it yourself in the reading, put it in your own words, and then look for the answer that comes closest in the question's answer set. As often as possible—and especially in the case of single-response question types—be sure to use the process of elimination to remove unlikely or easily disproven possibilities from the answer set and to more quickly arrive at a correct response. For common inference question types, keep in mind that the words "reasonably infer" as they are used on the GMAT mean something along the lines of "be able to directly prove through what is written on your screen." That is, you must be able to *point at the evidence* that you use to arrive at your answer. If you are unable to do so—or if the presented information suggests or supports a broader array of possible interpretations—take a moment to carefully consider whether such an answer represents a reasonable or defensible inference. As always, be on the lookout for extreme language in the answer set. Answers containing words like *must*, *always*, *never*, *no one*, and *everyone* should raise a red flag. Although such answers are not automatically incorrect, it is rarely the case that GMAT passages can or will substantiate such absolute positions. Be extra wary.

Note that once you have answered a question and moved on, you will be unable to return to it, so be sure you are comfortable with your responses before pressing ahead.

Set 13

Now it is time to answer GMAT multisource reasoning practice questions that have been designed to test your integrated reasoning skills. Good luck!

Use the following articles to answer questions 311 through 314.

Article One: Opinion Article in a Popular Political Journal
The incumbent candidate's protests aside, it is a matter of plain fact that some 47% of the country's residents currently pay no taxes—the largest share of nonpayers on record—and therefore live almost entirely off the largess of those who are now shouldering a greater part of the burden than ever before. Our concern is that, as this number continues to grow, a greater portion of the population will become habituated to life on various forms of public assistance and thus less and less likely to seek avenues of employment that would lead them to leave the rolls of public welfare.

Article Two: Speech Delivered by the Incumbent Candidate
It's true that more folks are having trouble making ends meet these days, but what you should keep in mind is that a smaller and smaller group of people in the top one percent of the income scale takes home a greater share of wealth than ever before, while people in the bottom half have seen their incomes frozen essentially since the mid-1970s. When my opponent and his supporters argue that almost half of taxpayers pay no taxes, you should remember that many of them pay no taxes because they simply don't earn enough money to do so.

Article Three: Assessment by Nonpartisan Tax Policy Think Tank
Although it is true that a greater portion of the public pays no *federal income* taxes, almost everyone pays taxes of some kind. These include payroll taxes (in the case of those drawing income from regular employment), state and local taxes, fines and fees of various kinds, as well as taxes on gasoline, groceries, clothing, and most other consumer goods. Meanwhile, it is worth keeping in mind that federal income tax is the relatively progressive instrument in the national revenue-raising mechanism, whereas other forms of taxation (particularly those at the state and local levels) tend to be markedly regressive.

311. Consider each of the following statements. Does the information in the articles support the inference as it appears here?

Yes　No The number of taxpayers paying no federal income taxes is currently the largest on record.

Yes　No Making the federal tax code even more progressive would alleviate much of the repressiveness of the tax codes at the state and local levels.

Yes　No The candidate for local office is unaware of the relatively progressive nature of the federal tax code.

Yes　No The fact that the country's top earners pay a greater share of the total national tax burden is proof that the federal tax code is unusually progressive.

312. Consider each of the following statements. Does the information in the articles support the inference as it appears here?

Yes　No The incumbent candidate is unaware that 47% of taxpayers currently pay no federal income tax.

Yes　No The author of the opinion piece is unaware that the 47% figure he or she employs does not include other forms of taxation, such as state and local taxes, payroll taxes, and taxes on consumer goods.

Yes　No Members of the top one percent of the income scale currently pay little or no payroll tax.

Yes　No At least some local fees are more regressive than the federal income tax.

313. It can be reasonably inferred that the Nonpartisan Tax Policy Think Tank mentions "income from regular employment" to suggest that
a. some taxpayers are evading legal taxation.
b. there are some forms of income not affected by payroll.
c. the 47% are the only ones who pay payroll taxes.
d. top earners are less likely than others to pay state and local fees.
e. payroll taxes are the most regressive of all those mentioned by the think tank in its article.

314. For each of the following statements, select *All Accept* (AA) if, based on the information provided, it can be inferred that the authors of the three articles would likely accept that the statement is true. If not, select *Otherwise* (O).

AA   **O**   47% of taxpayers currently pay no federal income tax.

AA   **O**   Top earners bear an undue burden under the current tax code.

AA   **O**   The distribution of employment income plays at least some part in the appearance of unbalance in the federal tax code.

Use the following e-mail correspondence to answer questions 315 through 317.

E-mail from the Convention Coordinator

Our upcoming comic book convention is running into a few unexpected snags, the most pressing of which is that we appear to have seriously underestimated likely attendance. Our idea to promote the attendance of industry professionals (who do not pay an attendance fee, once they are credentialed) by allowing them to bring along two guests is now threatening to cause us to overflow our assigned space in the convention center. There is an additional space available during the three days of the convention, but acquiring it would threaten our ability to pay our vendors and force us to rely on greater-than-anticipated volunteer assistance.

E-mail from the Convention Budget Officer

The change in guest policy has created a real problem then. We have currently budgeted $35,000 for three days to cover a wide array of vendor services, including security, transportation, and on-site medical personnel in the event of an accident or sudden illness. It has already been very difficult to find professionals who are both qualified and available to take on many of those skilled responsibilities. Worse, securing the use of expanded convention center space will cost an additional $7,000 over the long weekend, cutting into our already tight overall budget. Indeed, any additional expenditures will require the use of yet more (potentially underqualified) volunteers.

E-mail from the Events Coordinator of the Convention Center
We have considered your proposal for expanded use of the convention center facilities and (given the expected size of the convention's attendance) are prepared to let you lease the additional space at a 40% discount. More, the center is willing to offer you the use of its own security personnel, though only for Friday and Saturday (which together are expected to see far more traffic than Sunday), and only if you agree to also take on the additional convention space.

315. Consider each of the following statements. Does the information in the articles support the inference as it appears here?

Yes	**No**	Skilled professionals account for the largest contingent of the convention's vendor personnel.
Yes	**No**	Given the current budget restrictions, even with the discount offered by the convention center, it is likely that the convention will have to somewhat expand its use of volunteer personnel.
Yes	**No**	At least some volunteer personnel are unqualified to perform certain vendor duties required by the convention.
Yes	**No**	The convention center's offer of discounted additional floor space and security personnel will alleviate most of the "unexpected snags" mentioned by the Convention Coordinator in her e-mail.

316. The 40% discount on the expanded floor space, if accepted, would account for what percentage of the convention's total budget for vendor services?
   a. 15
   b. 9
   c. 8
   d. 11
   e. 6

317. For each of the following statements, choose *Definitely True* (DT) if the statement is absolutely true. Choose *Possibly True* (PT) if the statement can be true but might not necessarily be true all the time.

   DT   **PT**   In the past, the comic book convention had a different policy toward industry professionals and their guests.

   DT   **PT**   If every industry professional brought along only one guest, the convention center would not overflow its assigned space.

   DT   **PT**   If the comic book convention eliminates the guest policy next year, it will not overflow its assigned space.

Use the following e-mail correspondence to answer questions 318 through 322.

E-mail from Buyer

I recently noticed your listing in *Antiques Quarterly* magazine and am prepared to make an offer on the ceremonial sword you described. As a serious collector, however, it behooves me to double-check the authenticity of my acquisitions and to this end I insist on using experts who are known to me and who have earned my trust over the years. I find the current authentication open to some question. Because this is a somewhat costly endeavor, I ask that you consider my offer of $83,000 for the sword, an amount that will (in part, at least) offset this additional expense.

E-mail from Seller

Thanks so much for getting in touch. Your offer is some 15% less than my asking price, and (as such) is much less than I'd hoped to get for the sword. I assure you that this unusual item's authenticity has been confirmed by its country's leading experts on the era. More, weapons from this particular era are becoming more and more collectible as the ongoing upheaval in its country of origin has led many of these treasures to be destroyed. It is my hope that sometime during the next four years the value of the sword will more than triple. Still, I am willing to part with this exquisite piece of history if you are willing to increase your offer by an additional 7%. Please think it over.

318. For each of the following statements, choose *Definitely True* (DT) if the statement is absolutely true. Choose *Possibly True* (PT) if the statement can be true but might not necessarily be true all the time.

DT   PT   The value of the sword will increase during the next four years.

DT   PT   The buyer's expert appraisers are more highly skilled than any in the employ of the seller.

DT   PT   The buyer is not entirely certain that the value of the weapon will triple in the coming four years.

DT   PT   The cost the buyer will incur to confirm the sword's authenticity will exceed the value of 15% of the seller's original asking price.

319. According to his message, the seller would be willing to accept an offer of:
a. $79,500
b. $81,650
c. $88,810
d. $90,100
e. $95,450

320. Consider each of the following statements. Does the information in the correspondence support the inference as it appears here?

Yes   No   The buyer has legitimate concerns about the authenticity of the sword.

Yes   No   It is unlikely that the experts used by the buyer and seller overlap.

Yes   No   There is other evidence that the seller could produce to convince the buyer to accept the original asking price.

Yes   No   The seller does not inhabit the country of origin of the antique artifact in question.

321. The seller refers to "the ongoing upheaval" in the sword's country of origin as evidence to support which of the following?

   a. The sword is the last known example of its kind.

   b. The buyer's authenticators lack the expertise to confirm the sword's actual value.

   c. The seller expects the value of the sword to continue to increase.

   d. The buyer will be unable to acquire a similar artifact at the price he is offering.

   e. The sword's country of origin is well known for its political instability.

322. For each of the following statements, select Yes if true. Otherwise, select No.

Yes	No	The seller will not be able to afford to sell the sword at the buyer's current offer.
Yes	No	The buyer is not entirely convinced of the reliability of the seller's experts.
Yes	No	Other artifacts from the era in question are known to exist.
Yes	No	At least some of the experts on the item's authenticity reside in its country of origin.

Use the following to answer questions 323 through 328.

Internal Communication from Sports League

We appear to have reached a serious impasse with the umpires' union regarding their contract demands. Besides salary and cost-of-living increases amounting to 10% distributed evenly over four years, a refinement of the league's full-time umpire hiring policy, and improved physical fitness regimes and assessments, the union is demanding that our league continue to offer a defined-contribution retirement plan to all currently active umpires through the year 2021. Frankly, we find this latter demand unacceptable, as it is a benefit enjoyed only by the umpires. We may need to temporarily vacate certain standing policies related to umpires if we are to have replacements on the field in time for the regular-season opener.

Internal Communication from Umpires' Union

We appear to have reached a serious impasse regarding our demands from the sports league. First, the league is demanding that we permit the hiring of a greater number of full-time umpires. And, though the league has agreed in principle to our salary demands (though only to a six percent cost-of-living increase distributed evenly over four years), the issue of the pension plan remains, with the league insisting that we accept a more conventional 401k plan. The cost of the current plan, remarkably, is a mere $3 million per year and therefore well within the league's current ability to fulfill. Still, there has been no significant agreement on this front. We believe that the league will move soon to hire replacement umpires in hopes of having them on the field for the regular-season opener in two weeks.

323. For each of the following statements, choose *Definitely True* (DT) if the statement is absolutely true. Choose *Possibly True* (PT) if the statement can be true but might not necessarily be true all the time.

> **DT   PT**   The league's players do not have a defined-pension plan.

> **DT   PT**   The replacement umpires will be in place in time for the league's regular-season opener.

> **DT   PT**   The umpires' union would be willing to accept the sport league's current salary counter-offer.

> **DT   PT**   Prior to this impasse, the league had in place a physical fitness assessment program for its umpires.

324. According to the information presented by the umpires' union, which of the following can be most reasonably inferred about full-time umpires?
   a. There are currently no full-time umpires in the league, but they will soon outnumber the regular umpires.
   b. Full-time umpires currently represent a majority of the umpires, but will soon represent almost all umpires.
   c. At least some of the current roster of umpires are full-time umpires.
   d. None of the full-time umpires has a defined-contribution retirement plan.
   e. The umpires will be unwilling to accept any new hiring of full-time umpires.

325. For each of the following statements, select *Inferable* (I) if the statement is reasonably inferable from the information provided. Otherwise, select *Not Inferable* (NI).

> **I NI** The sports league has agreed to at least part of the umpires' salary demands.

> **I NI** The sports league brings in more than $3 million a year in revenue.

> **I NI** None of the umpires would be happy with a 401k pension plan.

326. The sports league's mention of vacating "certain standing policies related to umpires" can be more reasonably said to imply that:
a. The sports league is unconcerned with umpire safety.
b. The sports league will be unwilling to reconsider the umpires' salary demands.
c. The sports league does not expect the umpires to consider any new contract proposals for at least two weeks.
d. Certain policies related to umpires sometimes take longer than two weeks to implement.
e. None of the policies in question apply to full-time umpires.

327. Assuming that the information presented by the umpires' union is accurate, the author's use of the word "remarkable" most reasonably suggests:
a. The issues in question are not entirely financial in nature.
b. The umpires' union is surprised that contract negotiations have not already been resolved in its favor.
c. The league's insistence on hiring more full-time umpires will lead to a season-ending strike.
d. The umpires' union expects many of its members to quit if their cost-of-living demands are not met.
e. The impasse appears to be the result of a misunderstanding on the sports league's part about the nature of its pension plan.

328. Assuming an umpire's annual salary of $150,000, the difference between the sports league's cost-of-living increase and the umpires' union's demands amounts to how much per year?

    a. $2,500

    b. $1,500

    c. $3,000

    d. $3,100

    e. $5,100

Answers—Set 13

311. **Yes.** The various correspondents are in agreement about this fact, and therefore it can be reasonably inferred given the available information.

No. There is not enough information in the passages to support this prediction of what future actions might be taken by state and local governments to offset any attempts to add progressivity to the current tax system.

No. There is not enough information in the passage to support such a conclusion.

No. There are other explanations as to why this might be the case. Indeed, the passage suggests that top earners might be paying an expanded share of total taxes because their total share of the national income has increased disproportionate to the rest of the population.

312. **No.** There is not enough information in the passage to support such a conclusion.

No. There is not enough information in the passage to support such a conclusion.

No. There is not enough information in the passage to support such a conclusion.

Yes. This fact is explicitly stated in the Assessment by the Nonpartisan Tax Policy Think Tank and can therefore be supported as a reasonable inference.

313. **b.** The Nonpartisan Tax Policy Think Tank mentions "income from regular employment" to suggest a categorical distinction between types of income that might or might not be exposed to payroll taxes.

314. **AA.** All three of the passages appear to accept this information as fact.

O. Whereas the first passage appears to agree with this statement, it is clear that the second and third either do not or likely do not.

O. Whereas the second and third passages appear to agree with this statement, it is clear the third passage likely holds a contrary view.

315. **No.** It is clear that skilled professionals constitute a vital part of the convention's vendors but there is not enough information presented in the passages to suggest that they represent the greatest number of said vendors.

Yes. The e-mail from the Convention Budget Officer explicitly states that any further expenditures (even discounted ones) will necessitate the use of greater numbers of volunteers.

Yes. The communications make clear that certain transportation, security, and medical vendors require professional skills or credentialing.

No. While it is clear that the convention space issue is significant, there is no evidence to suggest that it constitutes the greatest number of possible problems with the convention's going forward.

316. **c.** Forty percent of $7,000 is $2,800, which is 8% of the convention's total operating budget of $35,000.

317. **DT.** The communications make clear the policy toward credentialed professionals is a new one.

PT. Because the number of invited professionals is not known— nor is some sense of the actual capacity of the convention center in question—there is not enough information available to fully substantiate this statement.

PT. There is not enough information available to fully substantiate this statement.

318. **PT.** Without much further detail, the seller's projection that the sword's value will increase is not enough to fully substantiate this statement.

PT. There is not enough information available to fully substantiate this statement.

DT. The buyer makes clear that he has questions both about the item's value and authenticity.

DT. The seller makes it clear that his asking price will only mostly offset the cost of the authentication.

319. **c.** The seller makes it clear that he will accept an 8% discount on an item fully priced at $95,450.

320. **No.** It is unclear whether the buyer's concerns are legitimate inasmuch as there is not enough information about the quality of his expert authenticators to substantiate such a statement.
Yes. Given the disdain on display in the passages, as well as the demands of the buyer, it is highly unlikely that the buyer and seller have any expert authenticators in common.
No. There is not enough information available in the passage to substantiate this statement.
Yes. The seller makes it clear that he does not currently inhabit the item's country of origin.

321. **c.** The seller mentions "the ongoing upheaval" in the sword's country of origin as evidence to support his contention that the item will continue to gain value.

322. **No.** There is not enough information available in the passage to substantiate this statement.
Yes. The buyer makes it clear that he does not entirely trust the expertise of the seller's authenticators.
Yes. The seller makes it clear that at least some artifacts from the era in question have escaped destruction.
Yes. The seller explicitly states that at least some of the experts on the item's authenticity reside in its country of origin.

323. **DT.** The sports league's communication explicitly states that the umpires are the only league members to have the defined-contribution plan.
PT. This is stated as a possibility, though whether it will happen remains an open question.
PT. There is not enough information available in the passage to fully substantiate this statement.
DT. The sports league's communication makes clear reference to "improved physical fitness regimes and assessments."

324. **c.** It is clear from both statements that a number of full-time umpires are already members of the umpires' union.

325. **I.** The umpires' union makes it clear that the league has, in fact, acceded to at least some of its demands.
I. The umpires' union communication makes it clear that the league brings in more than enough to cover the annual expense of the umpires' union's current pension plan.
NI. There is not enough information available in the passage to substantiate this statement.

326. **d.** The statement of the sports league—in conjunction with information that the regular-season opener is two weeks away— makes it clear that certain league policies related to umpires sometimes take longer than that amount of time to implement.

327. **a.** The fact that the league could easily cover the annual expense of the umpires' current pension plan strongly suggests that at least some of the issues at stake in the current impasse are not financial in nature.

328. **b.** Assuming this baseline salary, the difference between the cost-of-living increases in question distributed evenly over the projected time period is $6,000, or $1,500 per year.

SECTION 4

GMAT Quantitative Section

The GMAT quantitative section will measure your ability to reason mathematically, solve numerical problems, and analyze graphic data. These are common situations that you will be faced with in the business world.

GMAT quantitative questions fall across three disciplines:

- Arithmetic
- Elementary algebra
- Commonly known concepts of geometry

Most of the concepts tested on the GMAT were probably taught in your high school math classes.

You will have to answer 37 multiple-choice questions on the GMAT quantitative section. Of these questions, 15 fall into the data-sufficiency category and 22 into the problem-solving category. Problem-solving questions will assess your basic math skills, knowledge of elementary-level concepts, and aptitude for reasoning and solving quantitative problems. Data-sufficiency questions will assess your ability to interpret a math problem, identify relevant information, and evaluate whether there is enough information to solve a problem. Each data-sufficiency question on the GMAT is accompanied by information and two statements, labeled (1) and (2). You must decide whether the statements offer sufficient information for you to answer the question. Then, you'll choose from the following answer choices:

- Statement (1) ALONE is sufficient, but statement (2) ALONE is not sufficient.
- Statement (2) ALONE is sufficient, but statement (1) ALONE is not sufficient.
- BOTH statements TOGETHER are sufficient, but NEITHER statement ALONE is sufficient.
- EACH statement ALONE is sufficient.
- Statements (1) and (2) TOGETHER are NOT sufficient.

Arithmetic

Out of the three math topics, arithmetic usually accounts for one-half of the questions asked in the GMAT quantitative section. This chapter reviews basic arithmetic concepts and formulas, involving:

- number terminology
- order of operations
- absolute value
- factoring
- fractions
- decimals
- mean, median, mode, and range
- percents

Number Terminology and Properties

Integers are the numbers that you see on a number line. *Positive integers* are integers that are larger than zero. *Negative integers* are smaller than zero.

The result in an addition problem is called the *sum*. The result in a subtraction problem is called the *difference*.

Adding integers often involves the use of certain properties. The *associative property of addition* states that when you add a series of numbers, you can regroup the numbers any way you'd like:

$$1 + (9 + 7) = (1 + 9) + 7 = (1 + 7) + 9$$

The *commutative property of addition* states that when you add numbers, order doesn't matter:

$$8 + 2 = 2 + 8$$

The result in a multiplication problem is called a *product*. The result in a division problem is called a *quotient*.

The product of two integers with the same sign (+ and + or – and –) is always positive. The product of two integers with different signs (+ and –) is always negative. For example:

$$3 \times 4 = 12$$

$$-3 \times -4 = 12$$

$$-3 \times 4 = -12$$

$$3 \times -4 = -12$$

Likewise, the quotient of two integers with the same sign (+ and + or – and –) is always positive. The quotient of two integers with the different signs (+ and –) is always negative. For example:

$$4 \div 2 = 2$$

$$-4 \div -2 = 2$$

$$-4 \div 2 = -2$$

$$4 \div -2 = -2$$

When multiplying integers, you will often use the same properties you used with the addition of integers. The *associative property of multiplication* states that when you are multiplying a series of numbers, you can regroup the numbers any way you'd like:

$$2 \times (5 \times 9) = (2 \times 5) \times 9 = (2 \times 9) \times 5$$

The *commutative property of multiplication* states that when you multiply integers, order doesn't matter:

$$6 \times 5 = 5 \times 6$$

The Order of Operations

To remember the order of operations with numerical expressions, you can use a mnemonic, the word PEMDAS.

P	Do operations inside parentheses.
E	Evaluate terms with exponents.
M/D	Do multiplication and division in order from left to right.
A/S	Add and subtract terms in order from left to right.

Set 14

Use the order of operations to answer the following questions.

329. $5 + 10 \div 5 - 7 =$

330. $2 - 6 \times 4 \div 2 =$

331. $9 \div 3 + 3 \times 8 =$

Absolute Value

If you look at a point on a number line, measure its distance from zero, and consider that value as positive, you have just found the number's absolute value. The absolute value of 3, written as $|3|$, is 3. The absolute value of -3, written as $|-3|$, is also 3.

When using the order of operations, the absolute value symbol is treated at the same level as parentheses. Try this out:

$$5 \times |-13 + 3|$$

First, evaluate the expression inside the absolute value symbol:

$$5 \times |-10|$$

Now, evaluate the absolute value:

$$|-10| = 10, \text{ so } 5 \times 10 = 50$$

Set 15

Find the absolute values.

332. $|156| =$

333. $|-97| =$

334. $-|13| =$

335. $74 + |-23| =$

336. $35 - |-12| =$

337. $100 \div 5 + |-5 \times 3| =$

338. $5 \times -|9| =$

339. $99 \div |-33| =$

Factoring Numbers

A number is a factor of a second number if it can be divided into the second number without leaving a remainder. Let's look at the factors of 12: 1,

2, 3, 4, 6, and 12. The number 12 can be divided by each of these numbers without leaving a remainder.

$$12 \div 1 = 12$$

$$12 \div 2 = 6$$

$$12 \div 3 = 4$$

$$12 \div 4 = 3$$

$$12 \div 6 = 2$$

$$12 \div 12 = 1$$

If you start with 1 and the number itself when you write down factor pairs, you won't forget any of them. For 12, the factor pairs are as follows:

1 and 12
2 and 6
3 and 4

If a number is a factor of a given number, the given number is divisible by the factor. A few simple rules will help you quickly determine divisibility and factor problems.

- An integer is divisible by 2 if its ones digit is divisible by 2.
- An integer is divisible by 3 if the sum of its digits is divisible by 3.
- An integer is divisible by 4 if its last two digits form a number divisible by 4.
- An integer is divisible by 5 if its ones digit is either 0 or 5.
- An integer is divisible by 6 if it is divisible by both 2 and 3.
- An integer is divisible by 9 if the sum of its digits is divisible by 9.
- An integer is divisible by 10 if its ones digit is 0.

When an integer greater than 1 has exactly two factors (1 and itself), it is a prime number. Examples of prime numbers include 2, 3, 5, 7, 11, 13, 17, 19, 23, and 29. Note that the opposite (negative version) of these numbers are also prime. For example, the factors of –23 are 1, –23, –1, and 23. Thus, –23 is prime because it has exactly two positive factors: 1 and 23.

When an integer greater than 1 has more than two factors, it is called a composite number.

The numbers 0 and 1 are neither prime nor composite. Zero has an infinite number of factors. The number 1, on the other hand, has one factor—itself. When a number is expressed as a product of factors that are all prime, that expression is called the prime factorization of the number.

The greatest of all the factors common to two or more numbers is called the greatest common factor (GCF).

A multiple of a number is the product of that number and any whole number. The least of the common multiples of two or more numbers, excluding 0, is called the least common multiple (LCM).

Set 16

Answer the following questions.

340. What is the prime factorization of 60?

341. Find the greatest common factor of 20 and 30.

342. Find the greatest common factor of 63 and 81.

343. Find the least common multiple of 63 and 81.

Fractions

A *proper fraction* has a numerator that is smaller than its denominator:

$$\frac{9}{10}$$

Improper fractions have numerators that are bigger than their denominators:

$$\frac{15}{7}$$

A *mixed number* is a number that is represented as a whole number and a proper fraction. The following are all mixed numbers:

$$7\frac{3}{4}, 8\frac{1}{2}, -2\frac{5}{6}$$

To change a mixed number into an improper fraction, follow these steps:

1. Multiply the denominator of the fraction by the whole number.

2. Add that sum to the numerator.

3. Put that amount over the original denominator.

A fraction can be considered negative if either its numerator or denominator is negative. When a fraction receives any type of sign, particularly the negative sign, it can appear in three different places—in the numerator, denominator, or right before the fraction.

To add or subtract fractions, the denominators have to match. To add fractions with like denominators, just add the numerators. To subtract fractions with like denominators, just subtract the numerators.

To find the sum or difference of two fractions with unlike denominators, rename the fractions with a common denominator. Then, add or subtract and simplify your answer.

To multiply fractions, multiply the numerators, then multiply the denominators, and finally simplify if possible and necessary.

To divide one fraction by another, you need to flip the second fraction and then multiply the fractions. This flip of the second fraction is called the *multiplicative inverse* of a number or the *reciprocal*.

Sometimes, you may need to find the greatest fractions or put fractions in order from least to greatest or from greatest to least. To do this, you should first give all the fractions a common denominator.

Set 17

Answer the following questions.

344. Convert $\frac{19}{5}$ to a mixed number.

345. Convert $6\frac{5}{8}$ to an improper fraction.

346. $\frac{4}{3} - \frac{14}{15} =$

Decimals

The *decimal system* is a way to name numbers based on the powers of 10. The numbers to the right of the decimal point are fractional equivalents with denominators that are powers of ten. For example,

$0.1 = \frac{1}{10}$

$0.2 = \frac{2}{10}$

$0.3 = \frac{3}{10}$

Decimal numbers are easy to compare and order, when you remember that the place value has meaning. In mathematics, 2.4 is the same number as 2.400 because both numbers represent two and four tenths. A whole number is understood to have a decimal point to the right of the number. For example, 12 = 12. = 12.0 = 12.000. Each expression represents twelve with no remainder. To compare decimals, it is best to change each decimal into an equivalent decimal with the same number of decimal places.

To add or subtract decimal values, line up the decimal points and add or subtract.

When you are multiplying decimals, first you multiply in the usual fashion, and then count over the proper number of places. This is done by counting how many places are to the right of the decimal point in each number you are multiplying.

When you are dividing decimals, you move the decimal point of the dividend and divisor the same number of places.

Set 18

Answer the following questions.

347. Order from lower to higher: 0.03, 0.008.

348. $6.4 - 1.3 =$

349. $3.1 \times 4 =$

Mean, Median, Mode, and Range

When you are dealing with sets of numbers, there are certain measures used to describe the set as a whole. These are called measures of central tendency, and they include *mean*, *median*, *mode*, and *range*.

Mean is another way of saying average. To find the average, you total up all the values and then divide by the number of values.

When you are considering a list of values in order (from smallest to largest), the median is the middle value. If there are two middle values, you just take their average.

In a list of values, the mode is the number that occurs most often. If two numbers occur most often, you have two modes. This is called bimodal.

The range indicates how close together the given values are to one another in a set of data. To find the range, determine the difference between the largest and the smallest values in the set of data. Subtract the smallest value from the largest value in the set.

Set 19

350. Find the mean of the following set of data: {32, 34, 34, 35, 37, 38, 34, 42}

351. What is the mode of {71, 68, 71, 77, 65, 68, 72}?

352. The ages at the day camp were as follows: 9, 12, 9, 10, 9, 13, 11, 8, 17, 10. What is the median age?

353. What is the range of the temperatures listed: 43°, 47°, 43°, 52°, 42°, 78°, 84°, 80°?

Probability

Probability is the mathematics of chance. It is a way of calculating how likely it is that something will happen. It is expressed as the following ratio:

$$P(\text{event}) = \frac{\text{number of favorable outcomes}}{\text{number of total outcomes}}$$

The term *favorable outcomes* refers to the events you want to occur. Total outcomes refers to all the possible events that could occur.

A probability of zero (0) means that the event cannot occur. A probability of 50% is said to be random or chance. A probability of 100% or 1.00 means it is certain to occur. Probabilities can be written in different ways:

As a ratio: 1 out of 2 (1:2)
As a fraction: $\frac{1}{2}$
As a percent: 50%
As a decimal: 0.5

Percents

When you see a number followed by the percent symbol, think of the percent as a ratio comparing that number to 100. Percents can be expressed in two different ways:

1. as a fraction (just put the number over 100): $5\% = \frac{5}{100}$

2. as a decimal (move the decimal point two places to the left): $5\% = 0.05$

Recall that the word *of* tells you to multiply. When you take the percent of a number, you should multiply.

When you take the percent of a percent, all you need to do is multiply:

$$40\% \text{ of } 20\% \text{ of } 600 =$$

$$0.40 \text{ of } 0.20 \text{ of } 600 =$$

$$0.40 \times 0.20 \times 600 = 48$$

Set 20

Now it is time to answer GMAT problem-solving practice questions that have been designed to test your arithmetic skills. Remember:

- Solve the problem and indicate the best of the answer choices given.
- All numbers used are real numbers.
- A figure accompanying a problem-solving question is intended to provide information useful in solving the problem. Figures are drawn as accurately as possible EXCEPT when it is stated in a specific problem that the figure is not drawn to scale. Straight lines may sometimes appear jagged. All figures lie in a plane unless otherwise indicated.

354. List the following fractions in order from least to greatest.
$\frac{1}{2}, \frac{5}{7}, \frac{4}{6}, \frac{3}{4}, \frac{3}{8}, \frac{1}{3}, \frac{2}{5}$

   a. $\frac{1}{3}, \frac{3}{8}, \frac{2}{5}, \frac{1}{2}, \frac{4}{6}, \frac{5}{7}, \frac{3}{4}$

   b. $\frac{1}{2}, \frac{1}{3}, \frac{3}{4}, \frac{1}{5}, \frac{4}{6}, \frac{5}{7}, \frac{3}{8}$

   c. $\frac{1}{2}, \frac{1}{3}, \frac{2}{5}, \frac{3}{4}, \frac{3}{8}, \frac{4}{6}, \frac{5}{7}$

   d. $\frac{1}{3}, \frac{3}{8}, \frac{2}{5}, \frac{1}{2}, \frac{4}{6}, \frac{3}{4}, \frac{5}{7}$

   e. $\frac{1}{2}, \frac{5}{7}, \frac{3}{8}, \frac{3}{4}, \frac{2}{5}, \frac{1}{3}, \frac{2}{5}$

355. When processing iron ore into stainless steel, high-purity oxygen is blown through, removing 1.5% of all impurities. Then only 30% of the remaining metal alloy can be used to create rust-free stainless steel. If 5 kg of stainless steel is desired, how much starting iron ore is needed?

   a. 19.61 kg

   b. 16.9 kg

   c. 6.73 kg

   d. 7.64 kg

   e. 16.5 kg

356. The House of Representatives consists of 435 members divided into two parties. How many Daemocrats are seated in the House if their seats are equal to 20 more than two-thirds of the Republican Party seats?
  a. 249
  b. 186
  c. 162
  d. 273
  e. 229

357. In 2009, TechNet had an average net profit of $7.50 per item sold. In 2012, the profit decreased to $6.60 per item sold. What is the percent of profit decrease?
  a. 12%
  b. 11.3%
  c. 8.8%
  d. 9%
  e. 10%

358. A nutritionist creates the following diet. Four days a week the nutritionist eats three meals a day, starting with a 450-calorie breakfast, and adding 100 calories for each subsequent meal. The other three days the nutritionist eats five smaller meals, each consisting of 300 calories. At the end of four weeks what is the average caloric intake per meal?
  a. 386
  b. 411
  c. 394
  d. 425
  e. 488

359. A class is asked to record every book they read during their summer break. Find the median of the summer reading data set.

Jennifer	2
Roman	14
Javier	21
Sophia	1
Sergio	16
Valerie	5
Lizzette	7
Danny	10
Freddy	9
Michelle	22
Julia	2
Victor	3

a. 8
b. 9
c. 9.3
d. 9.5
e. 10

Set 21

Now it is time to answer GMAT data sufficiency practice questions that have been designed to test your arithmetic skills. Remember:

- All numbers used are real numbers.
- A figure accompanying a data sufficiency question will conform to the information given in the question but will not

necessarily conform to the additional information given in statements (I) and (II).

■ In data sufficiency problems that ask for the value of a quantity, the data given in the statement is sufficient only when it is possible to determine exactly one numerical value for the quantity.

360. The approximate average temperature for the second week in March was 75°.

    I. The sum of the seven-day forecast was 525.

    II. The average temperature from Sunday to Tuesday was 67°. The rest of the week was 81°.

  a. Statement (I) ALONE is sufficient, but statement (II) ALONE is not sufficient.

  b. Statement (II) ALONE is sufficient, but statement (I) ALONE is not sufficient.

  c. BOTH statements TOGETHER are sufficient, but NEITHER statement ALONE is sufficient.

  d. EACH statement ALONE is sufficient.

  e. Statements (I) and (II) TOGETHER are NOT sufficient.

361. Is x divisible by five?

    I. The sum of the digits is eight.

    II. The first digit of x is 3.

  a. Statement (I) ALONE is sufficient, but statement (II) ALONE is not sufficient.

  b. Statement (II) ALONE is sufficient, but statement (I) ALONE is not sufficient.

  c. BOTH statements TOGETHER are sufficient, but NEITHER statement ALONE is sufficient.

  d. EACH statement ALONE is sufficient.

  e. Statements (I) and (II) TOGETHER are NOT sufficient.

362. Which company had a higher growth in net profit?

    I. Company P's net profits rose by 2.5%.

    II. Company Q's net profits rose by 3.7%.

a. Statement (I) ALONE is sufficient, but statement (II) ALONE is not sufficient.

b. Statement (II) ALONE is sufficient, but statement (I) ALONE is not sufficient.

c. BOTH statements TOGETHER are sufficient, but NEITHER statement ALONE is sufficient.

d. EACH statement ALONE is sufficient.

e. Statements (I) and (II) TOGETHER are NOT sufficient.

363. How many female attendees at a 240-person concert bought a band T-shirt before the concert?

    I. 40% of the attendees were male.

    II. 127 T-shirts were sold at the gift shop before the show started.

a. Statement (I) ALONE is sufficient, but statement (II) ALONE is not sufficient.

b. Statement (II) ALONE is sufficient, but statement (I) ALONE is not sufficient.

c. BOTH statements TOGETHER are sufficient, but NEITHER statement ALONE is sufficient.

d. EACH statement ALONE is sufficient.

e. Statements (I) and (II) TOGETHER are NOT sufficient.

364. A jar is filled with blue and green marbles. What is the probability that two green marbles are drawn in a row?

    I. There are 36 blue marbles in the jar.

    II. The probability of choosing a green marble on the first try is $\frac{1}{4}$.

a. Statement (I) ALONE is sufficient, but statement (II) ALONE is not sufficient.

b. Statement (II) ALONE is sufficient, but statement (I) ALONE is not sufficient.

c. BOTH statements TOGETHER are sufficient, but NEITHER statement ALONE is sufficient.

d. EACH statement ALONE is sufficient.

e. Statements (I) and (II) TOGETHER are NOT sufficient.

365. How old is Roy if he is twice as old as his friend Jane, Jane is four times as old as Timmy, and Timmy is two year older than Ben?

    I. The sum of all their ages is 152.

    II. Ben is 9.

a. Statement (I) ALONE is sufficient, but statement (II) ALONE is not sufficient.

b. Statement (II) ALONE is sufficient, but statement (I) ALONE is not sufficient.

c. BOTH statements TOGETHER are sufficient, but NEITHER statement ALONE is sufficient.

d. EACH statement ALONE is sufficient.

e. Statements (I) and (II) TOGETHER are NOT sufficient.

366. Annie finished her race before Alexi.

    I. Annie ran the first 4 minutes at a 4 mph pace, and finished the last 8 miles of the race in 60 minutes.

    II. Alexi's top speed was 5.5 mph.

a. Statement (I) ALONE is sufficient, but statement (II) ALONE is not sufficient.

b. Statement (II) ALONE is sufficient, but statement (I) ALONE is not sufficient.

c. BOTH statements TOGETHER are sufficient, but NEITHER statement ALONE is sufficient.

d. EACH statement ALONE is sufficient.

e. Statements (I) and (II) TOGETHER are NOT sufficient.

Answers

Set 14

329. **0.** Using the order of operations, first you divide. 5 + **10** ÷ **5** – 7 becomes 5 + **2** – 7. Next, you add/subtract in order from left to right: **5** + **2** – 7 becomes 7 – 7 = 0.

330. **–10.** Using the order of operations, first you multiply: 2 – **6** × **4** ÷ 2 becomes 2 – **24** ÷ 2. Next, you divide: 2 – **24** ÷ **2** becomes 2 – **12**, which equals –10.

331. **27.** Using the order of operations, first you divide/multiply in order from left to right: **9** ÷ **3** + 3 × 8 becomes **3** + 3 × 8. Next, you multiply: 3 + **3** × **8** becomes 3 + **24**, which equals 27.

Set 15

332. |156| = **156**

333. |–97| = **97**

334. –|13| = **–13**

335. 74 + |–23| = **97**

336. 35 – |–12| = **23**

337. The absolute value symbol serves as a grouping symbol, and grouping symbols are evaluated first: |–5 × 3| = 15. Now, divide 5 into 100 to get 20. Finally, add 20 + 15 = **35**.

338. –9 is equal to the opposite of the absolute value of 9, or –9: 5 × –9 = **–45**.

339. –33 is equal to 33. What times 33 equals 99? Your answer should be **3**.

Set 16

340. $2 \times 2 \times 3 \times 5$

341. The prime factorization of 20 is $2 \times 2 \times 5$. The prime factorization of $30 = 2 \times 3 \times 5$. Because 2 and 5 are prime factors of both 20 and 30, the greatest common factor is 2 times 5, which is **10**.

342. Factors of 63: 1, 3, 7, 9, 21, 63
Factors of 81: 1, 3, 9, 27, 81
All factors have been listed. The largest one in common between 63 and 81 is **9**.

343. Multiples of 63: 63, 126, 189, 252, 315, 378, 441, 504, 567
Multiples of 81: 81, 162, 243, 324, 405, 486, 567
Multiples are listed until one is found in common. The least common multiple of 63 and 81 is **567**.

Set 17

344. $3\frac{4}{5}$. To convert an improper fraction to a mixed number, divide the numerator by the denominator: $19 \div 5 = 3$ with 4 left over. You express the remainder as a fraction. The improper fraction has a denominator of 5, so the remainder has a denominator of 5: $19 \div 5 = \mathbf{3\frac{4}{5}}$.

345. $\frac{53}{8}$. To convert a mixed number to an improper fraction, you begin by multiplying the whole number, 6, by the denominator of the fraction, 8: $6 \times 8 = 48$. Next, add to that product the numerator of the fraction: $48 + 5 = 53$. Put this number over the original denominator, 8, to get the improper fraction $\frac{53}{8}$.

346. $\frac{2}{5}$. First convert both fractions to the LCD ($\frac{4}{3} = \frac{20}{15}$). Subtract the numerators and write the result over the denominator. Don't forget to reduce! ($\frac{20}{15} - \frac{14}{15} = \frac{6}{15}$, which reduces to $\frac{2}{5}$).

Set 18

347. The correct answer is **0.008, 0.03**. Since 0.008 has three decimal digits, tack one zero onto the end of 0.03, making it 0.030. To compare 0.008 to 0.030, just compare 30 to 8. 30 is larger than 8, so 0.03 is larger than 0.008.

348. **5.1.** Line up the numbers so that their decimal points are aligned. Move the decimal point directly down into the answer and subtract: 6.4 − 1.3 = **5.1**.

349. **12.4.** Multiply 31 by 4: 31 × 4 = 124. The answer requires 1 decimal digit because there is a total of 1 decimal digit in 3.1 and 4. Move the decimal point one place to the left (**12.4**).

Set 19

350. To find the mean, add all the data values, and divide by the number of items, which is eight: 32 + 34 + 34 + 35 + 37 + 38 + 34 + 42 = 286; 286 divided by 8 is **35.75**.

351. There are two modes for this data set. Both **71** and **68** appear in the set twice.

352. First, arrange the data into increasing order: 8, 9, 9, 9, 10, 10, 11, 12, 13, 17. There is an even number of data values, so the median is the mean of the two middle values. The middle values are 10 + 10 = 20, and 20 divided by 2 is **10**.

353. The range is the difference between the highest and lowest values in the set of data. The highest temperature is 84° and the lowest temperature is 42°: 84° − 42° = **42°**.

Set 20

354. **a.** All fractions can be converted to decimals to verify whether they are in the correct order form least to greatest.

$$\frac{1}{3} = 0.33$$

$$\frac{3}{8} = 0.375$$

$$\frac{2}{5} = 0.4$$

$$\frac{1}{2} = 0.5$$

$$\frac{4}{6} = 0.67$$

$$\frac{5}{7} = 0.71$$

$$\frac{3}{4} = 0.75$$

Choice **b** is incorrect as it lists the fractions from least to greatest according to denominator. Choice **c** is incorrect as it lists the fractions from least to greatest according to numerator. Choice **d** is incorrect as it mixes up the last two fractions, $\frac{5}{7}$ and $\frac{3}{4}$.

355. **b.** Starting with the 5 kg product, you can work backward to find the metal alloy (m) middle product and the original total of iron ore (t).

5 kg = 0.30(m)

m = 16.67 kg

$t - 0.015t = m$

$t - 0.015t = 16.67$ kg

$0.985t = 16.67$ kg

$t = 16.9$ kg

The rest of the answers are incorrect because they do not set the equations up correctly ($0.015t = 16.66$) or they use the wrong percentile decimal (0.15 instead of 0.015)

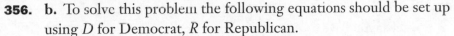

356. **b.** To solve this problem the following equations should be set up using D for Democrat, R for Republican.

$D + R = 435$

$\frac{2}{3}R + 20 = D$

Then substitute the second equation into the first equation.

$(\frac{2}{3}R + 20) + R = 435$

$\frac{5}{3}R = 415$

$R = 249$

Then substitute R into the first equation to solve for D.

$D + (249) = 435$

$D = 186$

Choice **a** is the number of the Republican seats, not Democrat seats. Choices **c** and **d** are the respective Democrat and Republican seats if you set your equation up incorrectly and subtracted 20, ($\frac{2}{3}R - 20$), instead of adding.

357. **a.** To properly solve this problem you would need to set up an equation, using p for percent profit.

$7.50 - 7.50(p) = 6.60$

$-7.5(p) = .9$

$p = -.12 \text{ or } -12\%$

This represents a 12% profit decrease. Choice **b** is the profit calculated using this incorrect equation: $7.5 \div 6.5 = p$.

Choice **c** is the profit calculated using this incorrect equation: $6.5 \div 7.5 = p$.

Choice **d** is incorrect because you just subtracted $7.5 - 6.6 = 0.9$.

358. **b.** To find the average caloric intake per meal during these four
weeks, you have to find the average during a one week cycle.

$(450 + 550 + 650) = 1,650 \times 4$ days $= 6,600$ (3 meals a day for
4 days $= 12$ total meals per week)

$(300 + 300 + 300 + 300 + 300) = 1,500 \times 3$ days $= 4,500$ (5 meals
a day for 3 days $= 15$ total meals per week)

$6,600 + 4,500 = 11,100$ total calories at the end of a week

$\frac{11,100}{27} = 411$ calories per meal

Choice **c** is incorrect because is it only the average of the two
different meal plans.

$(450 + 550 + 650 + 5(300)) \div 8$ meals $= 394$

Choice **d** is incorrect because it is the average of each day averaged
together:

$(550 + 300) \div 2 = 425$

359. **a.** The median is the number in the middle of the series when the
numbers are arranged in numerical order.

1, 2, 2, 3, 5, 7, 9, 10, 14, 16, 21, 22

Since there are an even amount of numbers, to find the median
you must find the mean of the middle two numbers. The mean of
7 and 9 is 8. Choice **b** is incorrect because it means you did not
include the second 2 in your series. Choice **c** is incorrect as it is the
mean of the series. Choice **d** is incorrect as it is the mean of the
series without including the double 2. Choice **e** is incorrect
because you forgot to list 2 twice when ordering the numbers from
least to greatest.

Set 21

360. **d.** Either statement will produce an average temperature of 75°.
For the first statement, if the sum of all seven days is 525, you can
divide by 7 (total days in the week) to find the average of 75°. For
statement (2), you can sum the first three days (Sunday–Tuesday)
and get 201 ($67 \times 3 = 201$) , and then sum the last four days
(Wednesday–Saturday) and get 324 ($81 \times 4 = 324$), add those
together, and divide by 7 to find an average of 75° ($201 + 324 =
525 \div 7 = 75$).

361. **c.** Both statements are needed together because if x is divisible by 5, the second digit must be either a zero or a 5. If the sum of the digits is 8, the only combination that would make x divisible by 5 would be 3 and 5 or 8 and 0. The second statement confirms that the first digit is 3, meaning the second digit has to be 5, so they can sum to 8.

362. **e.** It does not matter how much the profits rose if we do not know the actual profits. 2.5% of 1,000 would be larger than 3.7% of 100.

363. **e.** Neither statement is sufficient because they do not state how many females bought T-shirts. The first statement allows you to determine how many females are present at the concert. The second statement tells you how many total T-shirts were bought, but it cannot be assumed that equal ratios of males and females bought shirts.

364. **c.** In order to determine the probability, you would need to know both the total number of marbles and the ratio of blue to green marbles. Using the information from both statements you can determine both the total number of marbles and the specific number of each. If there are 36 blue marbles, and a $\frac{1}{4}$ chance of picking a green marble, that means there are 9 green marbles. $(\frac{1}{4} = \frac{\text{green marbles}}{\text{blue marbles}} = \frac{9}{36})$

365. **d.** You can use either statement independently to determine the age of Roy. To use either statement you would have to set up algebraic expressions for each variable.

$R = 2J$

$J = 4T$

$T = B + 2$

Given statement (I), you know the sum of all ages,

$R + J + T + B = 152$

but in order to solve you would have to put the expression in terms of one variable, say, B:

$2(4(B + 2)) + 4(B + 2) + (B + 2) + B = 152$, then solve for B:

$8B + 16 + 4B + 8 + B + 2 + B = 152$

$14B + 26 = 152$

$14B = 126$

$B = 9$

Then, using that, or the information given in statement (II), plug B back into the original expressions to solve for T, J, and R.

$T = (9) + 2$

$T = 11$

$J = 4(11)$

$J = 44$

$R = 2(44)$

$R = 88$

Roy is 88 years old.

366. **c.** To determine who won the race, both statements are needed for comparison. The first statement allows you to calculate Annie's average speed. If she ran the first 4 miles at 4 miles per hour, the last 8 miles in 60 minutes, she ran a total of 12 miles in 120 minutes (or 2 hours).

speed = distance ÷ time

Annie's speed = 12 miles ÷ 2 hours = 6 miles per hour.

The second statement tells you that Alexi's fastest pace was 5.5 miles per hour, meaning that could be his highest average speed, if he ran the entire race at his top speed. With both statements we can compare the two speeds and confirm that Annie did finish the race faster if she ran at a higher average speed.

10

Algebra

Algebra questions account for about 25% of the GMAT quantitative section. This chapter reviews key algebra concepts, including:

- sequences
- exponents
- roots
- expressions
- equations
- word problems
- inequalities

Sequences

Arithmetic sequences grow by adding or subtracting a constant number to each term. For example, look at the following series:

9, 13, 17, 21, . . .

Notice that each term is four more than the term that comes before it. This is an example of an arithmetic series with a common difference of 4. What will the next term be?

To solve, add 4 to 21:

$$21 + 4 = 25$$

Thus, the next term will be 25.

Geometric sequences grow by multiplying each term by a constant number to get the next term. For example, look at the following series:

$$5, 25, 125, 625, \ldots$$

Note that each term is five times the prior term. This is an example of a geometric series with a common ratio of 5. What will the next term be?

Multiply 625 by 5:

$$625 \times 5 = 3{,}125$$

Thus, the next term will be 3,125.

Set 22

Find the missing numbers in the following sequences.

367. What is the next number in the following sequence?
3, 16, 6, 12, 12, 8, __

368. What number should come next in the following sequence?
$0.2, \frac{1}{5}, 0.4, \frac{2}{5}, 0.8, \frac{4}{5}$

Exponents

An *exponent* tells you how many times the base is used as a factor. In the expression 4^3, the three is the exponent and the four is the base. The expression 4^3 shows that four is a factor three times. That means four times four times four.

When you are multiplying two identical bases, you add the exponents instead of multiplying them. For example:

$$x^2 \cdot x^3 =$$

$$(x \cdot x)(x \cdot x \cdot x) =$$

$$x^5$$

Set 23

Solve the following problems.

369. $5^2 =$

370. $2^3 =$

371. $a^3 a^4 =$

Roots

You know you need to take the square root of a number when you see a radical sign, which looks like this $\sqrt{}$.

To find the square root of a number, ask yourself: What number when squared will equal the number under the radical sign?

For example, you know that $2^2 = 4$, so $\sqrt{4} = 2$. Square roots are relatively easy to calculate for *perfect squares*, such as:

$\sqrt{4} = 2$
$\sqrt{9} = 3$
$\sqrt{16} = 4$
$\sqrt{25} = 5$
$\sqrt{36} = 6$

Other times, you can approximate the value of a radical by finding out which two perfect squares it falls between. For example, since $\sqrt{25} = 5$ and $\sqrt{36} = 6$, $\sqrt{30}$ must be a number between 5 and 6.

You know that $3 \times 3 = 9$, so $\sqrt{9} = 3$. But, $-3 \times -3 = 9$ as well. $\sqrt{9}$ has two solutions: 3 and -3.

However, for the most part, you will be solving for the *principle square root*, which will be the positive root.

If a problem is looking for both solutions, the problem will be written like this: $\pm\sqrt{9}$.

You can multiply and divide the square roots of different numbers, but you cannot add or subtract them.

$$\sqrt{a} + \sqrt{b} \neq \sqrt{a+b}$$

$$\sqrt{a} - \sqrt{b} \neq \sqrt{a-b}$$

$$\sqrt{a} \times \sqrt{b} \neq \sqrt{a \times b}$$

$$\sqrt{\frac{a}{b}} = \frac{\sqrt{a}}{\sqrt{b}}$$

If you are dealing with the root of the same number, you can combine the like terms:

$$\sqrt{a} + \sqrt{a} = 2\sqrt{a}$$

$$\frac{4\sqrt{a}}{2\sqrt{a}} = 2\sqrt{a}$$

Set 24

Solve the following problems.

372. $\sqrt{12} \times \sqrt{12} =$

373. $\sqrt{\dfrac{1}{4}} =$

374. $\sqrt{9} + \sqrt{16} =$

375. $\sqrt{9+16} =$

Algebraic Expressions

In algebra, letters are often used to represent numbers. These letters are called *variables*. The numbers in front of the variable or variables are called *coefficients*. Remember:

- A coefficient is a factor in an algebraic term, as are the variable or variables in the term.
- Like terms can have different coefficients, but the configuration of the variables must be the same for the terms to be alike. For example, $3x$ and $-4x$ are like terms, but they are different from $7ax$.

Mathematical expressions, like numbers, can be named in different ways. For example, here are three ways to write the same expression:

$x + -3$

$x + (-3)$

$x - 3$

For purposes of combining like terms, a variable by itself is understood to mean one of that term:

$n = +1n$

A term without a sign in front of it is considered to be positive.

To simplify expressions, clear any parentheses, combine like terms by adding coefficients, and then combine the constants.

When you are asked to evaluate an algebraic expression, you substitute a number in place of a variable (letter) and then simplify the expression.

Set 25

Simplify the following expressions by combining like terms.

376. $5a + 2a + 7a$

377. $7a + 6b + 3a$

378. $4x + 2y - x + 3y$

379. $27 - 3m + 12 - 5m$

380. $7h + 6 + 2w - 3 + h$

Simplify the following expressions by combining like terms.

381. Evaluate the expression $2b + a$ when $a = 2$ and $b = 4$.

382. Evaluate the expression $a^2 + 2b + c$ when $a = 2$, $b = 3$, and $b = 7$.

Equations

An *equation* is a mathematical tool that helps people solve many real-life problems. The word *equation* means *two equal expressions*. These expressions could be numbers, such as $6 = 5 + 1$, or variables, such as $D = rt$.

What does it mean to solve an equation? When you find the value of the variable, you have solved the equation. For example, you have solved the equation $2x = 10$ once you know the value of x.

Here's the basic rule for solving equations: *When you do something to one side of an equation, you must do the same thing to the other side of the equation.* You'll know you have solved an equation once the variable is alone (isolated) on one side of the equation and the variable is positive. In the example $-x = 5$, 5 is not the answer because the x variable is negative. Remember that $-x$ is the same as $-1x$. To make the variable positive, divide both sides by -1. Therefore, $x = -5$.

Solving Equations Using Addition or Subtraction

You can solve equations using addition and subtraction by getting the variable on one side by itself. Think about how you would solve this equation:

$x + 4 = 10$

Your goal is to get the variable x on one side by itself. To get x by itself, you need to get rid of the 4. If you subtract 4 from 4, the result is 0, and you have eliminated the 4 to get x on one side by itself. However, if you subtract 4 from the left side of the equation, then you must do the same to the right side of the equation.

Subtract 4 from both sides of the equation: $x + 4 - 4 = 10 - 4$

Simplify both sides of the equation: $x + 0 = 6$

Add 0 to x: $x = 6$

When you add zero to a number, the number does not change, so $x + 0 = x$. When you do this, you are using the additive property of zero, which states that a number added to zero equals that number. For example, $5 + 0 = 5$.

Set 26

Simplify both sides of the following equations.

383. $x - 5 = 9$

384. $a + 6 = 7$

385. $y - 11 = 8$

386. $-r + 9 = 13$

387. $d - 7 = 8$

388. $x - 5 = -6$

Solving Equations Using Multiplication or Division

In the equation $x + 10 = 2$, to get rid of the 10, you would subtract 10. In the equation $x - 5 = 6$, to get rid of the 5, you would add 5. So, in the equation $5x = 10$, how would you get rid of the 5?

The opposite of multiplying by 5 is dividing by 5; therefore, you would solve this equation using division:

$$5x = 10$$
$$\frac{5x}{5} = \frac{10}{5}$$
$$x = 2$$

When you divide a number by itself, you always get 1, so $5x$ divided by 5 equals $1x$. Remember, $1x$ is the same as x.

In the equation $\frac{x}{5} = 2$, how would you get rid of the 5 so the x will be on one side by itself? If you multiply $\frac{x}{5}$ times 5, you will get $1x$, which is the same as x.

Set 27

Solve the following equations.

389. $\frac{x}{2} = 13$

390. $\frac{x}{5} = 3$

Polynomials

A *polynomial* is a number, a variable, or a combination of a number and a variable. A polynomial can be one or more terms. Monomials, binomials, and trinomials are all polynomials.

A polynomial with one term is called a *monomial*. To multiply a polynomial with one term (monomial) by a polynomial with more than one term, use the distributive property. You multiply the term outside the parentheses by every term inside the parentheses. For example:

$$2(a + b - 3) = 2a + 2b - 6$$
$$3x(x^2 + 2x) = 3x^3 + 6x^2$$

A *binomial* is a polynomial with two terms. To multiply a binomial by a binomial, you will use a method called FOIL. This process is called FOIL because you work the problem in this order:

First
Outer
Inner
Last

Example: $(x + 2)(x + 3)$
Multiply the first terms in each binomial: $([x] + 2)([x] + 3) = \boldsymbol{x^2}$
Multiply the two outer terms in each binomial: $([x] + 2)(x + [3]) =$
$\quad x^2 + \boldsymbol{3x}$
Multiply the two inner terms in each binomial: $(x + [2])([x] + 3) =$
$\quad x^2 + 3x + \boldsymbol{2x}$
Multiply the two last terms in each binomial: $(x + [2])(x + [3]) =$
$\quad x^2 + 3x + 2x + \boldsymbol{6}$
Simplify: $= x^2 + 5x + 6$

A bicycle has two wheels; a tricycle has three wheels. Likewise, a binomial has two terms, and a *trinomial* has three terms. Here's how you would multiply a binomial by a trinomial.

$(x + 2)(x^2 + 2x + 1)$

To work this problem, you need to multiply each term in the first polynomial with each term in the second polynomial. You are doing exactly that when you use FOIL.

Multiply x by each term in the second polynomial: $x(x^2 + 2x + 1) =$
$\quad x^3 + 2x^2 + x$
Multiply 2 by each term in the second polynomial: $2(x^2 + 2x + 1) =$
$\quad 2x^2 + 4x + 2$
Simplify: $x^3 + 2x^2 + x + 2x^2 + 4x + 2 = x^3 + 4x^2 + 5x + 2$

Formulas

Formulas are special equations that show relationships between quantities. For example, you have probably worked with the formula $A = lw$. This formula tells you to multiply the length times the width of a rectangle to find its area. The formula $D = rt$ tells you to multiply the rate by the time to find the distance traveled.

When you substitute the information you know into a formula, you can use that to find the information you don't know. For example, if you travel 55 miles per hour (mph) for 3 hours, how far would you travel? Substitute what you know into the equation. Then, solve the equation for the variable you don't know.

Substitute what you know into the formula: $D = 55 \times 3$
Multiply: $D = 165$
You would travel 165 miles.

This technique works for any formula, even if the formula is very complex.

Example: Find the interest on a savings account with a balance of $2,400, when the interest rate is 3% for 3 years. Use the formula $I = prt$.
I = interest earned
p = amount of money invested
r = interest rate
t = time invested
$I = prt$

Substitute what you know into the formula:

$I = \$2,400 \times 3\% \times 3$ years
$I = 2,400 \times .03 \times 3$

Simplify the equation:

$I = \$216$

Set 28

Answer the following problems by substituting the information that you know into the formulas.

391. How long would you need to invest $3,000 with an interest rate of 3.5% to earn $630? (Use $I = prt$)

392. How long would it take to travel 300 miles traveling at a speed of 60 mph? (Use $D = rt$)

Setting Up Equations for Real-World Problems

Equations can be used to solve real-life problems. In an equation, the variable often represents the answer to a real-life problem. For example, suppose you know that you can earn twice as much money this summer as you did last summer. You made $1,200 last summer. How much will you earn this summer? You can use the variable x to represent the answer to the problem. You want to know how much you can earn this summer.

Let x = how much you can earn this summer.

$1,200 = amount earned last summer
$x = 2 \times \$1,200$
$x = \$2,400$

Set 29

Answer the following problems.

393. There are twice as many women in your yoga class as there are men. If there are 18 women in the class, how many men are in the class?

394. You are going to be working for Success Corporation. You got a signing bonus of $2,500, and you will be paid $17.50 an hour. If you are paid monthly, how much will your first paycheck be? Be sure to include your signing bonus, and assume that you have a 40-hour work week and that there are 4 weeks in this month.

395. Grace sells real estate and receives a 6% commission for every residential property that she sells. How much commission would she receive if she sold a home for $175,000?

396. There are 40 questions on a test. How many questions must you answer correctly to score 90%?

Inequalities

An *inequality* is two numbers or expressions that are connected with an inequality symbol. The inequality symbols are

<	(less than)
>	(greater than)
≤	(less than or equal to)
≥	(greater than or equal to)
≠	(not equal to)

Here are some examples of inequalities:

$2 < 5$	(two is less than five)
$9 > 3$	(nine is greater than three)
$4 \leq 4$	(four is less than or equal to four)
$2x + 5 \neq 11$	($2x$ added to five is not equal to eleven)

You can solve inequalities with variables just like you can solve equations with variables. Use what you already know about solving equations to solve inequalities. Like equations, you can add, subtract, multiply, or divide both sides of an inequality with the same number. In other words, what you do to one side of an inequality, you must do to the other side.

Example: $2x + 3 < 1$

Subtract 3 from both sides of the inequality:

$2x + 3 - 3 < 1 - 3$

Simplify both sides of the inequality:

$2x < -2$

Divide both sides of the inequality by 2:

$\frac{2x}{2} < \frac{-2}{2}$

Simplify both sides of the inequality:

$x < -1$

The answer for this example is the inequality $x < -1$. There is an infinite (endless) number of solutions because every number less than -1 is an answer. In this problem, the number -1 is not an answer because the inequality states that your answers must be numbers less than -1.

Did you notice the similarity between solving equations and solving inequalities? You can see that the previous example was solved using the same steps you would use if you were solving an equation.

However, there are some differences between solving equations and solving inequalities. Notice what happens when you multiply or divide an inequality by a negative number.

$2 < 5$
$-2 \times 2 < 5 \times -2$
$-4 < -10$

However, -4 is not less than -10. So $-4 < -10$ is a false statement. To correct it, you would have to rewrite it as $-4 > -10$.

You can solve inequalities using the same methods that you use to solve equations with these exceptions:

- When you multiply or divide an inequality by a negative number, you must reverse the inequality symbol.
- The answer to an inequality will always be an inequality.

Set 30

Solve each inequality.

397. $x + 3 < 10$

398. $2x + 5 < 7$

399. $-3x < 9$

400. $5x + 1 < 11$

401. You are treating a friend to a movie. You will buy 2 tickets and spend $8 on concessions. If you don't want to spend more than $20, how much can you spend on each ticket?

402. You are pricing lawn furniture and plan to buy 4 chairs. You don't want to spend more than $120. What is the most you can spend on one chair?

403. You are going to a restaurant for lunch. You have $15 to spend. Your beverage is $2.50, and you will leave a $2 tip. How much can you spend on the entrée?

404. You own a gift shop. You bought a case of candles for $144. There are 12 candles in a case. What do you need to sell each candle for to make a profit?

Set 31

Now it is time to answer GMAT problem-solving practice questions that have been designed to test your algebra skills. Remember:

- Solve the problem and indicate the best of the answer choices given.
- All numbers used are real numbers.
- A figure accompanying a problem-solving question is intended to provide information useful in solving the problem. Figures are drawn as accurately as possible EXCEPT when it is stated in a specific problem that the figure is not drawn to scale. Straight lines may sometimes appear jagged. All figures lie in a plane unless otherwise indicated.

405. Simplify $\dfrac{x^2 + 7x + 10}{3x^5 + 6x^4} \div \dfrac{x^2 - 25}{15x^8}$

    a. $\dfrac{15x^2}{3x^4\,(x - 5)}$

    b. $\dfrac{5x^4}{x + 5}$

    c. $\dfrac{-5x^4}{x - 5}$

    d. $5x^4(x - 5)$

    e. $\dfrac{5x^4}{x - 5}$

406. Factor the trinomial $4x^2 - 9x - 9$

    a. $(4x + 3)(x + 3)$

    b. $(4x + 3)(x - 3)$

    c. $(8x - 6)(x + 3)$

    d. $(4x + 3)(3x + 1)$

    e. $(2x - 3)(2x - 3)$

407. Simplify the expression $\dfrac{18x^4y^{10}z^6}{20x^{11}y^3z}$

    a. $\dfrac{9y^7z^5}{10x^7}$

    b. $\dfrac{9y^7x^7z^5}{10}$

    c. $\dfrac{z^5}{2}$

    d. $\dfrac{y^7z^5}{2x^7}$

    e. $\dfrac{9x^7}{10y^7z^5}$

408. Multiply $(x + 3)^2$

    a. $x^2 + 9x + 9$

    b. $x^2 + 6x - 9$

    c. $x^2 - 9$

    d. $x^2 + 6x + 9$

    e. $x^2 + 6$

409. $|3x + 9| < 15$

    a. $x < -2$ or $x > 8$

    b. $x > -2$ and $x < 8$

    c. $x < 2$ and $x > -8$

    d. $x > 2$ or $x < -8$

    e. none of the above

410. $\sqrt[3]{8} + \sqrt{81} =$

    a. 13

    b. 89

    c. 17

    d. 33

    e. 11

411. Annie has a total of 100 dimes and quarters. If the total value of the coins is $14.05, how many quarters does she have?

    a. 3

    b. 40

    c. 56

    d. 73

    e. 27

412. Which equation is part of the process of completing the square for $x^2 - 8x + 4 = 49$?

    a. $(x + 8)^2 = 11$

    b. $(x - 8)^2 = 67$

    c. $(x - 4)^2 = 61$

    d. $(x + 4)^2 = 19$

    e. $(x + 2)^2 = 11$

413. The sum of x^2 and $7x$ is –10. What is one possible answer for x?

    a. $x = -2$

    b. $x = 5$

    c. $x = 2$

    d. $x = 10$

    e. $x = -7$

414. In the following sequence, each term is 6 greater than the previous term. Which of the following could NOT be a term in the sequence?

    –36, –30, –24, –18, . . .

    a. –492

    b. 256

    c. 344

    d. 510

    e. 678

415. $(37)^3$

    a. 50,653

    b. 49,453

    c. 50,427

    d. 49,867

    e. 50,238

Set 32

Now it is time to answer GMAT data sufficiency practice questions that have been designed to test your algebra skills. Good luck!

416. Is $x > y$?

    I. x and y are both positive integers.

    II. $x \div y > 1$

    a. Statement (I) ALONE is sufficient, but statement (II) ALONE is not sufficient.

    b. Statement (II) ALONE is sufficient, but statement (I) ALONE is not sufficient.

    c. BOTH statements TOGETHER are sufficient, but NEITHER statement ALONE is sufficient.

    d. EACH statement ALONE is sufficient.

    e. Statements (I) and (II) TOGETHER are NOT sufficient.

417. In a sequence, what is the fifth term?

    I. The sum of the first term and fourth term is equal to the fifth term.

    II. All numbers are multiples of the first term.

    a. Statement (I) ALONE is sufficient, but statement (II) ALONE is not sufficient.

    b. Statement (II) ALONE is sufficient, but statement (I) ALONE is not sufficient.

    c. BOTH statements TOGETHER are sufficient, but NEITHER statement ALONE is sufficient.

    d. EACH statement ALONE is sufficient.

    e. Statements (I) and (II) TOGETHER are NOT sufficient.

418. Are x and y positive integers?

    I. xy is positive.

    II. x^2 and y^2 are both positive.

a. Statement (I) ALONE is sufficient, but statement (II) ALONE is not sufficient.

b. Statement (II) ALONE is sufficient, but statement (I) ALONE is not sufficient.

c. BOTH statements TOGETHER are sufficient, but NEITHER statement ALONE is sufficient.

d. EACH statement ALONE is sufficient.

e. Statements (I) and (II) TOGETHER are NOT sufficient.

419. Annie and Alexi are running a race. When the race starts Alexi starts running 9 ft. per second. Annie starts 10 seconds later because she forgot to stretch. She is running at a pace of 10 ft. per second. If they keep going at the same pace, who will win?

    I. Their distance after 20 seconds is equal.

    II. It is a 500 ft. race.

a. Statement (I) ALONE is sufficient, but statement (II) ALONE is not sufficient.

b. Statement (II) ALONE is sufficient, but statement (I) ALONE is not sufficient.

c. BOTH statements TOGETHER are sufficient, but NEITHER statement ALONE is sufficient.

d. EACH statement ALONE is sufficient.

e. Statements (I) and (II) TOGETHER are NOT sufficient.

420. A ball is dropped off a balcony 49 ft. high. How long will it take to hit the ground?

    I. The acceleration of the ball toward the ground is –9.8 m/s.

    II. The ball weighs 3 lbs.

a. Statement (I) ALONE is sufficient, but statement (II) ALONE is not sufficient.

b. Statement (II) ALONE is sufficient, but statement (I) ALONE is not sufficient.

c. BOTH statements TOGETHER are sufficient, but NEITHER statement ALONE is sufficient.

d. EACH statement ALONE is sufficient.

e. Statements (I) and (II) TOGETHER are NOT sufficient.

421. Are x and y consecutive integers?

    I. $x + y = 15$

    II. $x - y = 3$

  a. Statement (I) ALONE is sufficient, but statement (II) ALONE is not sufficient.

  b. Statement (II) ALONE is sufficient, but statement (I) ALONE is not sufficient.

  c. BOTH statements TOGETHER are sufficient, but NEITHER statement ALONE is sufficient.

  d. EACH statement ALONE is sufficient.

  e. Statements (I) and (II) TOGETHER are NOT sufficient.

422. Find the values of x and y.

    I. $3x + 2 = y - 7$

    II. $4x - 12y = 36$

  a. Statement (I) ALONE is sufficient, but statement (II) ALONE is not sufficient.

  b. Statement (II) ALONE is sufficient, but statement (I) ALONE is not sufficient.

  c. BOTH statements TOGETHER are sufficient, but NEITHER statement ALONE is sufficient.

  d. EACH statement ALONE is sufficient.

  e. Statements (I) and (II) TOGETHER are NOT sufficient.

423. The sum of the polynomials is $4x + 6$. What are the two polynomials?

    I. The difference of the two is 0.

    II. The product of the two polynomials is $4x^2 + 12x + 9$.

  a. Statement (I) ALONE is sufficient, but statement (II) ALONE is not sufficient.

  b. Statement (II) ALONE is sufficient, but statement (I) ALONE is not sufficient.

  c. BOTH statements TOGETHER are sufficient, but NEITHER statement ALONE is sufficient.

  d. EACH statement ALONE is sufficient.

  e. Statements (I) and (II) TOGETHER are NOT sufficient.

424. Eric was buying cookies and Pop-Tarts. He bought 5 cookies and 10 Pop–Tarts for $12.50. How much were the cookies?

    I. Pop-Tarts are $1.00.

    II. You can buy 20 cookies and 20 Pop-Tarts for $30.00.

a. Statement (I) ALONE is sufficient, but statement (II) ALONE is not sufficient.

b. Statement (II) ALONE is sufficient, but statement (I) ALONE is not sufficient.

c. BOTH statements TOGETHER are sufficient, but NEITHER statement ALONE is sufficient.

d. EACH statement ALONE is sufficient.

e. Statements (I) and (II) TOGETHER are NOT sufficient.

425. What is the value of x in the following expression?

$$\frac{4a^3b^4c^x}{12ab^7c^{12}}$$

    I. The simplified expression has a coefficient of 3 in the denominator.

    II. The resulting exponent of c in the simplified answer is 9.

a. Statement (I) ALONE is sufficient, but statement (II) ALONE is not sufficient.

b. Statement (II) ALONE is sufficient, but statement (I) ALONE is not sufficient.

c. BOTH statements TOGETHER are sufficient, but NEITHER statement ALONE is sufficient.

d. EACH statement ALONE is sufficient.

e. Statements (I) and (II) TOGETHER are NOT sufficient.

426. The expression $4x + 9 - 2(5x + 1)$ is equal to a number. What is the number?

    I. The number is 9 less than twice the value of x.

    II. The number is an integer and is less than x.

a. Statement (I) ALONE is sufficient, but statement (II) ALONE is not sufficient.

b. Statement (II) ALONE is sufficient, but statement (I) ALONE is not sufficient.

c. BOTH statements TOGETHER are sufficient, but NEITHER statement ALONE is sufficient.

d. EACH statement ALONE is sufficient.

e. Statements (I) and (II) TOGETHER are NOT sufficient.

427. Kline spent three hours on the phone with her brother. 20% of that time was spent talking about work. The rest of the time was spent talking about her boyfriend, weekend plans, and new kitten. How much time did she spend talking about her kitten?

    I. She spent twice as long talking about her boyfriend as on work and her weekend plans combined.

    II. She spent the same amount of time on the kitten as she did on her weekend plans.

a. Statement (I) ALONE is sufficient, but statement (II) ALONE is not sufficient.

b. Statement (II) ALONE is sufficient, but statement (I) ALONE is not sufficient.

c. BOTH statements TOGETHER are sufficient, but NEITHER statement ALONE is sufficient.

d. EACH statement ALONE is sufficient.

e. Statements (I) and (II) TOGETHER are NOT sufficient.

Answers

Set 22

367. This sequence actually has two alternating sets of numbers. The first number is doubled, giving the third number. The second number has 4 subtracted from it, giving the fourth number. Therefore, the next number will be 12 doubled, or **24**.

368. This is a multiplication sequence with repetition. The decimals (0.2, 0.4, 0.8) are repeated by fractions with the same values ($\frac{1}{5}, \frac{2}{5}, \frac{4}{5}$) and are then multiplied by 2. Thus, the next number will be 0.8×2, or **1.6**.

Set 23

369. $5^2 = 5 \cdot 5 = \mathbf{25}$

370. $2^3 = 2 \cdot 2 \cdot 2 = \mathbf{8}$

371. $a^3 a^4 = (a \cdot a \cdot a)(a \cdot a \cdot a \cdot a) = a^{3+4} = \boldsymbol{a^7}$

Set 24

372. **12.** Use the rule $\sqrt{a} \times \sqrt{b} = \sqrt{a \times b}$ to get $\sqrt{12} \times \sqrt{12} = \sqrt{12 \times 12} = \sqrt{144} = 12$.

373. $\frac{1}{2}$. Use the rule $\sqrt{\frac{a}{b}} = \sqrt{a} / \sqrt{b}$ to get $\sqrt{\frac{1}{4}} = \frac{\sqrt{1}}{\sqrt{4}} = \frac{1}{2}$.

374. **7.** Solve and add: $\sqrt{9} + \sqrt{16} = 3 + 4 = 7$

375. **5.** Add the numbers under the radical, then take the square root: $\sqrt{9+16} = \sqrt{25} = 5$

Set 25

376. Use the associative property of addition: $(5a + 2a) + 7a$
Add like terms: $[5a + 2a = 7a]$
Substitute the results into the original expression: $(7a) + 7a$
Add like terms: $7a + 7a = 14a$
The simplified result of the algebraic expression is: **14a**

377. Use the commutative property of addition to move like terms together: $7a + 3a + 6b$
Use the associative property for addition: $(7a + 3a) + 6b$
Add like terms: $[(7a + 3a) = 10a]$
Substitute: $(10a) + 6b$
The simplified result of the algebraic expression is: **$10a + 6b$**

378. Change subtraction to addition and change the sign of the term that follows: $4x + 2y + (-x) + 3y$
Use the commutative property of addition to move like terms together: $4x + (-x) + 2y + 3y$
Use the associative property for addition: $(4x + -x) + (2y + 3y)$
Add like terms: $[4x + -x = +3x = 3x]$
$[2y + 3y = 5y]$
Substitute the results into the expression: $(4x + -x) + (2y + 3y) =$
$(3x) + (5y)$
The simplified algebraic expression is: **$3x + 5y$**

379. Change subtraction to addition and change the sign of the term that follows: $27 + -3m + 12 + -5m$
Use the commutative property for addition to put like terms together: $27 + 12 + -3m + -5m$
Use the associative property for addition: $(27 + 12) + (-3m + -5m)$
Add like terms: $[27 + 12 = 39]$
$[-3m + -5m = -8m]$
Substitute the results into the expression: $(27 + 12) + (-3m + -5m)$
$= (39) + (-8m)$
Rewrite addition of a negative term as subtraction of a positive term by changing addition to subtraction and changing the sign of the following term: $39 - +8m = 39 - 8m$
The simplified algebraic expression is: **$39 - 8m$**

380. Change subtraction to addition and change the sign of the term that follows: $7h + 6 + 2w + (-3) + h$

Use the commutative property for addition to put like terms together: $7h + h + 2w + 6 + -3$

Use the associative property for addition: $(7h + h) + 2w + (6 + -3)$

Add like terms: $[(7h + h) = 8h]$

$\qquad\qquad\quad [(6 + -3) = 3]$

Substitute the result into the expression: $(8h) + 2w + (3)$

The simplified algebraic expression is: $\mathbf{8h + 2w + 3}$

381. Substitute 2 for the variable a and 4 for the variable b. When the expression is written as $2b$, it means 2 times b: $2b + a$

Multiply $2 \cdot 4$: $2(4) + 2$

Add the numbers: $8 + 2$

$= \mathbf{10}$

382. Substitute 2 for a, 3 for b, and 7 for c: $a^2 + 2b + c$

Find the value of 2^2: $(2)^2 + 2(3) + 7$

Multiply $2 \cdot 3$: $4 + 2(3) + 7$

Add the numbers: $4 + 6 + 7$

$= \mathbf{17}$

Set 26

383. 14. Add 5 to both sides of the equation: $x - 5 + 5 = 9 + 5$

Simplify both sides of the equation: $x + 0 = 14$

Add 0 to x: $x = 14$

384. 1. Subtract 6 from both sides of the equation: $a + 6 - 6 = 7 - 6$

Simplify both sides of the equation: $a + 0 = 1$

Add 0 to a: $a = 1$

385. 19. Add 11 to both sides of the equation: $y - 11 + 11 = 8 + 11$

Simplify both sides of the equation: $y + 0 = 19$

Add 0 to y: $y = 19$

386. **−4.** Subtract 9 from both sides of the equation: $-r + 9 - 9 = 13 - 9$
Simplify both sides of the equation: $-r + 0 = 4$
Add 0 to $-r$: $-r = 4$
The value of the variable must be positive, but in this equation, r is negative. You can make it positive by multiplying both sides of the equation by -1.
$(-1)(-r) = 4(-1)$
$r = -4$

387. **15.** Add 7 to both sides: $d - 7 + 7 = 8 + 7$
$d = 15$

388. **−1.** Add 5 to both sides: $x - 5 + 5 = -6 + 5$
$x = -1$

Set 27
389. **26.** Multiply both sides by 2: $\frac{x}{2} \times 2 = 13 \times 2$, $x = 26$.

390. **15.** Multiply both sides by 5: $\frac{x}{5} \times 5 = 3 \times 5$, $x = 15$.

Set 28
391. **6 years.** Substitute what you know into the formula: $\$630 = \$3,000 \times 3.5\% \times t$, or $630 = 3,000 \times .035t$. Simplify the equation: $630 = 105t$. Divide both sides of the equation by 105: $t = \frac{630}{105}$. Simplify both sides of the equation: $6 = t$. It would take 6 years to earn $630.

392. **5 hours.** Substitute what you know into the formula: $300 = 60t$. Divide both sides of the equation by 60: $t = \frac{300}{60}$. Simplify both sides of the equation: $5 = t$. It would take you 5 hours to travel 300 miles.

Set 29
393. **9.** Let x = the number of men in the class. Then, 2 times the number of men is equal to the number of women. You can represent that in the equation $2x = 18$. $x = 9$; therefore, there are 9 men in the class.

394. **$5,300.** Let x = first monthly paycheck. Then, $x = 4 \times 40 \times \$17.50$ + $2,500$; $x = \$5,300$.

395. **$10,500.** Grace sells real estate and receives a 6% commission for every residential property that she sells. To find how much commission she would receive if she sold a home for $175,000, label the commission with the variable c, and rewrite 6% as .06: $c = .06 \times \$175,000$; $c = \$10,500$.

396. **36.** There are 40 questions on a test. To find out many questions you must answer correctly to score 90%, rewrite 90% as 90 out of 100 and set up a proportion to see how many points, p, out of 40 are needed: $\frac{90}{100} = \frac{p}{40}$. Cross multiply: $40 \times 9 = 10p$; $360 = 10p$. Divide both sides by 10: $p = 36$.

Set 30

397. $x < 7$. Subtract 3 from both sides of the inequality.

398. $x < 1$. Subtract 5 from both sides of the inequality. Then, divide both sides by 2.

399. $x > -3$. Divide both sides of the inequality by -3. Remember, when you multiply or divide an inequality by a negative number, you must reverse the inequality symbol.

400. $x < 2$. Subtract 1 from both sides of the inequality. Then, divide both sides by 5.

401. $x \leq \$6$. $2x + 8 \leq \$20$; $x \leq \$6$. You can spend up to $6 on the tickets.

402. $x \leq \$30$. $4x \leq 120$; $x \leq \$30$. The most you can spend on a chair is $30.

403. $x \leq \$10.50$. $x + \$2.50 + \$2.00 \leq \$15.00$; $x \leq \$10.50$. You can spend up to $10.50 on the entrée.

404. $x > \$12$. $12x > \$144$; $x > \$12$. You need to sell each candle for $> \$12$.

Set 31

405. **c.** Start simplifying the problem by changing the second rational expression to its reciprocal and changing the division symbol to a multiplication symbol. Factor each numerator and denominator. The factored form of the rational expression is $\frac{(x + 2)(x + 5)}{3x^4(x + 5)} \times \frac{15x^8}{(x + 5)(x - 5)}$. The $(x + 5)$s and the $(x + 2)$s cancel. Reduce the $15x^8$ and $3x^4$ by dividing the coefficients by 3 and subtracting the exponents. Leave the x^4 in the numerator since the exponent in the numerator is bigger. The other choices have reducing errors, are still unsimplified, or do not have the correct terms in the denominator.

406. **b.** Find the factors of $4x^2$ and -9 that multiply and add to make $-9x$. $4x$ and x are both factors of $4x^2$. 3 and -3 are factors of -9. Testing them in the polynomials $(4x + 3)(x - 3)$ will yield the answer when multiplied together. The other choices include switched signs and added values instead of multiplication.

407. **a.** Simplify the coefficients and subtract the exponents. $\frac{18}{20}$ reduces to $\frac{9}{10}$, and when the powers of x are subtracted they yield x^7 in the denominator. When the powers of y are subtracted they yield y^7 in the numerator, and when the powers of z are subtracted they yield z^5 in the numerator. The other choices subtracted the coefficients, performed the wrong operation with the exponents, or have incorrect placement of x in the numerator.

408. **d.** A squared binomial means you can write out the binomial multiplied by itself $(x + 3)(x + 3)$. When each term in the first set of parentheses is multiplied by each term in the second set of parentheses it yields the answer. $x(x) + x(3) + 3(x) + 3(3) = x^2 + 3x + 3x + 9$. Combine like terms to get $x^2 + 6x + 9$. The other choices include squaring each term, multiplying when combining like terms, or sign errors.

409. **c.** Start by splitting the absolute value portion into its two possible outcomes $3x + 9 < 15$ and $3x + 9 > -15$. Solve each by subtracting 9 from both sides, yielding $3x < 6$ and $3x > -24$. In both inequalities, divide by 3, resulting in $x < 2$ and $x > -8$. Incorrect choices include reversed inequalities and incorrect signs.

410. **e.** The cube root of 8 is 2, and the square root of 81 is 9. 2 + 9 = 11. Choices **a**, **b**, and **c** are incorrect due to incorrect usage of order of operations and incorrect use of a cubed root.

411. **e.** Start by setting up two equations. $q + d = 100$ refers to the number of quarters added to the number of dimes equaling 100. $25q + 10d = 1,405$ refers to the value of the quarters added to the value of the dimes equaling their combined value of 1,405 cents. Using the method of linear combination, or elimination, multiply the second equation by –10 to cancel the ds. Then combine the two equations $-10q - 10d = -1,000$ with $25q + 10d = 1,405$. This results is $15q = 405$. Divide both sides by 15 to get $q = 27$. The incorrect choices are incorrect estimations with guess and check, and also the value of the dimes.

412. **c.** Start by subtracting on each side of the equation to isolate the constants on the right. This will give you $x^2 - 8x = 45$. Next find the value that will make $x^2 - 8x$ a perfect square trinomial. Add 16 to both sides, yielding $x^2 - 8x + 16 = 61$. Factor the left into $(x - 4)(x - 4)$ and rewrite as a binomial squared. This gives you $(x - 4)^2 = 61$. The incorrect choices contain incorrect factoring, missing negative signs, or incorrect addition and subtraction.

413. **a.** Start by setting up the equation $x^2 + 7x = -10$. Add 10 to both sides to get $x^2 + 7x + 10 = 0$. Factor the left side of the equation $(x + 5)(x + 2) = 0$. Using the zero product property, you can assume that $x + 5 = 0$ or $x + 2 = 0$. Solving both equations gives you the solution set $x = -5$ and $x = -2$. The incorrect choices are the values factored without using the zero product property and a number seen initially in the problem.

414. **c.** Because each term in the sequence is 6 greater than the previous term, every term, positive or negative, in the sequence must be divisible by six. Choice **c** is the only solution that is not evenly divisible by 6. ($344 \div 6 = 57.333$)

415. **a.** This problem is a lengthy multiplication problem: $(37)^3 = 37 \times 37 \times 37 = 50,653$. All the other choices are variations of multiplication errors.

Set 32

416. **b.** Statement (II) is the only sufficient statement because if $x \div y$ is greater than 1, it means x must be a larger number that y is able to go into it at least once. Statement (I) does not provide any information regarding the relationship between x and y.

417. **e.** The statements do not provide enough information to determine the numbers in a sequence. The first statement suggests that the sequence is increasing by the value of the first term, but it does not explicitly state the value of the first term. This pattern would work for any sequence increasing by the first variable (2, 4, 6, 8, (2 + 8 =10) 10) or (25, 50, 75, 100 (25 + 100 = 125) 125). The second statement tells you the numbers are all multiples of the first term but again does not explicitly state the value of the first term. The previously mentioned sequences could work for this pattern as well.

418. **e.** Neither of these statements can strictly determine whether both x and y are positive. Given the first statement, x and y could either both be positive, or both be negative. The same goes given the second statement. Both statements can be deceiving if you forget that the product of two negative numbers is a positive number.

419. **b.** If Annie runs at a rate of 9 fps with a 10-second penalty going a distance of 500 feet, her distance equation will be $500 = 9(T + 10)$ based on *distance = speed(time)*. Alexi's distance equation will be $500 = 10T$. When both are solved, we find that Alexi's time was 50 seconds and Annie's time was 45, which means Annie won the race. We cannot use the second piece of information because we don't know whether the race lasted for more or less than 2 minutes.

420. **a.** To find how long (or the time) it will take the ball to hit the ground, you would need to know its speed. The first statement gives you the acceleration, and from there you can find the time.
Speed = Distance ÷ Time
−9.8 m/s = 49m ÷ time
49 ÷ 9.8 = 5 seconds
The weight of the ball does not affect the answer, and the acceleration already takes the weight into account. Therefore, only the first statement is needed.

421. **b.** Statement (I) is not enough because x and y might be 7 and 8. Statement (II) is sufficient because if you subtract 2 consecutive integers, the difference should be 1.

422. **e.** Both statements together are insufficient because if the equations are manipulated, they become the same, and you cannot solve for each variable. You end up with only trivial solutions, which is to say x and y could be anything.

423. **d.** Statement (I) indicates that since the difference of the two polynomials is 0, they are the same. So you could take the sum of them and divide by 2 $\frac{4x + 6}{2} = 2x + 3$. Statement (II) is sufficient because the only trinomial that adds to $4x + 6$ are the two binomials $(2x + 3)(2x + 3)$ you get from factoring $4x^2 + 12x + 9$.

424. **d.** The problem gives you enough to set up the following equation, $5c + 10p = \$12.50$. The first statement gives you the value of variable p, and from there you can solve for c.
$5c + 10p = \$12.50$
$5c + 10(1.00) = \$12.50$
$5c + 10 = 12.50$
$5c = 2.50$
$c = 0.50$
The second statement gives you enough information to set up a second equation using both variables, p and c, and then you can use elimination to solve for each variable.
$5c + 10p = \$12.50$
$20c + 20p = \$30.00$
$-2(5c + 10p) = -2(\$12.50)$
$20c + 20p = \$30.00$
$-10c - 20p = \$-25.00$
$\underline{20c + 20p = \$\ 30.00}$
$10c\qquad = \$\ \ 5.00$
$c = 0.50$
Either statement (I) or statement (II) provides enough information independently to solve for the price of the cookies.

425. **e.** Statement (I) is insufficient because as long as $x > 1$ there will be a coefficient in the denominator of 3. Statement (II) is also insufficient because the exponent of c^9 could be in the numerator or the denominator, which leaves us two possibilities for the value of x, 21 and 3.

426. **a.** Statement (I) provides a way to set up an algebraic expression that is in terms of x. Replace the number in the original equation with its equivalent expression; an expression is formed that has a solution $4x + 9 - 2(5x + 1) = 2x - 9$. Statement (II) provides insufficient information because there are multiple instances in which the integer could be less than x. If x were 5, the number would be -23. If x were 6 the number would be -29.

427. **c.** Statement (I) alone is insufficient because if Kline spent twice as long talking about her boyfriend than talking about her work and weekend combined, the amount of time she spent talking with her boyfriend is still variable, and how long she talked about the kitten is still unknown. The addition of statement (II) puts everything in terms of one variable. An expression representing the time spent talking about her boyfriend is $2(20 + w)$, where w = time talked about work. Since time talked about work is the same as time talked about the kitten, both can be represented as w. An equation can be set up representing the situation: $(20) + (40 + 2w) + (w) + (w) = 100$, since each is a percent. The simplified expression is $60 + 4w = 100$, and when 60 is subtracted from both sides, the result is $4w = 40$, which when divided by 4 results in $w = 10$. With this information, you can tell that 10% of the time Kline talked about her kitten, and 10% of 3 hours is 18 minutes.

Geometry

Geometry questions account for about 25% of the GMAT quantitative section. The key to tackling geometry questions is to know the properties of different shapes and several key formulas, which are reviewed in this chapter, including:

- angles
- lines
- triangles
- quadrilaterals
- circles
- coordinate geometry

Classifying Angles

In geometry, an *angle* is formed by two rays with a common endpoint. The symbol used to indicate an angle is ∠. The two rays are the sides of the angle. The common endpoint is the vertex of the angle.

Angles that make a square corner are called right angles (see the following examples for more details about what makes an angle a right angle). In drawings, the following symbol is used to indicate a right angle:

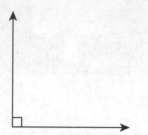

Opposite rays are two rays with the same endpoint that form a line. They form a straight angle. A straight angle has a 180° measure.

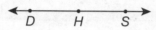

An acute angle has a measure between 0° and 90°. Here are two examples of acute angles.

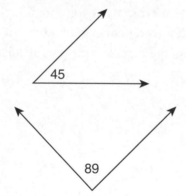

A right angle has a 90° measure. The corner of a piece of paper will fit exactly into a right angle. Here are two examples of right angles.

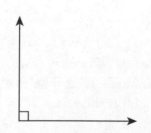

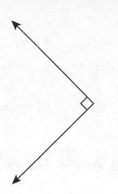

An obtuse angle has a measure between 90° and 180°. Here are two examples of obtuse angles.

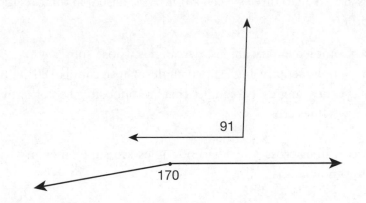

Set 33

Use the figure to answer the following practice problems.

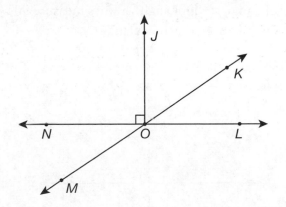

428. Name three acute angles.

429. Name three obtuse angles.

430. Name two straight angles.

431. Determine the largest angle shown, and write it two ways.

432. If ∠*MON* measures 27°, then ∠*JOK* measures _____ degrees.

Congruent Angles and Angle Pairs

When two angles have the same degree measure, they are said to be congruent.

Names are given to three special angle pairs, based on their relationship to each other:

- Complementary angles: two angles whose sum is 90°.
- Supplementary angles: two angles whose sum is 180°.
- Vertical angles: two angles that are opposite each other when two lines cross.

When two lines cross, the adjacent angles are supplementary, and the sum of all four angles is 360°.

Perpendicular and Parallel Lines

Perpendicular lines are another type of intersecting lines. Perpendicular lines meet to form right angles. Right angles always measure 90°. In the following figure, lines *x* and *y* are perpendicular:

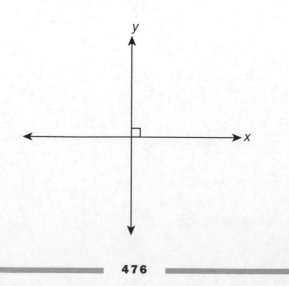

Parallel lines lie in the same plane and don't cross at any point.

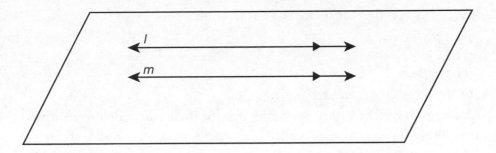

The arrowheads on the lines indicate that they are parallel.

Angle–Pair Problems

Angle–pair problems tend to ask for an angle's complement or supplement.

Example: If $m\angle A = 35°$, what is the size of its complement?

To find an angle's complement, subtract it from 90°:

90° – 35° = 55°
Example: If $m\angle A = 35°$, what is the size of its supplement?

To find an angle's supplement, subtract it from 180°:

180° – 35° = 145°

Set 34

Answer the following problems.

433. What is the complement of a 30° angle?

434. What is the complement of a 5° angle?

435. What is the supplement of a 5° angle?

436. What is the supplement of a 100° angle?

Triangles

You can classify triangles by the lengths of their sides. Below are three examples of special triangles called *equilateral*, *isosceles*, and *scalene* triangles.

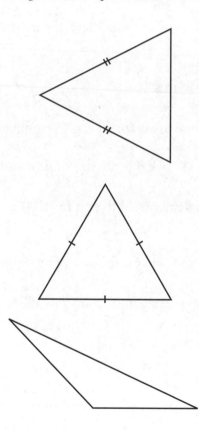

You can also classify triangles by the measurements of their angles. Here are four examples of special triangles. They are called *acute*, *equiangular*, *right*, and *obtuse* triangles.

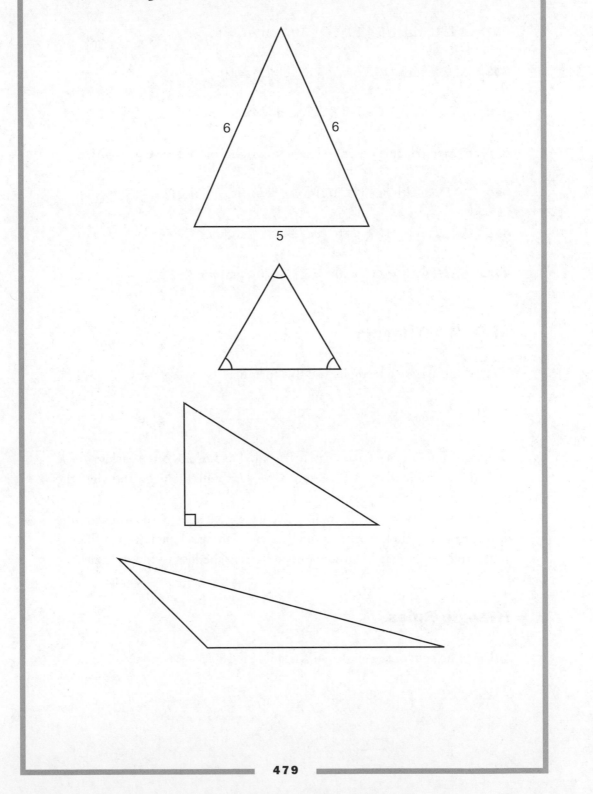

Set 35

Classify each triangle described as equilateral, isosceles, or scalene.

437. $\triangle ABC$ with $AB = 10$, $BC = 10$, and $AC = 8$.

438. $\triangle DEF$ with $DE = 6$, $EF = 8$, and $DF = 10$.

439. $\triangle XYZ$ with $XY = 7$, $YZ = 7$, and $XZ = 7$.

Classify each triangle described as acute, right, obtuse, or equiangular.

440. $\triangle MNO$ with $m\angle M = 130°$, $m\angle N = 30°$, and $m\angle O = 20°$.

441. $\triangle RST$ with $m\angle R = 80°$, $m\angle S = 45°$, and $m\angle T = 55°$.

442. $\triangle GHI$ with $m\angle G = 20°$, $m\angle H = 70°$, and $m\angle I = 90°$.

Area of a Triangle

To find the *area* of a triangle, use this formula:

$$area = \frac{1}{2}(base \times height)$$

Although any side of a triangle may be called its *base*, it's often easiest to use the side on the bottom. To use another side, rotate the page and view the triangle from another perspective.

A triangle's *height* (or *altitude*) is represented by a perpendicular line drawn from the angle opposite the base to the base. Depending on the triangle, the height may be inside, outside, or on the legs of the triangle.

Triangle Rules

Rule 1. The sum of the angles in a triangle is 180°:

$$\angle A + \angle B + \angle C = 180°$$

Example: One base angle of an isosceles triangle is 30°. Find the measure of the vertex angle.

Draw a picture of an isosceles triangle. Drawing it to scale helps. Since it is an isosceles triangle, draw both base angles the same size (as close to 30° as you can) and make sure the sides opposite them are the same length. Label one base angle as 30°.

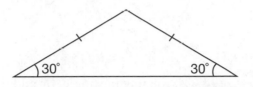

Since the base angles are congruent, label the other base angle as 30°.
There are two steps needed to find the vertex angle:

- Add the two base angles together: 30° + 30° = 60°
- The sum of all three angles in a triangle is 180°.

To find the measure of the vertex angle, subtract the sum of the two base angles (60°) from 180°:

180° – 60° = 120°

Thus, the measure of the vertex angle is 120°.
Add all 3 angles together to make sure their sum is 180°:

Rule 2. The longest side of a triangle is opposite the largest angle.
This rule implies that the second longest side is opposite the second largest angle, and the shortest side is opposite the smallest angle.

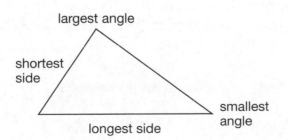

Example: In the following triangle, which side is the shortest?

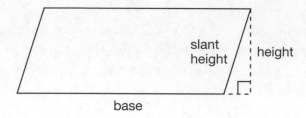

base

Determine the size of $\angle A$, the missing angle, by adding the two known angles and then subtracting their sum from 180°:

$90° + 46° = 136°$
$180° - 136° = 44°$

Thus $\angle A$ is 44°.

Since $\angle A$ is the smallest angle, side a (opposite $\angle A$) is the shortest side.

Rule 3. Right triangles have a rule of their own. Using the *Pythagorean theorem*, you can calculate the missing side of a right triangle.

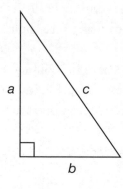

$$a^2 + b^2 = c^2$$
(c refers to the hypotenuse)

Example: What is the perimeter of the following triangle?

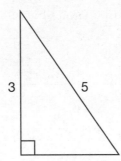

Since the perimeter is the sum of the lengths of the sides, we must first find the missing side. Use the Pythagorean Theorem:

$$a^2 + b^2 = c^2$$

Substitute the given sides for two of the letters. To solve this equation, subtract 9 from both sides:

$$3^2 + b^2 = 5^2$$
$$9 + b^2 = 25$$
$$9 - b^2 = 25 - 9$$
$$b^2 = 16$$

Then take the square root of both sides.

$$\sqrt{b^2} = \sqrt{16}$$
$$b = 4$$

Thus, the missing side has a length of 4 units.
Adding the three sides yields a perimeter of 12:

$$3 + 4 + 5 = 12$$

Quadrilaterals

A quadrilateral is four–sided polygon. Three common quadrilaterals are
shown here:

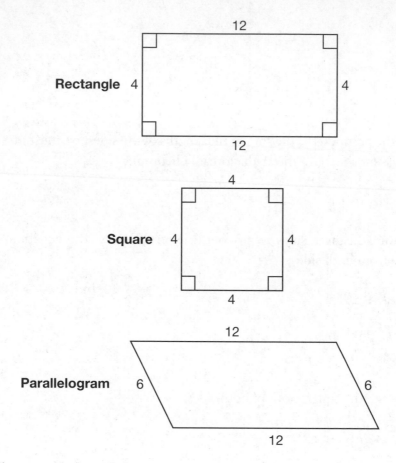

These quadrilaterals have something in common besides having four
sides:

- Opposite sides are the same length and parallel.
- Opposite angles are the same size.

However, each quadrilateral has its own distinguishing characteristics as given on the table that follows.

Sides Angles	Rectangle	Square	Parallelogram
	The horizontal sides don't have to be the same length as the vertical sides. All the angles are right angles.	All four sides are the same length. All the angles are right angles.	The horizontal sides don't have to be the same length as the vertical sides. The opposite angles are the same size, but they don't have to be right angles. (A parallelogram can look like a rectangle leaning to one side.)

The naming conventions for quadrilaterals are similar to those for triangles:

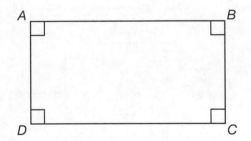

- The figure is named by the letters at its four corners, usually in alphabetical order: rectangle *ABCD*.
- A side is named by the letters at its ends: side *AB*.
- An angle is named by its vertex letter: ∠*A*.

The sum of the angles of a quadrilateral is 360°:

$\angle A + \angle B + \angle C + \angle D = 360°$

To find the perimeter of a quadrilateral, follow this simple rule:

Perimeter = sum of all four sides

To find the area of a rectangle, square, or parallelogram, use this formula:

Area = base × height

The *base* is the size of the side on the bottom. The *height* (or *altitude*) is the length of a perpendicular line drawn from the base to the side opposite it. The height of a rectangle and a square is the same as the length of its vertical side.

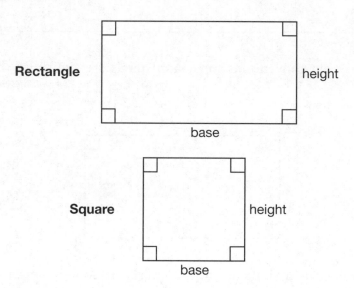

A parallelogram's height is not necessarily the same as the length of its vertical side (called the *slant height*); it is found instead by drawing a perpendicular line from the base to the side opposite it—the length of this line equals the height of the parallelogram.

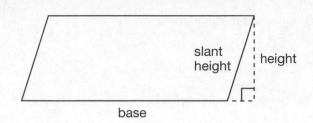

slant
height / height

base

The area formula for the rectangle and square may be expressed in an equivalent form as:

Area = length × width
Example: Find the area of a rectangle with a base of 4 meters and a height of 3 meters.

Draw the rectangle as close to scale as possible. Label the size of the base and height.

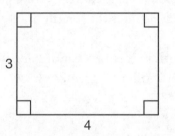

Write the area formula, then substitute the base and height numbers into it:

$A = b \times h$
$A = 4 \times 3 = 12$

Thus, the area is 12 square meters.

Set 36

Answer the following practice problems.

443. All squares are also rectangles.
    a. True
    b. False

444. All rectangles are also squares.
   a. True
   b. False

445. Some rectangles are also squares.
   a. True
   b. False

446. All squares and rectangles are also parallelograms.
   a. True
   b. False

447. What is the length of a side of a square room whose perimeter is 58 feet?

448. Find the dimensions of a rectangle with a perimeter of 16 feet whose long side is 3 times the length of its short side.

449. What is the length in feet of a parking lot that has an area of 8,400 square feet and a width of 70 feet?

Circles

A *circle* is a set of points that are all the same distance from a given point called the *center*.

You are likely to come across the following terms when dealing with circles:

Radius: The distance from the center of the circle to any point on the circle itself. The symbol *r* is used for the radius.

Diameter: The length of a line that passes across a circle through the center. The diameter is twice the size of the radius. The symbol *d* is used for the diameter.

The *circumference* of a circle is the distance around the circle (comparable to the concept of the *perimeter* of a polygon). To determine the circumference of a circle, use either of these two equivalent formulas:

$$Circumference = 2\pi r$$

or

$$Circumference = \pi d$$

The formulas should be written out as $(2 \times \pi \times r)$ or $(\pi \times d)$. It helps to know that:

r is the radius
d is the diameter

π is approximately equal to 3.14, or $\frac{22}{7}$

Example: Find the circumference of a circle whose radius is 7 inches.

Draw this circle and write the radius version of the circumference formula (because you're given the radius):

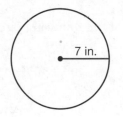

Substitute 7 for the radius:

$C = 2\pi r$
$C = 2 \times \pi \times 7$
$C = 2 \times \pi \times 7; \ C = 14\pi$

Example: What is the diameter of a circle whose circumference is 62.8 centimeters? Use 3.14 for π.

Draw a circle with its diameter and write the diameter version of the circumference formula (because you're asked to find the diameter):

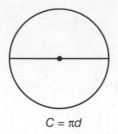

$$C = \pi d$$

Substitute 62.8 for the circumference, 3.14 for π, and solve the equation.

$$62.8 = 3.14 \times d$$
$$62.8 = 3.14 \times 20$$

The diameter is 20 centimeters.

The *area* of a circle is the space its surface occupies. To determine the area of a circle, use this formula:

$$Area = \pi r^2$$

The formula can be written out as $\pi \times r \times r$.

Example: Find the area of the following circle, rounded to the nearest tenth.

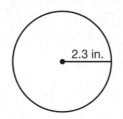

Write the area formula:

$$A = \pi r^2$$

Substitute 2.3 for the radius:

$$A = \pi \times 2.3 \times 2.3$$
$$A = 5.3\pi$$

Example: What is the diameter of a circle whose area is 9 square centimeters?

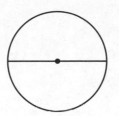

Draw a circle with its diameter (to help you remember that the question asks for the diameter), then write the area formula. (Note: Refer to Chapter 10 if you need help with square roots.)

$A = \pi r^2$

Substitute 9π for the area and solve the equation:

$9\pi = \pi r^2$
$9 = r^2$
$3 = r$

Since the radius is 3 centimeters, the diameter is 6 centimeters.

Set 37

Find the approximate circumference of each circle shown or described. Use 3.14 for π.

450.

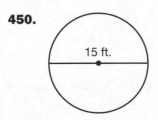

15 ft.

451.

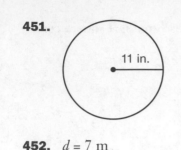

452. $d = 7$ m

453. $r = 25$ m

Find the approximate area for each circle shown or described. Use 3.14 for π.

454.

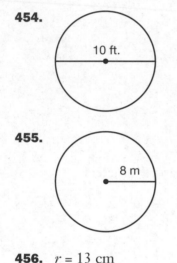

455.

456. $r = 13$ cm

457. $d = 24$ in.

Surface Area of a Cylinder

When you are looking for the surface area of a cylinder, you need to find the area of two circles (the bases) and the area of the curved surface that makes up the side of the cylinder. The area of the curved surface is hard to visualize when it is rolled up. Picture a paper towel roll. It has a circular top and bottom. When you unroll a sheet of the paper towel, it is shaped like a rectangle. The area of the curved surface is the area of a rectangle with the same height as the cylinder, and the base measurement is the same as the circumference of the circle base.

Surface area of a cylinder = area of two circles + area of rectangle

$$= 2\pi r^2 + bh$$
$$= 2\pi r^2 + 2\pi rh$$

Volume of a Cylinder

You can find the volume of a cylinder by finding the product of the area of the base and the height of the figure. Of course, the base of a cylinder is a circle, so you need to find the area of a circle times the height.

Theorem: The volume (V) of a cylinder is the product of the area of the base (B) and the height (h).

$$V = Bh \text{ or } V = \pi r^2 h$$

Volume of a Cone

A cone relates to a cylinder in the same way that a pyramid relates to a prism. If you have a cone and a cylinder with the same radius and height, it would take three of the cones to fill the cylinder. In other words, the cone holds one-third the amount of the cylinder.

$$V = Bh \text{ or } V = \pi r^2 h$$
$$V = \tfrac{1}{3}Bh \text{ or } V = \tfrac{1}{3}\pi r^2 h$$

Coordinate Geometry

The two axes divide the coordinate plane into four regions, which are called *quadrants*. The quadrants are numbered counterclockwise beginning with the upper-right region. The coordinates (x,y) of a point are an ordered pair of numbers. The first number is the x coordinate. The second number is the y coordinate. The coordinates of the origin are (0,0).

Each point on the coordinate plane has its own unique ordered pair. You can think of an ordered pair as an address. Now that you have located a point, you can also find the coordinates of a point on a graph.

Example: Find the coordinates of each point.

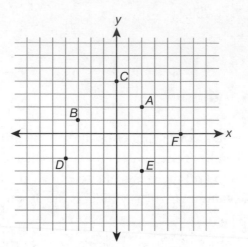

Solution:

$A(2,2)$
$B(-3,1)$
$C(0,4)$
$D(-4,-2)$
$E(2,-3)$
$F(5,0)$

The distance d between any two points $A(x_1,y_1)$ and $B(x_2,y_2)$ is

$$d = \sqrt{(x_2 - x_1)^2 + (y_2 - y_1)^2}$$

The *slope* of a line is the measure of its steepness. The slope of a line is determined by the ratio of its rise to run. When looking at a line on a coordinate grid, always count the run before you count the rise. When a line points up to the right, it has a positive slope. A line with a negative slope points up to the left.

You can also use a formula to determine the slope of a line containing two points, point $A(x_1,y_1)$ and point $B(x_2,y_2)$. Here is the formula:

$$\text{slope} = \frac{y_2 - y_1}{x_2 - x_1}$$

Set 38

Use a formula to find the slope of the line through each pair of points.

458. (0,0) and (5,6)

459. (−3,−2) and (−4,−3)

460. (1,−3) and (−1,−3)

461. (5,−6) and (−2,8)

Set 39

Now it is time to answer GMAT data sufficiency practice questions that have been designed to test your algebra skills. Good luck!

462. The area of a quadrilateral is $81 - 25x^2$; what is the value of x?
  I. Its base is $9 - 5x$ long.
  II. The shape is a square.
  a. Statement (I) ALONE is sufficient, but statement (II) ALONE is not sufficient.
  b. Statement (II) ALONE is sufficient, but statement (I) ALONE is not sufficient.
  c. BOTH statements TOGETHER are sufficient, but NEITHER statement ALONE is sufficient.
  d. EACH statement ALONE is sufficient.
  e. Statements (I) and (II) TOGETHER are NOT sufficient.

463. Is *BD* a perpendicular bisector of *AC*?
  I. Angle *AC* = 180°
  II. *AB* = *BC*

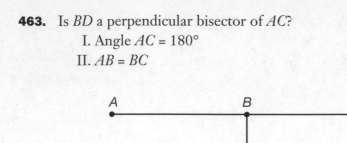

  a. Statement (I) ALONE is sufficient, but statement (II) ALONE is not sufficient.
  b. Statement (II) ALONE is sufficient, but statement (I) ALONE is not sufficient.
  c. BOTH statements TOGETHER are sufficient, but NEITHER statement ALONE is sufficient.
  d. EACH statement ALONE is sufficient.
  e. Statements (I) and (II) TOGETHER are NOT sufficient.

464. Are angle *A* and angle *B* supplementary?
    I. Angle *A* − angle *B* = 10°
    II. *LM* ∥ *ND*

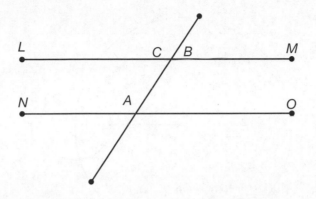

a. Statement (I) ALONE is sufficient, but statement (II) ALONE is not sufficient.

b. Statement (II) ALONE is sufficient, but statement (I) ALONE is not sufficient.

c. BOTH statements TOGETHER are sufficient, but NEITHER statement ALONE is sufficient.

d. EACH statement ALONE is sufficient.

e. Statements (I) and (II) TOGETHER are NOT sufficient.

465. Is the circumference of circle $B > 10$?

    I. Radius of the circle $A = 9$

    II. $XY = 2YZ$

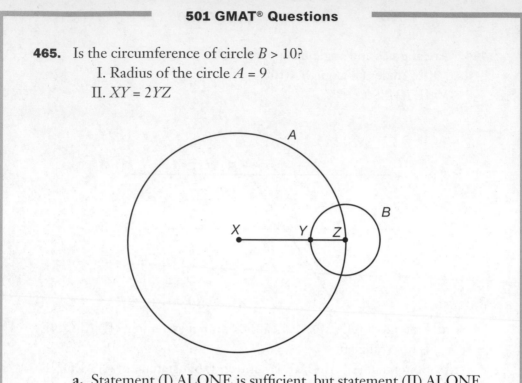

  a. Statement (I) ALONE is sufficient, but statement (II) ALONE is not sufficient.

  b. Statement (II) ALONE is sufficient, but statement (I) ALONE is not sufficient.

  c. BOTH statements TOGETHER are sufficient, but NEITHER statement ALONE is sufficient.

  d. EACH statement ALONE is sufficient.

  e. Statements (I) and (II) TOGETHER are NOT sufficient.

466. What is the measure of angle *A*?

    I. Angle *B* and angle *C* are complementary.

    II. Angle *B* = 30°

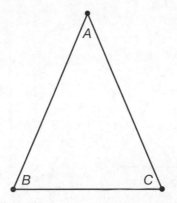

  a. Statement (I) ALONE is sufficient, but statement (II) ALONE is not sufficient.

  b. Statement (II) ALONE is sufficient, but statement (I) ALONE is not sufficient.

  c. BOTH statements TOGETHER are sufficient, but NEITHER statement ALONE is sufficient.

  d. EACH statement ALONE is sufficient.

  e. Statements (I) and (II) TOGETHER are NOT sufficient.

467. Are the areas of the rectangle and triangle the same?
   I. The triangle height is twice the height of the rectangle.
   II. The triangle and the rectangle have the same base.

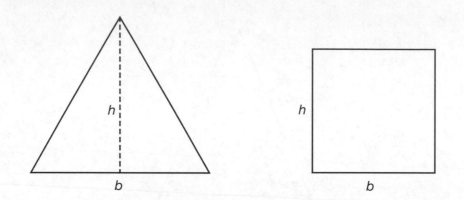

   a. Statement (I) ALONE is sufficient, but statement (II) ALONE
   is not sufficient.
   b. Statement (II) ALONE is sufficient, but statement (I) ALONE
   is not sufficient.
   c. BOTH statements TOGETHER are sufficient, but NEITHER
   statement ALONE is sufficient.
   d. EACH statement ALONE is sufficient.
   e. Statements (I) and (II) TOGETHER are NOT sufficient.

Use the following image to answer questions 468 and 469.

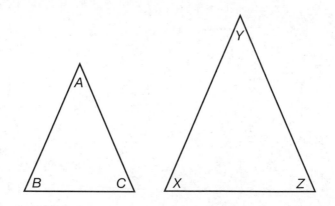

468. Are the triangles similar?

    I. Angle A = angle X

    II. $3AB = XY$

a. Statement (I) ALONE is sufficient, but statement (II) ALONE is not sufficient.

b. Statement (II) ALONE is sufficient, but statement (I) ALONE is not sufficient.

c. BOTH statements TOGETHER are sufficient, but NEITHER statement ALONE is sufficient.

d. EACH statement ALONE is sufficient.

e. Statements (I) and (II) TOGETHER are NOT sufficient.

469. Are the triangle areas congruent?

    I. They both have an inferior angle of 30°.

    II. They both have two sides that are 3 units and 5 units in length.

a. Statement (I) ALONE is sufficient, but statement (II) ALONE is not sufficient.

b. Statement (II) ALONE is sufficient, but statement (I) ALONE is not sufficient.

c. BOTH statements TOGETHER are sufficient, but NEITHER statement ALONE is sufficient.

d. EACH statement ALONE is sufficient.

e. Statements (I) and (II) TOGETHER are NOT sufficient.

470. Find the volume of both cubes.

    I. $a = 4$

    II. The volume of the small cube is 64.

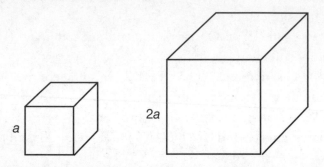

  a. Statement (I) ALONE is sufficient, but statement (II) ALONE is not sufficient.

  b. Statement (II) ALONE is sufficient, but statement (I) ALONE is not sufficient.

  c. BOTH statements TOGETHER are sufficient, but NEITHER statement ALONE is sufficient.

  d. EACH statement ALONE is sufficient.

  e. Statements (I) and (II) TOGETHER are NOT sufficient.

471. Is $BC \parallel$ to DF?

    I. Angle J + angle E = 180°

    II. Angle H = angle I

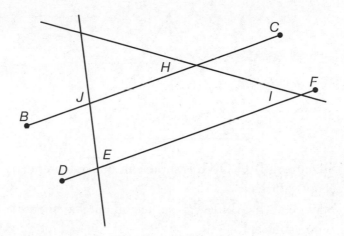

a. Statement (I) ALONE is sufficient, but statement (II) ALONE is not sufficient.

b. Statement (II) ALONE is sufficient, but statement (I) ALONE is not sufficient.

c. BOTH statements TOGETHER are sufficient, but NEITHER statement ALONE is sufficient.

d. EACH statement ALONE is sufficient.

e. Statements (I) and (II) TOGETHER are NOT sufficient.

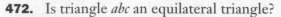

472. Is triangle *abc* an equilateral triangle?

     I. Angle *a* ÷ angle *b* = 1

     II. Angle *b* − angle *a* = 0

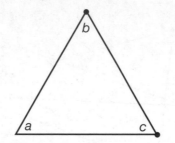

  a. Statement (I) ALONE is sufficient, but statement (II) ALONE is not sufficient.

  b. Statement (II) ALONE is sufficient, but statement (I) ALONE is not sufficient.

  c. BOTH statements TOGETHER are sufficient, but NEITHER statement ALONE is sufficient.

  d. EACH statement ALONE is sufficient.

  e. Statements (I) and (II) TOGETHER are NOT sufficient.

473. Find the surface area of a cube.

     I. The volume of the cube is 27 cm³.

     II. The surface area is six times the area of one side.

  a. Statement (I) ALONE is sufficient, but statement (II) ALONE is not sufficient.

  b. Statement (II) ALONE is sufficient, but statement (I) ALONE is not sufficient.

  c. BOTH statements TOGETHER are sufficient, but NEITHER statement ALONE is sufficient.

  d. EACH statement ALONE is sufficient.

  e. Statements (I) and (II) TOGETHER are NOT sufficient.

474. The circumference of a circle is $2x\pi$. What is the value of x?

    I. The radius is equal to x.

    II. The area of the circle is the same as double the diameter minus 1.

  a. Statement (I) ALONE is sufficient, but statement (II) ALONE is not sufficient.

  b. Statement (II) ALONE is sufficient, but statement (I) ALONE is not sufficient.

  c. BOTH statements TOGETHER are sufficient, but NEITHER statement ALONE is sufficient.

  d. EACH statement ALONE is sufficient.

  e. Statements (I) and (II) TOGETHER are NOT sufficient.

Set 40

Now it is time to answer GMAT problem-solving practice questions that have been designed to test your geometry skills. Good luck!

- Solve the problem and indicate the best of the answer choices given.
- All numbers used are real numbers.
- A figure accompanying a problem-solving question is intended to provide information useful in solving the problem. Figures are drawn as accurately as possible EXCEPT when it is stated in a specific problem that the figure is not drawn to scale. Straight lines may sometimes appear jagged. All figures lie in a plane unless otherwise indicated.

475. Find the slope of the line passing through the two points $(3, -5)$ $(-2, -5)$.

  a. $m = 2$

  b. $m = 0$

  c. $m = -2$

  d. $m = 5$

  e. undefined slope

476. Find the *y* intercept of the equation $3x + 6y = 12$
  a. 4
  b. $\frac{2}{3}$
  c. 3
  d. 6
  e. 2

477. What is the equation of the following graph?

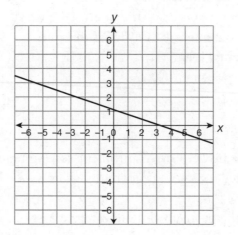

  a. $y = -3x + 1$

  b. $y = 3x + 1$

  c. $y = \frac{1}{3}x + 1$

  d. $y = -\frac{1}{3}x + 1$

  e. $y = -x + 3$

478. Which of the following statements about the lines $3x + 5y = 10$ and $-10y = 6x + 50$ is true?
  a. They have the same *y*-intercept.
  b. They have the same *x*-intercept.
  c. They are parallel.
  d. They are perpendicular.
  e. The slopes are additive inverses of each other.

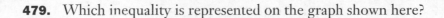

479. Which inequality is represented on the graph shown here?

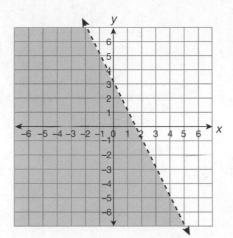

    a. $y > -2x + 3$
    b. $y \geq -2x + 3$
    c. $y < -2x + 3$
    d. $y \leq -2x + 3$
    e. $y \leq -3x + 1.5$

480. Which ordered pair is a solution to the system of equations?
$$\begin{cases} x + 3y = 7 \\ x + 2y = 10 \end{cases}$$
    a. $\left(\frac{7}{2}, \frac{13}{4}\right)$

    b. $\left(\frac{7}{2}, \frac{17}{5}\right)$

    c. $(-2, 3)$

    d. $(16, -3)$

    e. $(4, 1)$

481. Find the area of the rectangle.

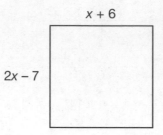

$x + 6$

$2x - 7$

    a. $2x^2 + 19x - 42$
    b. $2x^2 + 5x - 42$
    c. $2x^2 - 42$
    d. $6x - 2$
    e. $3x - 1$

482. If a public pool is a regular 25 m pool, with a 12 m width and an overall depth of 8 m, how many gallons are required to fill three-quarters of the public pool?
$1L = 001 \ m^3$
$1L = 0.26$ gallons
    a. 624,000 gallons
    b. 468,000 gallons
    c. 468 gallons
    d. 1,800,000 gallons
    e. 2,400 gallons

483. The distance between two coordinates, X and Y, is seven units. A third coordinate, Z, is five units away from Y. Which of the following could be the only distance from X to Z?
    I. 13
    II. 6
    III. 1
    a. I and II only
    b. II only
    c. II and III only
    d. III only
    e. I only

484. Find the value of *x*.

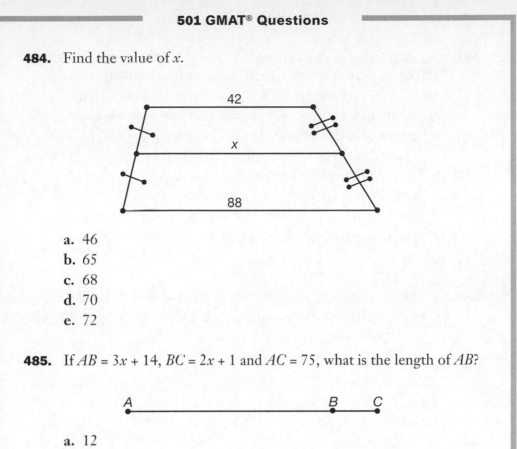

a. 46
b. 65
c. 68
d. 70
e. 72

485. If $AB = 3x + 14$, $BC = 2x + 1$ and $AC = 75$, what is the length of AB?

a. 12
b. 68
c. 44
d. 50
e. 13

486. In the three-dimensional coordinate plane, what is the approximate distance between (3,2,–4) and (7,–8,2)?
a. 11.8
b. 12.3
c. 13.1
d. 15.2
e. 16.5

487. A cylindrical silo and a rectangular silo are both being filled with 400 m³ of corn. The cylindrical silo has a base with an area of 20 m². The rectangular silo has a base with an area of 10 m². Assuming that the corn will not overflow in either, which statement will be true about the corn levels?

    a. The cylindrical silo level will be 20 m higher.

    b. The cylindrical silo level will be 10 m lower.

    c. The rectangular silo level will be 20 m higher.

    d. The rectangular silo level will be 40 m higher.

    e. The rectangular silo level will be the same as the cylindrical silo.

488. If triangle *ABC* is rotated 180° about point *C*, and then reflected over the *y*-axis, what will be the coordinate of *B*?

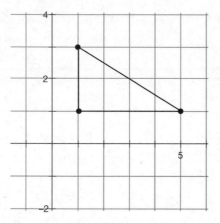

    a. (−1,−2)

    b. (9,1)

    c. (9,−1)

    d. (−1,2)

    e. (−9,−1)

489. Which list of a triangle's side lengths is impossible?

    a. 4, 7, 4

    b. 2, 3, 7

    c. 2, 8, 7

    d. 5, 6, 7

    e. 8, 5, 5

490. If angle *A* and angle *B* are supplementary angles, and the measure of angle *A* < 80°, then you can assume that the
  a. measure of angle *B* = 100°.
  b. measure of angle *B* = 10°.
  c. measure of angle *B* < 80°.
  d. measure of angle *A* > 80°.
  e. angle *A* is an obtuse angle.

491. Find the midpoint of segment *MN* if point *M* is (4,6) and point *P* is (−2,14)
  a. (2,1)
  b. (2,20)
  c. (6,8)
  d. (1,10)
  e. (10,12)

492. What is the measure of angle *x*?

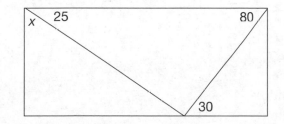

  a. *x* = 124°
  b. *x* = 15°
  c. *x* = 35°
  d. *x* = 30°
  e. *x* = 115°

493. The following net represents which shape?

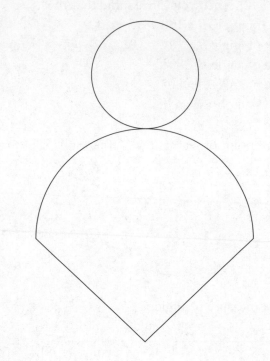

    a. a sphere
    b. a cone
    c. a dome
    d. a cylinder
    e. a triangle

494. Find the area of the shaded region.

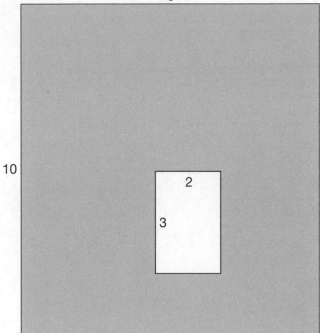

a. 6
b. 28
c. 48
d. 84
e. 90

495. A spherical model of the planet Earth has a diameter of 6 inches. The interior is a mantle surrounding a molten core. The core has a radius of 3 inches. What is the volume of everything outside of the core?

Volume of a sphere = $\frac{4}{3}\pi r^3$

a. 186π
b. 324π
c. 216π
d. 288π
e. 252π

496. A pyramid made of rectangular prisms has layers each half the width of the layer beneath it. The base is a square that is 8 meters wide. Each level is a meter high. If the outside of the pyramid was being painted (not including the bottom), what would the surface area be of the painted part?

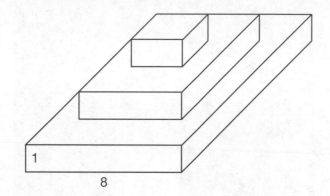

a. 84 m²
b. 120 m²
c. 208 m²
d. 248 m²
e. 268 m²

497. Which string of letters has two lines of symmetry?
a. OLLO
b. MEW
c. TAAT
d. OHO
e. IIBII

498. If the sum of the interior angles of a triangle is 180° and the sum of the interior angles of a quadrilateral is 360°, which equation represents the correlation between the sum of the interior angles (s) and the number of sides of a polygon (n)?
a. $s = 180n$
b. $s = 180n - 180$
c. $s = 180(n - 2)$
d. $s = 90n - 90$
e. $s = n + 177$

499. Use the Pythagorean theorem to find x. Round your answer to the nearest tenth.

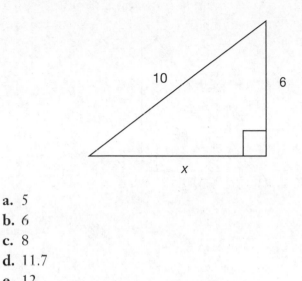

a. 5
b. 6
c. 8
d. 11.7
e. 12

500. What is the value of x?

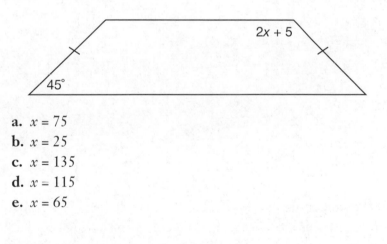

a. $x = 75$
b. $x = 25$
c. $x = 135$
d. $x = 115$
e. $x = 65$

501. What is the tangent of A?

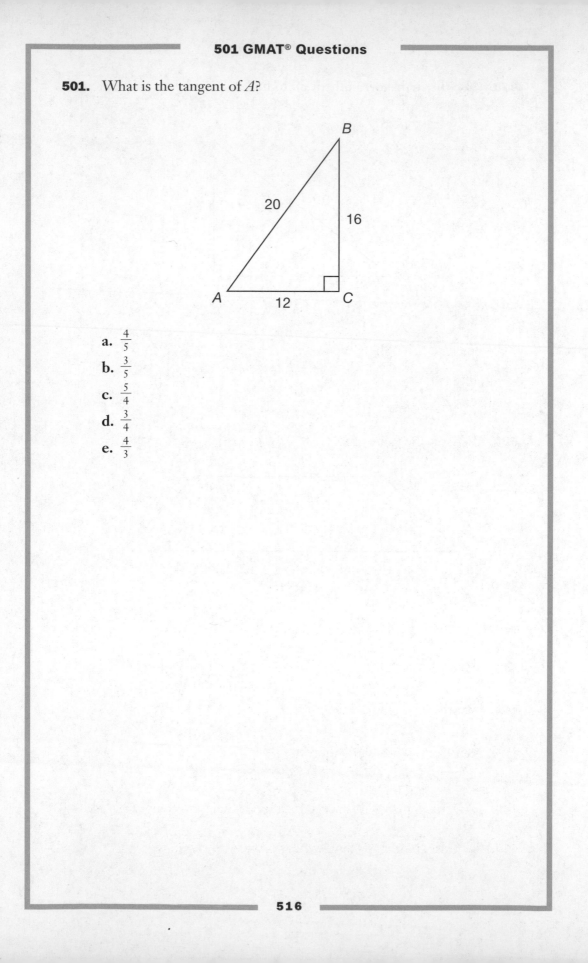

a. $\frac{4}{5}$

b. $\frac{3}{5}$

c. $\frac{5}{4}$

d. $\frac{3}{4}$

e. $\frac{4}{3}$

Answers

Set 33

428. ∠*KOL*; ∠*JOK*; ∠*NOM*

429. ∠*NOK*; ∠*MOJ*; ∠*MOL*

430. ∠*NOL*; ∠*MOK*

431. ∠*MOK*; ∠*KOM*

432. **63°.** $(180° - 27° - 90°)$

Set 34

433. **60°.** The sum of both angles must equal 90°.

434. **85°.** The sum of both angles must equal 90°.

435. **175°.** The sum of both angles must equal 180°.

436. **80°.** The sum of both angles must equal 180°.

Set 35

437. **Isosceles.** There are two equal sides.

438. **Scalene.** No sides are equal.

439. **Equilateral.** All sides are equal.

440. **Obtuse.** One angle is greater than 90°.

441. **Acute.** All angles are less than 90°.

442. **Right.** Note the right angle.

Set 36

443. **a.** True. Squares are special rectangles that have four equal sides.

444. **b.** False. Not all rectangles have four equal sides.

445. **a.** True. The rectangles that are also squares are those that have four equal sides.

446. **a.** True. Squares and rectangles are special parallelograms that have four right angles.

447. **14.5 feet.** Because the room is square, divide the total perimeter by 4: $\frac{58}{4} = 14.5$

448. **2 feet by 6 feet.** Use the formula $s + s + 3s + 3s$. Solve for s: $8s = 16$ feet, or $s = 2$ feet. The length of the short side is 2 feet, so each long side is 6 feet.

449. **120 feet.** $8,400 = \text{length} \times 70$. Solve for the length: $\frac{8,400}{70} = \text{length} \times \frac{70}{70}$, or 120 feet.

Set 37
450. **47.1 ft.** You are told the diameter: 15×3.14.

451. **69.08 in.** You are told the radius: $2(11) \times 3.14$.

452. **21.98 m.** You are told the diameter: 7×3.14.

453. **157 m.** You are told the radius: $2(25) \times 3.14$.

454. **78.5 ft.²** You are told the diameter, so you know the radius is 5: $5^2 \times 3.14$.

455. **200.96 m².** You are told the radius: $8^2 \times 3.14$.

456. **530.66 cm².** You are told the radius: $13^2 \times 3.14$.

457. **452.16 in.²** You are told the diameter, so you know the radius is 12: $12^2 \times 3.14$.

Set 38
458. $\frac{6}{5} \cdot \frac{6-0}{5-0}$.

459. **1.** $\frac{-2-(-3)}{-3-(-4)}$, or $\frac{-2+3}{-3+4} = 1$.

460. **0.** 3 – (–3) would result in a zero in the numerator.

461. **–2.** $\frac{8-(-6)}{-2-5}$, or $\frac{14}{-7} = -2$.

Set 39

462. **c.** If the area of the quadrilateral is $81 - 25x^2$ and the value of the base is $9 - 5x$, we can divide to find that the height of the quadrilateral is $9 + 5x$. We need to know it is a square because then we can set the base equal to the height and solve for x. In the equation $9 - 5x = 9 + 5x$, isolate variables and constants by adding $5x$ to both sides and subtracting 9 from both sides, yielding $0 = 10x$. Divide both sides by 10 to get $x = 0$.

463. **e.** In order to determine whether line BD and line AC are perpendicular, you would need to verify that the angle between them is 90°. Neither statement gives enough information to determine the angle between the lines. The first statement only tells you that line AC is a straight line, and statement (2) tells you that the lines are the same length.

464. **b.** The only piece of information you need to know in order to determine whether angle A and angle B are supplementary, or when added together are equal to 180°, is whether the two lines they intersect are parallel, as stated in the second statement. When given two parallel lines, the alternate interior angles of the transverse line are always supplementary.

465. **c.** Statement (1) indicates that the radius of circle A is 9, which means the circumference of the big circle is 18π or roughly 56.5, which is insufficient to tell determine whether the radius of circle B is bigger or smaller than 10. Statement (2) indicates that if $XY = 2YZ$, then $XZ = 3YZ$. The radius of A can be set equal to $3YZ$ to find the length of YZ. $9 = 3YZ$; divide both sides by 3 to get $3 = YZ$. This tells us that the circumference of circle B is 6π or approximately 18.8, which means yes, it is greater than 10.

466. **c.** Inside a triangle, all angles must add up to 180°. Complementary angles add up to 90°. To determine the value of angle A, both statement (1) and statement (2) are needed together. Statement (1) gives the relationship between angles B and C, yet this statement alone does not let you determine the measure of angle A. When combined with statement (2), all three angles can be determined. If angle B is 30°, then angle C must be 60° (90 – 30), and since the measures of all angles together must equal 180°, angle A is 90°.

467. **c.** Area of a rectangle = length × height. Area of a triangle = $\frac{1}{2}$ base × height. To determine whether the area of the rectangle and triangle are the same, you would need both statement (1) and statement (2). If the triangle height is twice the height of the rectangle and the bases/lengths are the same, you can set the equations equal to each other: length × height = $\frac{1}{2}$ length × 2 height.

468. **e.** Statements (1) and (2) together are insufficient because the only way to prove triangle similarity is to have 2 congruent corresponding angles. Since these two only have one set of corresponding angles, they could be 2 right triangles, one with a side triple the other and 2 other angles completely different.

469. **e.** In order to prove triangle congruence, you need to prove that they share two of the same corresponding sides and an angle that is in the same position on both of them. The information in statements (1) and (2) does not state that the sides and angle are in corresponding locations, so congruency cannot be determined.

470. **d.** Because of the direct relationship between the two cubes, either statement is enough information to calculate the volume of both cubes. Statement (1) gives the value of variable a, which can be used for both cubes. Statement (2) gives you the volume of the smaller cube, and if you work backward you can find the volume of a.

$a^3 = 64$

$a = 4$

Then from this you can find the volume of the second cube.

471. **d.** Statement (I) is sufficient because angle J is part of a straight angle with an interior angle on the parallel transversal. Since the supplements of J and E are equal, by the converse of the parallel line transversal theorem (if alternate interior angles of a transversal are congruent then they are transversing parallel lines) BC is parallel to DF. Statement (II) is sufficient because H is opposite to a straight angle and once again by the converse of the parallel line transversal theorem BC is parallel to DF.

472. **e.** Statement (I) only implies that angle a equals angle b. This could make the triangle an isosceles triangle. Statement (II) implies that if the difference between angle a and angle b is 0, they have the same measure, which still could possibly be an isosceles triangle.

473. **a.** To find the surface area of the cube, you would need to find the area of each side using the equation area = length × width. Since this is a cube, you can change the equation to area = length^2. Statement (I) gives you the volume, and if you work backward you will be able to find the length of one side. Volume of a cube = length^3.
27 = length^3
3 = length
Substitute this into the area equation and you will be able to solve for the area of each side and find the total surface area. Statement (II) does not give enough information to determine the length of one side needed to find the surface area.

474. **b.** Given that the circumference of this circle is $2x\pi$, and knowing that the circumference of a circle is $2\pi r$, then you know that $x = r$. This is stated in the first statement, but that does not give you enough information to determine the value for x. Statement (I) is insufficient. Statement (II) gives you enough information to find the value of x, as you should know the equation for both the circumference and area of a circle.

Set 40

475. **b.** Substitute the points in the form (x_1, y_1) and (x_2, y_2) into the slope formula. This yields $\frac{-5 - (-5)}{3 - (-2)}$, which simplifies to $\frac{0}{5}$, which equals 0. The incorrect choices contain operation errors and sign changes.

476. **e.** To find the y intercept of the line, substitute the value 0 for x. This resulting equation will be $3(0) + 6y = 12$. Simplifying this makes $6y = 12$. When both sides are divided by 2, the result is $y = 2$. Choices **a**, **b**, **c**, and **d** substitute 0 for y or have basic operation errors.

477. **d.** The line crosses the y-axis at the point $(0,1)$, which means the y-intercept (b) is 1. The change in y over the change in x (slope or m) is $-\frac{1}{3}$. Replacing these values in the slope-intercept form of a line yields the answer $y = -\frac{1}{3}x + 1$. The incorrect choices contain switched slopes and wrong signs for slopes.

478. **c.** In order to tell which statement is true, the equations must be put in slope-intercept form to check the y-intercept and slopes. Doing this results in the equations $y = -\frac{3}{5}x + 3$ and $y = -\frac{3}{5}x - 5$ respectively. These equations have the same slope, so they will be parallel. The other choices are incorrect because they don't have opposite reciprocal slopes; therefore, they aren't perpendicular. The y-intercepts in the equations are 3 and −5; they aren't the same, and if you replace y with 0 and solve for x in each equation, they do not share the same x-intercept.

479. **c.** Since the area below the line is shaded, the y will be greater than the other side of the equation. In addition, the line of the equation is a dashed line, so it will not be greater than or equal to and will not include the solutions on that line. The incorrect choices are all variations of reversed inequalities.

480. **d.** Using the method of linear combination or elimination, multiply the second equation by –1. Then combine the two equations $x + 3y = 7$ and $-x - 2y = -10$. This results is $y = -3$. Substitute the value of y into either of the original equations to obtain the x-value. $x + 3(-3) = 7$ when simplified yields $x - 9 = 7$. Add 9 to both sides to find that $x = 16$. The ordered pair $(16, -3)$ reflects the answers $y = -3$ and $x = 16$. The incorrect choices are all the result of addition error or leaving out a negative.

481. **b.** Area is equal to the base times the height. Multiply the terms in each binomial by the terms in the other binomial: $x(2x)$, $x(-7)$, $6(2x)$ and $6(-7)$. This yields the expression $2x^2 - 7x + 12x - 42$. Combine terms to get $2x^2 + 5x - 42$. Wrong answers were obtained through common calculation errors (choice **a**), not multiplying all terms (choices **c** and **d**), and finding the perimeter (choice **e**).

482. **b.** To start this problem you have to determine the volume of the pool when it is three-quarters full.
$V = l \times w \times h$
$V = 25 \text{ m} \times 12 \text{ m} \times \frac{3}{4}(8 \text{ m})$
$V = 1800 \text{ m}^3$
Then you need to convert the cubic meters into liters, and then gallons.
$1800 \text{ m}^3 \times \frac{1 \text{ liter}}{0.001 \text{ m}^3} \times \frac{0.26 \text{ gallons}}{1 \text{ liter}} = 468{,}000 \text{ gallons}$
Choice **a** uses 8 m to find volume, resulting in the overall depth, not three-quarters. Choices **c** and **d** are conversion errors. Choice **c** omits the conversion to liters and choice **d** omits the conversion to gallons.

483. **b.** If X and Y are seven units apart and Z is five units from Y, the absolute furthest distance between X and Z would be 12 $(5 + 7)$, and that would only be if angle XYZ was 180°, or they were all along a straight line. The absolute shortest distance between X and Z would be 2 $(7 - 5)$, and that would only be if angle XYZ was 0°, and Z was a point on the line between X and Y. All the other numbers are not possible.

484. **b.** Obtain the length of x by taking the length of each segment, adding them and dividing by 2 to find the mean value of both segments. $\frac{42 + 88}{2} = \frac{130}{2} = 65$. Incorrect answers are incorrect estimates and the result of subtracting the sides.

485. **d.** To find the length of AB, simply set up the equation $AB + BC = AC$. Substituting in values you get $3x + 14 + 2x + 1 = 75$, then solve for x. When like terms are combined, the equation becomes $5x + 15 = 75$. Using the additive inverse, $5x + 15 - 15 = 75 - 15$ yields $5x = 60$. Divide both sides by 5 to get $x = 12$. Substitute the value of x into the expression for AB: $3(12) + 14$. $36 + 14 = 50$, which is the length of AB. Incorrect choices include the value of x, the length of BC, and an answer with an incorrect operational error.

486. **a.** In order to find the distance between the points, use the distance formula and take the square root of $(x_1 + x_2)^2 + (y_1 + y_2)^2 + (z_1 + z_2)^2$. Replacing the values of x, y, and z with the coordinate components yields the square root of $(7 + 3)^2 + (-8 + 2)^2 + (2 - 4)^2$. Simplifying yields the square root of $10^2 + (-6)^2 + (-2)^2$, which equals the square root of $100 + 36 + 4$, which is the square root of 140, which is 11.8. Choices **b**, **c**, and **d** have operational errors used in the distance formula.

487. **c.** The height of each corn level in both silos can be obtained by using volume = that silo's base area times its height. The rectangular silo has a base of 10 cm^2, so $400 = 10h$, which means its height is 40. The cylindrical silo's height can be found the same way, $400 = 20h$, which means its height is 20. Hence, the rectangular silo will be 20 m higher than the cylindrical silo. The incorrect choices include the difference between the bases, the height of only one silo, or switching the heights.

488. **e.** When triangle ABC is rotated about point C, the new coordinate of B will become $(9,-1)$. When $(9,-1)$ is reflected over the y-axis, it will become $(-9,-1)$. The other choices have reflected over the wrong axis or have the wrong sign.

489. **b.** The triangle with sides 2, 3, and 7 is impossible to form because the sides 2 and 3 do not have lengths that could add to more than the third side. All three sides of the triangle would not connect. Each other triangle has two sides that add up to more than the third.

490. **d.** If angle A and angle B are supplementary, that means that $A + B = 180$. So if angle A is less than 80°, in order to add up to 180 angle B must be greater than 80°. The incorrect choices include mixups with complementary instead of supplementary, assuming that $A = 80°$, and greater than and less than mixups.

491. **d.** To find the midpoint of segment MN, one can average each component of the points. Average the x-values $\frac{4 + (-2)}{2}$ and get $x = 1$. Average the y-components $\frac{6 + 14}{2}$ and get $y = 10$. Together these yield the coordinate (1,10). The other choices are incorrect because of operational errors an adding the coordinates instead of averaging them.

492. **b.** Find the two other bottom angles in order to find x. The middle triangle's interior angles will all add to 180, so find the missing angle by using the expression $180 - 80 - 25$. The bottom angle will be 75°. Since 30 and 75 and the third angle on the bottom of the figure make up a straight angle, this is 180°. Subtract again to find the third angle. $180 - 75 - 30$ yields 75. Two of the angles in the triangle on the left are 75 and 90 degrees. $180 - 75 - 90$ gives the value of x, which is 15. The incorrect choices include other angles in the figure or angles that were yielded from operational errors.

493. **b.** When constructed, the circular part of the net becomes the base of the shape and the round part on the bottom wraps around the edge of the circle to create the point for the cone.

494. **d.** To find the area of the shaded region, the area of the inner rectangle must be subtracted from the area of the outer rectangle. The equation is area = length × height, so the area of the outer rectangle is $(10 \times 9) = 90$, and the area of the inner rectangle is $(2 \times 3) = 6$. Then, to find only the shaded area subtract $90 - 6$ and the correct answer is 84. Choices **a** and **e** represent the area of either rectangle if it is found alone.

495. **e.** To find the volume of everything outside the core in the model of Earth, the volume of the core must be subtracted from the volume of the total Earth. Find the volume of each by substituting radius values into the volume formula. The volume of Earth is $\frac{4}{3}\pi \times 6^3 = 288\pi$. The volume of the core is $\frac{4}{3}\pi \times 3^3 = 36\pi$. $288\pi - 36\pi = 252\pi$.

496. **b.** Find the area of each exposed surface face. All the upward-facing squares will have a combined surface area of a large 8×8 square, so the upward-facing area is $8(8) = 64$. The side wall for the base is 8×1 and there are four of them, so $8(1)(4)$. Add this to the side areas for each level to receive the expression $8(1)(4) + 4(1)(4) + 2(1)(4) = 32 + 16 + 8 = 56$. Add the side area (56) with the upward area (64) to get the total surface area 120 m². The other choices added extra sides or the bottoms of each shape not visible on the surface.

497. **d.** The string of letters OHO is the only choice that has two lines of symmetry, one vertical that divides it in half in the center of the H and a horizontal axis that reflects the top to the bottom and runs through the middle of the letters. Other choices only have one or no lines of symmetry.

498. **c.** A triangle is a 3-sided polygon, and a quadrilateral is a 4-sided polygon. The difference between the sums of the interior angles of these shapes is $360° − 180° = 180°$. A triangle is the polygon with the fewest number of sides (there cannot be a 1- or 2-sided polygon), so it can be reasoned that for each side added to a polygon above 3, the sum of the interior angles of that polygon increases by 180°. The equation for the sum of the interior angles of a polygon must hold true for all polygons, including triangles, so the equation must subtract the number of sides of the polygon by 2 before multiplying by 180°. This yields the equation $s = 180(n − 2)$, which holds true for the given sums of interior angles for triangles and quadrilaterals. When the given values are substituted into the other equations, they are not solutions.

499. **c.** When the values are plugged into the Pythagorean theorem, $a^2 + b^2 = c^2$ yields $x^2 + 6^2 = 10^2$. When simplified, it yields $x^2 + 36 = 100$. Subtract 36 from both sides to get $x^2 = 64$. Take the square root of both sides to find that $x = 8$. The other choices either replaced the wrong values in the Pythagorean theorem or are approximate lengths.

500. **e.** Since the bases of a trapezoid are parallel, it can be assumed that both bottom angles are equal and both top angles are equal, and since the sum of all interior angles of a quadrilateral are equal to 360°, the equation can be formed as $2(45) + 2(2x + 5) = 360$. Simplifying yields $90 + 4x + 10 = 360$, which simplifies to $4x + 100 = 360$. Subtracting 100 from both sides yields $4x = 260$, and when both sides are divided by 4, $x = 65$. The other choices assumed that $45 = 2x + 5$ or included common operational errors.

501. **e.** The tangent of an angle in a right triangle is equal to the opposite side of that angle divided by the adjacent side to that angle. The opposite side is 16 and the adjacent is 12. Reduce the fraction $\frac{16}{12}$ to get $\frac{4}{3}$. The wrong choices have other answers mixed up with ratios of the adjacent side, the hypotenuse, and the opposite side.

Notes

Niles
Public Library District

OCT 2 8 2013

Niles, Illinois 60714

Niles, Illinois 60714

OCT 2 2 2013

Niles
Public Library District

Notes

3 1491 01128 5594